AF449163

The Uncertainty of Analysis

Timothy J. Reiss

THE UNCERTAINTY OF ANALYSIS

Problems in Truth, Meaning, and Culture

Cornell University Press

ITHACA AND LONDON

A grant from the Office of the Dean of the
Faculty of Arts and Sciences of New York University
contributed to the publication of this book.

First published 1988 by Cornell University Press.

International Standard Book Number 0-8014-2162-4
Library of Congress Catalog Card Number 88-47741
Printed in the United States of America
*Librarians: Library of Congress cataloging information
appears on the last page of the book.*

*The paper in this book is acid-free and meets the
guidelines for permanence and durability of the
Committee on Production Guidelines for
Book Longevity of the Council on Library Resources.*

Contents

[vii]

It was a splendid mind. For if thought is like the keyboard of a piano,
divided into so many notes, or like the alphabet is ranged in twenty-six
letters all in order, then his splendid mind had no sort of difficulty in
running over those letters one by one, firmly and accurately, until it
had reached, say, the letter Q. He reached Q. Very few people in the
whole of England ever reach Q. . . . But after Q? What comes next?
After Q there are a number of letters the last of which is scarcely
visible to mortal eyes, but glimmers red in the distance. Z is only
reached once by one man in a generation. Still, if he could reach R it
would be something. Here at least was Q. He dug his heels in at Q. Q
he was sure of. Q he could demonstrate. If Q then is Q— R—. . . . He
could see, without wishing it, that old, that obvious distinction between the two classes of men; on the one hand the steady goers of
superhuman strength who, plodding and persevering, repeat the
whole alphabet in order, twenty-six letters in all, from start to finish;
on the other the gifted, the inspired who, miraculously, lump all the
letters together in one flash—the way of genius. He had not genius;
he laid no claim to that: but he had, or might have had, the power to
repeat every letter of the alphabet from A to Z accurately in order.
Meanwhile, he stuck at Q. On, then, on to R.

—Virginia Woolf, To the Lighthouse

Preface

This volume has been a long time in the making and remains perhaps somewhat haphazard and unsystematic in organization, if not in intention. Written over a number of years, its chapters form part of a more complicated project whose purpose is to understand how forms of conceptualization and the sociocultural environments within which they function, to which they help give shape, and for whose practice they provide meaning have come into being and continue to exist. *The Discourse of Modernism* (1982), using a rather narrow corpus, sought to show how such forms of conceptualization develop from elements within some quite different conceptual structure and how gradual development over centuries gives way to a "moment" of more abrupt transformation. That book took the case of the rather familiar transformation characterizing the European sixteenth and seventeenth centuries; it tried to indicate just how constraining were the new conceptual structure and its concomitant sociocultural environment. To be sure, the book concentrated far more, in its analysis of the *textual* corpus of science fictions and utopias, on structures of conception than on those of society. But it sought to examine the modernist development of such essential concepts as subject and individual, analysis and reference, contract and conflict, right and obligation, arguing that they developed into a conceptual totality the understanding of which is essential to our own comprehension of the past three hundred years. *Tragedy and Truth* (1980)—written, as it were, "inside" the work just mentioned—applied similar assumptions to the analysis of tragedy, arguing that that literary genre has played a singularly important role in the development of modern views of language and truth, subject and individual responsibility.

These two books left unresolved any number of questions, as they also raised new ones. Most clearly, they suggested that the structures of analytico-referentiality (as I called them, uncomfortably), consolidated in the late seventeenth century, had started breaking down in the late nineteenth. With respect to the period of Renaissance and neoclassicism, I argued that new dominant conceptual structures had developed not only by the use of what were at the time apparently quite new and unfamiliar elements but simultaneously by the incorporation of elements emerging from a previous different conceptual totality in which various aporias and contradictions had become overwhelmingly present. If such an analysis was at all "correct," then the understanding of how *that* occurred, the comprehension of contradictions and aporias within the analytico-referential itself and the grasp of elements seemingly new within it, should help us understand how similar transformations could occur in our own time. Such understanding is needed not because we might then hope to predict the processes, forms, and direction of change (a singularly foolish aspiration) but because we might then begin to comprehend what is already a changing sociocultural environment. To analyze certain fundamental analytico-referential discourses in their most contemporary form, to show some of the aporias, contradictions, and emergent elements within them, is the purpose of this volume, *The Uncertainty of Analysis*.

The previous books also implied that discourses (my use of the term is explained at length in the Introduction) fulfill certain specifiable functions within the sociocultural environment. Their particular implications concerned what we call "literature," and that is the issue to be attended to at length in my *Meaning of Literature* (which will follow the present volume). There I will also seek to link these until now textually oriented analyses with the sociocultural environment in its concrete and more "practical" manifestations (that opposition may well be queried, however). This is not an easy thing to do, but the underlying assumptions evidently necessitate the attempt. I will also make a later attempt to show the purpose and ongoing function of modern political philosophical discourse.

More generally, this work implies that the sociocultural environment as a whole is made comprehensible and practicable to those who live within it by a multitude of meaningful processes ("discourses") to which we give various names. Increasingly I would argue that these productions of meaning (not *separable* from the environment but integral to and defining of it) are what enable its participants to recognize the coherence of their culture and society, as well as to specify its difference from others. These issues will be examined in my *Discourse and Society*, which, in a sense, will offer the "general theory" (if the phrase is not too pretentious) underlying but developing with these various analyses.

This process of research explains why the chapters composing the present volume have all appeared in print in previous versions. They were responses to a variety of provocations, but they (and others) all sought to examine a process of profound questioning in our own time that appears in many ways analogous to what occurred in the European sixteenth and seventeenth centuries. These chapters, then, are part of an effort to understand a contemporary process of conceptual and sociocultural transformation—not a "crisis" but simply a particular kind of not unfamiliar historical movement. They have all received extensive revision (especially the earliest and those here translated from the French) whose nature, purpose, and limits are explained in the Introduction.

Chapters 1 and 2 first appeared in slightly different form in the *Canadian Journal of Research in Semiotics*, 4, no. 2 (Winter 1976–77), and 5, no. 1 (Fall 1977). This journal has been succeeded by *Semiotic Inquiry*. Chapter 1 also appeared in French in *Langages*, 58 (June 1980). Chapter 3 was published in different form and in French as "Archéologie du discours et critique épistémique: Projet pour une critique discursive," in *Philosophie et littérature* (Montreal: Bellarmin; Paris–Tournai: Desclée, 1979); and Chapter 4, also in French, as "Le non-lieu de la fête et le projet d'ordre," in *La fête en question*, ed. Karin Gürttler and Monique Serfati-Arnaud (Montreal: Université de Montréal, Etudes Anciennes & Modernes, 1979). Two small parts of Chapter 3 appeared in English as "Discursive Criticism and Epistemology" and "The Discourse of Criticism and the Uncertainty Principle" in, respectively, *Interpretation of Narrative*, ed. Mario J. Valdés and Owen J. Miller (Toronto: University of Toronto Press, 1978), and *Actes du VIIIe Congrès de l'Association Internationale de Littérature Comparée* (Budapest: Akadémiai Kiado, 1980). Chapter 5 appeared in French in *Sartre et la mise en signe*, ed. M. Issacharoff and J.-C. Vilquin (Paris: Klincksieck; Lexington, Ky.: French Forum, 1981), and Chapter 6 in *Europa*, 3, no. 2 (Spring 1980). Chapter 7 was published in the *Canadian Review of Comparative Literature*, 12, no. 1 (March 1985), and Chapters 8 and 9 in 13, no. 1 (March 1986), the second being published in French. I thank the editors and/or publishers of these various publications for permission to include these texts, however considerably changed, in this volume. The material of the Appendix is reprinted by permission of the Harvard University Press.

As always, I express my deep gratitude to all those whose friendship, conversation, and intellectual companionship contributed to the production of some or all of these essays: students in various seminars at the universities of Montreal and Toronto and at New York and Emory universities, as well as members of lecture audiences, always provided feedback, criticism, and provocation from which the following chapters have benefited even more than I am always aware.

To many colleagues at the institutions above mentioned I owe much of my thinking about these matters, and it would probably be pernicious to single out individuals beyond those who helped specifically with what are now chapters of this book. Pierre Beaudry, Françoise Gaillard, Pierre Gravel, Walter Moser, Lewis Pyenson, and Eugene Vance all gave careful attention to what is now Chapter 3. Sylvie Romanowski provided the opportunity for considerable discussion of Chapter 1, as did Paul Bouissac and David Savan for Chapter 2. Wladimir Krysinski gave me a careful reading of Chapter 7 and Alessandro Briosi and Paul Zumthor of Chapter 5, for whose very existence Alain Goldschläger is responsible. Without the original urging of Krysinski and Milan Dimič, Chapter 9 would certainly not exist in anything like its present form. I thank them all, as well as the two anonymous readers for Cornell University Press, whose lengthy comments on the original manuscript were essential.

Some of this material was further elaborated during a leave of absence in 1983–84. I am grateful to the Université de Montréal, which made possible the original arrangement, and especially to Emory University, which continued it, and to the Social Sciences and Humanities Research Council of Canada for the Faculty Fellowship facilitating it. I am likewise beholden to the American Council of Learned Societies and the Emory University Research Committee for, respectively, a Fellowship and a Faculty Research Award for the academic year 1986–87; although given primarily for work on *The Meaning of Literature,* these also enabled me to bring together and completely revise the essays that make up this volume. I also thank Patricia Sterling for her quite excellent copy editing, and Bernhard Kendler and Marilyn Sale for seeing the book through the Press.

A more general and evident debt is acknowledged in the dedication to Michel Foucault, whose work was far from completion at the time of his death, and to my father, whose sense of the importance of intellectual life and whose belief that even in seemingly trivial matters one owes a debt to the general welfare were, I think, more formative than I was ever able to let him know. And finally, without Patricia Hilden the beginning and end of this volume would have been very different, as indeed would have been the whole of the Introduction and Chapters 8 and 9 without her careful reading of their earlier versions. She has in fact forced me to look at a number of issues in a very different light and in a vastly more complicated context than I had previously done. Only glimmers of her influence can be seen here, but my gratitude is more profound than I can well say.

TIMOTHY J. REISS

New York, New York

A Note on Punctuation

Double quotation marks indicate citations of other authors, terms used in a commonly accepted sense to which I am referring as quotations (though no particular source may be provided), or, in some few cases, phrases cited from earlier parts of the book. Single marks, except where they indicate a quotation within a quotation, are used for other emphases—most often either to indicate the inappropriateness of some habitually used term or to signal that a term taken from one discursive logic (or class of discourse) is being unavoidably but unsuitably applied to a different such logic.

The Uncertainty of Analysis

Introduction

Written over nearly a decade, in the margins of other writing of my own and in response to that of others, the chapters that follow all have their starting point in one principal concept and theme: that of 'discourse' and discursive transformation as a principal factor for the understanding of how the sociocultural environment develops.

What is meant here by 'discourse'? Contrary to what is all too frequently assumed, I do not mean by this term something that originates in natural language. I mean a process that exists both within and beyond natural language: that is to say, any organized practice of sign systems creating meaning. To refer to all these as "languages" and then to believe that their model is to be found in some comprehension of natural languages is to be taken in by a metaphor.

In any sociocultural environment there are many such sign systems: 'art'—and more precisely, 'literature'—is one; others are 'science,' medicine, law, history, modes of production, and so forth.[1] I call these "discursive types." They are all ordered practices composed of identifiable elements that are meaningful both as separate entities and as composed whole sets. These disciplined practices therefore do not, as one might think, *have* sign systems; they *are* sign systems. Both their production and their comprehension depend upon the way in which they are meaningfully ordered.

Sign systems are present in and manifested through diverse *materials*: natural language, myth, painting, scientific experiment, music, historiography, legal practice, automobile production lines (means of production), and more. These cannot be thought of or grasped separately from the disciplined practices to which I have just referred, but the materials provide the *Stoff*, rather than the *meaning*, of the systems' elaboration.

'Meaning,' here, will have to be defined as something like the actual production of generalized comprehensible *effects* in the world. 'Effects'

---

1. Literature is considered in my *Meaning of Literature* (forthcoming) and all of these in my *Discourse and Society* (in preparation). I have made a brief exploration in "Société, discours, littérature: De l'histoire discursive," *Texte*, 5/6 (1986–87), 151–79.

are comprehensible in the sense that they enable their human originators and recipients to function in a manner *they* understand as coherent by leading to further effects considered to be anteriorly *predictable* and posteriorly *explicable* in terms of those other effects (not necessarily thought of as chronologically connected). Together they provide what is called an 'analysis' of *all* human activities (they may of course be said to 'allow for' such an analysis to be made, but within their sociocultural environment they provide the guiding and fully constraining conditions for analysis).

That analysis is generated in, out of, and upon such *material* activities (of which language may or may not be a part on any particular occasion). Yet the ascription of meaning to those activities by human interpreters is *essential* to them, not merely accidental. It is the case, as Christine Delphy observes, that human bodies, actions, and events are partly characterized by "a physical, non-social element," but they also possess "a social component." That alone makes them accessible to us, makes them human, situates them as a part of our history and of our 'nature' (as Marx also emphasized). Their meaning is "given" not simply by physical existence and act but, "like all *meaning*, by consciousness, and thus by society." "A particular culture," Delphy adds, "not only imposes a meaning on an event which, being physical, is in and of itself bereft of meanings. Society (culture) also imposes a material form through which the event is lived, or rather is moulded in a constraining way."[2] The way in which such meaning is imposed, the *means* of doing so, is what I referred to before as the disciplined practice of sign systems (the "discursive types"). The event, action, or phenomenon is the "material."

The meaning of acts, events, and even of physical existence depends therefore on the particular sociocultural environment dwelt in by the humans who experience such existence, acts, and events. That is the case for all human experience of whatever kind, which is by definition (*as* human and *as* social) understood as *meaningful*, trammeled with interpretation. This is not to say that human activities invent the world, objects of knowledge, moral obligation, and so forth. But it *is* to say that the world exists (for us) only within a particular kind of mediated relation. As Charles Sanders Peirce wrote, what especially needs explaining is the fact that *any* kind of lawfulness can be ascribed to the world; what requires analysis is how any understanding of a chaotic world is possible at all.

It was precisely this connection between human practice, social environment, and the world that Karl Marx in the 1844 manuscripts, sought to understand and to define with respect to the cognitive nature of hu-

---

2. Christine Delphy, *Close to Home: A Materialist Analysis of Women's Oppression*, tr. and ed. Diana Leonard (Amherst, Mass., 1984), p. 194.

mans and the process of their being in the world. On the one hand, the world of things exists for humans only "as a totality of possible satisfactions of" our needs, and for us (to use a Peircean phrase) that is absolutely all there is in it. On the other hand, "nature," for humans, is actually constituted out of our consciousness of it.[3] That is not in the least to say that humans create nature, as Jamesian pragmatism would have it (thus provoking Peirce's violent objections). It is to say, however, that nature "in itself" can only be the Peircean *idea* of Firstness; as such it is inaccessible and meaningless in the very strongest sense. In turn, this means that knowledge, truth, and moral action cannot be thought of in terms of some ever closer approach to a reality "out there," because we can never know what such reality might be. A definition in those terms, as Gottlob Frege came to assert, is strictly meaningless. There are (of course) "facts," and a fact may perhaps best be recognized as that which people suffer before they can understand and change it—or change to understand it. What we *can* grasp, therefore, is the great number of means we have for functioning within our world; these are the discursive types through which we compose our sociocultural environment.

The given sociocultural environment is thus made up of a potentially unlimited number of discursive types. Yet any particular environment lies under the dominance of one discursive 'class,' by which I mean a fundamental model of understanding and functioning manifest in the majority of discursive types (even though other, "subordinate," orders may function simultaneously). Such a dominant class does not exist in any transcendent way but is immanent in those types. Thus a participant in any sociocultural environment, and any observer of it, can recognize its specificity, both diachronically (with respect to other societies historically distant from it) and synchronically (with regard to societies spatially distant from it). In slightly different theoretical contexts the phenomenon has been diversely referred to as "hegemony" (Antonio Gramsci), as "structures of feeling" (Lucien Goldmann), or as "world model" (Aron Gurevich). This particular assumption carries with it a pair of corollaries that are of particular significance for the discussions that follow.

The first is that the functioning of language and mind, together with the activity of the so-called "subject" (the need for that adjective will be clear in a moment), cannot be considered in isolation from the sociocultural environment as a whole in whose functioning it is but a part. That is especially the case when the purpose of such consideration involves a transformation of that functioning (as it does in what follows). So to

---

3. These sentences are part paraphrase and part quotation from Leszek Kolakowski, "Karl Marx and the Classical Definition of Truth," in his *Toward a Marxist Humanism: Essays on the Left Today*, tr. Jane Zielonko Peel (1968; rpt. New York, 1969), pp. 38–66; this from pp. 42–43.

isolate it is to fall into what we may perhaps call the "idealist fallacy": the belief in the primacy of natural language or, perhaps more precisely, the belief that all significant forms of order may be reduced to language like processes. (Saying that is not to belittle the enormous difficulty involved in embedding language, mind, and subject, for example, in their total environment in ways other than trivial and simplistic—or to imply that I have been successful in doing so.)

The second corollary involves the role of literature and criticism in particular and the written text in general; indeed, it concerns the entire question of 'cultural' production in the narrow sense (as the development of "superstructural" processes). If all discursive types within the sociocultural environment are fundamentally under the direct sway of some dominant discursive class (or are obliged to take it into account even when they are not), then we cannot meaningfully speak of primary and secondary production. Once an environment is functioning as an identifiable sociocultural 'totality,' its particular manifestations of language and mind, of 'subject,' of aesthetic or ethical order, and so on, are varying manifestations of the dominant order of discourse. The functioning of different discursive types may therefore show various impasses, aporias, and contradictions present in the environment in its entirety. These cannot be solved (contrary to certain claims: "change the way we speak/write/think, and we change the social order") within any one discourse alone, but they can be *understood* there and then projected elsewhere.

All I have just been saying argues that discursive classes and the sociocultural environments corresponding to them have their history: a history of their more or less stable existence over a fairly long period of time and of their moments of transformation during a rather shorter one. We can trace their development, their passage from preceding forms of dominance and their gradual consolidation as a new one, and follow the gradual development from such 'inception' toward future change into something else.

In *The Discourse of Modernism* I argued that just such a period of transformation and consolidation occurred during the period from about the beginning of the European sixteenth century to the second third of the seventeenth. I sought also to claim that once what I have called the analytico-referential (or modernist) class of discourse was consolidated, it held sway until the end of the nineteenth century and indeed until our own time. As others have done, I also suggested that since the late nineteenth century it has been thrown into increasing disarray, partly as its own contradictions and aporias have become more evident, partly as emergent elements have been pursued and consolidated toward some more efficacious mode of human functioning ("efficacious," that is, in terms of a changing configuration of the entire environment).

This class of discourse functioned on the basis of an assumed division between thinking and the world. It depended, however, on the claim that the functional structures of world, mind, and language were in some way identical in that the well-ordered speech or text provided an exact analysis of the reasoning process and, in turn, a precise analysis of the world. It also asserted that words referred correctly to concepts, which, in their turn, adequately captured things and events in the world: that *reference*, in short, was entirely sufficient to correct, "commonsensical" understanding. Analysis and reference in this sense thus provided an idea of Reason founded upon two truths: the one of coherence, the other of correspondence. It was an *instrumental* reason whose *purpose* was to affect the world, but it was an *objective* reason whose processes were identical in their own sphere with those of the world in *theirs*.

It was objective just because of that structural identity, which implied all human mediating processes to be in fact *transparent* to their object. The instrument of analysis was assumed to intervene or interfere in no way whatsoever with a knowledge of the world. This meant that any consequent action was not, so to speak, idiosyncratic but corresponded both to the real nature of the world and to the authentic and permanent nature of humans. The representative *model* was provided by experimental science.

The subject of such understanding and action was therefore at once individual and genuinely representative of the entire species: individual because it perforce 'knew' itself and its own processes first; representative because those processes were common to all. That such an individual self might be but a hypostasis of the producer of a discourse was a matter gradually occulted. On the contrary, that self defined itself in terms of its will to impose (to capture and grasp—conceive, *concipere*, be*greifen*— the world and other), of its authority (provided by the truth of objective knowledge), of its right to property (given by combining the previous two).

The form of that understanding was linear and temporal, one of cause and effect, or of narration, grounded on the claim that natural, rational, and linguistic processes all followed such a trajectory. In the nineteenth century John Stuart Mill's view of the right method of history provided an exemplary case of the transfer of such an analytico-referential scientific model into another domain, where its purpose was to attempt "by a study of the general facts of history to discover . . . the law of progress; which law, once ascertained, must . . . enable us to predict future events, *just as after a few terms of an infinite series in algebra we are able to detect the principle of their regularity in their formation, and to predict the rest of the series to any number of terms we please*." Mill, to be sure, asserted that this could not, where society and history were concerned, be anything but an "empirical law"; it lacked the rigid uniformity of a mathematical sequence. Nonetheless, the assumption remained that such a succession corresponded sufficiently to the truth of the natural sequentiality of societies to provide real and true understanding of their functioning.[4] We have small difficulty in understanding Mill's view (*intended* as a critique of Auguste Comte's stricter mechanistic materialism) as a transposition into the domain of social history of the Marquis de Laplace's claim that if one knew the current position and motion of every atom, one could predict the future of the universe to all eternity: a simple matter of mathematical projection. Unlike Peirce, such thinkers assumed the universal, ubiquitous, and fundamental being of natural, social, and historical laws; for them, chaos and chance were merely the sign of an entirely provisional ignorance.

As the preceding example makes evident, the initial separation of mind and matter meant that what was conceived as true *knowledge* was always a methodic generalization, a universalization of particular instances (as was the very Subject itself). Reason provided a more truthful version of reality than reality itself. This was the view of Enlightened rationality that Virginia Woolf debunked with ironic glee in *To the Lighthouse*, when she told how Lily Briscoe thought of Mr. Ramsay's work:

> She always saw clearly before her a large kitchen table. It was Andrew's doing. She asked him what his father's books were about. "Subject and object and the nature of reality," Andrew had said. And when she said Heavens, she had no notion what that meant. "Think of a kitchen table then," he told her, "when you're not there."
>
> So now she always saw, when she thought of Mr. Ramsay's work, a scrubbed kitchen table. It lodged now in the fork of a pear tree, for they had reached the orchard. . . . Naturally, if one's days were passed in this seeing of angular essences, this reducing of lovely evenings, with all their flamingo clouds and blue and silver to a white deal four-legged table (and it was a mark of the finest minds so to do), naturally one could not be judged like an ordinary person.[5]

The subject, the authority, the owner of property is for this discursive class ineluctably masculine. The way in which the discourse became thus gender-specific (as to its *dominance*) is too complex to be dealt with here.[6] Woolf's novel provides, however, a good idea of its functioning, through the character of Lily Briscoe. What she understands as masculinist ana-

4. John Stuart Mill, *Logic*, VI, x 3; quoted in Karl R. Popper, *The Poverty of Historicism* (1957; rpt. New York, 1964), pp. 117–18. See also Mill, *Philosophy of Scientific Method*, ed. Ernest Nagel (New York, 1950), pp. 344–46.

5. Virginia Woolf, *To the Lighthouse* (1927; rpt. New York, 1937), p. 38.

6. The question is discussed at length in my *Meaning of Literature*.

lytical discourse is to her neither unfamiliar nor outlandish but merely an imposition. She (like Mrs. Ramsay) is the victim of Ramsay's oppressive discourse, of his authority and his supposed legitimate power. She is the 'object' captured within a practice whose authority and possession are justified and confirmed by the very success of its undertaking. In *To the Lighthouse*, the imposition is in place from the outset, in the form of that patriarchal and analytical discourse. The novel recounts Mrs. Ramsay's ambiguous acceptance of its dominance: she plays the role set out for her by her husband as representative of familiar forms of societal control, giving men "chivalry and valour" and all power in the public domain, receiving for herself "something trustful, childlike, reverential." These are aspects of an attitude, remarks the narrator with biting irony, that "no woman could fail to feel or to find agreeable." At the same time the novel presents Lily Briscoe's rejection of such an imposition and her constant search for a personal vision capable of withstanding the constant interference of that dominance; even if, under present conditions, it might mean exclusion from society: the picture she is striving to finish "would be hung in attics . . . it would be destroyed. But what did that matter? she asked herself," painting the last essential stroke upon the canvas. For, after all, she had "had [her] vision" and thereby established her own identity.[7]

In the opposition between Mrs. Ramsay and Lily Briscoe we have a glimmer of what this book is about, for on the foundation laid by all I have been saying rest the main arguments of what follows. These are threefold.

The first has already been proposed: it is that analytico-referential discourse has provided the dominant model for all understanding, practice, and action in Western cultures from about the middle of the seventeenth century to the present; since the middle of the nineteenth century, however, its ability to account thoroughly for human understanding and to facilitate consequent action adequate to sociocultural conditions has been increasingly questioned. Indeed, such action has increasingly become not only inadequate but misdirected and counterproductive, when not downright abusive.

The second principal argument is that the doubts expressed from the mid-nineteenth century onward have inspired a number of attempts to fortify analysis by strengthening (usually unintentionally) the terms of the very discursive dominance being questioned. In logic and in theory of science, I discuss such as Gottlob Frege, Bertrand Russell, and the early Ludwig Wittgenstein; in linguistics and philosophy of language, Ferdinand de Saussure, Algirdas Julien Greimas, and Noam Chomsky; in

---

7. Woolf, *Lighthouse*, pp. 13, 309–10. This conclusion is of course rather despairing, for it implies that under current social conditions a woman can establish her separate identity only at the price of exclusion from both the public and the accepted private domain.

political theory, Jean-Paul Sartre and some few other Western Marxists; in literary criticism and related areas, Terry Eagleton, Geoffrey Hartman, and Jacques Derrida.

The third argument is that some unfamiliar forms of discourse appear to be working their way out of the more familiar, older hegemony (Peirce, or Wittgenstein in his later work, perhaps). These are forms that need eventually to cope with the entire sociocultural environment but have begun to become visible in various areas of practice. In some spheres they clearly will not depend upon written forms alone: political and economic relations, legal practice, scientific work, forms of labor, and so on. In others, they will obviously be far more constrained by writing: hence the linguistic and literary focus of this book, which seeks nevertheless to be aware always of the wider ramifications of its arguments.

The opposition between Mrs. Ramsay and Lily Briscoe is in some sense emblematic, then, of the second and third arguments, as it is of the oppositions explored in many of the book's chapters. I begin by confronting the work of Peirce with that of Frege, for these two thinkers in many ways embodied opposing modes of thought at the turn of our century as they strove to respond to the ever more obvious dilemma of the late nineteenth—of which I have already spoken. Both did so in answer to what was then seen as a fundamental crisis in logic and mathematical thought, themselves understood by philosophers and scientists to correspond to the basic forms of all human reason.

Frege has been of clear and increasing importance in the strain of 'empiricist' analytical thinking that includes the logical atomists, the Vienna positivists, modern Anglo-American analytical and linguistic philosophy, and speech-act theory. In contemporary France, his work is coming to be viewed and used as a viable alternative to the non-Marxist and 'apolitical' Heideggerian line of thought (I put it thus to avoid assimilating Sartre's efforts) that has terminated in "deconstruction" and its avatars. France, especially, was prepared for such a reception by the long-standing influence of Saussure's *Cours de linguistique générale*, which had applied similar assumptions (as Chapter 2 indicates) to an analysis of language. Through the textual and linguistic work of Vladimir Propp, Louis Hjelmslev, and Emile Benveniste, this strain has culminated in the semiology of Greimas and his school. Here we find a projection of Saussurean linguistics toward a textual and literary linguistics, widely offered as a scientific analysis of sign functioning entirely the equal of any analytical science. This semiology has certain similarities to speech-act theory (which it has increasingly sought to incorporate) and though relatively unfamiliar to English speakers, has become widely known and used in Europe. Indeed, it has made specific claims for itself as a tool for analyzing texts in a way no other semiotics has (with the possible exception of some German versions of 'Peirce' and of *Textlinguistik*).[8] The structural linguistics explored in Noam Chomsky's work (whose implications are examined in Chapter 7) may be inserted within this same project. It is one seeking to revalorize the terms of analytico-referential discourse.

Peirce's work was more akin to that of the later Wittgenstein and seemed to foreshadow some of the consequences of quantum theory and indeterminacy, of the questioning of individualism, of binary logics, linear rationality, and the rest. The strain of political thinking embodied in the Frankfurt School and that of what one might call critical 'Marxist' semiotics, prefigured in the work of Mikhail Bakhtin and his companions, were not unrelated to this thinking (as Jürgen Habermas's and Karl-Otto Apel's writings have ably demonstrated with respect to Peirce, using his thought quite differently than do the textual semiotic German analyses). We can also look at such figures as Umberto Eco, Roland Barthes, and Julia Kristeva. The very difficulty of classifying their work in terms of any traditional "discipline" is itself a mark of the opposition being explored. For as we will see from the outset, Peirce managed to make use of certain frustrations, constraints, contradictions, impasses, and aporias—by which Frege ultimately found himself blocked—in order to start developing unfamiliar forms of argumentation and logic. In many ways they bear certain fascinating resemblances to those found in the scientific thinking of such as Werner Heisenberg and the philosophical explorations of the later Wittgenstein (the matter of Chapter 3). Out of elements already present in analytico-referential discourse, but in ways that seem to circumvent Frege's difficulties, Peirce started to forge an entirely different kind of "semeiotic" (his preferred spelling), one that could lead to entirely new forms of understanding and practice.

Once we are able to view the extremely complex opposition with relative clarity, we must also explore and condemn the efforts to found some sociopolitical and conceptual transformation upon the basis of a utopian or quasi-mystical "Other." However attractive and readily available such an attempt may be, it has shown itself to be rather more a reactionary trap than a future hope. Chapter 4 makes that argument; Chapter 7 asserts that neither can effective general transformation be based on an idea of individual or collective revolutionary fiat (though it may well achieve a just 'catching-up' in particular instances). Both history and reason, it argues, suggest that the outcome of such effort has almost always been counterproductive, perhaps largely because change of reason must then ever lag behind change of history. That is precisely why the historical verdict

8. For much of my knowledge of this "German version" I am indebted to Jean-Claude Rochefort, "La réception de Charles S. Peirce en Allemagne: Période 1960–1980" (Ph.D. diss., Université de Montréal, 1981). As for Greimas, recent translation of most of his work into English will doubtless overcome the unfamiliarity.

cannot yet be in; bets must necessarily be well hedged. Various mis-apprehensions about events in western Europe (and elsewhere) in 1968 and the subsequent failures and disillusionment, I suggest, were by no means foreign to what seemed simply *theoretical* concerns. The relation-ship between these discursive transformations and the apparently more concrete aspects of the sociocultural environment increasingly occupies the second half of this volume, which examines matters of cultural and political transformation through philosophical, political, and literary crit-ical writings.

Taken together, these chapters explore not simply the nature of the dis-cursive class whose impossibility seems by now quite manifest and the forms of what appears to be some emergent class; they seek also to ask the questions that inevitably accompany such a proposition. How is dis-cursive transformation possible at all? What may be the actual effects of revolutionary-style efforts? What is the place and the meaning of *evolution*? How *do* mind, society, and culture function together? How are discursive change and sociocultural transformation and/or development linked? How, especially, do they affect social and political formations? To these questions, too, the answers must remain moot. For we cannot know what the outcome may be until some new form of discourse is in fact func-tioning *in conjunction with* its sociocultural environment.

We can, however, look back at some past moment of transformation and see what appeared to take place. We can examine in some detail the functioning of discourses in the seeming uncertainty of our own time and see the consequences of certain failures. We may even be able to draw some provisional conclusions as to which emergent elements are proving significant. But until such elements provide the dominant means of func-tioning for the entire sociocultural environment, we can do no more.

The failures are examined at length in much of what follows; nonethe-less, it will be useful, I think, to observe here some of those that appear common, in our time, to literature and to science, to religion and to philosophy, at the very least. The search for some coherent series of signs able to be *interpreted*, endowed with one or more specific, limited mean-ings (in accordance with familiar habit), seems frequently to peter out and collapse. The (enunciating) subject's will to impose itself *as* ordering sub-ject upon objects leads only to a sort of discursive isolation—comprehen-sible to others, no doubt, but providing an entirely subjective and perspectival ordering of whatever seems beyond discourse itself; the will becomes either impotant or autotelic and solipsist.

Discursive transparency becomes impossible, because discourse itself reveals no correspondence whatever between its own order and that of things or of (daily) experience. It would always have been correct to say, as Leszek Kolakowski and others have now done, that language was "a set of tools we use to adapt ourselves to reality and to adapt it to our needs—active tools, tools of construction, not of exploration." But analytico-referential discourse always in fact assumed an entire adequacy of expression, of the conception it rendered, and of the action it made possible—hence the general frustration of the late nineteenth century. Frege could then observe, with something like despair, that logic had lost its ability and all aspiration to prove referentiality and found itself confronting a world of incapacitating "flux." To grasp a thing, of course, we must be able to provide either a nominal designation or a description of its properties. But we should not then suppose that things are actually "composed of their abstractly understood properties," for such "general terms only enable us to describe the individual."[9] Analytico-referential thought, however, all too frequently conflated that individual with its abstract description—because it understood the commonsensical, "objective" view of the "real" world to be identical with mathematical reason. "At bottom," wrote Laplace in a familiar and celebrated statement of that idea, "probability theory is only good sense reduced to calculus."[10]

Once that conflation became visible, once people began to see that the world's lawfulness had no clearly discoverable reality among things (which, precisely, were not then immediately identifiable with their abstract analysis), the hope of any simple *objective* and universal knowledge appeared to have been lost. The enunciating subject then seemed to have to take responsibility for the 'creation' of events (adopting an attractive, but false, appeal to the opposite pole from analytico-referentiality's previous certainties). But that could 'work,' like the scholastics' syllogism, only for matters already given; confronting events, phenomena, and situations it could not appropriate, the subject had either to accept its own incomprehension or to claim complete command over events (a difficulty faced with special acuity in subatomic physics, for example). Under such conditions, the only possible discursive meaning finally became that of the very process itself of producing signification, of only and always inscribing one's own signature (as I have described it elsewhere) within and upon discourse.[11] For Frege, this was a retreat to a theory of truth emphasizing the self-sufficiency, independence, and inner coherence of logical systems. And there the subject enfolds itself in the private language so beloved of analytical philosophy, making any relation with others impossible and indeed frustrating all and any social activity.

Precisely this kind of withdrawal, I think, is what explains the rapid success of deconstruction (and of growing religious sentiment), especially

9. Kolakowski, "Karl Marx," pp. 45, 49.

10. Pierre Simon Laplace, *Essai philosophique sur les probabilités* (Paris, 1986), p. 206.

11. Timothy J. Reiss, "Cosmic Discourse; or, The Solution of Signing (Gombrowicz)," *Canadian Journal of Research in Semiotics*, 8 (Winter 1980–81), 123–45.

in North American academic culture. These various failures of analytico-referential discourse, vestigial elements of a previously sufficient functioning, have been granted the status of some almost mythic, nostalgic *Other*. Yet to emphasize *errance* or *dérive, supplément* or *différance*, indecidability or chaotic flux as providing some sort of primordial 'place' of *archi-écriture* (in Derrida's term) or semiotic "chora" (as Kristeva would have it), is to turn away with a vengeance from the public sphere and to fall into that separation of fragmented selfhood long since criticized by Schiller in his *Letters on the Aesthetic Education of Man* or by Hegel in his *Aesthetics*.[12] To make a nostalgic virtue of those false trails is to wish the reinstatement of the very order their practitioners sought to query; nor is it at all irrelevant to add how frequently they claim to derive their dicta from some form of "post-Freudianism"[13]

Peirce, too, confronted a world envisioned as one of chaotic flux. He

12. That "turning away" or retreat is certainly why Julia Kristeva, whose current writing describes "melancholy" as the individual psychological version of her "chora," finds herself asserting that such melancholy proceeds more frequently from loss of love or of the beloved than from loss of work. As she puts it, "Il est vrai [!] qu'un chômeur est moins suicidaire qu'une amoureuse délaissée" (it is true that an unemployed man is less suicidal than an abandoned [female] lover): *Soleil noir: Dépression et mélancolie* (Paris, 1987), p. 18. Among other things, one wonders just how often an unemployed worker consults a psychoanalyst. But even were one ready to accept so simplistic a notion of causality, the suicide rate among, e.g., the unemployed young in North America belies such a dubious assertion. Similarly, Kristeva ascribes the "sociologically attested" greater frequency of "female depressions" to woman's greater difficulty in distancing herself from the "maternal Thing" (*la Chose maternelle*), the primary chora (p. 81). If such attestation is indeed the case, one might well suppose it to have at least as much to do with women's sociopolitical situation and status. Indeed, although Kristeva locates this particular situation in the Western tradition (pp. 77–78), such a privatizing and individualist view comes perilously close to biological determinism—whence there is no escape. The consequent inevitability of oppression might then induce *all* its victims to commit suicide. I emphasize here that the remarks critical of some aspects of deconstruction and its implications were all written (and in most cases published) long before anyone was aware of those wartime writings of the young Paul de Man, which have become in 1988 such a *cause célèbre*. It may indeed be that there is a relation between the historical and biographical purport of the sympathy there expressed for the ugliest aspects of German fascism and certain of the theoretical implications of deconstruction. Any such connection will surely be extremely complex and must await a reading of the early texts in question. Then, too, they will have to be understood in the context of Belgian socialism, of the cultural and ethnic conflicts between Walloons and Flemings as well as of class struggles within those groups, of German occupation during two world wars, and (doubtless not least) of the de Mans personal odyssey. This is not a matter of excuse, but of understanding, and the case is by no means so simple as to permit facile associations and kneejerk abuse—most often for reasons of academic politics. Furthermore, a personal itinerary must be kept separate from a general critical and theoretical movement. The profound seriousness of the issues raised is readily evident, but the meaning of such relation as must certainly exist (unless one denies any unity to a historical and thinking subject—a denial contrary to the experience of most of us), requires pondering. Moreover, the answers will have bearing not only on deconstruction, but on the political and ideological meaning of any and all criticial and theoretical effort.

13. I have elsewhere sought to show how Freud adopted and extended modernist discourse: "Science des rêves, rêves de la science," *Etudes Françaises*, 19, no. 2 (1983), 27–61.

rejoiced, however, in seeking not its separate 'reality' (whatever that might be) but the laws that marked the genuine interrelation of mind and world. What we need above all to explain, he wrote, is not the world's chaos and random contingency but *how* humans may grasp anything lawful about it at all, and just *what* the laws we are able to derive may tell us about the mediatory relationship between humans and the world, whether natural or social. For Peirce, such derivation and development were always ongoing, were always the practice of a group, and always resulted in some fruitful effect in the social and natural world. Individuality would thus give way to community (not some "Other"). Division would yield to continuity (not to "free play" of meaning, to *errance*). Identity would cede to a concept of "field" (not "difference"). Stability would be absorbed in process ordered as an ongoing production of communal "habit" (without fear of chaotic flux). Privacy and self-possessiveness of mind would be replaced by mind conceived of as inseparable from the public and social community of which it is constitutive and which constitutes it (so that a notion such as that of "undecidability" becomes irrelevant). Notions of individual authority or a subject's right to property would of necessity yield up their place.

Put thus, these Peircean principles appear as a series of disembodied and idealistic utopian abstractions. I try to show how they develop fruitfully from the very discourse they indeed do put in question and to indicate some of their concrete consequences. That the latter is necessarily a more complex, difficult, and long-range collective project is one of the inevitable aspects of writing on questions of contemporary urgency, of participating in discussion that is, after all, ongoing. Indeed, the very nature of the matter requires me to provide some explanation, I think, as to why I have incorporated few substantive changes in chapters whose original versions first saw print some years ago.

Michael Dummett wrote about his work on Frege that "almost every thought one has, or encounters in the work of another" about the writings and discussions in question "is apt to change what one is disposed to say in expounding or commenting on" them.[14] Certainly most of these chapters could well be rewritten in the light of what has since been said about their subjects—but such a process would by definition be never-ending; no book or argument could ever appear before the public, and debate would cease forthwith. "Each of us," as Jonathan Steinberg put the matter, "belongs to an invisible community of living and dead minds in constant and often random communication with each other" [15] (that randomness

---

14. Michael Dummett, *Frege: Philosophy of Language* (London, 1973), p. x.

15. Jonathan Steinberg, " 'Real Authentick History,' or What Philosophers of History Can Teach Us," *Historical Journal*, 24, no. 2 (1981), 474.

may sometimes appear in these pages). Peirce, on the basis of just such awareness, understood human culture, society, and history as a constant process of understanding, analysis, and meaningful praxis.

If these chapters were entirely updated for their present publication, they would lose their interest (if any) as developing elements in current discussion and as what I take to be a coherent intellectual progression. Further, nothing I have read since on the way in which they present these issues suggests any profound alteration in their underlying argument (alterations in detail I *have* sought to take into account, either in the rewriting or in the notes). One possible exception is some current work being done on Frege, suggesting that he was much closer to Peirce than I propose and indeed that he was advancing toward some entirely original conceptual breakthrough. As far as I am aware, however, Claude Imbert's work on that question, save for an occasional essay, has yet to appear. She is now working especially on conceptual parallels with Walter Benjamin, and we can only await the outcome of her researches with eagerness. In any case, these would not alter the purpose of my opposing Peirce to Frege, which concerns not so much their work as such as it does the matter of discursive and environmental stasis and change.

Another possible exception concerns the question of the individual and the collective subject. The appearance of the long-suppressed second volume of Sartre's *Critique* might change my view of his discussion of the matter, although his own dissatisfaction with it requires us to be chary of any dramatic assumptions.[16] The work of Lev S. Vygotsky and his school, only now becoming properly known and appreciated in the West, may well help develop some useful concept of the collective nature of "individual" psychology and a better awareness of its profoundly social nature. But the political and cultural dimensions of this elaboration remain to be seen. The alterations I have indeed made in the chapters of this book serve for the most part to bring them more into line with one another and with my own present thinking on their topics, to compose a

---

16. Just prior to the appearance of the second part of the *Critique*, Thomas R. Flynn published a wonderfully subtle study of the tension in Sartre between the seeming need for, but absence of, a "collective subject," and the simultaneous demand for collective responsibility, arguing that Sartre was in fact working toward a solution to this tension and that his work reveals an entirely coherent development in this respect: *Sartre and Marxist Existentialism: The Test Case of Collective Responsibility* (1984; rpt. Chicago, 1986). More recently, in what is essentially a commentary upon *Critique II*, Ronald Aronson has found himself obliged to conclude that "Sartre's starting point of individual praxis, meant as a heuristic device, becomes the substantive core of the entire analysis. The problem is that as Sartre construes individual praxis, its intrinsic links with larger totalities can never appear. Without presuming these social links at the outset, as the very basis for the individual's identity, we will never understand how this individual, alone or as a member of a class in conflict, will naturally build larger totalities": *Sartre's Second Critique* (Chicago, 1987), p. 235. I return to these questions in the second half of this book (starting with Chapter 5).

coherent whole, and to link them more clearly with the ongoing work mentioned earlier.

From this essentially retrospective collection there is, nonetheless, one major omission: no discussion of feminism appears in these pages and only a few references to its fundamental issues. Quite simply, it increasingly seems to me that a new discourse is emerging here whose dual preoccupations with discursive and social transformation make of it a genuinely *political* instrument. By this I mean that unlike Freudianism, for example (which I consider not a renewal but the mark of the end of a discursive dominance; see note 13), and unlike most if not all Western Marxisms (which have proved incapable of escaping the trammels of *their* history by renewing a social, economic, and political analysis that has long since revealed itself to be quite inadequate to the realities of late industrial conditions), some feminist thinking and action are necessarily and inevitably aimed at changing the organization of the power relations ordering our sociocultural environment. That such feminism undertakes to do so by attacking present discursive norms and all social relations is the principal part of its action. And there, of course, it is joined by the explorations in this book, though they have come from different sources and rather different preoccupations.

To be sure, some 'feminisms' may be accounted profoundly regressive: the 'rightist' ones that seek to argue for old ideals of "femininity," and the 'leftist' ones asserting an "earth-mother" syndrome or the like. In both, woman (the preferred use of the generic term, rather than the particularizing "women," itself reveals a reifying, estranging, and alienating form of consideration) is conceived of as "nurturing," "boundless," "all-embracing," "generous," "whole," and receptively "patient." Clearly, these two are in fact allies, the one arguing that femaleness is so different from maleness as to be incommensurable (Hélène Cixous, Mary Daly); the other affirming that that same difference justifies something very near the social roles made familiar to us in recent Western life (Phyllis Schlafly, Anita Bryant, Midge Decter—not to mention much of the work on so-called "female psychology").

Delphy is right to observe that these need to be understood as evidence of that false consciousness inevitable among oppressed groups (which is why "reification" and "alienation" are appropriate descriptions); those male writers who are aware of the issue at all can do little more, in that regard, than take note. Speaking in a recent interview about the altogether analogous situation of totalitarian imposition, Václav Havel made the similar point that in old totalitarian societies (as in old liberal ones, we may add), *overt* domination of one group by another is not the "most typical feature." Rather, "what is typical is the domination of one part of each of ourselves by another part of ourselves. It's as if the régime had an outpost inside every single citizen."[17] And in such a case, those who cannot avoid benefiting within the oppressive order cannot, without ceding to their own false consciousness, criticize those who suffer within it. We must avoid the "arrogance" of those who set themselves up as sympathizers with the very group of which their own sort are the oppressors.[18] One can and must, however, try to acknowledge forms of consciousness that have *not* yielded to the old familiar order of things. Indeed, the beneficiary's responsibility is all the greater.

Other feminists are satisfied to use liberal arguments to seek equality of opportunity and achievement, so that all may participate in what is viewed as so far the best form of society. In urging that what matters is women's equal access to the advantages of a dominant order, their argument is of a piece with the old Marxist socialist one—maintained by such as August Bebel, Clara Zetkin, Rosa Luxemburg, and Simone de Beauvoir in *Le deuxième sexe*—that the freeing of the working class would also free women. (So far as the liberal argument is concerned, Zillah Eisenstein has shown both its hope and its limits; Delphy has made perhaps the strongest and most compelling arguments against the Marxist socialist one.)[19] In practice, of course, if such 'equality' were achieved, it might well coincide with what seems most valuable in current feminist theory: the awareness that, as humans, men and women are always equal (in any understanding

17. "Doing without Utopias: An Interview with Václav Havel" [by Erica Blair, tr. A. G. Brain], *Times Literary Supplement*, January 23, 1987, pp. 81–83; this quotation, p. 81. Miklós Haraszti has recently devoted an ironic and profoundly complex book-length study to this matter, remarking at one point that at the end of a long history such imposition "is not like a garment but more like our skin: it grows with us" (*The Velvet Prison: Artists under State Socialism*, tr. Katalin and Stephen Landesmann, with Steve Wasserman [New York, 1987], p. 77).

18. The reference is to Ngugi Wa Thiong'o, *Homecoming: Essays in African and Caribbean Literature, Culture, and Politics* (1972; rpt. London, 1982), pp. viii–xix. Ngugi accuses those described here as acquiring "the most proprietorial air when talking of" the group they have decided to support. They "carve out a personal sphere of influence and champion the most reactionary and the most separatist cause" of the group among which they happen to live. In the context he describes, such "poisonous and divisive flattery" is as racist as outright opposition. That kind of "sympathy" is entirely analogous to the chauvinism just indicated. None of this implies either a refusal of criticism or a studied incuriosity toward all and any argument, but it does mean that men must undertake such criticism and curiosity in regard to putting their own house in order. It is therefore by no means enough to say, as do John Rajchman and Cornel West in the preface to their recent collection of contemporary U.S. philosophy (*Post-analytic Philosophy* [New York, 1985], p. vi), that the fact of their contributors being all white males reflects not on the editors' selection but on the profession or on the state of society, because that is how things are at the present time. I doubt this is to be entirely so, but even were it the case, the expression of sympathy would seem to require that such a collection not be compiled. Rather would they have to explain why it could not—or should not—be done. It would be one thing to work *that* matter out; it is quite another to present an encomiastic compilation, taken to represent the state of present U.S. philosophy, in which a brief *nostra culpa* is belied by all that follows.

19. See Zillah Eisenstein, *The Radical Future of Liberal Feminism* (New York, 1981). For the sense of urgency with which I now understand these issues, as well as discussion and in-

of the term that makes sense), that gender differences are created by and within the sociocultural environment, that these can and must be changed so as to enable a quite different sociocultural environment to emerge.

Lawrence Lipking has written of the expanding domain of feminist literary history, theory, and criticism that not only must it shed new light on works by women but that it will inevitably revise "our view of the masculine canon." "Not even," he concludes, "our secret places—our language, our habits of reading—can be immune from [its] fire." Aristotle's so-long silent sister, "Arimneste, is learning to speak."[20] Indeed, every area of human activity must and will rethink and reorder itself within new parameters appropriate to its specific domain. In more general terms, the intellectual approach represented by (materialist?) feminism will not, as Delphy has urged, be limited to a single population or to any single issue—hence its radically fundamental importance. It applies to all populations, to all issues, and to "knowledge" in any sense whatever. "It will not leave any aspect of reality, any domain of knowledge, any aspect of the world untouched."[21]

But why is that the case? the skeptic, the cynic, or the disbeliever may still ask. The major answers are two, though they are based upon a more elementary premise. In the first place, the *political* aim of reordering society inevitably implies entirely new kinds of concrete relationships, therefore of understanding and meaning, therefore of acts and events, and therefore of consciousness (there being no particular order in these changes, since they would by definition be simultaneous and ongoing). In the second place, the analytical and still political goal of understanding and laying bare hidden structures of oppression—of comprehending both how they have functioned and to what (and whose) ends, interests, and advantages—implies simultaneously a renewed understanding of old forms of meaning and their rejection in favor of others.

Yet these 'answers' must be held subordinate to the very basis of the arguments making the implications apparent. That basis is a political struggle corresponding to the principal contradictions inherent in our supposedly 'egalitarian' societies: their exclusion of fully one-half of their

creased reading in and around them, I am indebted to Patricia J. Hilden (though she has no responsibility for the views expressed here and may well take exception to some of them).

20. Lawrence Lipking, "Aristotle's Sister: A Poetics of Abandonment," in *Canons*, ed. Robert von Hallberg (Chicago, 1984), p. 103. Of course, women have *always* spoken, and while Lipking's general assertion seems to me correct, Joan DeJean is quite right to criticize him for having sought to put *him*self once again in women's place: he speaks of *masculine* literary and critical depictions of women (as "abandoned"), not of their self-portraits. See Joan DeJean, "Fictions of Sappho," *Critical Inquiry*, 13 (Summer 1987), 787–805, esp. 787–90. The dangers of men's *not* putting their own house in order first are admirably captured in this confrontation between DeJean and Lipking.

21. Delphy, *Close to Home*, p. 218.

populations from the ostensible benefits of their culture, and indeed the actual and objective oppression of that half by the other. And such exclusion and oppression occur in addition to the hierarchies of class with which those societies (as has long since been recognized) are fraught. *That*, needless to say, implies a fundamental error or flaw in the theoretical and practical foundations of our societies themselves.[22] Of course, if one then expands the issue to that of the relation between 'our' societies and others, the flaw becomes even graver.

This view of feminism (perhaps along with some 'Marxisms') quite evidently offers a transformational goal, if not yet a "model," that not only cannot be ignored but must become an essential ingredient of any eventual solution to the critical matters being raised and the diverse contradictions being increasingly suffered in our time. That is why the omission of any thoroughgoing assimilation of feminism within the following pages (and indeed, by and large, within the debates themselves of which they treat) is a major one. That is also why, nonetheless, the political feminism of which I have just spoken has a natural ally in the analyses and debates, criticism and theory represented here. This volume is, then, intended as a contribution both to a further understanding of the many discursive constraints, impasses, and contradictions already indicated and to furthering the consequences of their abrogation.

22. Londa Schiebinger has shown how Enlightenment arguments about natural rights required that (theoretical) *natural inequalities* be found to justify *real* social inequities. In their study of the human skeleton, for example, eighteenth- and especially nineteenth-century anatomists set out to unearth just such inequalities. Indeed, she has demonstrated how the very claim of universality actually underwrote the legitimation of male dominance: both spoken of above as fundamental in modernist discourse. In their drawings of male and female skeletons—used to support the claim of natural inequality—their idea was not to draw with precision any particular skeleton but to collect data from several, so as to discover the "perfect" one. Which aspects were "perfect" and which were not depended of course on some prior cultural decision, upon culturally established norms of beauty and perfection: one such norm was indicated by the female skeleton's "underdevelopment" in relation to the male's—in all except the pelvis. The very fact of creating a universal notion of the human was necessarily "laden with cultural values," one of whose aspects was the masculinity of that "universal." ("Skeletons in the Closet: The First Illustrations of the Female Skeleton in Eighteenth-Century Anatomy," *Representations*, 14 [1986], 42–82; citations, pp. 61–62). I mention this not only as an exemplary case of a foundational "flaw" but also because it demonstrates both how the elements indicated as essential within modernist discourse are entirely imbricated, and how the analyses in this volume correspond to aspects of the specifically feminist analysis of the Enlightenment.

Peirce and Frege:
In the Matter of Truth

Although we no longer accept the correspondence theory, we remain *realists au fond*; we retain in our thinking a fundamentally realistic conception of truth. Realism consists in the belief that for any statement there must be something in virtue of which either it or its negation is true: it is only on the basis of this belief that we can justify the idea that truth and falsity play an essential role in the meaning of a statement, that the general form of an explanation of meaning is a statement of the truth-conditions.

—Michael Dummett, "Truth"

In fact, and to conclude briefly on the question of binarism, we may wonder whether this is not a classification which is both necessary and transitory: in which case binarism also would be a metalanguage, a particular taxonomy meant to be swept away by history, after having been true to it for a moment.

—Roland Barthes, *Elements of Semiology*

The discourse of classical (or "modernist") thought, consolidated as the sole mode of genuine knowledge after the work of Francis Bacon, Galileo, Thomas Hobbes, René Descartes, and their contemporaries, can be characterized above all by two particularities: as a process of analysis and as a system of reference. The latter characteristic has behind it the assumption that thought and language are quite separate *operations* and the idea that language is no more than the instrumental medium of expression serving a thought that is capable of grasping representations of reality. The former is associated with that other apriori according to which the fundamental *structures* of language are identifiable with (as) those of thought: hence the attempt to discover in "general grammar" the universal workings of thought processes.

If, on the other hand, we can suppose thought to be composed of adequately precise representations of the actual—mediated in language— and if, on the other, we can identify the grammatical structures of language with the logical structures of thought, then, evidently, a properly organized discourse will provide us in its very form with the correct analysis of the objects it presents to us in its content, the objects to which its propositions are taken to refer. At the same time, it permits us to grasp them, to possess them, and use them as *ours,* the belongings of the owners of right thought.

I am well aware that this is a distinctly schematic review of a very complex matter; I have dealt with it at considerable length in *The Discourse of Modernism.* Suffice it to say here that I am referring to this set of elements whenever I use the phrase "analytico-referential discourse," abbreviated in the title of this volume to "analysis." In this chapter, I seek to show how the logical model of this discourse was at once questioned and reasserted (Frege) and how elements from the model and its questioning were extended toward something apparently quite new and potentially different (Peirce).

I suggest, indeed, that logical atomism—as it appeared, for example, in the Wittgenstein of the *Tractatus* (1921), who developed his analysis largely out of Frege—is an extreme form of a classical analytico-referential epistemology. It assumed that an ideal language lies hidden, so to speak, in ordinary language, an ideal truth-functional or extensional language whose basis is the sum of atomic propositions taken as picturing atomic facts in the external world. A fact is not, let it be said right away, anything "in itself," but the existence of certain "states of affairs" taken as "a combination of objects."[1] In his introduction to the English translation, Bertrand Russell underscored Wittgenstein's comparison of the process of reference involved in these assumptions with projections in geometry, whereby the projective properties of the original remain the same, whatever the actual projection of a given figure (each of whose possible different projections "corresponds to a different language"). "These projective properties correspond to that which in [Wittgenstein's] theory the proposition and the fact must have in common, if the proposition is to assert the fact."[2] Francis Bacon had long since invented just such a logical atomism with his concept of elements in the material world as an alphabet whose organization corresponds to the letters and words composing a phrase. This, he argued, meant that a correct understanding of the world was one in which the *projection* of the elements of written language and of the elements of the world coincide in some way.[3]

Wittgenstein, like the other logical atomists, was at pains to separate the propositions of a truth-functional language from those of ordinary language, for they are clearly incompatible. Nonetheless, his analysis showed clearly that the latter was taken as somehow *containing* the former (as

1. Ludwig Wittgenstein, *Tractatus Logico-Philosophicus,* tr. D. F. Pears and B. F. McGuiness (London, 1961), §§2–2.01.
2. Ibid., introduction by Bertrand Russell, p. xi.
3. See Timothy J. Reiss, *The Discourse of Modernism* (1982; rpt. Ithaca, 1985), pp. 208–11.

George Dalgarno, John Wilkins, and especially Gottfried Wilhelm von Leibniz had maintained in the seventeenth century), while it emphasized the classical separation of thought and the language held to be its relatively straightforward expression: "Everyday language is a part of the human organism and is no less complicated than it. It is not humanly possible to gather immediately from it what the logic of language is. Language disguises thought. So much so, that from the outward form of the clothing it is impossible to infer the form of the thought beneath it" (*Tractatus*, 4.002).

These classical assumptions posed the difficulty, as Peirce had recognized very early (and as Wittgenstein would himself discuss at length in *Philosophical Investigations*), that one cannot separate knowledge from the functioning of the organism that collects or makes it, and that the forms taken by knowledge must be *essentially* affected by the forms of discourse available to us at any given time, because the system of signs in which we are involved is a part of the knowledge that we acquire progressively through the practice of the system itself.[4] Nothing in our experience or in any logic provides a basis for the assumption of a separation between thought and language, or for the supposition that ordinary language conceals the skeleton of an ideal form of expression. Frege was entirely aware of this difficulty and deliberately, specifically, and constantly separated the truth of logical laws from referential truth.

The difficulty in such a division was not only that it divorced systematic knowledge from everyday experience (which, after all, was the very reverse of what classical science and the technology derived from it sought to

4. For Peirce, see the series published in 1868 in the *Journal of Speculative Philosophy*, reprinted in *Collected Papers of C. S. Peirce*, vol. 5, ed. Charles Hartshorne and Paul Weiss (Cambridge, Mass., 1931–58). The series has now been published in the second volume of *Writings of Charles S. Peirce: A Chronological Edition*, ed. Christian J. W. Kloesel et al. (Bloomington, Ind., 1984), pp. 162–307 (including other materials). I have nonetheless retained references to the *Collected Papers*, since this enables uniformity (only three of the proposed twenty volumes of the *Chronological Edition* have so far appeared, though they will necessarily become *the* edition of reference), hereafter citing it by volume and section number (in Arabic numerals) as is customary; these references are 5.213ff., 5.264ff., 5.318ff. As far as Wittgenstein is concerned, I do not wish to add to the now traditional (but changing) Anglo-American view of the incompatibility of the *Tractatus* and the *Investigations*. Wittgenstein himself urged that the latter be understood only in the light of the former, and the *Notebooks* of 1914–16 certainly point up many similarities. More important, his insistence on the closed nature of logical formalism, on the 'grammatical' foundations of knowledge, on the inexpressibility of extrapropositional 'reality,' and thence on the possible corollary of its inaccessibility and the *nonsensical* nature of attempts to 'know' it all form some of the many explicit or implicit links. The massive publication of Wittgenstein's 'marginalia' in recent years has confirmed these connections. See too Sylviane Agacinski, "Découpages du *Tractatus*," in *Mimésis des articulations* (Paris, 1975), pp. 19–53.

achieve) but also that it tended to remove any justification whatsoever for discussing such concepts as truth and falsity.[5] Obviating this perplexity, there always appeared in Frege's writings, therefore, an implied element of referentiality, if only by the fact that the problem was dismissed with such speed. While Frege did insist that logico-mathematical discussion need not be concerned with truths to be established by extralogical means, such a position tended to leave begging the question of the practical application of mathematical logic. If it did not in fact do so, it could only have been because there was a tacit assumption regarding experimental truth at the time Frege was writing, and because that assumption was— generally speaking—accepted. The difficulty *there* was that the question of the nature of experimental truths had become an extremely controversial one during the second half of the nineteenth century. Russell and, some- what later, Wittgenstein were well aware of the lacuna (as indeed were all the foundational mathematicians and logicians at this time, George Boole, Peirce, Ernst Schroeder, Guiseppe Peano, Edmund Husserl, Alfred North Whitehead, and others were all wanting to fill it). In seeking to restore the shaky edifice, however, at least initially, the logical atomists and their kin tended to return to the classical analytico-referential position.

Now the presupposition that "ordinary" language and thought were in some way separate yet that their fundamental *structures* were identical, and that adequate mental representations of the external world were available and 'present' to human judgment, controlled the precise forms taken in classical European thought by those oppositions of identity and differ- ence, of same and other, of mind and matter, of inside and outside. These were essential to the functioning of instrumental reason. The assumption of ground and origin was built into the discursive form itself by the claim that behind all particular language operations there lie these general and universal structures; the constant search for the 'original' language is merely one particular form that the assumption took.

The concept of time, like that of cause and effect, was also built in, for the necessary linearity of all verbal expression appeared to mean that predication was essentially diachronic, and predication (at least after Port- Royal) was taken both as the elementary purpose of all discourse and the discursive form of judgment. Predication reproduced the judgment con- cerning a truth: the order subject-predicate was necessary for this and given as the basic logical form of all discourse. Bertrand Russell has re- marked on the way such claims are linked to specific forms of language

5. See Michael Dummett, "Truth," *Proceedings of the Aristotelian Society,* 59 (1958–59), 141–62. The essay has been reprinted in Peter F. Strawson, ed., *Philosophical Logic* (Oxford, 1967), pp. 49–68, and in Dummett's own collection, *Truth and Other Enigmas* (London, 1978), pp. 1–24.

(though I think he might better have linked them to specific ways of *using* language—that is, to discourse): "The influence of language on philosophy has, I believe, been profound and almost unrecognized. . . . The subject-predicate logic, with the substance-attribute metaphysic, are a case in point. It is doubtful whether either would have been invented by people speaking a non-Aryan language."[6]

The fact that discourse reproduced the power of the possessive individual was included almost by definition: all linear enunciation of a predicate marks an imposition by the subject. Less evident but equally hegemonic is the certainty that such possessive individual power is always primarily *masculine.* Evelyn Fox-Keller, for example, has observed that this made science itself (the very model of the dominant class of discourse under modernism) a "parochial" activity, and that it requires of us, *now,* "a transformation of the very categories of male and female, and correspondingly, of mind and nature."[7]

For his part, Peirce fully accepted the idea that human activities, our conception of the world itself, and even what the world and society *are* for us are the result of what I would call discursive creation. He noted at one point how certain theories typical of the late nineteenth century were no more than a concretization, a reification of these discursive processes. Commenting upon political economic theory, he recorded its claim that "intelligence in the service of greed ensures the justest of prices, the fairest contracts, the most enlightened conduct of all dealings between men, and leads to the *summum bonum,* food in plenty and perfect comfort. Food for whom? Why, for the greedy master of intelligence" (6.290). He then concluded this sarcastic summary of a heavily Mandevillian laissez-faire, by adding: "The 'Origin of Species' of Darwin merely extends politico-economic views to the entire realm of animal and vegetable life" (6.293).[8]

---

6. Bertrand Russell, "Logical Atomism," in *Logic and Knowledge: Essays, 1901–1950,* ed. Robert Charles Marsh (1956; rpt. New York, 1971), p. 330. Frege's replacement of the subject-predicate relation by that of argument and function no doubt partly reduced this aspect. See *Conceptual Notation: A Formula Language of Pure Thought Modelled upon the Formula Language of Arithmetic* (1879), in Gottlob Frege, *Conceptual Notation and Related Articles,* tr. and ed. T. W. Bynum (Oxford, 1972), p. 107 (this translation of the *Begriffschrift* is henceforth cited as *Notation*). Frege remarks: "It is easy to see how regarding a content [in a proposition] as a function of an argument leads to the formation of concepts" (though this is actually perhaps not foreign to the notion of "projective properties" advanced by Russell and Wittgenstein, a function being, then, a possible projection of the argument). Apart from Dummett's work, an extremely important essay on the *Begriffsschrift* is Claude Imbert, "Le projet idéographique," *Revue Internationale de Philosophie,* no. 130 (1979), 621–65.

7. Evelyn Fox-Keller, *Reflections on Gender and Science* (New Haven, Conn., 1985), p. 178.

8. While Victoria Lady Welby did not share her future correspondent's opinion of Darwin, she did join in his view of discursive *meaning* as primary for humans: we function necessarily within a particular "universe of discourse," she wrote, foreshadowing the later Wittgenstein; see *What Is Meaning? Studies in the Development of Significance* (London, 1903),

Analytico-referential discourse, then, was always dual and opposi-
tional—what Peirce called dyadic: subject/predicate, subject (self)/other,
internal/external, then/now, cause/effect, and so on. And since, according
to (grossly simplified) classical theory, the relational structures of this
discourse reproduced (or were reproduced in) the different objective
series of which it spoke, the analytical and referential instrument that
related them—that was the 'place' of our knowledge—might be taken as
transparent, as not affecting the objects (events, phenomena, concepts . . .) whose expression it was; language became a neutral area of
mediation, doing no more than marking the space of separation between
mind and matter—and successfully bridging it. Matter and its mental
description had been for all practical purposes conflated.

For Frege, the concept of referential truth was finally a given, a state of
affairs that exists but whereof we cannot speak and that must therefore
remain inexpressible. For his own work, the only truth available for discussion and analysis was one able to be considered only in terms of an
intralogical function. He was concerned, he was to write late in life, with
the "laws of truth," asserting that logic "has the same relation to truth as
physics has to weight or heat. To discover truths is the task of all sciences;
it falls to logic to discover the laws of truth. . . . Laws of nature are the
generalizations of natural occurrences with which the occurrences are
always in accordance. It is rather in this sense that I speak of laws of
truth."[9] In his later thinking (from, say, the early 1900s), Frege accepted
the presupposition common to most formal logics that any statement may
be true or false: "A real proposition expresses a thought. The latter is
either true or false: *tertium non datur.*"[10] And he assumed that there exist
"extra-logical ways of finding out whether they are true or false (e.g. by
observation)."[11] Thus, logic, and the knowledge it provided, seemed to be
given almost as a self-contained automaton of analysis: "About what is
foreign to it logic knows only what occurs in the premises; about what
is proper to it, it knows all" (*Formal Theories*, p. 110). This axiom of

---

facsimile rpt., intro. Gerrit Mannoury, pref. Achim Eschbach (Amsterdam, 1983), p. 5.
Welby argued that this "universe" changes as humans evolve and adapt to the world; for this
reason, she naturally queried all the underlying concepts, oppositions, and metaphors of
analytico-referential discourse—including that of masculine primacy. On this, see Timothy
J. Reiss, "Significs: The Analysis of Meaning as Critique of Modernist Culture," in *Essays on
Significs*, ed. H. Walter Schmitz (Amsterdam, 1987), pp. 63–82.

9. Gottlob Frege, "The Thought: A Logical Inquiry" ("Die Gedanke," 1919), tr. A. M.
and Marcelle Quinton, *Mind*, 65 (1956), 289.

10. "On the Foundations of Geometry (1906)," in Gottlob Frege, *On the Foundations of
Geometry and Formal Theories of Arithmetic*, tr. E. -H. W. Kluge (New Haven, Conn., 1971), p.
97 (henceforth cited as *Formal Theories*).

11. J. O. Urmson, *Philosophical Analysis: Its Development between the Two World Wars* (1956;
rpt. London, 1971), p. 8.

separation led Frege (and after him the logical atomists) into an episte-mological impasse that Peirce was able to avoid; he did so by assuming the instrument of analysis to be anything but self-contained, while avoiding the aporias of classical referentiality.

Frege had always appeared to accept this division, indeed, to depend upon it. He remarked, for example (in 1884), that after the reasoning process has been completed, it rests "with observation finally to decide whether the conditions included in the laws thus established are actually fulfilled."[12] Only the specific sciences, he argued, are able to decide on the nature of the relationship between the actual and the reference provided by any single sign. For insofar as that reference has meaning— sense—for us only in terms of a propositional context, logic cannot possibly decide on external relationships. Still, in the same 1884 text, Frege slipped in con-siderably more ambiguity at the conclusion of his analysis:

> To apply arithmetic in the physical sciences is to *bring logic to bear on observed facts: calculation becomes deduction.* The laws of number will not . . . need to stand up to practical tests if they are to be applicable to the external world; for in the external world, in the whole of space and all that therein is, there are no concepts, no properties of concepts, no numbers. The laws of number, therefore, are not really applicable to external things; they are not laws of nature. They are, however, applicable to judgements holding good of things in the external world: they are laws of the laws of nature. They assert not connexions between phenomena, but connexions between judgements; and among judgements are included the laws of nature. [*Foundations,* p. 99, § 87; my emphasis]

Such a statement implied that a considerable adjustment needed to be made in our concept "truths of nature." That need was reinforced by the note Frege added to the words "observed facts": that "observation itself already includes within it logical activity." In so saying, Frege was coming very close to arguing that there *are* no facts except inasmuch as they are *already* involved in the activity of mediation—that they are, in more con-temporary parlance, already deeply theory-laden.

He did not actually say that; he said rather that logic has nothing to do with such facts. Nonetheless, it may be useful here to take a quick glance (in advance of more detailed discussion) at a passage from Peirce's 1901 review of Karl Pearson's *Grammar of Science* (not to be confused with a review of the first edition of the same book, published in 1892). Peirce was strongly critical of Pearson's nominalistic view of the natural sciences. Frege's view of their functioning, as expressed in the quotation above, was

12. Gottlob Frege, *The Foundations of Arithmetic: A Logico-Mathematical Enquiry into the Con-cept of Number,* tr. J. L. Austin, rev. ed. (Oxford, 1953), p. 23, §17 (henceforth cited as *Foundations*).

that there is a triple relationship (to whose complexities I will return in a moment) between sense, reference, and object. Sense and reference are both given by the word sign or the sentence sign (actually, he eventually adopted the view that a word can refer only if it is part of a complete proposition). At the propositional level, the sense is a judgment "holding good of things in the external world." This holding-good is the reference to the relational nature of externals. These externals are known to us by observation, already partly a matter of logic, and since the images (ideas, *Vorstellungen*) of observation become meaningful only inasmuch as they function as signs, so the formation of laws about them and the laws themselves can be only part of the mediating process. They are generalizable because they can be 'verified' by the particular sciences. This view, though Frege certainly did not elaborate upon it, was very similar to that expressed by Peirce in his 1901 Pearson review:

> Professor Pearson, not having fully assimilated the truth that every object is purely mental or psychical, thinks that when he has shown that the content of natural law is intellectual, he is entitled to conclude that it is of human origin. But every scientific research goes upon the assumption, the hope, that, in reference to its particular question, there is some true answer. That which that truth represents is a reality. This reality, being cognizable and comprehensible, is of the nature of thought. Wherein, then, does its reality consist? In the fact that, though it has no being out of thought, yet it is as it is, whether you or I or any group of men think it to be so or not. . . . But my argument to show that law is reality and not figment,—is in nature independent of any connivance of ours,—is that predictions are verified. [8.153]

This is precisely the answer Francis Bacon had given to exactly the same question.[13] One thinks of Frege's point that while the idea *(Vorstellung)* associated with a particular sign is perfectly individual and unusable in terms of knowledge, its sense (for example, a law of nature) is public property and as such does not depend upon the individual who may assert a proposition with that sense as being true.[14]

Because Frege is generally considered one of the founders of the line leading to modern analytical philosophy, it is perhaps worthwhile to take another look at the important works that preceded the turn of the century. In these, although the expressed intention was always the elaboration of a purely conceptual language, one could yet find an awareness of the *application* of this language for the acquisition of (observational) knowledge; hence, the separation of the two frequently became almost impossible. It

13. On this, see Reiss, *Discourse of Modernism*, pp. 211–14.

14. See esp. "On Sense and Reference" ("Ueber Sinn und Bedeutung," 1892), in *Translations from the Philosophical Writings of Gottlob Frege*, ed. Peter Geach and Max Black (Oxford, 1952), pp. 59–60 (henceforth cited as *Philosophical Writings*).

may well be that in the later works no analysis was ever given of the relationship of facts to sentences, and indeed that no full analysis was ever provided,[15] but the latent intuition of applicability, together with the ambiguities of certain later statements, certainly provided suggestions toward such an analysis. Indeed, it is my contention that his insistence on the formal separation of conceptual language and experimental (and experiential) fact led Frege into an impasse to which Peirce's work offers a solution. Moreover, it is a solution appearing to render operative certain elements implied in Frege's work that the latter chose to shunt to one side.

In his essay "On the Scientific Justification of a Conceptual Notation" (1882), written to explain the *Begriffsschrift* (1879), Frege had already started to break down certain of the suppositions of analytico-referential discourse. From the outset he argued that we could not consider the external world as entirely separate from us, because, unlike animals, we do not rely on our sense impressions to determine "the course of our ideas" or, therefore, of all our activities, as would be the case "if the outer world were not to some extent dependent on us."[16] The reason we are not thus limited is that we have the use of signs, which can place before our mind "that which is absent, invisible, perhaps even beyond the senses [*unsinnlich*]." He went on to add that only as the image becomes a sign, as it must, does it allow the creation of something like the center of a field. Failing that, the image is useless: "If we produce the symbol of an idea which a perception has called to mind, we create in this way a firm, new focus about which ideas gather. We then select another [idea, *Vorstellung*] from these in order to elicit *its* symbol. Thus we penetrate step by step into the inner world of our ideas and move about there at will, using the realm of sensibles itself *(das Sinnliche selbst)* to free ourselves from its constraint" (*Notation*, pp. 83–84). The sign itself, as sign, no longer signifies an individual. That it can become a point of focus in the accumulation of sign series (already forms of proposition?) is due to its capacity to refer to similar things—or, rather, to what they have in common: the concept.

Linguistic signs of course share this characteristic (by definition, as signs, they must). For this very reason, ordinary language, because of its utter lack of univocity, displayed an ambiguity fatal to the accumulation of 'true' knowledge. And no help was to be had from emphasizing linearity as a structural means to escape this ambiguity, or from seeking to suggest such means as a basis for a general and universal grammar. The obstacle to philosophical and scientific knowledge would not thereby be reduced at all: "Language is not governed by logical laws in such a way that mere

---

15. See, e.g., Jeremy D. B. Walker, *A Study of Frege* (Oxford, 1965), pp. 132–37.
16. *Notation*, p. 83. The last statement separates his view from that of the Cartesians, as the first does from that of the empiricists.

adherence to grammar would guarantee the formal correctness of thought processes" (*Notation,* pp. 84–85).

Logical thought differed in essential ways from ordinary language, and the division between them was inescapable and fundamental. Thought is revealed, Frege believed, more at the surface of language, so to speak; the formal laws of thought must try to take *that* into account. Ordinary language and such a formal language had their separate purposes. The grammar of ordinary language sought to maintain "a certain softness and instability . . . which nevertheless is necessary for its (ordinary language's) versatility and potential for development" (*Notation,* p. 86). Ordinary language rendered the flow of individual thought and feeling; it was not usable for the logician's purpose, which must be (argued Frege) the fixing of concepts and the analysis of the laws governing them. Ordinary language, on the contrary, presented the *dynamism of thinking.* This opposition (indeed, incommensurability) was the source of Frege's criticism of all linearly organized logics. That is why he insisted on the need to develop a two-dimensional logic as corresponding best to "the diversity of logical relations through which our thoughts are interconnected" (*Notation,* p. 87).

These suppositions imply a radical critique of the Cartesian tradition, which assimilated general grammar—as the basic underlying structure of all natural languages—to the universal forms of reason. According to Frege, traditional logical thought had allowed itself to be buried in a false view of the possible applications of ordinary language. Thereby, it had fallen into the trap of such confusions as that between object and concept (because in ordinary language a proper name and a concept word must often have the same form),[17] of such beliefs as that of the necessary linearity of thought, of such assumptions as the diachronicity of thought (as opposed to that of *thinking*), and therefore of such notions as those of origin, of absolute time, and so on, without being able to understand them as creations of the very logic that sought to justify their axiomatic nature.[18] Traditional logic was thus formed from a false valorization of a

17. Such a linguistically derived confusion could easily be corrected, of course. I have argued elsewhere that the reason for this assimilation of object and concept is in fact far more essential to the claims of analytico-referential discourse and far more deep-seated: Reiss, "The *concevoir* Motif in Descartes," in *La cohérence intérieure,* ed. Jacqueline Van Baelen and David L. Rubin (Paris, 1977), pp. 203–22. See Introduction above, p. 11.

18. See, e.g., the following comment by Frege: "A logical concept has no development, no history. . . . I do not agree . . . that it is very necessary to talk of the development of a concept. . . . Instead, it could be said that 'there is a history of defining that and that concept,' or 'there is a history of attempts to understand that concept,' and that would be more pertinent. A concept is something objective which we do not construct and which also has not developed in us; but something which we try to understand, and in the end we do understand, provided we have not sought erroneously after something where there is nothing" ("Uber des Trägheitsgesetz" ["On the Law of Inertia"], quoted in *Notation,* p. 31).

'well-formed' natural language, which supposed its grammar to be serving the same purpose as that of a possible science of the "laws of truth." Insofar as "the relations of concepts" were concerned, Frege sought "to break the power of the word over the human mind."[19]

Frege used a particular image to make the distinction between the two quite clear. The difference, he wrote, is one that concerns the achievement not so much of a form as of an *activity*. In both cases that activity is to be understood as an ongoing and accumulative one:

> I believe I can make the relation of my "conceptual notation" to ordinary language [*Sprache des Lebens*] clearest if I compare it to the relation of the microscope to the eye. The latter, because of the range of its applicability and because of the ease with which it can adapt itself to the most varied circumstances, has a great superiority over the microscope. Of course, viewed as an optical instrument it reveals many imperfections, which usually remain unnoticed because of its intimate connection with mental life. But as soon as scientific purposes place strong requirements upon sharpness of resolution, the eye proves to be inadequate. On the other hand, the microscope is perfectly suited for such purposes; but, for this reason, it is useless for all others. [*Notation*, pp. 104–5]

The whole purpose of a "conceptual notation," then (or of any adequate logic), was to be seen in terms of an instrument devised to show more clearly and to make usable the relations between the sense generated by the instrument's own mediatory relation with an objective reference on the one hand, and an idea *(Vorstellung)* become sign on the other.

The nature of these various relations with the particular relation concerning the exterior remained (in Frege) beyond explicit consideration. But it is no accident in this connection that Frege should later choose as his model demonstrating the order of mediating instrument, sense, reference, and idea the very one that was taken as marking the instauration (as Bacon put it) of classical science and modernist discourse: the telescope aimed at the moon, as recorded by Galileo in his *Sidereus Nuncius* of 1610. I return later to this matter. Here it is enough to observe that Galileo was always aware of the distinction to be made between an exact mathematical language and a largely analogical ordinary language: the former productive of predicative laws of nature and of truths about the order of things and events in the world; the latter useless for obtaining any knowledge of this sort, having quite other communicative and expressive uses. Only after Galileo—and indeed Newton—did science acquire the

---

19. Preface to *Conceptual Notation, Notation*, p. 106.

configuration it was to maintain at least until the end of the nineteenth century.[20] Frege's use of the metaphor was thus remarkably apposite.

From the beginning of his work, then, Frege made the distinction between an ordinary language, revealing the actual process and dynamism of individual thinking as available to us through a familiar discursive form, and a conceptual language that organized the laws governing the production of "true" statements about *concepts*. Let us take the case of two propositions whose form of expression differs but from which largely similar inferences may be drawn; then "the part of the content which is the *same* in both [may be called] the *conceptual content*." This, wrote Frege, is *all* we can be concerned with in a formal logic. However, we must remain aware that a proposition as a representation of the conceptualizing process is always limited and that what we say tends toward the approximative. Thus, he added, "the subject is the concept with which the judgment is *chiefly* concerned" (*Notation,* p. 113; my emphasis). Nor must we confuse the fact that "a proposition may be thought" with the quite different fact that "it may be true."[21] Ordinary language can communicate the former, but only a conceptual notation is able to tell us anything about the truth value attached to such a proposition.

Frege made the relationships more precise in his 1892 essay "On Sense and Reference," in which he generalized the "conceptual content" of a proposition into a notion of "sense" *(Sinn).* He argued that "connected with a sign (name, combination of words, letter), besides that to which the sign refers, which may be called the reference [*Bedeutung*] of the sign, [there is] also what I should like to call the *sense* of the sign, wherein the mode of presentation is continued. . . . The reference of 'evening star' would be the same as that of 'morning star' but not the sense" (*Philosophical Writings,* p. 57). One fundamental difference between the sense and the reference is that while we do grasp the reference by means of the sense (insofar as we are able to grasp it with any sort of clarity whatever), the sense is the common property of all those who participate in the same discursive field. While the reference is, generally speaking, subject to the laws produced in the field of sense, in its immediacy as a *particular* reference it makes contact only with its individual *Vorstellung,* and that, as we have seen, is unusable except as it becomes a sign—and therefore acquires sense.

20. On this matter, see esp. my essay "Espaces de la pensée discursive: Le cas Galilée et la science classique," *Revue de Synthèse,* no. 85–86 (January–June 1977), 5–47. The telescope metaphor has been discussed at some length in my *Discourse of Modernism,* pp. 25–27, 363–73, and in more detail yet in my "Science des rêves," pp. 27–61.

21. *Foundations,* p. vi: "Man . . . verwechselt das Gedachtwerden eines Satzes nicht mit seinem Wahrheit!"

This leaves us with the same difficulty as before where the ability to express truths about facts is concerned—unless, and only unless, the concept of truth is taken to be a statement not about things but about our mediation of them: "The sense of a proper name is grasped by everybody who is sufficiently familiar with the language or totality of designations to which it belongs; but this serves to illuminate only a single aspect of the reference, supposing it to have one. Comprehensive knowledge of the reference would require us to be able to say immediately whether any given sense belongs to it. To such knowledge we never attain" (*Philosophical Writings*, pp. 57–58).

Such a statement once again queried a logic, based on ordinary language usage, of a kind such as "Cartesian linguistics" had sought to establish. Doubt was thus thrown on the very search for some kind of necessary, though arbitrary, relation between a word and a thing (its denotation) that could be 'known.' Indeed, the very notion of the direct referentiality of word to thing tended to become moot. The proposition was that referentiality *must* pass through sense, and because sense is the possession of all those "familiar with the language," the result of previous conceptualization, there can be no royal way to the grasping of objects. Sense is already and always caught in established discourse: "The regular connexion between a sign, its sense, and its reference is of such a kind that to the sign there corresponds a definite sense and to that in turn a definite reference, while to a given reference (as object) there does not belong only a single sign. [What is more,] the same sense has different expressions [signs] in different languages or even in the same language" (*Philosophical Writings*, p. 58).

This was to say that ordinary language complicates the matter even further, because the signs for a given sense are multiple. Yet even in conceptual language the reference was given by the sense in a definite relationship that was not reversible, and that was because the reference was conceived not to produce a sign complete in itself but rather to multiply them. This meant that the relation of reference to sign (through sense) in *any* sign system must be a constantly multiplying one. Here, though Frege insisted elsewhere that such a process would render knowledge impossible, he seemed to come very close (if only implicitly) to Peirce's continuously developing and evolutionary triadic sign system.

Frege refused to see in this, however, any possible means of equating the process of sign production, and therefore of mediation itself, with an evolutionary process in the world:

If everything were in continual flux, and nothing maintained itself fixed for all time, there would no longer be any possibility of getting to know anything about the world and everything would be plunged in confusion. We suppose,

> it would seem, that concepts sprout in the individual mind like leaves on a tree, and we think to discover their nature by studying their birth: we seek to define them psychologically, in terms of the nature of the human mind. But this account makes everything subjective, and if we follow it through to the end, does away with truth. What is known in the history of concepts is really a history either of our knowledge of concepts or of the meaning of words. [*Foundations*, p. vii]

All this is no doubt the case, but it failed to take account of his own distinction, in the same text, between the objective and the actual: "The axis of the earth is objective, so is the centre of mass of the solar system, but I should not call them actual in the way the earth itself is so." Or, again: "What is objective . . . is what is subject to laws, what can be conceived and judged, what is expressible in words. What is purely intuitable is not communicable."[22] Under that assumption the notion of flux would not apply to the "objective" but could be taken as applying to the "actual" without arousing fear of epistemological anarchy. The notion of flux is not able to be assimilated in some a priori manner to what is given as an entirely individual subjective process. Indeed, Wittgenstein's view was that such a notion could well become the conceptual launching pad for all useful knowledge: "I should like to start (a book) with the original data of philosophy, written and spoken sentences, with books as it were. And here we come on the difficulty of 'all is flux.' Perhaps that is the very point at which to start."[23] The fact that Frege saw reference as multiplying sense could have been taken merely to mean that the laws of nature, inasmuch as they apply to objects only through concepts,[24] are multiple and *multipliable*. That would be something like Peirce's concept of "chance." To say that an object can be 'reached' only through a concept, the sense of a proposition, is to say that it can be known only in a conceptual *field*, one form of which we call the "laws of nature."[25]

22. Ibid., p. 35, §26. Cf. again: "What we cannot speak about we must pass over in silence" (Wittgenstein, *Tractatus*, §7).

23. Ludwig Wittgenstein, *Culture and Value*, ed. G. H. von Wright with Heikki Nyman, tr. Peter Winch (Chicago, 1980), p. 8 (written in 1930). Wittgenstein actually remarked quite frequently (a) that all thinking always starts from others' thoughts and (b) that we are always in the midst of ongoing processes, never able to fix upon anything like an "origin." Here there was a certain kinship with Peirce.

24. See the essay "On Concept and Object" (1892) in *Philosophical Writings*, p. 45: "An object's falling under a concept is an irreversible relation."

25. The notion of a conceptual field, a field within which alone a sign refers to a sense and thence to a reference, appears very close to Peirce's "phaneron": the contextual field, the manifold, or sometimes Gestalt, within which alone all signs must function. "Instead of linking our chain of deductions direct [*sic*] to any matter of fact," wrote Frege, "we can leave the fact where it is, while adopting its content in the form of a condition [*ihren Inhalt als Bedingung mitführen*]. By substituting in this way conditions for facts throughout the whole of a train of reasoning, we shall finally reduce it to a form in which a certain result is made

Actually, the bidimensionality of Frege's conceptual notation might it-self appear as an attempt to escape the difficulty of linear univocity that classical logic had sought to formulate through what it saw as the main characteristic of the natural languages. We have seen that Frege conceived of the functioning of ordinary language in a very different way, and he viewed the assumption that our thought processes could be depicted as linear and univocal as entirely misbegotten. That did not mean, however, that conceptual language and ordinary language could be identified on different principles. What it did mean was that we should see ordinary language as *showing* us thought in process and proceed from there to build a notation capable of *explicating* what the other only shows. To start from a primary assumption of the identity of linguistic and mental *struc-tures,* even if we did not follow the traditional norms in doing so, was, Frege opined, to court disaster. But at one level, therefore, conceptual notation was to be an analysis of the actual discursive process.

The facts of univocity and linearity are a limitation in linguistic expres-sion that we overcome in everyday communication and exchange, by means both linguistic and extralinguistic, but that ordinary writing ac-centuates as its primary characteristic. Indeed, one might well say (*pace* Derrida, perhaps) that our understanding of speech functioning has been through writing, rather than vice versa, and that that fact explains both why logic was thought to be derivable from natural language and why linguistics, especially of a Saussurean variety, has by and large ig-nored speech in favor of an underlying system *(langue)* that is—though covertly—writing. Univocity and linearity correspond to an actual discon-tinuity of the signs (written or so conceived) and *not at all to the discursive field of sense or to the matter of reference through that field.* Rousseau had long since spoken of writing as such a deformation: "Writing, which it would seem should stabilize language, is precisely what alters it. It changes not the words but the spirit, substituting exactness for expressiveness."[26]

---

dependent on a certain series of conditions. Thus truth would be established by thought alone. . . . It would then rest with observation finally to decide whether the conditions in-cluded in the laws thus established are actually fulfilled" (*Foundations,* p. 23, §17). The advantage of this procedure over a direct linking of individual propositions to facts them-selves, he argued, is that the propositions would be general, related to the nature of certain sets of conditions (*Foundations,* p. 24, §17). The truth concerning a particular case is then the extent of its inclusion in the propositional complex and the manner in which it can thus be included. There seems little doubt expressed here that signs could not function in the production of knowledge other than in terms of a field (= phaneron) or that knowledge is none other than that field.

26. Jean-Jacques Rousseau, *Essay on the Origin of Languages,* in Rousseau and J.-G. Herder, *On the Origin of Languages,* tr. John H. Moran and Alexander Gode (New York, 1966), p. 21. I have brought this closer to the original: *Essai sur l'origine des langues,* ed. Charles Porset (Bordeaux, 1970), p. 67.

The mid-nineteenth-century French philosopher and economist Augustin Cournot addressed himself quite precisely to this question:

> Condillac and the logicians of his school—whose ideas agree on this point with those of Descartes and Leibniz, a fact which should be noted because it is so rare—by perhaps exaggerating the power of the institution of language in general, exaggerate above all the imperfection of individual languages, as usage has fashioned them, by contrasting them endlessly to that ideal type which they call a "well-made language." Now on the contrary, it is in its abstract nature or in its general form that language must be considered essentially defective, while spoken languages, slowly formed under the lasting influence of infinitely varied needs, have warded off that radical disadvantage (of univocity and linearity), each in its own way and depending on its degree of suppleness. . . . What would augment and perfect our intellectual faculties by multiplying and varying the means of expressing and transmitting thought, if it were possible, would be to arrange all spoken languages to suit our liking, and in accordance with the need of the moment and not to find already constructed this systematic language which would be, in most cases, the most imperfect of instruments.[27]

"What we do want," Lady Welby was to write some fifty years later, "is a really plastic language," one that can "store up" in some way "all our precious means of mutual speaking" and enable people "to master the many dialects of thought."[28] In a different context but not from entirely different premises, Evelyn Fox-Keller has argued more recently that such a view needs to be applied to the very scientific ideal itself: "A healthy science is one that allows for the productive survival of diverse conceptions of mind and nature, and of correspondingly diverse strategies. In my vision of science, it is not the taming of nature that is sought, but the taming of hegemony."[29]

But it may well be that such a 'feminist' perspective had long since enabled the querying of a masculinist view of that hegemonic model: "Sciences, indeed, have been invented and taught long ago, and, as Men grew better advis'd, new modelled. So that it is become a considerable Piece of Learning to give an Account of the Rise and Progress of the Sciences, and of the various Opinions of Men concerning them."[30] So wrote Mary Astell in 1706, adding immediately and with a certain ironic tone that "Certainty and Demonstration are much pretended to in this

27. Antoine Augustin Cournot, *An Essay on the Foundations of Our Knowledge* (1851), tr. Merritt H. Moore (New York, 1956), pp. 317–18.

28. Welby, *What Is Meaning?* pp. 60, 97.

29. Fox-Keller, *Gender and Science*, p. 178.

30. Mary Astell, *Some Reflections upon Marriage, with Additions*, 4th ed. (1730; facsimile rpt. New York, 1970), p. 112; the citation is from the Appendix, which is an extended version of the original preface.

present Age." Cartesian that she was, she did not question that so much as, in the later manner of a Fox-Keller, question its hegemony. All these views seem very close to what I am suggesting was *implied* by Frege throughout the early texts (we will see the degree to which they coincide with Peirce's arguments.) The Cartesian tradition, however, sought to give words in discourse so precise a denotative capacity that one could obtain, through their 'proper' use, an adequate knowledge not only of what Frege called the objective but likewise of what he called the actual. The picture theory of the logical atomists, though corresponding not to the word but to the proposition, had a similar intention. Both argued that they had been sufficiently successful to make true scientific knowledge possible—certain and demonstrative, as Astell might have put it.

Frege, however, was at pains to divorce any "picture" we might have from any more general truth: "The reference and sense of a sign are to be distinguished from the associated idea [*Vorstellung*]." It may of course be disputed that this thought has anything whatever to do with logical atomism's 'image.' Perhaps not—but for Frege, anything more would be a matter of pure intuition, at once inexpressible and uncertain. The idea, he wrote in "Sense and Reference," though always based in previous memories and cognitive acts, is absolutely subjective: "This constitutes an essential distinction between the idea and the sign's sense, which may be the common property of many and therefore is not a part of a mode of the individual mind. For one can hardly deny that mankind has a common store of thoughts which is transmitted from one generation to another. In the light of this, one need have no scruples in speaking simply of *the* sense, whereas in the case of an idea one must, strictly speaking, add to whom it belongs and at what time" (*Philosophical Writings,* pp. 59–60). That is a challenge the Vienna School was to take up with the concept of the "protocol."

For Frege, then, the notion of sense was not simply a matter of situating a reference in a conceptual field. It was also characterized by its *public* nature. The ideal notational logic had to conform to the fact that conceptual thinking is common to all humankind, as are the structural elements composing it. Indeed, sense would be quite meaningless if it were not to belong to the community: more precisely, we could not speak of sense *unless* we also spoke of community. Such a thought corresponded to that principal point put forward by Peirce, that the idea of conceptual logic is inseparable from the idea of society. "Have you ever written," Lady Welby asked Peirce in 1904, "on the idea of order as part of that 'freedom,' and conversely? What is Order? (asked by Mr. Russell) is to me a twin question to What *is* Meaning?" Peirce replied to this kind of question that "an inference is 'logical,' if, and only if, it is governed by a habit that would in the long run lead to the truth. I am confident you will assent to this. . . .

It is a part of our duty to frown sternly upon immoral *principles;* and logic is only an application of morality. Is it not?" So indeed it is, Welby immediately wrote back, assenting to his "definition of a logical inference, and agree[ing] that Logic is in fact an application of morality in the largest and highest sense of the word."[31] The logic in question is, as Peirce had said in 1898 (in his lecture "Detached Ideas on Vitally Important Topics," 1.616–48), more an instinctive than a rational one—and Welby was quite right to conclude her agreement by adding: "That is entirely consonant with the witness of Primal Sense" (by which she meant, precisely, an instinctual form of "reason" going beyond and subsuming the ratiocination of Enlightenment).[32]

This bond between logic, morality, responsibility, and public order goes much further than Frege was willing to go. Thought and society, discourse and the whole sociocultural environment would be linked in inextricable ways. And those ways would be very different from the divisions and classifications fundamental to analytico-referentiality—as the development of this book from earlier to later chapters seeks to suggest. But something potentially similar seems at least implied in Frege's telescope metaphor:

> The reference of a proper name is the object itself which we designate by its means; the idea, which we have in that case, is wholly subjective; in between lies the sense, which is indeed no longer subjective like the idea, but is not yet the object itself. The following analogy will perhaps clarify these relationships. Somebody observes the moon through a telescope. I compare the moon itself to the reference; it is the object of the observation, mediated by the real image projected by the object glass in the interior of the telescope, and by the retinal image of the observer. The former I compare to the sense, the latter is like the idea or experience. The optical image in the telescope is indeed one-sided and dependent upon the standpoint of observation; but it is still objective, inasmuch as it can be used by several observers. [*Philosophical Writings,* p. 60]

The area covered by sense in the formation of knowledge was thus precisely analogous to Peirce's description of truth as the possibility of ("habitual") verification, as we saw in the Pearson review, for example, or in the exchange with Welby.

So far we have been examining, rather cursorily perhaps, a number of fairly important elements in Frege's thinking. At this stage I may usefully sum them up. The implication of evolutionism or continuity in a

31. *Semiotics and Significs: The Correspondence between Charles S. Peirce and Victoria Lady Welby,* ed. Charles S. Hardwick with James Cook (Bloomington, Ind., 1977), pp. 39, 83, 91 (letters of November 20, 1904; December 23, 1908; January 21, 1909).
32. See Reiss, "Significs."

developing mediatory relation, the hint of the necessarily communal nature of the concepts of logical propositions and of the form taken by such propositions, the notion of a conceptual field—three of the major premises of Peirce's triadic organization of thought and logic—were all in evidence in Frege's analysis. The last two, at least, were explicitly present. Further, we have seen the suggestions that thought cannot be considered as entirely separated from the external world, that there is no basic similarity at a structural level between the grammar of ordinary language and the logical foundations of thought, that referentiality is always at least partly obtained from previous cognitions and dependent upon already established relations. These provide us with a considerable number of the elements essential to the Peircean 'solution' to the matter of truth. From that, however, Frege himself seemed to shy away.

In response to the whole matter of the difficulty of attaining to any positive truth, if propositions refer only via their sense, via the conceptual field (both a common property and the result of prior cognition), Frege made use of the logical category of truth value. Yet we have to recognize that his use of the truth value itself became an obstacle: he remained unable to escape from the idea that he could separate his conceptual language from ordinary language (though not, as we have seen, in any traditional way), so that truth and falsehood as involving the laws of the excluded middle and of contradiction came back to haunt him. His logic finally obliged him to aver that science could discover no *facts* about the external world that any conceptual language could 'reliably' label as true, save only to the extent that we may say, "A fact is a thought that is true." The category of truth value, that is, was a kind of last resort permitting one to say that at least *something* could be taken as "true." That something is simply the existence of the thought itself in its supposed verifiability, or agreement with what Peirce would call habit. Thus, Frege concluded, the "work of science does not consist of creation but of the discovery of true thoughts."[33] The trouble with *that* is that Frege had already cut the ground from beneath the possibility of such verifiability, in any way other than as the mere outcome of any given single experiment or experience. Truth value could come to be limited to the Vienna School's protocol, recounting but a unique and individual instance. And even then. . . .

Earlier than the text just mentioned, in his 1891 essay "Function and Concept," Frege had proposed the truth value as the "reference of the sentence" (*Philosophical Writings*, p. 31). Truth value, of course, was to apply not to objects but to propositions. A function acquired a truth value when combined with an argument in a proposition about what is denoted by the proper name (for example) that satisfies the argument. It was a

33. Frege, "The Thought," pp. 307–8.

category applied to the satisfying of the relational aspect of a function. Any proposition could thus have two values: its truth value and its "objective" value. This last was its value in virtue of the reference contained in its argument: "The two truth values have already been introduced as possible values of a function; we must go further and admit objects without restriction as values of functions." Since they are the reference of a proposition, "the two truth values are objects"[34] (objective, rather than actual). The truth value relative to a thought (= sense of a proposition) should not be considered as a part of the thought but rather, Frege constantly insisted, as occupying an entirely different level: it is that to which the thought refers if the proposition containing that thought is complete. Truth values cannot therefore be affected if "part of the sentence is replaced by an expression having the same reference." But that argument forced him to go yet further and to assert that truth value provides all propositions with the same reference, be it the True or the False (for it was in fact but a category serving to affirm the completeness of the proposition):

> If now the truth of a sentence is its reference, then on the one hand all true sentences have the same reference and so, on the other hand, do all false sentences. From this we see that in the reference of the sentence all that is specific is obliterated. We can never be concerned only with the reference of a sentence; but again the mere thought alone yields no knowledge, but only the thought together with its reference, i.e., its truth value. Judgements can be regarded as advances from a thought to a truth value. . . . Judgements are distinctions of parts within truth values. Such distinction occurs by a return to the thought. To every sense belonging to a truth value there would correspond its own manner of analysis. [*Philosophical Writings*, pp. 64–65]

The relation between reference (truth value), sense, and sign was thus a 'dialectical' one: every advance of knowledge required a continual circulation within the common conceptual and discursive field, between the truth value as reference of an asserted proposition, the sense of the proposition, and the reference of that sense.[35] But truth value itself could be

34. *Philosophical Writings*, pp. 31–32. Cf. "On Sense and Reference," *Philosophical Writings*, p. 63.

35. In a letter to Edmund Husserl of May 24, 1891 (*Formal Theories*, p. xxxiv), Frege suggests the following model:

proposition	proper name	concept-word
↓	↓	↓
sense of the proposition (thought)	sense of the proper name	sense of the concept-word
↓	↓	↓
reference of the proposition (truth value)	reference of the proper name (object)	reference of the concept-word (concept) →
		object falling under the concept

seen as only dubiously useful: either it must be unique (as we saw), and then it is meaningless because identical with "objective" truth; or it must be universal, the single value of *all* complete propositions, and then it becomes pointless.

Indeed, the use of the truth value was severely criticized by Bertrand Russell, who objected that such a category would of necessity make all "asserted propositions . . . strictly and simply identical." For what would be asserted would be "the meaning (sense) of the unasserted proposition together with its truth-value."[36] In fact, we have just seen this expressly stated by Frege. The idea of a truth value was based on what Russell called (following the first volume of Frege's *Grundgesetze* of 1893) the three elements of judgment: "(1) the recognition of truth, (2) the *Gedanke,* (3) the truth value."[37] Of these, the second is the sense referring beyond itself. Such a configuration implied that what valorized the sense of a proposition was neither more nor less than its insertion into something of the nature of a 'field.' The matter of truth or falsehood as regards the reference of a sense would then be included as—shall we say?—a limit case of the truth-value element in judgment (which is at a quite different level). The logic implied would be something one might call a field logic. And while it is true that truth value, as applied there, is binary, it seems to have been 'elongated,' as it were, by the object/sense/sign axis that traverses the triple relation of judgment itself.

It is scarcely surprising that Russell criticized the very form Frege considered essential to facilitating the discovery of laws of truth—that is, his conceptual notation—as "unfortunately so cumbrous as to be very difficult to employ in practice." The notation is indeed very far from linear, 'atomistic' thinking. Possibly for the same reason, the same philosopher argued that Peirce's philosophy in its entirety could not be accepted but that there remained nonetheless "very many suggestions that, in a receptive mind, are capable of giving rise to large developments of great importance."[38] Both Peirce and Frege introduced, at the very least, a duplicity in meaning.

In Frege's case, that duplicity remained only a possibility, really, and one he seemed to renounce after Russell's criticisms (though that has given rise to debate).[39] Finally, he argued that all attempts to define truth must collapse: "For in a definition certain characteristics would have to be stated. And in application to any particular case the question would always

36. Bertrand Russell, *Principles of Mathematics* (1903; rpt. New York, n.d.), Appendix A: "The Logical and Arithmetical Doctrines of Frege," p. 504.

37. Ibid., p. 502.

38. Ibid., p. 501, and foreword to James K. Feibleman, *An Introduction to the Philosophy of Charles S. Peirce Interpreted as a System* (1946; rpt. Cambridge, Mass., 1970), p. xvi.

39. See, e.g., the two essays by W. V. Quine and Peter T. Geach, both entitled "On Frege's Way Out," in *Essays on Frege,* ed. E. D. Klemke (Urbana, Ill., 1968), pp. 485–504.

arise whether it were true that the characteristics were present. So one goes round in a circle. Consequently, it is probable that the content of the word 'true' is unique and indefinable." Whatever may be the case, the question of being true can have nothing to do with any notion of correspondence, because if it did, "the question of truth would reiterate itself to infinity" (so much for the classical discursive ideal of referentiality). Nonetheless, the assertion of a thought always carries with it the property of being true.[40] Frege's conclusion therefore appears to be that *that* kind of truth is axiomatic—but it seems no more than tautological. So he appears to have reached an impasse. Obliged to use a term whose ordinary acceptance he was unable to define, he remained unable to provide any new, alternative definition capable of furnishing a basis for understanding how a particular kind of sign system might function in terms of truth. He had been seeking to make available a new foundation for the familiar conceptual system, one seeking to mediate an exterior conceived of as composed of knowable facts. And without such a new foundation in truth (as Frege and others had seen) the system's very idea of knowledge was thrown into confusion.

Posited axiomatically, however, the concept of truth was no longer any use at all. Michael Dummett has remarked:

> We must abandon the idea which we naturally have that the notions of truth and falsity play an essential role in any account either of the meaning of statements in general or of the meaning of a particular statement. The conception pervades the thought of Frege that the general form of explanation of the sense of a statement consists in laying down the conditions under which it is true and those under which it is false (or better: saying that it is false under all other conditions); this same conception is expressed in the Tractatus in the words, "In order to be able to say that 'p' is true (or false), I must have determined under what conditions I call 'p' true, and this is how I determine the sense of the sentence" (§4.063). But in order that someone should gain from the explanation that P is true in such-and-such circumstances an understanding of the sense of P, he must already know what it means to say of P that it is true. If when he inquires into this he is told that the only explanation is that to say P is true is the same as to assert P, it will follow that in order to understand what is meant by saying that P is true, he must already know the sense of asserting P, which was precisely what was supposed to be being explained to him.[41]

A possible way out of this impasse was offered by Peirce, to whose sign theory of knowledge we have already seen certain similarities in Frege's work. Peirce took an idea of the continuing evolution of the world and of

40. Frege, "The Thought," pp. 291–93.
41. Dummett, "Truth," pp. 55–56.

human interaction with it as the basis for developing a general theory of signs capable of dealing with knowledge as a dynamic series of interrelations and transformations. The implicit elements of evolution, continuity, community, and semiotic field from which Frege constantly seemed to back away (fearful perhaps of allowing psychology to interfere with logic), with the consequent dilemma we have seen, were basic to a sign theory of which logic, in any narrow sense, was merely one part—whatever its relative importance. Thus logic, for Peirce, if considered simply as a self-contained conceptual process, might indeed be dyadic and able to be considered in terms of the excluded middle and contradiction. But so considered, it was itself a "Secondness" that could give no knowledge of anything because it had not yet entered into the triadic relationship peculiar to all forms of mediation. Applying the opposition true/false to a binary system (Peirce ultimately implied) is idle because it is merely to define the relation of Secondness. Only when that system is subsumed under a triadic process can the question of truth and knowledge be raised with any degree of appositeness.

Once a triadic relationship exists, assuming it to be "genuine" (that is, such that its 'parts' are each necessarily related together and individually to each of the 'others'),[42] it can no longer be separated from the evolutionary nature of the actual. The excluded middle can no longer hold, because the 'truth' expressed is never limited: it is not an either/or but rather the point of departure for thought activity in the world (though it is not, properly speaking, a point of departure either, for there is no such thing as an *original* triadic relation: it is but a moment in an always ongoing process). Thus, wrote Peirce, when we express a fact, we actually express a semiotic relation in which our expression of the fact is affirmed as well as what is given therein as the fact: "Not only is every fact really a relation, but your thought of the fact *implicitly* represents it as such" (3.417).

Peirce presented two principal definitions of the concept of truth. The first of these (as the foregoing discussion suggested) is extraordinarily similar to Frege's consideration of truth value: "All propositions refer to one and the same determinately singular subject, well understood between all interpreters and utterers; namely, to the Truth, which is the universe of all universes, and is assumed on all hands to be real" (5.506). The second definition explains truth as a process of knowing, the aspect that Frege ultimately found himself obliged to leave undefined and to consider undefinable: "Truth is that concordance of an abstract statement with the ideal limit towards which endless investigation would tend to

---

42. The quotation marks are needed here because the members of such a set cannot be meaningfully considered as separate entities.

bring scientific belief, which concordance the abstract statement may possess by virtue of the confession of its inaccuracy and one-sidedness, and this confession is an essential ingredient of the truth" (5.565).

"This confession" is also the mark of the permanent distance between these two truths and the measure of human fallibility: "It is almost impossible," the young Peirce had precociously written around 1854, "to conceive how truth can be other than absolute; yet man's truth is never absolute because the basis of Fact is hypothesis."[43] Such fallibilism, as Peirce eventually called it, had to be incorporated within the second, epistemological definition of truth—and not only in its definition, of course. It had also to be included in some meaningful way in its 'actualization'—say, in scientific experiment. In that sense, truth is the attainment of "a state of belief unassailable by doubt" (5.416), he wrote in 1905, confirming what he had already written in 1877 concerning the "conception of truth as something public" (5.384) and what he was to write to Welby at the end of 1908.

All that is to say (Peirce was arguing in this direction from the very earliest of his available notes, and such thoughts were fundamental to his first important series of articles, published in the *Journal of Speculative Philosophy* in 1868) that the concept of an actual, objective fact about which we can assert *the* (singular) truth is *a creation of the very idea we have of truth.* That is doubtless why Frege was obliged to admit that the epistemological idea of truth must be either tautological or indefinable, so long as he denied that logic (and thus its truth) did indeed have a history.

Peirce's view, therefore, was that we could not avoid starting out from certain given mental positions as to the logical means of inquiry, and that to be aware of these and then to use them was the only viable way to proceed. These means could then be made 'dialectical' through constant interplay with their 'object,' to which 'they' would adjust 'themselves,' and 'it' to 'them,' ever more nearly in terms of the probability of their conclusions concerning the object (of knowledge, that is to say). One of the problems faced, as we will see, was that of vocabulary, since to speak (as here) in terms of atomistic individuals was to allow traditional discourse to impede his thinking: "We think," wrote Welby in 1903, "in specks and lumps of stuff; we must learn to think in throb and complex whirl or intricate convolution."[44] That problem helps explain both the unfinished

---

43. Peirce, *Chronological Edition,* I:8. I have discussed the growth of the concepts of fallibilism, hypothesis, language as semiotic process, and triadicity in relation to other aspects of Peirce's thought, as these matters develop through the early works, in "The Young Peirce on Metaphysics, History of Philosophy, and Logic," *Recherches Sémiotiques / Semiotic Inquiry,* (March 1984), 24–47.

44. Welby, *What Is Meaning?* p. 78.

nature of Peirce's work and his constant elaboration of new nomenclatures and classifications.

Peirce's rejection of the Cartesian position, especially in "Some Consequences of Four Incapacities" (1868), was based on the argument that to deny our inbuilt "prejudices" in claiming to free ourselves from them by a universal doubt was merely a form of repression (or, more precisely perhaps, of what I have elsewhere called an "occultation": the concealment in discourse of a foundational element in fact essential to the ongoing functioning of that discourse).[45] It actually led to a serious blindness, for one would then philosophize merely *as though* those premises were not operative. Peirce's point was that by consciously situating these prejudices within our method, we would be in a position to place them in the dialectic of triadicity, together with the method itself and its 'objects.' In that way, he later wrote (1878), we would be able to approach that "final opinion" which could be our only truth about reality (2.693).

He was asserting, then, that traditional epistemology had made concrete, had hypostatized, a mental concept: that of truth. Having done so, it had then tried to 'discover' those concrete reals that would satisfy and justify it. The problem of the relationship between the actual world and the reference of a proposition was one of discourse's own making, the result of conceiving logic (and thought processes in general) as essentially separate from that of which it spoke and *therefore* concerned with its true rendering as an 'otherness.' This distortion has since been recognized with particular acuity in quantum physics and its philosophy (of which more in Chapter 3), and I may usefully give its example here (in Banesh Hoffman's words) for purposes of clarification: "The quantum paradoxes are of our own making, for we have tried to follow the motions of individual particles through space and time, while all along these individual particles have no existence in space and time. It is space and time that exist through the particles. An individual particle is not in two places at once. It is in no place at all."[46]

The concepts of space and time, like that of truth itself, were generalizations from 'immediate' sense impressions. These had been taken as primary intuitions, correct *in the world* (paralleling, no doubt, the Cartesian clear and distinct ideas, correct in the mind), rather than as results of prior calculation.[47] From the point of view of discourse, the dispute was

45. Reiss, *Discourse of Modernism* (see "occultation" in its index).

46. Banesh Hoffman, *The Strange Story of the Quantum* (1947; rpt. New York, 1959), p. 198.

47. From the time of the 1868 articles to the end of his life, Peirce continued to maintain that there was no such thing as an intuition free of prior cognitions. I quote from a 1901 paper on David Hume: "All our knowledge may be said to rest upon *observed facts*. . . . Thus, it is a fact that I see an inkstand before me; but before I can say that I am obliged to have impressions of sense into which my idea of an inkstand, or of any separate object, or of an

the same as the earlier one as to whether light was a collection of particles or of waves. Such disputes, Peirce's argument asserted, were the residue of dualism and the logic of the excluded middle, the discursive type of Newtonian physics (becoming, however, the model for the dominant analytico-referential discursive class): thus, for example, in what sense, except discursively, can wave and particle be considered 'opposites'? Only to the degree, it would seem, that they participate in different *theories;* only in terms of a particular epistemic history could two such discourses (types of discourse) be confronted and called 'opposites.' Such arguments, like that of the position of subatomic particles, depend upon a supposedly 'primary' intuition of space and time—themselves a reification of a mode of analysis. To confuse them with a fundamental element of the world (without any way of *knowing* one way or the other) was simply "the dementia of our metaphysics," as Welby put it, commenting on the mind/ body, inner/outer opposition: "mind and its presumed 'states' are internal—*inside* some nonentity not specified. Matter is all *outside* this nonentity."[48]

It is not at all surprising that Peirce seems to have foreseen quite clearly (by 1891) at least the possibility of the developments of quantum physics just indicated, for they stem not from a change in whatever the facts may be but from a change in our conception of how laws can be applied to them and of the mediatory relationship of laws and 'facts': "There is room for serious doubt whether the fundamental laws of mechanics hold good for single atoms, and it seems quite likely that they are capable of motion in more than three dimensions" (6.11). As he put it in more general terms in 1896: "[Science] advances by leaps; and the impulse for each leap is either some new observational resource, or some novel way of reasoning about the observations. Such a novel way of reasoning might, perhaps, be considered as a new observational means" (1.109). Laws of nature are in fact, he constantly asserts, *the momentarily fixed (habitual) statement of the evolutionary relationship that holds between the mind and the world*—a constant proposition. And that processive idea of scientific law may help explain why Peirce has no hesitation in jumping from Sir Joseph Thomson's new image of the atom to an otherwise astonishingly prophetic suggestion of the indefinite proliferation of subatomic particles confronted by

---

'I,' or of seeing, enter at all; and it is true that my judging that I see an inkstand before me is the product of mental operations upon these impressions of sense" (6.522).

48. Victoria Lady Welby, *Significs and Language: The Articulate Form of Our Expressive and Interpretative Resources* (London, 1911), facsimile rpt. with additional, previously unpublished, articles by V. Welby, ed. and intro. H. Walter Schmitz (Amsterdam, 1985), p. 16. In a footnote, she adds: "The obvious fact that space is 'internal' precisely as much—or little— as it is 'external' is, strangely enough, ignored. We might as well treat the spatial as 'upward' while using 'downward' for the non-spatial."

contemporary particle physics. In 1911 he wrote to Welby: "You know Thomson's . . . theory that atoms are vortices in a fluid. . . . If it be true, analogy would suggest that that underlying fluid really consists of separate bodies, and that those atoms of the second class were in their turn vortices of a second class in a second underlying fluid, itself composed of atoms of a third class, and so on, *endlessly.* Very well, there would be, then, not 64 or whatever the number of chemical elements is this afternoon—but an endless series of kinds of plausible matter in which to embody spirits."[49]

Peirce's assumption of Thirdness made perceived reality an essential ingredient of the mediatory process, which is not only ongoing but in which also the roles of the meaningful elements are interchanging, depending upon their place at any given time in the continuum of the knowledge process. These elements, as is well known, he gives as triple: object, sign (representamen), and interpretant. To take the example of Frege's three places of judgment: the recognition of truth is an interpretant, the *Gedanke* is the representamen, the truth value is the object. Or again: the proposition is the interpretant, the sense the representamen, the reference the object (this last in judgment; the order of the first two would be reversed in communication).

The concept of truth involved here became that of an efficacious, communal activity; an object or a fact was not subject to a statement of truth in any classical (modernist) sense. Meaning was achieved in terms of a mental activity that coincided with reality for the production of a probable effect in the world—and vice versa. Thus Peirce wrote in 1905 that he "formed the theory that a *conception,* that is, the rational purport of a word or other expression, lies exclusively in its conceivable bearing upon the conduct of life; so that, since obviously nothing that might not result from experiment can have any direct bearing upon conduct, if one can define correctly all the conceivable experimental phenomena that the affirmation or denial of a concept could imply, one will have therein a complete definition of the concept, and *there is absolutely nothing more in it*" (5.412). Peirce's solution to Frege's impasse, therefore, was to be found in a particular kind of dialectic, which made use of a notion of objectivity akin to that used by Frege when distinguishing between the objective and the actual. What was objective in this sense was shown to be so, simply by the fact that our activity verified past predictions about it (that made it "habitual"—probable; it did not make it a permanently true actuality).

The assimilation in this way, and for all practical purposes, of 'inside' and 'outside' (compare Welby's remarks above, and note 51) receives specific confirmation, according to Peirce, in our mental life. For what we

---

49. Peirce to Welby, postscript (dated May 22) to letter of May 20, 1911, in *Semiotics and Significs*, p. 144.

desire to do (a desire itself being the product of an activity: an interpretant) will correspond to the possibilities contained in the objectivity expressed. That is so because of the triadic relationship that includes those desires and activities in the process of mediation. In a note of 1903 to his article "The Fixation of Belief" (originally published in *Popular Science Monthly* in 1877), Peirce wrote: "Truth is neither more nor less than that character of a proposition which consists in this, that belief would tend to satisfy the desires we should then have [i.e., as a result of our belief in the proposition]. To say that truth means more than this is to say that it has no meaning at all" (5.375 n. 2). Truth, therefore, is a *mode of relationship* between fact, logical proposition (representamen), and human action (interpretant: here, for example, satisfaction of desires) such that these three factors remain in a stable (repeatable, predictable, 'verifiable') relationship. *Truth* is simply the name given to such a relationship. Insofar as it concerned human action and the human as sign, Peirce called that stability the formation of *habit*. Thus habit, as far as any idea of truth was concerned, becomes the final logical interpretant.[50]

So far I have only indicated the ultimate solution of Frege's impasse. Earlier, I argued that the concepts of continuity, of evolutionary process, of logical (or semiotic) field, and of the public nature of sense and the logic enabling its grasp—which Frege had precariously and ambiguously eschewed—were all to become essential to Peirce's semiotics of knowledge and action. The starting point in understanding how Peirce made use of them must be his three categories of being. I need not linger over them, because they are by now well known, but a rapid glance is necessary: "First is the conception of being or existing independent of anything else. Second is the conception of being relative to, the conception of reaction with, something else. Third is the conception of mediation, whereby a first and a second are brought into relation" (6.32 [1891]). Firstness, he wrote elsewhere, is "the being of actual fact"; and Thirdness is "the being of laws that will govern facts in the future" (1.23 [1903]).

With perhaps greater clarity, he elaborated: "Firstness is the mode of being which consists in its subject's being positively such as it is regardless of all else. That can only be a possibility" (1.25). By very definition, then, such Firstness is inexpressible. Secondness consists in a two-sided relationship "of effort and resistance," a relationship of reaction; it is "a mode of being of one thing which consists in how a second object is" (1.24).

---

50. See, e.g., Peirce's essay "How to Make Our Ideas Clear" (1878): "The whole function of thought is to produce habits of action. . . . To develop its meaning, we have, therefore, simply to determine what habits it produces, for what a thing means is simply what habits it involves" (5.400). In 1906 he wrote: "Thinking [consists] in the living inferential metaboly of symbols whose purport [as *habit*, not *purpose*] lies in conditional general resolutions to act" (5.260n).

Thirdness is that due to which "future events are in a measure really governed by a law," according to the degree in which they become mediately predictable. The concept of Thirdness registers that process of mediation in which the formation of laws occurs: "A rule to which future events have a tendency to conform is *ipso facto* an important thing, an important element in the happening of those events. This mode of being which *consists*, mind my word if you please, the mode of being which *consists* in the fact that future facts of Secondness will take on a determinate general character, I call a Thirdness" (1.26).

The triadic process referred, therefore, entirely to the functioning of signs, to the production of events that are *humanly* meaningful. For Peirce, as we have seen, the problem of truth could not be divorced from the process of mediation. All possible knowledge shared this nature: "The content of consciousness, the entire phenomenal manifestation of mind, is a sign resulting from inference" (5.313 [1868]). "All thought is in signs" (5.253 [1868]), and because a sign is a sign only inasmuch as "it translates itself into other signs in which it is more fully developed" (5.594 [1903]), the process of knowledge is both continuous (since every interpretant becomes the representamen for a succeeding interpretant) and evolutionary (since they become progressively "more fully developed"). Humans themselves, as creatures of *habit,* as mediators between reference and law, between world processes and mental processes, are themselves signs: each individual, in its triadic relationship with its environment, is "a sign [it]self" (6.344 [1909]). "And why do we seek for Significance," asked Welby, "and resume the value of innumerable observed facts under formulae of significance like gravitation or natural selection? Because we are the Expression of the world, as it were 'expressed from' it by the commanding and insistent pressure of natural stimuli not yet understood."[51] For her, as for Peirce, the entire content of consciousness is a sign and composed of signs; the factual 'world' is an interpreted environment of events to which we ascribe, and from which we derive, meanings. Truth resides, then, in a habitual, stable identity of sign ordering.

For this analysis, however, signs could not be simples. On the contrary, not only were they "genuinely" triadic (Peirce's term), but they functioned in reference to the 'other elements' of the triad only insofar as they were within a "ground" (2.228 [1897]) or, as Peirce called it elsewhere, within the "phaneron." The phaneron was understood to be the "collective total of all that is in any way or in any sense present to the mind, quite regardless of whether it corresponds to any real thing or not" (1.284 [1905]). He also used the word in the plural (1.286), and then appeared to think of it as synonymous with the grounds of sign relationships.

51. Welby, *What Is Meaning?* p. 6.

In his 1903 Lowell Lectures, Peirce defined this relationship as follows: "By a *sign* I mean anything which conveys any definite notion of any object in any way. . . . Now I start with this familiar idea and make the best analysis I can of what is essential to a sign, and I define a *representamen* as being whatever that analysis applies to. If therefore I have committed an error in my analysis, part of what I say about *signs* will be false. For in that case a *sign* may not be a *representamen*." (1.540). He gave many other definitions, but I prefer this one because in its actual process of defining the relationship of which he is speaking, it *performs* the relationship to be defined: the word "sign" is a Firstness; "representamen" is a Secondness; what is said about analyzing the one into the other is a Thirdness. It produces a complete definition of the triadic nature of all mediation, as Peirce argued the case, a complete definition of all thinking and therefore of the very idea of truth: "My definition of a representamen is as follows: *A REPRESENTAMEN is a subject of a triadic relation TO a second, called its OBJECT, FOR a third, called its INTERPRETANT, this triadic relation being such that the REPRESENTAMEN determines its interpretant to stand in the same triadic relation to the same object for some interpretant*" (1.541).

The process was thus conceived as itself a continuously developing and evolving one. nor must we forget that each element was understood as set in a ground, or, as Charles Morris put it, in a *locus*: "A distinction is to be made between the *locus of signifying,* the *locus signified,* and the *locus of confirmation.*"[52] The essence of the human was, then, the continual interpretation and establishing of signs, and the essence of the human environment (society, culture, material world), *as* human, was as an arena of actions and events understood as a constant production of meaningful relations.

The sign relationship explored by Peirce may now be indicated in a diagram wherein each circle represents the ground or phaneron of the triadic element marked within it.

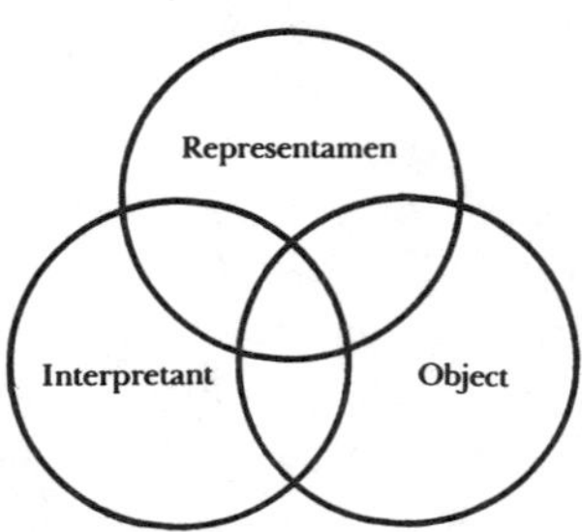

52. Charles Morris, *Signs, Language, and Behavior* (1946), in his *Writings on the General Theory of Signs* (the Hague, 1971), p. 189.

This diagram appears to capture, much better than the so-called "triangle of meaning," the "genuine" triadicity of the sign process. The area where all three overlap may be taken as representing the area of truth, of acquired belief, of settled habit. And the diagram would seem to satisfy this definition of logic offered by Peirce in 1896: "Logic may be defined as the science of the laws of the stable establishment of beliefs.[53] The *exact* logic will be that doctrine of the conditions of establishment of stable belief which rests upon perfectly undoubted observations and upon mathematical, that is, upon diagrammatical, or iconic, thought" (3.429). (The reference was to his logic of existential graphs.) As far as the diagram is concerned, we may add that the area where only two grounds overlap corresponds to the area in which it is possible to make hypotheses: those processes of discovery enabling us to get from Secondness to Thirdness.

Such a view of knowledge was also Lady Welby's. We need to understand, she wrote, "that the true advance (in thought) is spiral, that is, must sweep back on itself to take up ancient things and set them in new light and on new quests in new directions." The diagramming of thought processes is difficult, she remarked, for "unless we used a solid or hollow globe or screw, we should still only represent plane-thinking, whereas we have to learn to think in sphere."[54] To be a completely accurate representation of what both she and Peirce had in mind, the model would have to be composed of spheres in constant expansion in three dimensions; even then, the edges would have to blur imperceptibly into the 'empty' space around them (that of the inexperienced and the untried). More important still, it could neither imply nor indicate any originating point for its own ongoing processes, since Peirce's description sought to be one of praxis always and already in motion. The difficulty of a model fixed on plane paper is, of course, all there in the verbal attempt to make a visual diagram sufficient. But that attempt is not idle, for everyday thinking appears to require that it can in some way be visualized, at least vaguely, and Peirce's analysis therefore requires something other than a familiar plane-and-line diagram.

Indeed, this diagram satisfies another important consideration, one allied for Peirce with the whole matter of evolution, continuity, and the gradual fixation of law and habit. As the area of the phanera, the contextual fields, becomes larger, so too does the area of overlap: that is to say, the area representing habit, belief, truth. At the same time, of course, the area escaping overlap becomes larger. And this will always be the case:

53. We may note in passing how this corresponds to Frege's definition of logic as defining the "laws of truth." The parallel reinforces, perhaps, the suggestion that Peirce's work responds in some way to Frege's impasse.

54. Welby, *What Is Meaning?* pp. 16, 44.

"Notwithstanding all that has been discovered since Newton's time, his saying that we are little children picking up pretty pebbles on the beach while the whole ocean lies before us unexplored remains substantially as true as ever, and will do so though we shovel up the pebbles by steam shovels and carry them off in carloads" (1.117 [1896]).

All this implies that the acquisition of mental habits (laws) must always be imperfect and always subject to growth, for these habits could never cover all possible areas of activity, of knowledge. The establishment of mental law, as regards any given field of triadic relationships, "essentially involves a limitation of possibilities" (6.132 [1892]). That, of course, is why and how it acquires stability: it represents an *ordering* project. However—and this is where the Peircean analysis became enormously significant and why he was able to start speaking of the equation between mind and matter forged by mediation (Frege's indefinable truth)—such a limitation corresponds to the 'phenomenal' evidence for the laws of nature and those of a natural evolutionary process:

> Now the only possible way of accounting for the laws of nature and for uniformity in general is to suppose them the results of evolution. This supposes them not to be absolute, not to be obeyed precisely. It makes an element of indeterminacy, spontaneity, or absolute chance in nature. Just as, when we attempt to verify any physical law, we find our observations cannot be precisely satisfied by it, and rightly attribute the discrepancy to errors of observation, so we must suppose far more minute discrepancies to exist owing to the imperfect cogency of the law itself, to a certain swerving of facts from any definite formula. [6.13 (1891)]

Laws themselves are the result of evolution, he argued: "Law is *par excellence* the thing that wants a reason" (6.12). Laws must be supposed the results of the action of the second law of thermodynamics in nature, of entropy: "An idea can only be affected by an idea in continuous connection with it. By anything but an idea, it cannot be affected at all. This obliges me to say, as I do say, on other grounds, that what we call matter is not completely dead, but is merely mind hide-bound with habits" (6.158 [1892]). Such an evolutionary law of matter has its precise analogue in thought processes: "There is but one law of mind, namely, that ideas tend to spread continuously and to affect certain others that stand to them in a peculiar relation of affectibility. In this spreading they lose intensity, and especially the power of affecting others, but gain generality and become welded with other ideas" (6.104). Not surprisingly, perhaps, that relation between evolution and order, between the mind and the world, thought processes and material development in the world, was echoed by Peirce's correspondent Lady Welby: "In the 'spiritual' as well as in the physical world, there is of course no Rest as the ultimate goal or as the antithesis of Motion. The changeless is less than the dead, it is the non-existent. The secret here again for me lies in the unexplored conception of Order."[55]

Such a view of the relation between mind and matter seems, likewise, not at all distant from that held by Marx in the 1844 manuscripts. "If it is correct," Kolakowski has written of Marx's view, "to say that consciousness is things represented, then it is even more accurate to summarize his thought by saying that things are consciousness made concrete." Of these two statements, the first simply refers to the way in which consciousness necessarily begins in human contact with the environment as a whole, as a kind of "pre-existing 'chaos.' " The second, however, "takes into consideration the world of things already shaped and differentiated from each other."[56] Only the latter has anything at all to do with human action and meaning. Only the latter, therefore, considers the world as the place of all human activity of whatever sort—even though it is made collectively out of material drawn from the "chaotic" environment making consciousness possible, both as it supplies its material and as consciousness is itself an aspect of that "chaos."

Such being the case as regards the "equivalence" of mind and matter, it is clear that Peirce (like Marx) would insist that thought, belief, and their fixation were rooted in the community (5.378 [1877]) and vice versa: "The social principle is rooted intrinsically in logic" (5.354 [1868]). Logic, as we saw, was taken to permit the ordering of desire to action, of desire to habit (as opposed to doubt); and that in turn allowed the continuing order of the community in which the individual is inserted in the same way as the individual 'fact' in the natural order of matter. This was implied to some degree in Pierce's correspondence with Welby, who also presented an argument linking social, logical,and linguistic order: "It must be remembered that, [in linguistic and logical] as in the case of social order, the more complete the freedom conceded, the more inexcusable becomes the licentious use of such freedom. Such license degrades the nobility of the free citizen to the level of the mobsman and lowers voluntary or spontaneous consent to the reign of order, into all-destructive anarchy."[57]

55. Welby to Peirce, November 20, 1904, in *Semiotics and Significs*, p. 39. At one point Freud seems to imply something very similar indeed. In *Civilization and Its Discontents* (1930), he wrote: "To our dull eyes the play of forces in the heavens seems fixed in a never-changing order; in the field of organic life we can still see how the forces contend with one another, and how the effects of the conflict are continually changing" (*The Standard Edition of the Complete Psychological Works*, tr. James Strachey et al., 24 vols. [London, 1953–74], XXI:141). Peirce's "mind hide-bound with habits" was to receive startling 'confirmation' in relativity theory, as suggested in this precise respect by the recent use of the sentence: "Matter turns out to be frozen energy ($E = mc^2$)"; see Marcia Bartusiak, review of Clifford M. Will's *Was Einstein Right? Putting General Relativity to the Test* (New York, 1986), in *New York Times Book Review*, October 5, 1986, p. 46. Chapter 3, below, is evidently apposite here.

56. Kolakowski, "Karl Marx," p. 55.

57. Welby, *What Is Meaning?* p. 61.

Humans are none other than the thought/sign they have of experience and of the possibility of habitual action: it is as Morris's "locus" or a field of interpretation and consequent practice that they participate in the sociocultural (historical) environment. Habit is the field of possible ordered action that follows the formation of codes. But, saying this, one must never forget that the sign—the entire process of mediation—has sense, is meaningful, only insofar as that process itself participates in the continual transformation of the triadic relations. That circuit is essential to it. One may say that for Peirce, as for Welby, the arena of the social is made possible by the combination of habit and the circulation of signs. For Peirce, this essentially discursive practice and the forms taken by it (what he would probably refer to as an endless process of semiosis) replaced the whole epistemological concept of truth.

The Peircean project would seem, then, on the basis of those precise concepts considered inadmissible by Frege (and others), to have achieved at least a functional notion of truth. The fact that many of his predictions concerning the relationship of new laws and their objects have proved efficacious (they have *worked,* that is to say) suggests that the idea of a binary logic was at least inadequate, if not actually untenable, as far as the 'acquisition' of knowledge is concerned, and not very useful in explaining the laws governing that acquisition: hence Peirce's addition of a third logic of discovery—that of hypothesis, of ab- or retroduction—to the traditionally accepted ones of deduction and induction. The silence at the end of Wittgenstein's *Tractatus* (foreshadowed by Frege) was almost a confirmation.

The mediatory concept of Thirdness was to be essential in relativity theory (though not in any explicit way—as it could not be). Consider Arthur Eddington's remark in explaining the significance of Einstein's Special Theory of Relativity concerning the 'reality' of the Fitzgerald-Lorentz Contraction; "When a rod is started from rest into uniform motion, nothing whatever happens to the rod. We say that it contracts, but length is not a property of the rod; it is a relation between the rod and the observer. *Until the observer is specified the length of the rod is quite indeterminate.*"[58] That represents a quite precise illustration of the importance of what Peirce called the continuity between the triadically related 'parts' of a semiotic relation and a "genuine" triad as to the whole. Banesh Hoffman's remark (recorded above) about the relation between space, time, and individual particles illustrates the same point.

Such a result of Peirce's general theory of meaning was also indicated

58. Quoted in Ronald W. Clark, *Einstein: The Life and Times* (New York, 1972), p. 120. I have been unable to locate the original of this remark, but see as well Arthur Eddington, *The Nature of the Physical World* (1928; rpt. Ann Arbor, Mich., 1958), pp. 141–47, and *The Philosophy of Physical Science* (1939; rpt. Ann Arbor, Mich., 1958), pp. 71–86.

in the arguments he was able to make about the relations of cause and effect. Since his theory implied that the *particular kind* of lawful ordering an interpreter or observer employed was a matter of discursive evolution, he saw the law of cause and effect as a fixed habit of interpretation, itself subsumed in a general theory of processive meaning—much as Newtonian mechanics has been thought of as a particular case within a more general theory of relativity, a closed case within which limits are placed on certain variables. In an analysis of cause and effect undertaken in 1898 (6.68–69),[59] Peirce seemed to come close to arguments made within quantum mechanics some thirty years later—and the consequences apply in areas other than those of the natural sciences. The belief in cause and effect relations (itself the outcome of a given conceptual/discursive nexus) had clearly certain specific conceptual results. The centuries-old dispute as to whether sensation or intuition preceded in cognition, for example, can be seen as bound directly to this pseudo problem of causality and its essential or nonessential objective status (and let it be said right away that within the field of analytico-referential discourse it was not, *could* not be, a "pseudo-" problem, because it was a central part of that universe of discourse, of that logical and semiotic field). Not until the later work of Hermann von Helmholtz, perhaps, was it possible to view the question in terms that did not oppose sensation and intuition but made them, rather, interact. Then, a Cartesian "clear and distinct" and innate idea (intuition) would appear not so much in that familiar form, but as a form of dogma: that is, as a "habit" instilled by venerable discursive practice. Then, too, the way in which the dogma of linear cause and effect was caught up in a "desire" to fix upon some point of unequivocal and positive *origin* would seem equally apparent. (It is far from clear that we are not still caught up in this entire system.)

One might almost say that the manner in which this questioning of cause/effect relations, of familiar oppositions between such as rationalism and empiricism, of the notion of origin, and indeed of the manner in which relativity and quantum mechanics all operate, are special cases of the general theory of meaning upon which Peirce worked all his life (just as he conceived "logic" to be subsumed under semiotics). That achievement suggests that a triadic discourse, with its concept of knowledge as communal action-in-the-world, could provide an adequate basis for our discourses and could successfully replace the discourse that took the truth function as its ideal.

Contemporary continental semiology, by contrast (as it came from Saus-

---

59. See Appendix to Chapter 1. The cause/effect relation has of course been massively discussed in the present century. Two essays by Michael Dummett are useful (though somewhat arid): "Can an Effect Precede Its Cause?" (1954), and "Bringing About the Past" (1964), in his *Truth and Other Enigmas*, pp. 319–32, 333–50.

sure through Greimas), cannot be compared to the Peircean semiotic. In fact, it directly recalls classical positivism in the sense of a search for positive, objective truth; whether it seeks to grasp some singular common process for all human reason (semiotic square or/and linear narrative) or whether it wants to show how an inevitable system of signification is built from the relation of such reason to an objective world (rather than allowing for some more interactive process). In concluding this chapter, I may rapidly indicate how that is the case by alluding to the perplexity of a writer in this tradition, Emile Benveniste, when he found himself dealing with Peirce's work:

> The difficulty preventing any particular application of Peircean concepts, other than the well-known tripartition, which however remains too general a framework, is finally that the sign is taken to underlie the entire universe, and that it functions simultaneously as a defining principle for every element and as an explicative principle for every set, whether abstract or concrete. The whole man is a sign, his thought is a sign, his emotion is a sign. But ultimately, these signs, all being signs of one another, of what could they be the sign that IS NOT a sign? Will we find the fixed point where the FIRST sign relation may be anchored?[60]

Such fear of losing one's footing echoes Frege's fear of flux. And Benveniste's cry of despair is rooted in a basic misunderstanding. For what he calls a "tripartition" cannot be considered a *partition* at all. Working in the same tradition, Henri Meschonnic appeared just a little later to make a similar error: "Peirce's semiotic is not dialectical. It accepts and reinforces the metaphysics of the sign as an absence, the metaphysics of the sign as a unity."[61]

Both objections, however representative they may be of the important tradition discussed in Chapter 2, are quite simply wide of the mark. Such statements are possible only if the critic ignores the *practice* of signs, *semiosis,* the progressive circuit (or spiral, if, following Welby's suggestion, one wishes to signify its openness and progressivity, as well as its constant "return" upon itself) that proceeds from the idea that any given element of a given triadic relation changes its place continually, entering into a successive Thirdness in the process of thought. Neither the concept of the sign as absence nor that of partition can enter into the Peircean semiotic. Indeed, it is almost as though Peirce had himself foreseen those positivistic objections as they would be put forward by continental semiology. As early as 1861 he ironically congratulated Sir William Hamilton on his

60. Emile Benveniste, "Sémiologie de la langue (1)," *Semiotica,* 1, no. 1 (1969), 2, reprinted in his *Problèmes de linguistique générale II* (Paris, 1974), p. 45 (my translation).
61. Henri Meschonnic, *Le signe et le poème: Essai* (Paris, 1975), p. 156 (my translation).

system of definitions: "By his system of nomenclatures, Sir William Hamilton has conferred an immense boon not alone on his own school but on all English philosophers who believe in anchoring words to fixed meaning. I deeply regret that I am not one of these. That is the best way to be stationary no doubt. But, nevertheless, I believe in mooring our words by certain applications and letting them change their meanings as our conceptions of the things to which we have applied them progress."[62]

It is of course the case, as Benveniste urges, that Peirce's conception of semiotic allowed for no "DIFFERENCE between the sign and the signified," but that is because Peirce's practice accorded with a quite different norm. The notion of continuity replaces that of difference; the binary opposition (of which the distinction sign/signified is clearly but a special form) is subsumed under the triadic circuit; there is no "SIGNIFYING condition [*condition de SIGNIFIANCE*]" fixed in a "sign *SYSTEM*" because the *sense* of the sign in Peirce's analysis is produced within the triadic circuit of performed conceptual and discursive fields. To speak of a tri-*partition* is to falsify completely the practice of a thinker who insisted above all that the triadic relationship of the production of meaning is *irreducible*.

62. Peirce, *Chronological Edition*, I:58.

CHAPTER TWO

Semiology and Its Discontents:
Saussure and Greimas

Those attempts made to construct a linguistic model without any connection to a speaker or a listener and which therefore hypostatize a code detached from actual communication, risk reducing language to a scholastic fiction.
—Roman Jakobson, *Essais de linguistique générale*

As medieval philosophy was forced to remain rigidly within orthodox lines, and thus become scholasticism, so now all thought has still to present itself in orthodox philosophical and literary form. . . . We are running the risk of a modern linguistic scholasticism, more fatal than the original.
—Victoria Lady Welby, *What Is Meaning?*

In the 1647 letter-preface to the French translation of his *Principia (Principes de la philosophie)*, René Descartes remarked that the proper application of his methodical science would lead to the discovery of yet concealed truths and, in time, "to a perfect knowledge of the whole of philosophy." He admitted that "several centuries may pass before all the truths that can be deduced from these principles will be deduced from them, because most of those that remain to be found depend on particular experiments that are not met with by chance but must be sought after." In his *Description of a Natural and Experimental History,* Francis Bacon had already made a strikingly similar prediction: "The investigation of nature and of all sciences will be the work of a few years."[1] The methodical discourse of truth by analysis and reference was thereby endowed with a measure of temporal certitude whose project was made the communal goal of a particular cultural environment. At the same time, the dynamic process toward the acquisition of knowledge was understood to result and conclude in an entirely static mastery of all possible information: a kind of sealed "treasure-house" (as Addison called it somewhere) of complete conceptual wealth.

1. René Descartes, "Lettre-préface de l'édition française des *Principes*," in *Oeuvres philosophiques*, ed. Ferdinand Alquié, 3 vols. (Paris, 1963–73), III:783, 784; *The Works of Francis Bacon*, ed. James Spedding, Robert Leslie Ellis, and Douglas Denon Heath, 15 vols. (Boston, 1861–64), VIII:356.

The preceding chapter sought to show, in the area of scientific logic and epistemology, how many of the premises of this project were being questioned by the second half of the nineteenth century, and questioned in that very same discursive type which provided the exemplary model of analytico-referential discourse. In Frege's writings one could see some of the occultations, contradictions, and impasses being confronted even within the attempt to refurbish the logico-mathematical foundations of classical (or modernist) scientific discourse. Nonetheless, the goal of objective analysis and referential truth still characterizes most epistemological thinking in our own day, as well as the kinds of social and political, scientific and cultural activity dependent upon it.

This chapter seeks to show how this is the case for what I may call "continental" semiology—though I limit the analysis to the immediate line proceeding from Ferdinand de Saussure's work at the turn of the century. This semiology has been (and continues to be) viewed as some kind of alternative to, opponent of, a Peircean semiotics—even though, I would argue, they are qualitatively different in means, intention, and potential usefulness. Despite this difference (with the clear superiority of Peircean semiotics in terms of prospective change), the analysis of semiology undertaken here is not in vain, just because both *have* been widely conceived as offering a new kind of knowledge, at once more general than was possible through the "disciplines" inherited from the seventeenth and eighteenth centuries and less closed in, precisely, by such "disciplinary" thinking. Those claims are, I think, irrelevant, but the opposition is not, because semiology and semiotics do in fact appear to represent different ways of thinking.

This chapter's title alludes to the opposition suggested by Freud between individual desire and social exigencies. A similar opposition is to be traced in all discourse that claims to be scientific. A sort of conflict is played out between the 'dialectical,' processive, or dynamic nature of discursivity itself (Peirce's constant semiosis) and the demand of and for conclusive, static knowledge. Semiology's scientific goal, based upon the axioms characterizing all analytico-referential discourse, seems to bear with it those contradictions and impasses already indicated. It thus suffers from a kind of "discontent," as though within semiology's own functioning and the metadiscourse with which it tries to understand it a constant struggle were taking place between the demands of analysis, reference, the intention and truth particular to science, and what I have been referring to as the dynamic process of discourse and meaning themselves: perhaps, if you will, a struggle between what have been called *pouvoir-* and *vouloir-dire*. On the one side lie intention, will, truth, the imposition of authority; on the other the flow of discourse and meanings themselves, in all their ambiguity and potential equivocation: truth versus flux. That struggle undermines from within semiology's very project. (Let it be said right away that both 'opponents' are produced out of analytico-referential or modernist discourse; the *struggle,* or opposition, simply reproduces the familiar sets—inside/outside, same/other, here/there, now/then, true/false—that are essential to that discourse in which *tertium non datur*—a matter explored at greater length in Chapter 4).

Albeit in rather different terms, the issues confronted by Peirce and Frege, in their respective searches for acceptable and effective concepts of "truth" and "meaning," underlie semiology's explorations as well and are fundamental to my analysis. For that reason, it is well to sum them up with some clarity.

In the first place, I take two matters for granted. The first is that what we call knowledge is composed of our discourses, taken in the sense of ordered signifying processes as they are actually practiced; human action of any kind depends upon such "knowledge." The second is that approximately since the late seventeenth century in Europe, our episteme (the dominant functioning of all our discourses: the controlling "discursive class") has been organized by analytico-referentiality.

What I mean by this last term may bear repeating, if only because linguistic and semiological theory depends upon it so profoundly (a theme, indeed, running through this entire volume). Analytico-referential discourse, then, was that discourse taken to signify, through a conceptualizing thought of which it was supposed at once the container and the transparent mediator, a referential truth considered to be outside discourse and perfectly independent of it. At the same time, the linguistic "grammar" that discourse uses was assumed to be identical with the logic of reason whose strictly linear form would provide—indeed, would *be*— the analysis of the concepts composing thought. Those concepts were the elements of that logic and were taken as adequate to the external objects to which they referred. The *right* use of language thus gave us, through its grammatical structure, an analysis not merely of concepts but also of an exterior to which those concepts were entirely adequate.

That idea of truth not only dominated the forms of our knowledge but—as we saw implied in Frege and explicitly specified by Peirce— directed the conditions of society. The connection was inescapable, because all communication (for example) inevitably depended upon that idea. The model and ideal of such a discursive practice was provided by the physical sciences, as they developed most particularly from Galileo to Isaac Newton.

Throughout the nineteenth century, that discourse and its model functioned increasingly less surely as uncertainty about the acceptability of its foundations grew. The search for new foundations in logic and mathematics was joined at the beginning of the twentieth century by the 'master' strokes of general relativity and the development of quantum mechanics. In many ways these seemed to correspond to the first traces of semiotic theories of the Peircean variety; to the questioning of critical theory; to systematic changes in the forms of the visual arts, in music, in the theories of human 'sciences,' and so on (but I do not wish to repeat this familiar litany). Frege's thought and subsequent developments in logical atomism and logical positivism mark an attempt to rework foundations that had become deeply problematic. The attempt remained caught within the same discursive class. It was possible only at the cost of that series of dissimulations and occultations whose consequent impasse (in Frege) Peirce appeared to avoid by dint of including in a semiotics precisely those elements that Frege had set aside.

Frege, we saw, began by rejecting the traditional notion of direct correspondence between ordinary language and logical (conceptual) thinking at the level of some underlying syntax or deep structure. He initially wished to create a conceptual language that could produce true propositions concerning the concepts it adumbrated. The particular sciences would be responsible for precisely formulating the relationship between concept and object. Gradually, Frege was led to posit the concept of truth as axiomatic. Some concept such as that of truth was essential to him, simply because the question of the objectivity and reality expressed in a signifying process would be suspended, in Frege's view, if there were no such idea as that of true denotation. Yet he himself remained unable to provide any basis for this concept of truth in scientific discourse other than axiomatically (and other than the 'truth' of logical order itself: a [tautological] truth of the *form* of analysis, which has nothing to do with referential knowledge).

Frege resisted a series of notions whose occultation appears responsible for this impasse (an impasse also confronted by the Wittgenstein of the *Tractatus*). These notions are (1) the multiplication of signs in the passage from reference to sense; (2) the possibility of identifying the process of sign production, of composing meaning (and therefore all mediation), with an evolutionary process in the world: of not separating the world from thought—a nonseparation to be maintained in terms of productive ordering processes, not in those of some form of representation; (3) the communal, social nature of all and any manifestation of signification—at all levels; and (4) the idea of a semiotic (or conceptual?) *field* (as opposed to linear sequences) and of the complete and genuine interdependence of the elements of thought (signs) within this field.

Peirce elaborated a triadic sign theory on the very basis of this series of occulted principles and practiced a general semiotic theory capable of deploying a concept of knowledge as a dynamic series of interferences and transformations (Chapter 3 makes some propositions in this regard).

Systematically, he questioned the forms of knowledge, scientific and other, based within an analytico-referential formulation and functioning. He thus developed an idea of truth as a stable mode of ongoing relations between object, 'logical' proposition (representamen), and human action (interpretant) such that these three 'elements' (which in this relation could never be considered discrete) at once remained in a stable relation—able, that is, to be repeated, predicted, 'verified'—always presupposing its own development and expansion.

Peircean semiotics thus seemed to answer a difficulty in signifying any object whatsoever (including the so-called "object-language" of semiological inquiry itself) that continental semiology between Saussure and Greimas has remained unable to solve: the difficulty that analytico-referential discourse grasps its object ostensibly as an alterity and, while it works that object into its own conceptual image, supposes it to be given 'in itself.' That difficulty was responsible for the distinction A. J. Greimas sought at one time to make between two semiologies: the one of narrativity (linear system), the other of discursivity (seeming to emphasize a processive movement). He apparently hoped that the second would respond to the conceptual difficulties of the first. In fact, the assumption necessary to the elaborating of such a discursive semiology (as we will see) would seem to make that of narrativity untenable—and what is again being marked here is the opposition between the movement of discourse(s) and the demands of modernist science.

The difficulty was also responsible for Benveniste's criticism of Peirce's semiotic on the ground of an unworkability due to its allowing no place for any "fixed point," for any *origin* of the sign process. For what could such a fixed point be if not some supposed 'real' object (since otherwise the origin escapes fixity) offered to the grip of a semiological explanation? *That* would then have been inscribed within semiology as its point of departure, only to become the 'freshly discovered' and described object (otherness) of its conclusions.[2]

---

2. I should say immediately that the epistemological criticisms to be set forth in this chapter do not appear to apply altogether to Umberto Eco's work (itself heavily and directly influenced by Peirce), who has written, e.g., that in order to be considered scientific, semiotics must be "governed . . . by such methodological criteria as the indeterminacy or complementarity principles": *A Theory of Semiotics* (Bloomington, Ind., 1976), p. 129. It is also not clear how much these criticisms would apply to Julia Kristeva's writings. In *Semiotiké* she argued that the text *(littérature)* is a practice of the signifier which she called *signifiance* and viewed as "working upon" language and being in the realm of what I have referred to as *pouvoir-dire. Sémanalyse* itself, however, was not placed in such a situation, using, rather, the kind of instrumental analysis seen as going to the 'root' of such practice: "*Sémanalyse* will study *signifiance* and its types in the *text*, and it will thus have to traverse the signifier together with the subject and sign, as well as the grammatical organization of discourse, in order to reach the zone where the *germs* of what *will signify* come together in the presence of lan-

Saussure's text repeated (and indeed was contemporary with) Frege's attempt at renewal; it installed a science of linguistics that prefigured a more general semiology, only at the price of a similar series of occultations (and similar intellectual agonizings on the part of its author). It is therefore worth remarking that early on, Greimas explicitly rejected "any intention of situating F. de Saussure in the more general framework of the epistemology of his time."[3] His refusal has been repeated, and it does not appear entirely innocent, for underlying the Saussurean enterprise was the previous Cartesian one. In Descartes, too, one can follow a series of occultations complementary to those we saw in Frege's work and whose exclusion alone made possible a scientific discourse of analysis and reference.[4] They have been repeated specifically, if unsystematically, in the work of Greimas and his disciples.

---

guage" (*Semiotiké: Recherches pour une sémanalyse* [Paris, 1969], p. 9). The privilege of literature, analytical otherness, the place of origin are all here fundamental. In *La révolution du langage poétique* (Paris, 1974) and in *Polylogue* (Paris, 1977), Kristeva situated these "germs" in the realm of the "semiotic," now opposed to that of the "symbolic," in which society's (the "Father's") order has been imposed. The realm of the semiotic is that of "chora," a kind of 'space' of as yet unordered and merely potential meaningfulness. In more recent and more frankly psychoanalytical work—*Histoires d'amour* (Paris, 1983); *Au commencement était l'amour: Psychanalyse et foi* (Paris, 1985)—this space of what Derrida has called *athèse* (to contrast with the ordered rationality of *thesis*) is provoked into order not by the imposition of the "Father" but by the working of what Kristeva calls "melancholy." Most recently she has expressed this view at length in *Soleil noir:* "Rather than seeking the sense of despair . . . let us admit that sense proceeds only from despair. . . . Semiology, which is concerned with the zero degree of symbolism, is inevitably brought to examine not only the amorous condition, but also its somber corollary, melancholy. It immediately realizes that while there is no writing that is not amorous [an allusion to Barthes's textual pleasure or *jouissance*], there is no imagination that is not, openly or secretly, melancholic" (p. 15). Melancholy is what permits (indeed, obliges) the individual subject either to retreat into the silence (for communicative expression) of the chora or to move toward some form of symbolism. These claims clearly privilege the Subject, individualism, forms of biological determinism (as I argue here, e.g., in Introduction, n. 12; Chapter 4, n. 21; Chapter 5, n. 18). Some form of unreason has replaced the control of rationality. Need I recall that Jacques Derrida has studied at least twice the epistemological premises and consequences of the Saussurean enterprise (which, for him, date from Plato): *De la grammatologie* (Paris, 1967), pp. 46ff.; and "Sémiologie et grammatologie," in *Positions* (Paris, 1972), pp. 25–50. Cf. *Epistémologie de la linguistique*, in a special issue of *Langages* (1971) edited by Kristeva; and also V. N. Vološinov (M. M. Bakhtin), *Marxism and the Philosophy of Language* (1929), tr. Ladislav Matejka and I. R. Titunik (New York, 1973), pp. 58–61, 65–82, and Matejka's appendix, "On the First Russian Prolegomena to Semiotics," pp. 162–67. I would note as well the mixture of scholarly critique and scornful polemic characterizing Sebastiano Timpanaro's long analysis of structural linguistics and its avatars, condemning them as various types of idealism: "Structuralism and Its Successors," in his *On Materialism*, tr. Lawrence Garner (London, 1975), pp. 135–219. Many of these matters recur, esp. in my last three chapters.

3. Algirdas Julien Greimas, "L'actualité du saussurisme," *Le Français Moderne*, 24 (1956), 191–203; this from p. 192 n.3.

4. See Timothy J. Reiss, "Cartesian Discourse and Classical Ideology," *Diacritics*, 6, no. 4 (1976), 19–27. For similar arguments respecting the case of Francis Bacon, see Reiss, *Discourse of Modernism*, pp. 198–225.

To avoid misunderstandings, I should doubtless make quite clear at the outset that the series of occultations and the setting-up of an analytico-referential linguistics as they occur in Saussure are to be found in the *published* text of the *Cours de linguistique générale* (1916). We know now that this posthumous compilation, quite apart from some few actual additions by its editors,[5] neither revealed Saussure's own hesitations nor corresponded to the order he would apparently have selected for presenting his material. In a recent admirable edition, Tullio de Mauro has observed that the text as edited departed in significant ways from the linguist's own preferred order of discussion in the courses as actually given.

Saussure began with historical and evolutionary considerations rather than with theoretical discussion. His habit was to start with how languages were actually manifested rather than with how they might be conceptualized in linguistics, to undertake an analysis of several different languages in order to demonstrate the historical contingency of their signs. In the courses Saussure actually gave, he followed those matters with a consideration of diachrony and next of synchrony; only then did he turn to linguistic universals and thence to the question of how to deal with language in use or, in his interpretation of that notion, of how to deal with speaking.[6]

Some indications of this original order remained in the published text, but they were not explored there in terms of that discursive semiotics they seem to require. Indeed, they were already contaminated by the odd but perfectly traditional point of view that the individual subject of an utterance (*énonciation*, the *act* of speaking; as opposed to locution, *énoncé*, the speech actually uttered) is always primary in speaking, is always the origin of a speech act: "Nothing enters language without having been tested in speaking, and every evolutionary phenomenon has its roots in the individual" (F 231; E 169); the same view underlies contemporary Anglo-American speech-act theory.

If speaking is the only fact of human language immediately available to the scientific observer, then it is clear that to determine the object of linguistics as some 'objective,' hierarchical, and well-ordered system of human speech, language, and speaking (*langage, langue,* and *parole*)

5. Including, most notably, the well-known final statement that "*the true and unique object of linguistics is language studied in and for itself*": Ferdinand de Saussure, *Course in General Linguistics,* ed. Charles Bally and Albert Sechehaye with Albert Riedlinger, tr. Wade Baskin (1959; rpt. New York, 1966), p. 232. My text of reference is *Cours de linguistique générale,* ed. Tullio de Mauro (Paris, 1975). Page numbers cited hereafter indicate the respective languages of the two editions by the letters E and F; where no E is given, any translation is my own from de Mauro's critical apparatus. Square brackets in English quotations enclose my own emendations. I have also made use of another important edition: *Cours de linguistique générale,* ed. Rudolf Engler, 2 vols. (Wiesbaden, 1967–74).

6. See F 354–55, 406 n.12, 474 n.269, 476 n.291.

implied the invocation of an epistemology that is by no means implicit in that object of study (if such an epistemology ever could be). But if such a system were denied, then some very different idea of science would be required to cope with it. Had Saussure not presupposed such a system, he would also have been suggesting that that kind of conceptualization could not be aprioristically assumed.

In this regard, in an 1893–94 introduction to a proposed general linguistics (which in fact never appeared), Saussure wrote: "One never has the right to consider one side of language as anterior and superior to others, and as having to be used as a point of departure. . . . It is incorrect in linguistics to admit any one fact as being defined in itself. There is truly, therefore, a necessary absence of any point of departure, and if some reader is willing to follow our thought with care from one end of this volume to the other, he will realize, we are convinced, that it was impossible to follow a very rigorous order" (F 362). In a sense, such a passage could be taken as based upon the assumption that the *facts* are *given* objectively, and we need but to follow along with them as a passive and naive observer (that is, we can act as though our discourse had no control over its object, as though it were a transparent instrument). Nonetheless, at this point Saussure appeared to be leaning toward the idea that the object of linguistics was a far more fluid process than the published *Course* finally assumed.

To get from the process of uncertainty to a firm point of departure required that Saussure repeat the Cartesian epoche, so criticized by Peirce (in his 1868 "Questions concerning Certain Faculties Claimed for Man," for example), and that he argue for the possibility of returning to a kind of zero moment in thinking. And that would represent an occultation of the very *act* of thinking itself and thus a moment when its (potential) object disappeared from view, as it were: "From whatever direction we approach the question, nowhere do we find the integral object of linguistics" (F 24; E 9). Such an assertion implied that the entire project faced an obstacle at the very outset: that it would have to create its specific object of knowledge. A creation of that sort would imply a denial of language as a stable referent for objective analytical knowledge. In that case, linguistics as a 'traditional' form of science could not exist.

Such an obstacle could be overcome only by occulting the act of thought that constituted the object of this linguistics (that is, "language" as an objective, structured, and stable system) as existing prior to the linguistics that was to absorb, analyze, and explain it. For despite the statement just quoted (or rather because of it, since to accept its denial at face value would indeed be to renounce the science in question), no further emphasis was placed upon the existence or inexistence of this linguistic object. Then it could be no longer a question of constituting it but 'simply' of *finding* it. The science of language could then act *as though* the linguistic object were always and already 'there.' All that was needed was to take the right slice from among the mass of actual data.

Nowhere did the *Course* take a statement expressing objective doubt (such as that quoted earlier, which remained unpublished: F 362) the logical next step. This would have been to suggest that because the object of scientific study is always bound up with the functioning of the discourse studying it, because the two necessarily evolve together (in, for example, a Peircean triadic process), no systematically static science of linguistics is possible. Except perhaps in the anagrammatical studies, Saussure did not pursue such a thought.[7] The passage quoted might have served to introduce an initial ambiguity and equivocity, but general linguistics was in fact taken to be constituted by means of a deductive process elaborated upon the basis of first simples taken as real. Having occulted the moment establishing its object—in such a way that it could be understood as a *discovery*, not as a *making*—he presented linguistic science (in the *Course*) as having found its object in some sort of pristine, unsoiled state ("unsoiled," that is, by prior ways of thinking about language).

The main lines of the *Course in General Linguistics* are now quite familiar, and I do not intend to run through them once again as such. What I wish to show, in accordance with the project I mentioned at the beginning, is how they reinscribe the principles of analytico-referential discourse and at what cost they do so. I have already indicated the *Course*'s first occulting gesture, one necessitated by its initial and primary goal: the constitution of a scientific linguistics that could analyze language as a stable, determinate referent of its knowledge (and, no doubt, as ultimately actual). To establish the certainty of its own scientific ground and to situate its own potential flaws elsewhere, in a 'prescientific' discourse, the *Course* thus ran swiftly through its predecessors. By such means the absence of objective foundation could be situated in some *other* discourse. The act of making was not only then occulted; it was also *displaced*.

One of the earliest of the predecessors in question was philology. The *Course* criticized that discipline on the grounds that it had (precisely) no object: it *used* texts but did not seek to know what constituted them or how they were constituted. It did not bring order from disorder but, rather, multiplied disorder. It could not fulfill the first role of a science, because it failed to discover the invariant laws capable of accounting for the variations within its object, and that, in turn, was just because it had failed to constitute such an object. And if the lack of an objective system was philology's first sin, its second was that it applied itself to a subordinate object:

7. See Jean Starobinski, *Les mots sous les mots: Les anagrammes de Ferdinand de Saussure* (Paris, 1971).

it stood accused of a too "servile attachment" to written language and of neglecting "the living language" (F 14; E 1–2). The *Course* directed the former accusation at comparative grammar as well, affirming that it never sought out "the nature of its object of study" (F 16; E 3). Nor did comparative grammar ever examine self-critically "the meaning of (its) comparisons or the significance of the relations that (it) discovered" (F 16; E 3–4). That the *Course,* like Noam Chomsky later, should then plump for the Port-Royal *Grammar* as showing the way to a true linguistic science is naturally no accident. Yet it, too, was flawed, in this case by being prescriptive rather than simply descriptive (wrote Saussure in the *Course,* thus copying the *Grammar*'s own assumption of the possibility of descriptive naiveté). The *Grammar,* however, at least knew what its object was and had a clear idea of a universal system—though at the same time confusing written and spoken language, among some other uncertainties (F 118; E 82).

Those various criticisms delimited precisely the *Course*'s objectives: (1) the description and tracking of "all observable languages": that is, the constitution of its object; (2) the determination of "the forces that are permanently and universally at work in all languages": that is, the constitution of the system 'behind' that object, or underlying it; and (3) the delimitation and definition of linguistics itself (F 20; E 6).

In the *Course* as published that order was reversed, with far-reaching consequences. Actually (2) and (3) were initially worked out simultaneously, and the first problem clearly posed is, once again, that of all sciences of analysis and reference, though here made specific to linguistics, where, "far from . . . being the object that antedates the viewpoint, it would seem that it is the viewpoint that creates the object" (F 23; E 8). We have already glimpsed that difficulty, which implied that the aim of the original systematic linguistics had to be that of finding the way to bring linguistics into line with more advanced sciences in the tradition. These laid claim to generality and universality, as well as objective treatment of objects truly existing in the world. The linguist, however, was apparently confronted with a heterogeneous mass of facts, the chief characteristic of any one of which—any given locution—was, according to the *Course,* to be irreducibly individual.

The way around this difficulty was through recourse to the familiar epistemological tradition. A locution represents an act of communication; it must, therefore, be a communication of something. That "of" separates the thing from the act: a sound "is only the instrument of thought; by itself, it has no existence" (F 24; E 8). This claim produced the idea of a "speaking circuit" in which everything could be put in its hierarchical place in a system, a circuit "where mental facts ([which we call] concepts) are associated with representations of linguistic [signs] (sound-images) that are used for their expression. [Let us suppose that] a given concept unlocks a corresponding sound-image in the brain" (F 28; E 11). The system behind the linguistic object was beginning to be 'discovered.'

Given that the speech act is (as an *act*) entirely individual ("the individual is always its master": F 30; E 13) and yet that we succeed in communicating, we must suppose the area in which the individual makes a choice of sound-images to be social, communal; therefore, *"from the very outset we must put both feet on the ground of language* [i.e., the *system* of sound-images and their relations] *and use language as the norm of all other manifestations of speech"* (F 25; E 9: my emphasis). In addition, since we do in fact communicate, we must suppose not only that the relationship concept/ acoustic-image/locution is 'correct' but that it is more or less stable: "All will reproduce—not exactly, of course, but approximately—the same signs united with the same concepts" (F 29; E 13). Thus the system behind the linguistic object (observable enunciation) has defined linguistics itself: the science of *language,* as the system of relations and acoustic-images common to the possibility of all locutions and behind the possibility of all utterance.

With a pair of swiftly applied strokes, the *Course* has thus *excluded from the object of study its putative heterogeneity and evolutionary nature.* Further, the 'social,' 'communal' aspect of that object, manifest in the fact of speaking *(parole)* has been set 'behind' its 'actual' manifestation, so to speak, and placed within the system of language. That aspect is thus situated within the individual's control. By this means, individual 'liberty' can be maintained: "Speaking is an individual act. It is willful and intellectual" (F 30; E 14). Such a claim is ideologically suggestive because, as we saw in a slightly different context, actual utterances are made the initially prime material from which linguistic evidence (and *language*) is composed. Now on the one hand the locutions that are the end product of such utterances clearly provide the immediate observational data, but on the other they are *in themselves* unusable for such systematization. At the same time, if we go around them, as it were, we lose the individual. Such loss would not merely be a matter of 'political' ideology (though it would certainly also be that); it would mean that the concept/expression relation had to be conceived as primarily a matter of *social, public* order. It would mean (a) that the relation was entirely prescribed by culture and the historical development of any given culture and (b) that it thereby lost all pretension to eventual objectivity (or forced a reconsideration of the meaning of 'objectivity').

The way around what an analytico-referential science could see only as an obstacle and a difficulty was found, as one would expect, by recourse to a tradition that viewed individual freedom as *defined* by its situation and its function within a lawful, ordered system. The political and ideological nature of such a rule of law is simply one case, its manifestation within a particular discursive *type*. The relationship in fact holds good in all types of analytico-referential discourse and is constitutive of that dominant class.[8] In the specific case discussed here, it operated by making the concept/expression system of relations originate in the individual speech act, and it then existed "only by virtue of a sort of contract signed by the members of a community" (F 31; E 14).

Language, then, and the individual's place within it, corresponded precisely to the constitution of the contractual state established between individuals in willed association, much as Thomas Hobbes had elaborated it. What the *Course* offered here was a kind of abstract origin of language: "abstract," because the *Course* was consistently adamant about the individual's impotence to change the system thus constituted. We read on the one hand, therefore, that language "is purely social and independent of the individual" and on the other that "speaking is necessary for the establishment of language, and historically its actuality always comes first" (F 37; E 18). We might well be inclined to wonder what can conceivably be the meaning of the term "historically" here, except as a reference to an epistemological tradition whose order is to be found most notably in the writings of Bacon, Galileo, Hobbes, Descartes, and others.

Be that as it may, the *Course* now has an *origin* for language, situated in the individual act of enunciation. But that situation has simultaneously been occulted by the affirmation that it no longer operates; it is claimed to have been replaced by the lawful system that makes such an utterance possible. The *Course*, it seems to me, has found a way to avoid the problem that it constitutes its own objects. It can then proceed to set up "the true science of linguistics" with its "basis in reality," whence it describes "the facts of speech" ("les véritables conditions de tout langage": F 16–17; E 3–4).

Such a demand also means that the system itself has to be constituted as in some way real: that is to say, the *Course* needs to argue that its linguistics is not a deduction from some mode of discourse, is not simply some hypostatized derivation from scientific discourse itself, but *preceded* it; it was not simply logically but also *onto*logically primary. But that seems to imply a contradiction: if the system of language is truly primary, then how can its *origin* (the linguistic contract) be located clearly in a particular discursive elaboration?

---

8. I have elsewhere explored this relation in regard to other discursive types: with regard to psychoanalysis, in "Sciences des rêves," esp. pp. 42–48, 55–58; with regard to literature, in "Power, Poetry, and the Resemblance of Nature," in *Mimesis: From Mirror to Method, Augustine to Descartes*, ed. John D. Lyons and Stephen P. Nichols, Jr. (Hanover, N. H., 1982), esp. pp. 238–45. See also below, Chapters 7 and 9.

The answer lay in the *Course*'s celebrated dualism. The origin (in every way comparable to Benveniste's fixed point) was situated in a diachronic analysis and understanding of languages, which thereby had a past and a future as a *process*. Systemic primacy, on the other hand, became the object of a synchronic study of languages, which was thereby constituted as a stable network of relations in *stasis*. That dualism may well help to explain why some of Saussure's successors and contemporaries felt that his general linguistics contained a certain tension, and indeed that the two viewpoints were to some degree incompatible—though the *Course* itself denied such incompatibility. For our part, we have seen that the process/stasis conjuncture was inseparable from the modernist scientific enterprise.

General linguistics, then, has been constituted as an undertaking within the familiar framework of normative science; it has, that is to say, delimited and defined itself, linguistics, as a science; and it has constituted its object (a) as dependent upon a lawful system capable of analysis, and (b) as constructed of facts (locutions) able to be observed and possessing historical development. It has posited the "concrete" nature of language (F 31; E 15), asserting that it is defining "things rather than words" (F 31; E 14). The "things," needless to say, are the elements composing the system of relations that is given as *language*.[9] Linguistic science has thus given itself a referent: the elements in 'reality' that are the 'facts of speech,' the facts of language, and the facts concerning *their* components and ordering (that is, the facts of the underlying lawful system making those other facts possible).[10]

De Mauro dismissed the *Course*'s claim to be speaking of "things" as a "professor's mirage" of no importance or as a merely unfortunate metaphor (F 423 n. 68). One cannot treat the case so lightly, however, if one allows that the object of linguistics is the definition of the lawful set of relations applying to a real collection of linguistic facts (as de Mauro, for example, continued to do). For if such facts are only "words" (as some of them obviously are, in another sense) and not, shall we say, words/things, or perhaps events, states of affairs composed of words, then general

9. Such an idea would pose a difficulty later on, when language was defined as "a form and not a substance" (F 169; E 122), for in what sense could one then speak of defining "things"? Within the *Course*, no difficulty seems to have been raised by this, perhaps because the two statements were so far apart.

10. If there appears to be a confusion here between 'referent' as 'object' of discourse and as some notion of 'thing-in-the-world,' that is deliberate. Indeed, from the point of view of the 'metadiscourse' using such a concept as that of 'referent,' it makes no difference which meaning is given to it; in either case it will be understood as an element *exterior* to that metadiscourse's elaboration. As far as the metadiscourse's *functioning* is concerned, the logical and epistemological status of 'referent' will be the same, whichever of these meanings we may choose to give it. Regardless of the status claimed for 'referent,' the functional scientificity of the discourse is the same.

linguistics cannot hope to attain the scientific status the *Course* elaborates and takes for granted (as do all linguists themselves): a status confirmed by its capacity both to describe the *system* of language and to grasp the manner in which it comes to signify. Indeed, de Mauro himself relied on just such an idea of the *Course* in dismissing its suggestion of a distinction between a "linguistics of speaking" and a "linguistics proper, whose sole object is language" (F 38–39; E 19–20), and agreeing with its claim that the first would be fundamentally nonscientific because its objects would be the unique and discrete speech facts of a constantly fluctuating reality (F 428 n. 81). That proposition is reminiscent of Frege's fear: "If everything were in continual flux, and nothing maintained itself fixed for all time, there would no longer be any possibility of getting to know anything about the world and everything would be plunged in confusion."[11] Where could we cast our anchor?

Greimas likewise reaffirmed the need for a concept of stable objectivity, based on facts-in-the-world, when he remarked that among human sciences only linguistics could pride itself on a 150-year-old tradition of rigor and progress—"unless," he added, "one perceives no value at all in human knowledge of the world."[12] The question needing to be asked there is, in what possible way can a practice of producing meaning between *discourses* (the metadiscourse of linguistics and the language system upon which it is exercised) correspond to that ideal of objective science, working on some concrete material in the world? Linguistic sciences confront problems here very different from those faced by their model, natural science.

If one imagines such a question to be without importance, as de Mauro did, one might do well to compare the claim to be defining "things," to be dealing with a knowledge of concrete objects, with Peirce's definitions of representamen as *his word* for a particular moment in the signifying process, such that if a given sign did not function as he described under the name 'representamen,' then that description and his definition were at least partly false.[13] In all likelihood, of course, there could be no way of his knowing this in any case, for his ability to describe the sign situation depended upon that very definition. The importance of Peirce's observation, however, is its forcing us to understand that in order to be able to claim that one is dealing with untrammeled and pristine objects, one must perform the same occultation of utterance with regard to synchrony as that already carried out with respect to diachrony (see above, p. 67).

The *Course* repeated Descartes's scientific doubt, so criticized by Peirce in his "Four Capacities" essay. The scientific observer was supposed to be

11. Frege, *Foundations*, p. vi.

12. A. J. Greimas, "Sémiotique narrative et textuelle (entretien)," *Pratiques*, 11/12 (November 1976), 10.

13. Peirce, *Collected Papers*, 1.540 (see Chapter 1, pp. 48–49).

able to achieve a kind of zero point of knowledge: pure conception, an intransitive act of thinking, the *cogito* itself. The text of the *Course* speaks of what it knows and what it can communicate; it describes its own scientific activity and seems to assume that this activity can be unmediated, can be some transparent relation of thinking and 'material' substance: "Starting from words in defining things is a bad procedure" (F 31; E 14). But since we are in discourse and dealing (in linguistics) with discourse, it would seem impossible to do otherwise; it could be only self-deception to suppose that we can. Once again, the speaking subject has been occulted and transformed into an origin situated somewhere within linguistic facts: the thing that will enable science to define the laws of its relations with other things. *That* is now given as *independent* of any scientific discourse *about* it.

Peirce's remark to the effect that we do better to assume our own frailties—or, as he put it later, to include fallibility in all scientific analysis—seems entirely apposite here. Indeed, the *Course* was neglecting its own earlier sentence that "in dealing with speech it is an entirely false idea to think that the problem of origins differs from that of its permanent conditions" (F 24; E 9).[14] If, as this sentence implied, human speech must be thought of as having no point of origin either conceptually useful or (in any case) discoverable, then why should such a role be given to the object/word? If we look a little more closely at the matter, it becomes apparent that the positioning of language *(langue)* as the major principle of classification plays an important role in the establishment of this new scientific linguistics.

Speaking, said the *Course*, is a willful and intelligent act (F 30; E 14), which (a) results from a choice made among the elements of language present to the individual's mind and (b) links together the selected elements in an organized locution. According to the *Course*, such choice is made in terms of conceptual possibilities that the potential speaker associates with "representations of linguistic [signs] (sound-images) that are used for their expression" (F 28; E 11). Because the sound-image is a *representation* of a linguistic *sign* (the English translates *signe* as "sound"), it is clearly secondary; thus any origin in locution (in concrete linguistic 'fact') has been entirely repudiated. Not facts of language but a *concept* unlocks *(déclanche)* the representation in question. The speaker's choice, then, is made in terms of a possibility of speaking *from* a set of elements called "language." Both speaking as an act and language as a lawful system are thereby seen, *primarily,* as *used* (and use*ful*) for the instrumental expression of concepts.

14. My translation; the English differs altogether here from the French. The sentence is Saussure's but was displaced by the original editors, actually occurring later and in a different context (F 417 n.49).

Because, in the order now depicted in the *Course,* the concept is given as first in the order of utterance/locution, the speech act has found its fixed point of origin. The concept becomes the "thing" behind the shadow that the word is, or at least the concept as it is linked to the verbal sign. Now that its object has achieved such concrete status, the order of language has become a *natural* one (F 25; E 9). By getting rid of certain potential ambiguities, the *Course* has thus been able to do what Frege had sought to do for logic and axiomatic mathematics. It has provided a single invariant lawful foundation for the intended (eventually) total description of sets of variants.

If such a lawful basis is to be 'scientific,' it must also permit the assumption that it is generalizable. It was apparently in this sense that the *Course* referred to it as fundamentally social and public. However, the idea of the social that it presented was an extremely abstract one (F 104–5; E 71–72). And it is not without interest, in this regard, that the chapter whose primary purpose was the treatment of this matter was placed between two chapters that have hypnotized the specialists—as though to distract attention from unsatisfactory handling of an essential question. On one side is the chapter on sign/signified/signifier and the arbitrary; on the other is the chapter concerning the opposition between diachrony and synchrony (I.1 and I.3). Observing this, de Mauro also adds that the editors were following the order used by Saussure himself in the courses as presented orally (F 448 n. 146). The consequence of such abstraction and obfuscation is that we end up with a very odd notion indeed of the "social": one that replaced environmental reality (actual speaking, for example) with the rule of lawful competence (the ability to use *language* correctly).

The *Course* elaborated its notion of the public, lawful, and systematic foundation of *language* on the basis of a telling metaphor: "Language is comparable to a symphony in that what the symphony actually is stands completely apart from how it is performed; the mistakes that musicians make in playing the symphony do not compromise this fact" (F 36; E 18). In just what way this underlying model of the performed symphony may be considered public and social is hard to conceive. If anything is 'social' here, then it is surely the actual performance—unless one wishes to consider the culturally prescribed nature of scales, tone patterns, and so on. But that is an *active* competence only in a small minority of cases. Composition and playing, unlike language and speaking, are not a general competence. Is it too much to see in this metaphor a latent idea of the "qualified language user," the "competent" speaker? That is to say, may we not see here a transfer to the level of the system itself of the willful and intelligent speaker? And what is public and social is not actual practice but the *possibility* of a legitimate performance made available to competent users and indeed—thanks to the patterns of linguistic science as elaborated within the *Course*—endowed with a more profound reality than the merely superficial appearance from which *speaking* could benefit. (This idea of competence has since been carried over into the area of literary criticism in particular and of cultural criticism more generally, with ideological implications whose consequences require lengthy examination.)[15]

The metaphor as used in the *Course* prefigured, therefore, the later ideas to be explored in Chomskyan linguistics (see Chapter 7) and in the continental semiology with which I am concerned here. Common to these is the idea that language, deep structure, semiotic square, or narrative form in some way underlies not only the actual manifestation of discourse (locutions as produced) but a level even subsidiary to that, a level where meaning is 'put into place.' Greimas's semiotic square, for example, underlies a semic level (where a meaningful formula has already been elaborated, though not yet given form in an audible or visible sign) in a kind of belated throwback to the thought/language division, a division that precedes any actual manifestation in speaking. But that square is also a kind of universalized form of the Saussurean signified/signifier dichotomy, in which the latter—still bearing its trace of discreteness—has been transformed into a local, contingent form of a more universal meaning, now placed in a more or less entirely relational context. Thus an *origin* had been discovered in the very depths of the synchronic system; it could be called deep structure, semiotic square, or even the fundamental narrative form of all human thinking. What it did was locate a supposedly more universal and generalizable human mental structure 'beneath' all actual manifestations.

The project has much akin to the seventeenth-century ideal of a universal language, taken as derivable from basic concepts arranged in what was supposed to be their necessary and universal order: Wilkins, Dalgarno, Leibniz, and others took up a variant of the Cartesian idea that a perfect universal language could be derived directly from the possession of clear, distinct, and rightly ordered concepts. And Chomsky was quite right to seek a pattern for his own transformational grammar in such a "Cartesian linguistics" (though, as has been shown, the ideal in question goes back to Latin grammars of the sixteenth century). By the very nature of the case, however, there can be no evidence at all for the originary nature of *any* (inevitably verbally derived) concept of "deep structure," and Montaigne has long since provided a suitably ironic commentary: "I

15. In this connection, see, e.g., Stanley Fish's notions of "interpretive communities" and "informed reader," Michael Riffaterre's master reader, Jonathan Culler's "literary competence," or the more general notion of a "horizon of expectation" common to participants in a given culture. One may well wonder just how far these views differ from the traditional one encompassed by I. A. Richards's "expert in matters of taste" (*Principles of Literary Criticism* [1925; rpt. New York, n.d.], p. 36)—ideologically, not at all, one would think. I deal with further implications of this sort of thing in my forthcoming *Meaning of Literature*.

ask what is Nature, Pleasure, a Circle, and Substitution. The question is couched in words, and is answered in the same coin. A stone is a body. But if you press the point: And what is a body?—A substance.—And what is a substance? and so on, you will end by driving the answerer to exhaust his dictionary." I am reminded, too, of Molière's mocking 'analysis' (in *Le Malade imaginaire*) of the soporific power of opium, explained by its innate *vertu dormitive.*[16]

All this may be facile, but it is by no means irrelevant. The question confronting Saussure in particular, linguistics more generally, and positivistic science most broadly is that of origin and its effects: where does science "start"? Where may its object be fixed? In what may the analysis be anchored? The supposition that language was in some way the underlying structure of speaking, that language itself was in turn supported by a deep and strictly ordered rational network composed of potentially meaningful concepts (Cartesian innate ideas), enabled linguistic science to compose a linear story about the nature and development of language, to relate its strictly causal evolution, and to explain the functioning of its transparent instrumentality. And none of it depended upon the elaboration, even less upon the utterance, of the metalanguage itself—or so, at least, it could then be assumed.

Such linguistics thus became ever more disembodied. It may well be the case that producing meaning in a process of communication is one essential aspect of the individual's participation in society, even in the theory expressed by the *Course,* and would thus be as profoundly historical as de Mauro insisted. But it is hard to see how the *Course* in fact dealt with such a process, and certainly at the level of the structures it sought to conceive and analyze, it was deeply and entirely ahistorical. What, we may well ask, for instance, was historical in language thought of as a "symphony," composed of facts whose actualization was taken to be a matter of insignificant contingency? (And I use the word "insignificant" advisedly.) When the *Course* insisted that in discussing these structures it referred not to "words" but to "things," it strove to furnish a foundation corresponding to the modernist idea of *reality.* Such a concept of *real facts* assumed that they were the same at all times and in every place; it postulated that the possibility of their analysis depended not at all upon their disposition as formulated within linguistic discourse but upon the (a priori) composition of an invariant natural law controlling *our grasp* of their ordering but ontologically inherent to them. This natural law ordered both the linguistic facts themselves and the production of all discourse *about* them.

16. Michel de Montaigne, *Oeuvres complètes,* ed. Albert Thibaudet and Maurice Rat (Paris, 1962), p. 1046; translation by J. M. Cohen in Montaigne, *Essays* (Harmondsworth, 1958), p. 349.

In practice, it would appear rather that all we could study would be discourse: that is, the *use* of language (*not* to be confused with some kind of Bloomfieldian atomism). But the *Course*'s legal-theoretical economy of language implied that what was most important was a structure at once hidden and revealed by speaking. The justification for that supposition remained that we understand one another despite the supposed individuality of any given utterance. Just as Frege could separate sense (*Sinn*) from the individual image (*Vorstellung*), so the *Course* separated the common basis for comprehension (*langue*) from individual manifestation (*parole*). That might have been a useful and justifiable step had it remained simply a heuristic device, but the leap was made from methodological utility to the assumption that the new linguistics was actually dealing with things in themselves—a postulate whose warranty was the requirement of a particular scientificity.

To achieve the network of origin/cause-effect/enunciating subject/ analytical order, the *Course* repeated Frege's occultations. First, signs were viewed as essentially stable transmitters (their own "fixed points") of meaning that operated by means, as it were, of blocking and cutting out a set form from within "a shapeless and indistinct mass," a "nebula," a "floating realm of thought" (F 154; E 111–12).[17] That conception, while giving primacy to the realm of (as yet unordered) thought, enabled language not simply to be made an *effect* (since an 'intentional' *choice* must be made in terms of something preexisting both the choice and the linguistic material available to it, as well as providing the substance, *content,* for that material) but to be made also a necessary attribute of ideas as actualized. (In one way, that serves to confirm the need for a linguistics: if there were no such necessity, then it would obviously be futile to study language.)

The *Course* here has its cake and eats it: language is the instrument of the thinking that preceded it, but language is also a necessary (though not sufficient) part of that thinking. Had the *Course* posited, say, that thought was subsequent to expression (a kind of linguistic "reader-response criticism"!) rather than prior to it—the sea upon which floats the vessel of language, wrote Saussure—or had it even made thought simultaneous with its expression, then the difficulty of a "scientific" linguistics would

17. Though I think it has remained unacknowledged, this idea was to have a considerable future. It appears to be the Derridean *athèse* (otherwise manifest as *différance, supplément, dissémination, parergon,* and so forth), the not yet differentiated place of *archi-écriture* out of which all particular writing and speaking must be elaborated, following ("historically") the moment of the Platonic *thesis;* it is also Kristeva's arena of the semiotic, opposed and prior to the elaboration of a symbolic order; and it appears in the work of Hélène Cixous (and others) as the boundless Lacanian "pre-Oedipal" sphere of the "Great Mother," before the imposition of a dominant masculine symbolic order.

have been compounded a thousandfold. For what could we then do, for example, with the thoughts produced by linguistics about language? In the system of the *Course* such a problem would be insoluble; thought would then be entirely and solely the result of an individual and willful discursive act. Science would be reduced to subjectivity and flux. (That problem did not arise in a Peircean semiotics, in which the sets individual/society and subject/object were not inscribed in the system—and certainly not as oppositions.)

For the Saussurean enterprise the sign had first to be essentially stable, singular, and univocal—able to enter as such into a network of relations; this corresponds to Frege's occultation 1 (p. 59, above). Second (after this constitution of stable, originary signs), the abstract, "social" place of language was controlled by the individual and made functional by the individual, but on the basis of a general and readily available system of language and concept relations in every way parallel to that good sense that the Cartesian philosophy had presented as the most widely shared attribute of humans—otherwise known as "common sense." The public system of language was a stable order; social reality as actually manifested was understood to be in constant fluctuation. Thus a second occultation was achieved: flux had been excluded from the object of linguistic knowledge, and language made into a self-contained system. This corresponds to Frege's occultation 2. Third, any consideration of manifested discourse, where the social and the communal might appear as primary, was rejected: Frege's 3.

Fourth, any danger from so uncertain a concept as that of a semiotic *field* was obviated: Frege's 4. Initially, the *Course* appeared to maintain that last concept, but what it actually developed was what one might think of as two sets of linear relations: the syntagm of language on the one hand, and the hierarchy of the order concept/language-sign (signified/ signifier)/locution. When the signifier was defined as "arbitrary" and the arbitrary as "unmotivated" (F 101; E 68–69), the direction of the relation was made clear in a negative manner. The sign was clearly not arbitrary in terms of usage (which was excluded, however, from consideration). The relation of arbitrariness thus marked a relation between the signifier and the signified/concept. To use the word "unmotivated" was clearly to place the signified in a situation of potential primacy, since motivation could be provided only there (if anywhere). The *Course* thus proceeded as though there must have been at some time (and still must be) thoughts to be put into words, though the words found and made had no intrinsic relation to those thoughts. However, if thoughts depend on the delimitation given them by words in a certain linguistic context, how can we speak of the precedence of thoughts? We are not actually very far from falling into the name/thing order we have already seen criticized in the *Course*: "This rather naive approach can bring us near the truth" (F 97; E 65).[18]

However "unmotivated," signifiers nonetheless remained in their proper place in a right and legitimate order. If they did not, if we were serious about words making possible the selection ("blocking and cutting out") of concepts, we would once again confront the impossibility of a scientific linguistics. In actual use, therefore, the putative opposition expressed by "unmotivated" versus "motivated" was something of a red herring, as is the opposition between subjectivity and objectivity (see Chapter 3); both stemmed from the axiomatic adoption of causal, linear relations. Then why, one may ask, did the question of arbitrariness appear so important? And why did this idea strike linguists as so insightfully original (though explored by both Bacon and Descartes at some length in the beginnings of our modernist tradition) and as such a breakthrough? Its benefits, I think, were largely negative: without some such concept as this to get around the difficulty of causality, there was a terrible problem to resolve. If the signifier was not arbitrary, then language could not be treated as though it were an isolated system; it could not be dealt with as a system of abstract signs. The discipline of linguistics would promptly find itself (a) without a clear and unequivocal object and (b) without any borders. In semiotics, Peirce (and apparently Eco) had no hesitation in accepting that realization, with all the immense difficulties it posed. Saussure and Greimas were less adventuresome: thus the signifier would be turned into an unmotivated abstract entity, and semiosis (Peirce's *phaneron*) slotted into a double linearity.

Finally—and this was an occultation essential to *all* analytico-referential science—the enunciating subject of discourse was worked out of the process, to "become" (or be replaced by) the 'objective' origin in the now stable, discrete system of linguistic relations (I have discussed this at length in *The Discourse of Modernism*).

Between Port-Royal and Peirce, the *Course* (like Frege and others at the same time and in other areas of knowledge and action) performed the

---

18. Benveniste has observed how the interference of reality was even more pronounced: "[Saussure] asserts in precise terms . . . that 'the linguistic sign unites, not a thing and a name, but a concept and a sound-image' [F 98; E 66). But he asserts immediately afterwards that the nature of the sign is arbitrary because '*in reality*' it 'has no natural connection with the signified' [F 101; E 69]. It is clear that this reasoning is vitiated by an unconscious and surreptitious recourse to a third term that was not included in the initial definition. This third term is the thing itself, reality. It is all very well for Saussure to say that the idea of '*soeur*' is not bound to the signifier *s-ö-r;* he is nonetheless thinking of the *reality* of the notion. When he speaks of the difference between *b-ö-f* and *o-k-s,* he is referring in spite of himself to the fact that these terms are applied to the same *reality.* Here then is the *thing,* expressly excluded at first from the definition of the sign, being reintroduced by a subterfuge [*détour*] and establishing a permanent contradiction" (Emile Benveniste, "Nature du signe linguistique" [1939], in his *Problèmes de linguistique générale* [Paris, 1966], p. 50).

role of Copernicus, Tycho Brahe, Johannes Kepler, and Galileo between Ptolemy and Newton: the phenomena continued to be saved (more or less); the more dubious axiomatic and observational borders were blurred; the conceptual and epistemological order was maintained. As far as linguistics was concerned, the consequences were far-reaching. Any theory making "sentences the concrete units of language" (F 148; E 106), for example, was rejected with little ado. The unlimited variety of the sentence, the *Course* asserted, showed it to be a part of speaking, not of language. Explicitly, Saussurean linguistics could not deal with actual *usage*. And that is not simply a matter of delimiting a field of study; the discursive order whose establishment I have just been tracing made usage formally, axiomatically, subsidiary to the language *(langue)* that was taken as making it possible. In establishing that order as fundamental to the science of linguistics, the *Course* in fact rejected from that science any notion of dealing with real manifestations of language (Benveniste, as we will see, raised just this objection).

I have already indicated what that order was: individual thinking (place of concepts), language (place of 'social,' 'public' constraints), speaking. We know that the first two could be articulated together by means of the concept of a *sign*, binding together *signified* and *signifier*. Both, however, are conceived as actually *cut off* from speaking, which nonetheless proceeds from them. That order corresponds to the one established through a particular interpretation of Descartes, understood as allowing "nature" to be *fixed* in discourse (or rather, in "thought"): mechanical structure of nature (able to be *discovered* by the philosopher/scientist), methodical philosophy (the common order of human thought), discourse.[19] For linguistics, the place of concepts provided an 'inexhaustible' set of fixed, concrete objects and events—just as 'nature' did for, say, physics or chemistry, as 'civil society' did for political theory, or as 'mind' (in diverse conceptualizations) did for philosophy, psychology, and neurology. Thus was 'resolved' the problem of a science about the production of meaning between discourses.

For linguistics of the Saussurean variety, those underlying premises suggest certain difficulties (to say the least) where writing is concerned, the writing of "literature" in particular. Indeed, the subsidiary nature of usage, the rejection of "fluctuating realities," implies that literature—understood in any traditional sense—cannot enter the domain of linguistics at all. For the familiar view of literature was that its texts emphasized *speaking* at least as much as *language*, usage as much as what was "proper" and lawful (though that relationship is clearly most complicated). Such a

19. I have discussed this issue in "Cartesian Discourse," and in "The *concevoir* Motif." See also my *Discourse of Modernism*.

view placed some obstacles in the way of a semiology based on the "master-pattern" provided by this linguistics (F 101; E 68)—not only Greimas's, for example, but also that proposed by the Roland Barthes of *Elements of Semiology* (1964). Whatever Barthes may have written about that semiology's treatment of "larger fragments of discourse referring to objects or episodes whose meaning *underlies* language," the fact remains that they "can never exist independently of it" and therefore find themselves reduced to fixed language objects of just the same nature as those already seen.[20]

Two possible solutions appear to present themselves. The first of these has been adopted by literary structuralism and much continental semiology (including the German and French versions of Peirce as represented by Max Bense, Elisabeth Walther, and Gérard Deledalle). They proceed by trying to find the deep structure assumed to underlie the actual manifestation of the literary text; in an extreme view, such as Michael Riffaterre's, all literary texts could be reduced to the embroidering of one unifying structure, or "matrix."[21] In Greimas's narrative semiology the set of relations coordinated within the semiotic square is transformed into a text (whether "literary" or not) by being filled out with variously different semes (as the variants within a formal logic) or, as semiological practitioners are frequently thrilled to say, provided with an axiology. This solution has more than a little in common with the attempt by Geoffroy Saint-Hilaire in comparative anatomy at the beginning of the nineteenth century to derive all animals from the *one* originary animal form: embryology and skeletology had their contributions to make. (We may perhaps think of this as the *hilarious* solution.) It has been an application of Saussure's *Course* as recorded by its editors, and filtered through such as Benveniste,

20. Roland Barthes, *Elements of Semiology,* tr. Annette Lavers and Colin Smith (1967; rpt. New York, 1985), p. 11. Barthes stated earlier (p. 10) that while all kinds of "objects, images and patterns of behaviour can signify," they "never" do so "autonomously," being always subordinate to natural language: "It appears increasingly more difficult to conceive a system of images and objects whose *signifieds* can exist independently of language: to perceive what a substance signifies is inevitably to fall back on the individuation of a language: there is no meaning which is not designated, and the world of signifieds is none other than that of language." The obstacle alluded to here may well explain the gradual change occurring today in the meaning of the word "literature": a "textuality" that is "self-productive" rather than worked out by an author *using* language. *Text* would then simply be the actualized transformation of innate "grammatical" and "syntactical" possibilities of language and mind (exactly on the pattern of a transformational generative grammar), and the problem of coping with usage is displaced onto the "reader" and interpretation: hence, e.g., "reader-response criticism." "Literature" is thus being transformed, perhaps, to be better adapted to the demands of the "sciences" wishing to deal with it. In later, nonsemiological work Barthes himself responded at length to these matters.
21. Michael Riffaterre, *Semiotics of Poetry* (Bloomington, Ind., 1978), and *La Production du texte* (Paris, 1979).

Louis Hjelmslev, Roman Jakobson, and Noam Chomsky—however much some of these may have sought to escape its constraints.

The second possible solution is very different. The model for the method dependent upon fixed anchorages and causal, expansive development from them is, and has been since the European seventeenth century, the discourse of the physical sciences. Scientific linguistics of the kind discussed here and its semiological successors have attempted to follow that model—despite the very profound self-questioning those sciences have undertaken since the late nineteenth century (and precisely with respect to its own assumptions concerning its function). That examination, among other things (and to remain within my present area of discussion), has made it unclear whether the traditional distinction between, for example, the literary and the nonliterary is at all possible, and certainly whether its terms do not need complete reappraisal. If the distinction does not hold, then we can no longer suppose that literature is either *like* science in its underlying structures (as semiology supposes) or that it differs from it. The dichotomy itself would become sense-less: at least in terms of assumed structures of thought and language.

It is the case that some other differential element might then come importantly into play. It might also then appear that what they have in common is not deep structure but the fact that they are *discourses,* ways of elaborating meaning within a given sociocultural environment. The former basis for distinction or similarity would become not so much an irrelevancy as the mark of one such environment. For the contemporary critic, this solution might take the form of a 'Peircean' semiotics of discursive process: a practice of the practice of discourse. By this, however, I mean not a kind of free play of signifying (whatever that might be— perhaps what the French have referred to as a *pratique signifiante* transformed into *errance, dérive,* and the rest) but an activity seeking to change the nature of the processes upon which it works, aware that it can do nothing else. As Eco has put it: "To 'speak' about 'speaking,' to signify signification or to communicate about communication cannot but influence the universe of speaking, signifying and communicating."[22] (I return to these issues in Chapter 3.)

The anagrams aside, Saussure excluded writing altogether from linguistic consideration. He swiftly allotted it its place in the scheme of things: subsidiary to the "living language," its influence on this last is, according to the *Course,* monstrous and unnatural (F 54; E 31–32). Such a view was necessary because of the originary order of cause-effect set in place by the concept-language-speech sequence. De Mauro's argument notwithstanding (F 429 n.86), the *Course* did *not* maintain or even imply

22. Eco, *Theory,* p. 29.

that writing was a different but equal system to that of speaking. The *Course* viewed writing either as the passive representation of speaking or, when its signs no longer "match" those of speaking (whatever that means: synchronically it is nonsense), as a deformation. Indeed, the *Course* referred to such "displacements" (of meaning) as "pathological" (F 53; E 31) and to their study as that of "teratological cases" (F 54; E 32). They were due, it insisted, "to external influence" ("un facteur . . . étranger"), and they were monstrous because, were it to be granted a status equal to that of *language (langue),* say, writing would subvert the entire structure established in the *Course.*[23] If its subordinate status were canceled, then the cause-effect procedure would no longer work, and the entire system of relations would be thrown out of kilter. "Science" would disappear through the window of its firm building, or, rather, the window would disappear with the falling wall.

Literature had to be banished from linguistics less because it could not in theory be treated by a linguistics of *langue* (though its elements would have to be reduced to static atoms in a stable system of relations) than because, for any adequate treatment, emphasis would have to be placed on precisely those discursive *processes* whose exploration would throw into doubt the structural principles of that linguistics. The *Course* therefore sought a 'replacement' for writing in its own scientific activity—though it is worth recalling once again that Saussure himself did not publish the work and that much of the editorial difficulty was due to his having burned many of his notes. Be that as it may, the *Course* sought to establish itself as an act of memorial writing, necessary to avoid chaos: "When writing is suppressed in favour of thought, whoever has been deprived of this perceptible image runs the risk of no longer perceiving anything but a shapeless and unmanageable mass. It is as if the beginning swimmer were deprived of a life belt" (F 55; E 32: I have brought the English closer to the French). Science, said Saussure, has brought order to that initial chaos by using phonology as an "auxiliary science that has freed [linguistics] from the written word" (F 55; E 33). In fact, that is yet another red herring, for language has already been given to us as describable and comprehensible, as a fixed, ordered anchorage. But it was a red herring because what threatened chaos was not the suppression of writing; on the contrary, it was (as I have suggested) its continued presence in the scientific domain of linguistics. The *Course*'s argument was that only by removing the monster of false mimetic clarity could the true clarity of scientific method be achieved. The suppression of writing and the

23. At a personal level, one cannot help wondering whether the strange violence of the vocabulary here was not due in some part to Saussure's struggle with the anagrams and his eventual failure to analyze or explain their functioning in any satisfactory way. The attempt occurred before he conducted the classes in linguistics that now compose the *Course.*

elaboration of phonology actually meant "a first step in the direction of truth" (F 55; E 32).

A pleasant problem was thus set for the purveyors of a literary semiology. How could the chaos that writing introduced into the conceptual order of a scientific linguistics be reduced to a lawful system? How could a semiology that referred to such a linguistics as its "master-pattern" avoid the same monstrous chaos?

In his commentary on Vladimir Propp's *Morphologie du conte* (1970), Claude Lévi-Strauss recalled three things: (1) that the total system of elementary structures, Propp's "functions," in the folktale could never be empirically realized; (2) that one could never know this unless one had analyzed *all* such tales; (3) that to make such an attempt would be impossible in practice.[24] Because Propp's analysis lay explicitly behind the development of Greimas's semiology, these reminders were timely and important—even though, for precisely those reasons, the necessarily provisional, statistical, and probabilistic nature of the natural sciences had long been recognized and practiced. That nature was illustrated in the nineteenth century by Maxwell's demon and Peirce's fallibilism, but Bacon and others had been well aware of those limitations two centuries before.[25]

In Propp's case the difficulty did not arise, because he simply exhausted the possibility of finding any new functions in a corpus limited to one hundred tales and did not seek to extend in any detail the particular conclusions beyond the corpus investigated (though he could obviously have set to work on a further corpus). An initial response to the "pleasant problem" thus lay in reducing the corpus and raising writing to the same status as speaking, so that the *langue* or "grammar" behind it could be discovered. But Lévi-Strauss's reminders clearly intervened with a vengeance as soon as either the corpus itself was indefinitely expanded, or the method was applied to enormously more complicated phenomena: the written short story, novel, play, poem, and so on. In the oral or quasi-oral tale (Propp's corpus), as Millman Parry and Albert Lord seem definitively to have shown, what Propp called the "function" appeared to correspond to a kind of minimal semantic unit: the singer composed *by means of* such elements and not with individual words as such.[26] Once writing took over, that was clearly no longer the case.

<hr>

24. Claude Lévi-Strauss, "La structure et la forme: Réflexions sur un ouvrage de Vladimir Propp," in his *Anthropologie structurale deux* (Paris, 1973), p. 144. Propp's study was in fact available in English long before its translation into French: *Morphology of the Folktale* (Bloomington, Ind., 1958).

25. See Reiss, *Discourse of Modernism*, esp. pp. 211–14.

26. Albert Lord, *The Singer of Tales* (Cambridge, Mass., 1960).

Nonetheless, the series of analytical concepts established by Propp for studying the composition and meaning of his limited number of folktales could not but look singularly appealing to any putative literary semiologist—or, come to that, any other student of literature conscious of the attack of subjectivity, as well as any linguist fearing the chaos of writing but aware that sentences and other gross verbal structures have properties different from those of smaller units. Propp established the concept that underlying the composition of the folktales in his corpus was a finite number of "functions." He seemed to have shown that these functions always followed an invariable order (though not all were necessarily present in any given folktale). He argued that each function could be defined intrinsically (by means of the action it "bears") and extrinsically (with respect to its verbal and conceptual context, to the relational constraints working upon it). Functions thus operated both analytically and referentially, thereby further confirming the universality of modernism's idea of human mind and action. Taken separately and together, each of these concepts and the entire series had obvious properties of at least quasi-scientific law. The difficulty was that there were thirty-one functions, of which some or all would appear in any given text, and that if the analysis were to be applied to *any* literary text of whatever kind (not to mention, eventually, any text of any kind whatever), then the number of parameters involved in the analysis would be so multiplied as to render any statistical science virtually impossible; one would be likely to end up with a private analysis for each text.

In response to the *Course* (and to Propp), therefore, only one alternative seemed likely to bear fruit—assuming one wished to follow, broadly speaking, the path it had traced out. That response was to reduce the freedom of functions. If they could be made simpler, more 'absolute' and 'infrastructural'—less dependent, for example, on a massive context of surface relations—then the statistics might become manageable. Better still, might they not be reduced to a genuine minimum?

That was what Greimas set out to do. He accomplished it by establishing a set of actantial relations, a mere six "actants" being needed to account for all and any narration. They formed the minimal 'skeleton' common to all telling, any given textual exposition simply being a different way of putting flesh on those bones. Nor were they simply the laws of fictional telling. Beneath them an even more fundamental and deeper structure of mind organized all thinking itself and every other play of semiosis: the semiotic square, representing the essential relations of contradiction, opposition, and affirmation. Greimas thus provided a single generative model of meaning: in form a proposition of binary logic, in action a readily manipulated automaton, in apprehension an astonishing piece of reductionism. That model corresponded to the conceptual 'necessity' for whose achievement Greimas argued as he praised the objectives of a Hjelmslevian linguistics: "The theory of language will be perfect as soon as the axiomatics permitting its construction rejoins the general model that will have been established on the basis of the description of particular linguistic structures, and that subsumes them all."[27]

Greimas therefore set off, as he once put it in folkloric terms, on a "quest for the hidden hero" of signification. The remark occurred in a text reprinted in *Sémiotique et sciences sociales* and became, in fact, the closing phrase of that volume. The comment revealed that Greimas had remained within the axiomatics first fully expounded in *Sémantique structurale* ten years before.[28] By 1976 he was beginning to confront the increasingly worrisome difficulty of the reductionist nature of the axiomatics he had laid down, and the first chapter of *Sémiotique* can be read as an attempt to bring back the elements earlier occulted. To achieve this, Greimas proposed a second semiology: a semiology of discourse, which would be able, he thought, to avoid many of the earlier difficulties.

However, the two semiologies corresponded precisely to the system and process split (synchrony and diachrony) originated by Saussure, emphasized by Hjelmslev, and fully bound up within the conceptual basis of the narrative semiology:

27. Algirdas Julien Greimas, "Préface," to Louis Hjelmslev, *Le langage,* tr. Michael Olsen (Paris, 1966), p. 17. For a bibliography of Greimas's writings into the late 1970s, see Frédéric Nef, "Introduction to the Reading of Greimas: Toward a Discursive Linguistics," *Diacritics,* 7, no. 1 (1977). I have referred very little to the later texts now collected in *Du sens II: Essais sémiotiques* (Paris, 1983), because the pretensions to 'objective' scientificity there become even more explicit and exaggerated (my few comments in Chapter 9 may suffice in this respect). At the same time, those claims become rather more complex, as they do *attempt* to avoid reifying and fetishizing the sign as a static and clearly bounded object of knowledge. On this subject a useful overview has been provided by the editors' "Introduction: Exigences et perspectives de la sémiotique," in *Aims and Prospects of Semiotics: Essays in Honor of Algirdas Julien Greimas,* ed. Herman Parret and Hans-Georg Ruprecht (Amsterdam, 1985), I: xxiii–li. Greimas's principal writings are now appearing in English (making the present critique perhaps the more pertinent): A. J. Greimas and J. Courtès, *Semiotics and Language: An Analytical Dictionary,* tr. Larry Crist et al. (Bloomington, Ind., 1982); A. J. Greimas, *Structural Semantics: An Attempt at a Method,* tr. Daniele McDowell, Ronald Schleifer, and Alan Velie (Lincoln, Neb., 1983); A. J. Greimas, *On Meaning: Selected Writings in Semiotic Theory,* tr. Paul Perron and Frank Collins (Minneapolis, Minn., 1987). For the sake of consistency, I have maintained my own translations of all citations from Greimas.

28. A. J. Greimas, *Sémiotique et sciences sociales* (Paris, 1976), p. 216, and *Sémantique structurale* (Paris, 1966); these texts are hereafter cited as *Sémiotique* and *Sémantique,* respectively. Greimas actually extended this claim to *all* the human sciences, arguing that their enunciating subject always conceals its diverse ruses beneath a seemingly linear narrative of truth, ruses needed to overcome a series of obstacles placed before "its quest for true knowledge [*sa quête du savoir vrai*]." The human scientist *is* thus the hidden hero of knowledge, the director of reason, its *destinateur* and its *destinataire*: "Des accidents dans les sciences dites humaines: Analyse d'un texte de Georges Dumézil" (1979), in *Du sens II,* pp. 171–212; my quotation is this essay's concluding phrase.

When Saussure defined language as a system of signs, he posed the foundations of linguistic semiology. But we can now see that though the sign indeed corresponds to the signifying units of language, we cannot make it the unique principle of language in its discursive foundation. Saussure did not ignore the sentence, but he was visibly seriously embarrassed by it and relegated it to speaking, which resolved nothing. The Question is precisely to know how one can get from the sign to "speaking." In reality the world of the sign is closed. From sign to sentence there is no transition, either by the setting into syntagm or otherwise. They are separated by a hiatus.[29]

Benveniste added that because of the division the two semiologies would indeed require different conceptual bases. But the split in question was already inscribed in the *Course,* and the same conceptualizations underlie all these arguments.

Thus, a discursive semiology is implicitly secondary to a narrative one, just as speaking—or writing and the chaos it threatened—was explicitly secondary to *language* in the *Course.* In fact, the discursive semiology remained always reminiscent of its patron (as we may call it), the narrative.[30] Nor can it be accidental that *Sémiotique,* whose beginning sought to problematize the project of a scientific semiology, concluded with the mark of the hidden hero: the final subject of narration, the provider of purpose in narrativity, the origin of a teleological process. That hero was (ostensibly) to be found, however, *après coup,* and *destinataire* of the semiologist's gift of life and therefore the final (justifying) signal of a system constituted in its *truth*: "he" was the fixed point that offered an origin of signification and at the same time a final goal for the semiologist's quest.

The hidden hero was the general semiotic model whose discovery Greimas had made the praiseworthy goal of linguistics in the preface to Hjelmslev (note 27). Though elusive, it would be discovered by means of a supposedly naive description of its various elaborated manifestations. Though actually existing as a potential object of knowledge, it would be revealed as isomorphic with that very axiomatics making possible the description in question—but *that* would not be taken to mean that the axiomatics had in any way influenced (far less, created) the *found* model. The choice of elements corresponding to the axiomatics of that scientific semiology, that is to say, was not understood as an open one; the elements were provided from the outset by the identity of the lawful systems of

29. Benveniste, *Problèmes II,* p. 65. Paul Ricoeur has of course discussed these questions many times: three important texts are *Le conflit des interprétations* (Paris, 1969); *La métaphore vive* (Paris, 1975); and *Interpretation Theory: Discourse and the Surplus of Meaning* (Forth Worth, Tex., 1976).

30. See, e.g., A. J. Greimas, "The Cognitive Dimension of Narrative Discourse," with J. Courtès, *New Literary History,* 7 (Spring 1976), 433–47.

language, mind, and world; the sought-for generative model was *rightly* identical to the conceptual system that made the terms of the search and the search itself possible. That is why the "hidden hero" could be extended to all the "human sciences" (see note 28).

From the beginning, Greimas had situated the problem of meaning in a "place" considered to be quasi-autonomous with respect to any relation with language: "We propose considering perception as the nonlinguistic place where the apprehension of signification is to be located." That enabled him to posit the existence of some kind of general semantic virtuality—capable of being actualized in linguistic forms but quite independent of them—such that there would be no "autonomous classes of linguistic meanings (*significations*)."[31] Greimas later suggested that "the best point of departure for understanding semantic structure consists, for the present, in the Saussurean conception of two levels of language."[32] He would appear already to have gone further than that, however, by arguing that the level of the signified, of system, was the actualization of a virtuality of sense (the sphere of concepts underlying *langue*, that Saussurean amorphous mass which Greimas will be able to reduce to order through the device of the semiotic square, as Chomsky had done through his deep generative grammatical structure).

The traditional division of language and thought, but their similarity of structure, was picked up anew by a device similar, therefore, to that used by Saussure. Signification was amorphous, no doubt, but it *existed* prior to its linguistic manifestation. Furthermore, its Saussurean status as a "thing," available objectively to knowledge, could also be reinstituted, though in a slightly different form: "Semantics openly acknowledges itself, therefore, as an attempt to describe the world of sensible qualities" (*Sémantique*, p. 9). A sensible quality was obviously not a "thing" in the sense of some object-in-the-world; it was a phenomenon posited as independent insofar as the proposed semantics was concerned.

31. *Sémantique*, p. 8. Greimas argued the phenomenological bent of this choice by referring it to Maurice Merleau-Ponty. He had actually asserted the need for such a choice ten years earlier when he wrote that it was supported by "Merleau-Ponty's efforts, which are tending to elaborate a psychology of language in which the dichotomy of thought and language is abandoned in favor of a conception of language where sense is immanent to the linguistic form and which . . . appears . . . as the natural continuation of Saussurean thinking" ("L'actualité du saussurisme," p. 193). Roman Jakobson has observed the "close and effective connections" between the early protagonists of structural linguistics and "phenomenology in its Husserlian and Hegelian versions": *Main Trends in the Science of Language* (London, 1973), p. 13. One might also point to remarks by Barthes, as well as to studies on the matter by both Kristeva and Derrida. "Immanent" it may have been, as Greimas insisted, but sense had regained an autonomy appearing to require rather more than a mere adjustment.

32. A. J. Greimas, *Du sens* (Paris, 1970), p. 39.

To have situated the object of scientific study in "perception separated it from the discursive process that sought to talk about it as an "otherness." It was thus possible to assume the total independence of an object and a subject, with the result that a scientific "knowledge" became communicable and specifiable in terms of difference, objectivity, inside/outside, and so on. And it is indeed worth remarking that the form of that process of knowledge would be set quite precisely in the terms of a certain reading of the *cogito.* I have elsewhere argued that *cogito ergo sum* depicts exactly the order of analytico-referential discourse: the *cogito* is the place of thought, the *sum* that of body (the material world in general), and the *ergo* the communicative instrument (language, for example) that links them together. In abstract terms it repeats the telescope metaphor: mind's eye, instrument of understanding, material world. In this semiology the ordinary place of sense (the 'first' object of "perception") corresponds in this *ordering system* to the *cogito;* actual manifestation (available for study) corresponds to the *sum;* the process allowing the passage from one to another corresponds to the *ergo*: "Semiotic theory must be conceived in such a way that between the fundamental instances *ab quo,* where the semantic substance receives its initial articulation and constitutes itself in a signifying form, and the final instances *ad quem,* where signification is manifested through a multiplicity of languages, a vast space may be disposed [*amenagé*] for the installation of an *instance of mediation* where the semiotic structures that possess an autonomous status would be located."[33]

Not only are these three instances, *ab quo, ad quem,* and *of mediation* (all italicized by Greimas) posited as autonomous, but they are laid down as the necessary pattern of all possible knowing: "must [*on doit*]." One need hardly be surprised, after that, to discover that the epistemological order accompanying this interpretation of the *cogito* is confirmed as the fundamental, general semiotic/semantic axis: *vouloir* → *savoir* → *pouvoir* ⇒ *faire* (*Du sens,* p. 179, and throughout Greimas's work). (These were the terms of the psychology of political order as analyzed, for example, by Descartes's contemporary Cardinal Richelieu, in his *Political Testament.*[34] But they were also those of Descartes's psychological theory, explored in the 1649 *Passions of the Soul.*)

That order had two distinct advantages: first it potentially situated the object of analysis, assuming one could be found able to fit the pattern. Second, it allowed the scientist to fit *his* own discourse into the same

33. Ibid., pp. 159–60. Cf. earlier: *"The generation of signification does not pass, first of all, through the production of locutions and their combination in discourse, but is relayed in its course by narrative structures, and it is these that produce meaningful discourse articulated in locutions"* (p. 159).

34. Armand-Jean du Plessis, Cardinal-Duc de Richelieu, *Testament politique,* ed. Louis André (Paris, 1947). On this, see, e.g., my *Tragedy and Truth: Studies in the Development of a Renaissance and Neoclassical Discourse* (New Haven, Conn., 1980), esp. pp. 220–21, 228.

pattern and to take *his* own *ergo* as nonconstructive (I use the masculine possessive deliberately). In the later texts, Greimas started to reveal a profound worry with respect to the second point, but his narrative semiology, at least, continued to keep that worry at a relatively safe distance. So, for instance, the potentially perilous remark that the very process of discourse itself constituted at once the discursive subject and, as an inevitable corollary, the sense it produced was not conceived as redounding against the "scientific" semiology producing the remark but as bearing only upon the object-language, the goal of its study: "The subject of discourse is, therefore, the instance that does not stop, according to the Saussurean conception, at ensuring the passage from the virtual to the real state of language: it appears as the place where the set of mechanisms that makes it possible for *language to be made into discourse* is put together. Located in a place where the *being of language* is transformed into a *linguistic act,* the subject of discourse may be said to be productive of discourse, without this being just a bad metaphor."[35]

The structural semanticist followed, then, a hallowed order. Nor was this establishment of a particular epistemology indifferent, of course. It marked the semiological project as an institutional activity. From the didactic intention *(vouloir)* to the foundation in truth *(savoir)* to the possibility of right reading *(pouvoir)* to the actual production of such operations *(faire),* one could follow with entire accuracy both the stages of the semiological project as a scientific analysis of reality, and the inscription within its own order of the axiomatic epistemology that it asserted was alone able to make the project realizable. As one might expect from so self-conscious a thinker, Greimas himself confirmed this view: the scientific project of semiology "consists first of all in reducing the part played by the ideal intuitive competence of the 'gifted' reader, by making explicit the process of reading, by formulating it univocally, by formalizing it if necessary; these are the antecedent conditions for the transmissibility of knowledge [*savoir*], guarantor of the *operational* character of the constructed models. . . . Discourse whose aim is scientific and one with didactic purpose once again find themselves possessed of the common concern of being founded in truth" ("Sémiotique narrative," pp. 11–12). To set up such an ideal of scientific knowledge required a certain amount of agility, the play of some ambiguity, the admission of certain paradoxes. These had to be overridden, concealed, occulted—at least initially.

The principal ambiguity occurs at the very point in Saussure where Greimas located the origin of his own text: in the distinction and the relation between the signified and the signifier. "Whatever may be the

35. *Sémiotique,* p. 11. It should be acknowledged nonetheless that in this same text Greimas did seek to confront science itself with the problem—unresolvably, in his terms. I return to this at the end of the chapter.

status [sensuous or other] of the signifier, no classification of signifieds is possible by starting from signifiers. Signification, accordingly, is independent of the nature of the signifier through which it is manifested" (*Sémantique*, p. 11). However, he had already defined the signified as "the signification or significations that are covered [*recouvertes*] by the signifier and manifested thanks to its existence" (*Sémantique*, p. 10). They were, that is to say (and this is entirely in agreement with Saussure), logically inseparable: no signifier without a signified, no signified without a signifier.

In this there were two difficulties. The first proceeded from the ambiguous nature of the scientific *ergo*, which surreptitiously inscribed causality as the primary categorical intuition. The fact that no classification of signifieds was possible through signifiers did *not* imply the consequence of their independence. At least for practical purposes, it was tied to the apparent fact that the 'bounds' of the signifier did not correspond to those of 'its' possible signified, because the boundaries were fluid and because there was no such thing as an absolutely bounded signifier. Signification was not independent of the signifier, but neither would the one be defined by the other in a simple relation of difference and/or opposition. But such a conclusion *would* make an *independent* science of semantics impossible, for it would mean that semantics could no longer define its own object with any clearly delimited frontiers. That signification be defined as independent of the signifier was thus necessary *for semantics*.

The very element, it would seem, that ought of necessity to be accepted as the first given—discourse in actual functioning and as manifest in use—had therefore to be dismissed as not pertinent. Worse yet, it appeared as a real obstacle to scientific knowledge: the truth of the world would be revealed only when the false appearance had been removed. In semantics, however, there could quite clearly be no means of validating such an assumption except through and within that very manifestation already rejected as an obstacle to knowledge. Greimas thus found himself obliged to write: "This recourse, first and last, to linguistic reality thus constitutes for (the linguist) the unique and homogeneous reference— referent—of his scientific activity [*faire scientifique*]. That is the paradox of that level of signs which is their manifestation: though it is a level not pertinent for his activity, it is nonetheless necessary because it provides a foundation and justifies it" (*Sémiotique*, p. 16).

The second difficulty was evidently connected with the scientific necessity of constituting an object as exterior to the process analyzing it, and of establishing casual relations. At the beginning of his attempt to create a science of semiology, Greimas appeared to elaborate this requirement by mixing two levels. When he wrote that signification was manifested by means of a signifier and noted, consequently, that the two presupposed each other, he was commenting upon a given instance of meaning: the *fact*, as he put it, of an *"ensemble signifiant"* (*Sémantique,* p. 10). When he wrote of the status of the signifier and of the "classification of signifieds," he was at a rather different level of analysis: that of his supposedly separate metalanguage ("separate," of course, from the discursive objects about which it was speaking). It was there that the other notion crept in: the notion that the signified was independent of the "nature of the signifier through which [*grâce auquel*] it is manifested," indeed, in which it is *contained* ("les significations qui y sont éventuellement contenues"; *Sémantique,* p. 11). Because the distinction of metalanguages had not yet been elaborated, what happened here was that the object of study—meaning, sense—was confirmed in its status as an otherness available to scientific study, and, once again, actual manifestation might be set aside.

That series of developments, a projection from the signified/signifier doublet, corresponded to the earlier definition (in *Sémantique*) of the object of a structural semantics: signifieds are "apprehended"; they are sensible qualities not in themselves linguistic. Semantics sought to deal with those. Semantics wanted to be "structural" (or assumed it must be). It could be structural only if there were structures to examine, and, by definition, structures could be found only among the sensible qualities that were to be the objects of study. These had therefore to be a set of objects capable of arranging themselves in ordered relations, but the set had to be of a given order and closed, for otherwise the structure could not be delimited. Thus Greimas spoke quite rightly of "our efforts to establish . . . the principles and rules of the narrative organization underlying the unfurling of discourse" ("Sémiotique narrative," p. 7).

If the members of the set were of a single order, then signifieds and signifiers clearly had to be kept separate. *In order for a structural semantics to have an object, it had to assume distinct sets of meanings that were independent of any specific manifestation.* That meant that all the arguments we have so far been examining were *all* already inscribed within the very project of a structural semantics.

The debate about the signifier/signified relation permitted that *necessary* referent of the science to be endowed with a status in reality: because one signifier could have several signifieds, because several signifiers could possess one signified (a rather more dubious notion), because signifiers of a different sensorial kind might be needed to 'convey' a given signified, and so on, *therefore* the 'two' were independent within reality. That claim was necessitated, of course, by the particular scientific project itself. And since that is the case, it is of considerable interest to come across a text explicitly denying it: "The question of knowing whether the semantic structure is immanent to and underlies the semantic universe, or whether it is only a metalinguistic construct accounting for the given universe, may be considered as nonpertinent" (*Du sens,* p. 39). On the contrary, what is in question is the very status of the science and of its analytical object of reference. Perhaps that science would at least like to be able to consider the raising of the question *im*pertinent.

The referent selected would be the object of the scientific analysis to be elaborated. But it was also its subject, because it was the major postulate allowing that science to be established: the existence of a structured order of meaning separate from what signifies it. If we are to be able to speak about this, then the subject of utterance must be occulted so as to be (re)constituted, as it were, *as* the object of science. And it had to be constituted as a potential object in knowledge dependent on scientific discourse only to the extent that it is supposed to be "revealed," "laid bare," by it. Thus Greimas could speak of "the problematics of the instance *ab quo* of the generation of discourse, of a place originating the first elementary articulation of signification, at once simple and open; a new conception of discourse brings us, indeed, to situate 'denotation' no longer at the surface of discourse but at its deepest level."[36]

That reminiscence of a certain *cogito,* however, with its simples situated as a denotative place of origin, had to be assumed situated in object, not in subject—in *sum,* not in *cogito,* as it were: "The truth value of [a given] assertion can only be founded upon what is contained in the locution in question and in the act of uttering this locution made explicit, that is to say, upon a *knowledge that is logically anterior* to what was necessary for the production of this linguistic formulation; a knowledge that can go from 'intimate conviction,' founded upon an axiological universe assumed by the subject, to knowledge 'proved,' for example, by a previous experimental discourse" (*Sémiotique,* p. 21). This led to the categorical assertion that "one must admit that the 'semiotic' is located between signs, that it is presupposed by and anterior to signs" ("Entretien," p. 19).

All that is, of course, essential. Saussure had confronted the same difficulty: if sense were ascribed to the discursive act, what could be the status of linguistics, semantics, or a semiology of language? The problem is especially grave in the present case, for if meaningfulness could not be separated from the order of the signifier, how would it be possible to constitute a scientific semantics at all? The problem was a general one, but posed with special acuity for a science seeking to signify the nature of signification (one is reminded of Eco's remark quoted earlier). All sciences must obviously define their object with some clarity; must they also invent them? A structured mass of signifieds ("places" of signification) was by no means a given; it could be no more than a hypothesis. Indeed, it was a

36. A. J. Greimas, "Entretien avec Frédéric Nef," in *Structures élémentaires de la signification,* ed. F. Nef (Brussels, 1976), p. 20.

hypothesis the real existence of whose object remained undemonstrable and unprovable.

Yet if one accepted the 'alternative' notion (which *is* a given) that meaning is the discourse as actually produced, in all its flux and movement, then the Greimasian hypothesis became itself only the result of a particular type of discursive production. Discourse, clearly, does exist as an apparently structured given. But does anything like "meaning" exist separately from it? In a sense, Chomsky's deep structure was an affirmative response, and so was Greimas's idea of signification as sensible quality, whose basic structural form was the semiotic square.[37] The implications were far-reaching. The pattern was exactly that of an analytico-referential science the limits of whose efficacy have long since been firmly set. The occultation of the subject of utterance was essential to that.

Once the basic epistemological model had been set in place, once the scientific object had been constituted, once the enunciating subject had been occulted (thus allowing those first two to maintain their "objective" status), the final step had to be to affirm in some way the adequacy to its object of the science so established. To this end, Greimas called upon Russell's hierarchies of language. He established a 'firm' division between different levels of language, some sort of arboreal taxonomy.

The object of analysis (object-language), wrote Greimas, had to be closed, because the tools of analysis were the same as the elements to be analyzed. Signification could not be a relation of signs, for we remain always within what Wittgenstein called the same "language game." Semantics, therefore, could not deal with the problem of referents (*Sémantique*, pp. 13–14; Frege had postulated the same exclusion, exactly, with regard to logic). That restriction posed the evident difficulty that the same limitation had to apply to all discourse, including the scientific one Greimas was hoping to be able to use. Greimas (like others) believed he could escape the apparent impasse by positing a metalinguistic system.

First, the object-language was confronted by a secondary language, a metalanguage asserted simply to describe the other. That does not get around the problem of closure, needless to say, so a tertiary language was brought in. The descriptive metalanguage was supposed to achieve a level of transparent instrumental mediation thanks to the fact that all its terms had been thoroughly defined (*Sémantique*, p. 15). Clearly, such definition could be accomplished by means of a 'descriptive' model based on one of two possible premises: either it was bound in some 'dialectical' way to the object to be analyzed, or it was not. If Greimas chose the first case, then the descriptive metalanguage could be neither transparent nor

---

37. Despite his continued use of the square alone, Greimas has expressed some doubt as to its universality. "The 'semiotic square' that usage is seeking to impose is only one of [the] possibilities [of elementary structures]" (ibid., p. 19).

indifferent to its object; if the second, then it could be nothing but an axiomatic projection from within the definitional metalanguage (the tertiary language).

Greimas chose the second alternative—as he had to in his system. There might conceivably be some kind of mild play between the "descriptive or translative metalanguage" and the "tertiary language" defining it, but there could not be such give and take between the object-language and the descriptive level; *that* would destroy objectivity and the permanent fixed reality of that object. However, it was immediately clear that one could not stop at the tertiary language, either; a fourth level was needed in order to ground the value of the definitions, the level where the question of "truth" was posed (and the level, in Greimas's terms, at which I am writing in this chapter).

Greimas was trying to respond to two exigencies. The first was that of "internal coherence"; it had to be situated within the descriptive metalanguage and its tertiary definition. The second lay in the relation between the descriptive metalanguage and the object-language-posed, as was long since established, as the referent of this science (*Sémantique*, p. 17). To be scientific, the descriptive metalanguage was to take the form of symbolic notation; thus, Greimas argued, univocity, precision, operational facility, and the needed simplicity would all be achieved. Pending proof, he wrote, this new semantics would posit the existence of a quite restricted "inventory of concepts" (*Sémantique*, p. 17), and the discovery of that inventory would be the principal scientific objective. Furthermore, the concepts composing that inventory had to be assumed to correspond to reals in the object-language. The complete goal was thereby set: to discover, as a reality, the most restricted possible structure of signification capable of generating all *ensembles signifiants* within natural (or *a* natural) language(s). If the structure could then be used for purposes of such generation, it was claimed (and already hypothesized here), we would have the proof of the pudding: "The possibility of . . . using [symbolic notation] in a given area brings with it the indirect proof that the ground for the chosen research has been fairly well cleared" (*Sémantique*, p. 17). The symbolic notation would correspond to the elementary structure of signification, itself capable of enveloping the restricted inventory of concepts in question; indeed, the inventory of concepts caught within the elementary structure would turn out to be the real process of thinking and organizing thought into communication about the reality underlying the process. Whatever Greimas might have been claiming, it would be hard to conceive of a more closed system—however defined.

In fact, he seemed eventually to suggest that the hierarchy and its claims were seriously flawed in practice. On the one hand, there was no way of avoiding the need for endless further definition and thus, the accumulation of an unlimited series of metalanguages (as, I fear, we have begun to see in the kinds of discussion published in or refused by learned journals). On the other, there was no means of 'filling the distance' between any two languages within the hierarchy: that is, of exhausting all the definitional requirements that would be necessary to make any instrumental language entirely transparent and adequate to its own object-language (to do *that*, it would have to be identical). "I even have the impression," Greimas somewhat wistfully admitted, "that the progress of semiotic analysis runs the risk of increasing considerably the number of these levels" ("Entretien," p. 24). It did.

Any attempt to seek an adequacy of relationship between this science of semiology and its object (as reality) seemed doomed to doubt and paradox. Yet that has not in practice prevented it from supposing that it casts an innocent eye upon its object and mediates it transparently. So, in 1970, when Greimas undertook the study of a legal document, he could write: "It must remain understood that the projected analysis can only lead to naive results, that is to say (giving the term *naive* its scientific meaning), to banal and sometimes unexpected conclusions. *The naïveté of the analyst's observation* ["regard"] is therefore the first ordinance of this investigation" (*Sémantique*, 79–80). Such scientific innocence presupposes (a) that the descriptive metalanguage is adequate to its object-language, (b) that the secondary language has been *entirely* and *exhaustively* defined by the definitional metalanguage, and (c) that that tertiary language is thoroughly grounded in a metaphysical justification taken to have been set forth (or simply assumed) within a fourth metalanguage. And what grounds that?

The divisions Greimas and his followers have made with regard to the object of study—this hierarchy of languages—and the goal of "science" follow directly from the instauration we saw: the distinction of natural and artificial significations (the first being privileged), the positing of *all* signification as dichotomous, and so forth (*Sémantique*, pp. 11–13, 19). It is surely no accident that the very first "semic system" to be examined in Greimas's 1966 *Sémantique*, following an opening chapter on the elementary structure of signification, was that of space—or, more precisely, the systems of space and of extension in space. The project was thus placed squarely within a very particular scientific tradition. At the same time, that implied a familiar epistemological justification for the use of spatial models in the scientific discourse itself (pp. 30–34). The Cartesian-Kantian background served to fit the entire project into the common sense tradition.

It hardly seems necessary to pursue the results of this instauration in detail. It is entirely clear, now, that this semiology sought to establish itself as a science by following a specific interpretation of a familiar Cartesian tradition, recertified, as it were, for the domain of linguistics by the impact of Saussure's *Course in General Linguistics.* The *cogito* was adopted as the epistemological model. The language/thought division thereby established was subject to a familiar (though not entirely successful) occultation. There was a general occultation of the enunciating subject. An analyzable object was introduced as exterior and mediated. By means of the hierarchy of languages the scientific discourse (the descriptive metalanguage) was posited as adequate to the 'referent' it sought to analyze. The scientist's passiveness was continually asserted (almost aggressively, one might paradoxically say). In the wake of Saussure, then, the development of this type of semiology has repeated in detail a particular Western scientific tradition—a tradition that had long since been problematized.

When Greimas posited the sign relation as one between two objects (that is, existent, *as such,* within the object-language), he did so by arguing that that relation "0———0" is significant independent of any interpretant or, rather, that no interpretant "enters" that relation of signification; in fact, he deliberately rejected such an idea in the guise of the problem of "presence": the expression *presence,* he said, "implies the mode of existence of terms/objects in perception: at this level it is not analyzable" (*Sémantique,* p. 19). Indeed, it is not, as Frege had also observed—chiefly because such an interpretant could not be understood in terms of a "place" (topos?) within the set of "terms/objects." But to make it an element within a second- or third-level language, or descriptive of the relations between such languages, removes it altogether from the signifying process. In doing so, Greimas and his followers have a serious difficulty to confront: how can one speak of a relation "0———0," lying entirely within the object-language, as "significant" in any meaningful way whatever?

Here Peirce would seem to be correct. The factor one might call the "interpretant" (the triadic 'moment' in a relation of signification that makes it possible to speak of *meaning* at all) cannot but pose a difficulty for any "science" trying to exclude it. Insofar as it is a *genuine* factor in the semiotic relation (I use the term "genuine" with its Peircean implications), its exclusion suggests an insufficiency in what Greimas called the metalanguage (indeed, in the very idea of a metalanguage) which is enough to limit severely the reach of any science purporting to do without it. For it interferes with both analytico-referential versions of "truth" (coherence and referential adequacy) and can only undermine them. It invalidates the notion of any gap between metalanguage and object-language and, therefore, that very idea of analysis and referentiality. Finally, it invalidates the idea of some "indifferent," transparent metalanguage and of its imposition as a right and legitimate "description."

In this sense, semiology was a science that could not but undermine its own scientificity, "scientificity" being here understood as a certain kind of activity of a discourse that creates its own objects as points in a metalinguistic system and 'reads' them as reals external to that system. Such a science sets up static places within an otherwise uncontrollable (for it, un-"knowable") process: the establishment of these static points is the mark of Frege's fear of flux, which fear it is that makes them necessary. To establish such points was to repudiate any participation in the production of that process. (In the terms of the analytico-referential discursive model, it was to repudiate what I have elsewhere called "the responsibility of enunciation," the presence in discourse of the subject's act of speaking, its participating in the production of knowing and doing—not just in the "what" but in the "how").[38]

We have seen that semiology at once sets up its objects and depends upon them for its own functioning (as subject). Only through the occultation of this last process could it hope to establish as the object of its study some static system, one based, for example, on the so-called semiotic square as the alleged universal generator of signification. It could survive, as Greimas pointed out, by a constant fabulation of metadiscourses—but then semiology would conclude by speaking only of its own 'previous' discourse, at an even further remove from the 'original' ambiguously named object-language. And what, in such a system, permits one to establish the fixed point making *any* of the languages *original?*

Peircean semiotics avoided that difficulty by situating itself within a triadic relation in constant evolution. The branch of Continental semiology we have just been examining has not managed to avoid the aporias to which Frege and others were seeking a response at the end of the nineteenth century. Greimasian semiology remains torn between the will to system and the need to account for its own production as a process. After all I have said to this point, the fact remains that within his 'School' it has been Greimas himself who has made clear the profound doubt of which the semiologist may be victim: "Thus, if we leave science conceived as system, we may represent it as a process, that is to say as a scientific *activity* [*un faire scientifique*] that is manifested in the discourse it produces, always incompletely and often defectively. And these discourses are only recognizable, at first view, thanks to the sociolinguistic connotations of "scientificity" with which they are endowed. . . . It is on this dual ground, at once as subject and object of reflection on scientific discourse, that semiotics is engaged."[39]

<hr>

38. Reiss, *Tragedy and Truth*, pp. 101–2; *Discourse of Modernism*, p. 34 (and see the indexes of both books).

39. *Sémiotique*, pp. 9–10. This is a peculiar idea of what a "science" is, even as a "first view," though such a remark serves to underscore the difficulty with semiology conceived as a ("traditional") *science of semantics.* Greimas has continued to have these difficulties; e.g., more recently, in "Le contrat de véridiction" (1980; in *Du sens II*, pp. 103–13), he has sought to discuss the question of how 'truth' may result from a kind of social contract. The text is

The will to system (as providing knowledge) marked the attempt to discover the discursive functioning of *our* discourse (but posited by this semiology as the universal form and model of *all* signifying processes). The difficulty was that the system was therefore posited as the basis for its own operation as well, so that the possibility of "process" escaped the system's examination, not to mention its analysis—unless it could posit simultaneously the necessity of undermining its own establishment as/of such an unalterable and universal system. To do that, however, would quite clearly have been to repudiate such a systematic semiology's avowed goal of revealing those very structures of signification. Thus *it could not produce new structures of meaning, because all such structures were posited as lying before, not within, discursive functioning.* That implied that there could be no evolution in the objects of semiology's study, either: the possibilities of sense were always and already fixed.

Torn, like Frege, between escaping the fear of flux through the imposition of system, on the one hand, and accepting the seeming necessity of a kind of Peircean evolutionary semiotics, on the other, French semiology has in the main opted for the former. To this decision, an appropriate response is perhaps that of Freud's conclusion to his *Civilization and Its Discontents*. The particular appropriateness of that response comes from the fact that it, too, signals its own system as a trap. Taken seriously, it would rock the foundations of psychoanalysis itself, much as Greimas's comments on the "scientific" nature of semiology would undermine its claim to discover any universal structure of meaning (both should, as Montaigne might have said, set their respective systems of knowledge *en branle*): "One thing only do I know for certain and that is that man's

---

brief and profoundly unsatisfactory, however, using so wild and extraordinary a generalization as that whereas the French view language as a "falsifying screen destined to hide a reality and a truth lying beneath it," Americans understand discourse as "clinging to things and expressing them innocently" (p. 108). Even apart from the identification of language and discourse, the opposition is as condescending as it is preposterous. It provides a salient instance of the sense of superiority only too common in French intellectual life, which finds similar expression in Kristeva's nostalgic view of Americans as somehow closer to the originary (childish) nonverbal "chora." She has thus written of North America as "a complete, new, vibrant culture, producing itself without speaking to itself": "D'Ithaca à New York," in *Polylogue*, p. 500; see, too, her "Why the United States?" in *The Kristeva Reader*, ed. Toril Moi (New York, 1986), pp. 275–78. Such ludicrosities may be taken as rather foolish aberrations. Greimas has done rather better in his "Le savoir et le croire: Un seul univers cognitif" (*Du sens II*, pp. 115–33), although even there (a text apparently dating from 1982 or 1983) he goes no further than to assert that our "cognitive universe" is "a network of formal semiotic relationships from which the epistemic subject selects those equivalences it needs in order to be receptive to the veridictory discourse" (p. 133). And if the subject is itself composed out of that network? What then may be meant by such "selection"? And so on. So expressed, the notion seems little more than a truism of analysis and reference, saying little about the status of truth, knowledge, and the rest.

judgements of value follow directly his wishes for happiness—that, accordingly, they are an attempt to support his illusions with arguments."[40]

Contemporary science has not hesitated to respond to the challenge set for it by the doubts of modernist, analytical discourse, just as that discourse itself had been an immensely effective response to the doubts and failures of an earlier discourse and its sociocultural environment.

40. Freud, *Standard Edition*, XXI:145.

CHAPTER THREE

Project for a Discursive Criticism

Every science contains an element of caprice and hence of transitoriness in its very structure, a defect which cannot be eradicated because it is rooted in the nature of the case.

—Max Planck, *Philosophy of Physics*

The concepts "particle" and "wave" or, more exactly, "spatially discontinuous event" and "spatially continuous event" appear therefore as interpretations demanded by the forms of our perception for processes that are no longer immediately perceptible.

—C. F. von Weizsäcker, *The World View of Physics*

The analysis undertaken in this chapter begins with a rather free understanding of Michel Foucault's concept of *episteme* and of a notion of *discourse* as an organizing, productive, and constructive operation of human sign systems, resulting in certain forms of action and what is called "knowledge." The totality of discourses at a given time and place (their *"types"*—though these concepts are themselves products of *our* discourses) is the episteme.

The word *episteme* marks an abstraction whose concrete side is named by the word *society:* the use and practice of a given *class* of discourse.[1] The terms used here are not intended to indicate a dichotomy, for in this view discourse—semiotic systems in use and as used—is only 'meaningful' as the result of a constant dialectical tension between the elaboration of its own processes and the concrete social activities from which it derives and to which it gives 'meaningfulness' or, better, *for which it provides a practice of sense.*[2] 'Together' (but they can perhaps not be conceived of at all as being

1. For more precision with respect to this understanding of discourse, see the Introduction. Let me reemphasize here that discourse is not at all to be equated with natural language, which merely provides one kind of material in which and through which discursive practices operate.

2. Cf. Allan Janik and Stephen Toulmin, *Wittgenstein's Vienna* (New York, 1973), p. 127: "Fritz Mauthner continually refers to language as the 'common sensorium' of a culture. Conversely, however, the contours and practices of a culture are the source and meaning of its language." The quotation marks around the word 'meaningfulness' in my text are

apart or separated) they compose what may be called the sociocultural environment.

Discourse and society are a total praxis, "society" designating a kind of concrete anchorage of discourse, "discourse" designating the way in which society makes itself meaningful to itself. Such a concept provokes a series of questions. What discursive class could render this dialectic operative, could make it visible, could embody it fully? What kind of "object," what kind of "knowledge" would it presuppose? What sort of communication—and therefore what sort of society? And so on. These are not questions this chapter will seek to answer, even though they necessarily lie in its background. They do, however, provide the *reason* for this chapter as that reason is manifest within our present analytico-referential discourse. These are the questions raised by the aporias noted in the preceding chapters.

Discursive Criticism and Epistemology

In our everyday usage, discourse seems always to suppose a certain realism; it does not hesitate to take its referents as in some way real existents adequately rendered in discourse in the guise of "objective" and *real* knowledge. The use of this analytico-referential discourse assumes that without objective and real truth, what it calls "meaningful communication" is not possible. At the same time, such truth is founded upon an analytical order of nomination and predication, understood as the sole reliable order of rational language. These ideas in turn would seem to presuppose that discursive meaning has been fixed once and for all. Explicitly or implicitly, that is the assumption behind much literary hermeneutics, for example, of a North American or a German cast, which distinguishes between "meaning" and "sense" precisely on the basis that the invariance of the former for interpretation provides an anchor for the varieties of criticism respecting the latter. In this view an author's meaning can be more or less precisely *interpreted* once and for all (whether or not some principle of probability is allowed to lie behind it).[3]

---

necessary because the very concept, here as elsewhere, will be in question whenever the term or any derivative is used.

3. The distinction in question is made especially by E. D. Hirsch, Jr., *Validity in Interpretation* (New Haven, Conn., 1967), and again in his *Aims of Interpretation* (Chicago, 1976), but traces of a similar point of view are to be found, e.g., in Wolfgang Iser, *Der implizite Leser* (Munich, 1972). Iser, working in a kind of watered-down Ingarden tradition, therefore refers back to such as Friedrich Schleiermacher and Wilhelm Dilthey. See too Iser's *Der Akt des Lesens: Theorie ästhetischer Wirkung* (Munich, 1976).

Such a view of discursive functioning is scarcely an isolated one. E. D. Hirsch's ideas (note 3) are avowedly based upon certain aspects of logical empiricism. And these aspects, whatever the supposedly "antimetaphysical" stance of certain of their adherents, represent an extension of a Cartesian viewpoint. Until at least the end of the nineteenth century and, by and large, to the present the basic characteristics of Eurocentric discourse were those of linearity, of distance, of difference, of analysis and reference, of the discursive imposition of the (masculine) enunciating subject. All these 'functions' were considered essential to the Cartesian principle of truth as an eventually "correct" agreement within a sign system between the elements of a given proposition (its "coherence"), and as an eventually precise agreement between those elements and their order within the sign system and some reality taken (as) outside it— whether conceptual or material. Such *truth* was the function enabling the discourses of analytico-referentiality to operate.

Applied more specifically to the discursive *type* of (literary) criticism, the *taking* of reality appears to follow two directions: (1) the study of the (literary) text as an expression of some fixed reality, which thus becomes a matter of biographical or psychological evidence, of historical sources or influence, or of sociological, economic, philosophical, or other commentary supposedly aimed at what the text *says* (signifies); and (2) the study of the text either as a fixed entity, reality, or system (as the object, for example, of linguistic or semiotic analyses) or as a revelation of its author's meaning, intention. The first represents a rather discredited positivism and assumes that the text possesses a specific reference (even if this may be multiple). The second is the area in which certain forms of semiotics and hermeneutics continue to do battle; both of these emphasize the internal (analytically coherent) order of the text, the one accentuating the logical processes that obtain within the system as such, the other underscoring its existence as product of an individual consciousness that precedes it (though comprehensible only in and through that 'product'). Both meet to a degree in the assumption of hermeneutics that any individual consciousness is representative and its processes generalizable (otherwise the interpreter could have no claim to its comprehension), and in that of continental semiology (at least) that the logical coherence of a textual system corresponds to its extension from the universal conceptual order represented by the "semiotic square," "narrative reason," or the "deep structure" of a generative grammar.

The claims made upon the basis of internal coherence—direction (2) above—assert most originality for themselves. Yet when, instead of reading literary discourse as itself a commentary upon reality (the realistic novel's upon society, say, or lyric poetry's upon the poet's persona), criticism seeks to isolate the "specificity" of literary discourse and obtain a classification of its "unique" and "universal" structures, it undertakes a project clearly akin to the Cartesian one of constructing a general grammar and formulating a universal reason. Not for nothing did Noam Chomsky have recourse to Port-Royal to unearth his ancestors, or A. J. Greimas—affirming "narration" to be "the basic form of human expression" and the one permitting "man [*sic*] to think himself [*sic*, again] and the world"—propose, upon that foundation, a taxonomy of genres in terms of "an arborescence of restrictive rules" representing the "canonical forms" through and in which this fundamental expression, an underlying "grammar," would be manifest.[4] By such means, literary discourse can remain a privileged world (with its own "specificity," located in "literariness" itself), whose elements may be analyzed by the very methods used by classical science to examine the world of things.[5]

All this is in spite of manifest quandaries long since raised within that model itself. As soon as it had been shown—explicitly by Peirce, Welby, and others; implicitly by someone like Frege—that meaning was all and always a production and imposition of *that* class of discourse, and as soon as that demonstration had been practiced by such as Virginia Woolf and James Joyce, then the concept of truth in its terms was invalid; the discourse was entirely crippled. Its a prioris were discredited or, more exactly, situated within the limits of their possible application. They could be seen, for example, as a language game (in Wittgenstein's terms), as the practice of a discursive class. That is just what Ernst Cassirer asserted: "What scientific cognition calls the 'truth' of phenomena [means] nothing other than the totality of the phenomena themselves, insofar as they are not taken in their concrete existence but are transposed into the form of a *relationship*, a relationship which is based to an equal degree and with equal necessity on acts both of logical synthesis and of logical analysis."[6] Of course, one may debate whether science does in practice function in such a way, or whether it does not rather continue to adopt the pattern suggested by Michael Dummett's epigraph to Chapter 1. As a rule, science does not in any way include the elaboration of its own discourse

4. Greimas, *Sémiotique*, pp. 205, 211. Chomsky was actually wrong in his dating, as G. A. Padley has demonstrated at length: *Grammatical Theory in Western Europe, 1500–1700: The Latin Tradition* (Cambridge, 1976). More recently, Padley has published *Grammatical Theory in Western Europe, 1500–1700: Trends in Vernacular Grammar I* (Cambridge, 1985). He observes that the arguments about which Chomsky is speaking were made throughout much of the sixteenth century; the point is important, because it links these conceptual disputes with much broader sociocultural developments, whereas Chomsky tended to limit them to the sphere of specifically "Cartesian" philosophy: Noam Chomsky, *Cartesian Linguistics: A Chapter in the History of Rationalist Thought* (New York, 1966).

5. A longer analysis of this last claim is to be found in Reiss, "Espaces de la pensée discursive."

6. Ernst Cassirer, *The Philosophy of Symbolic Forms*, tr. Ralph Manheim, 3 vols. (1953–57; rpt. New Haven, Conn., 1968), vol. II: *Mythical Thought*, p. 62.

within the experimental process. Indeed, as a general rule, how could it? For in such a case, the matter of determinate laws of nature (however statistical or probabilistic) would have to be treated as the case for particular theories, not for particular phenomena; in effect, all laws would be provisional and dependent upon scientific habit.

As we will see, Werner Heisenberg in particular went a long way toward such an argument, and an attempt to cope with it is the object of this chapter. Indeed, the chapter's intention is to propose a discursive criticism (literary, among others) capable of 'going beyond' certain others—in its ability to take account of its own processes, of its 'environmental' limitations, and of the considerable achievements of Enlightened rationalism—without falling back into a simplistic representational positivism on the one hand or surrendering to an indecisive, cynical, and/or pessimistic relativism on the other. To this end, it may be useful to look once again at certain aspects of the analytico-referential discursive class that already seems at the end of its tether, and at certain of its limits.

I may perhaps approach the matter by means of a parallel that emphasizes the essentially spatial conceptualization underlying that discourse. The Cartesian *cogito ergo sum* is the exemplary formal expression of this discursive class. Within this phrase is set up the image of an ideal self: perceiving, uttering, and conceiving. The *cogito* as simple thought is put into a discursive relationship with the *sum* as simple being. Taken separately, these two elements have no meaning; the connecting *ergo* supplies it. The triple set provides the exemplary analysis whose projection is our own epistemological process: the place of simple thought, the space of mediation, the place of (concrete, actual) existence. It will not have escaped the reader's attention that this order is that of the functioning of Galileo's or Frege's telescope.

I refer to the "space" of mediation rather than its "place" because—unlike the other two terms—mediation is not conceived of as a definite entity/substance. It is the field where the other two are put in contact and where they are taken to "explain" each other: the idealist will argue that thought explains being, the empiricist that being explains thought. Where the other two elements are 'substance' (in whatever specific sense of the term may be implied), the *ergo* is supposed an indifferent, or transparent, mediator whose presence does not affect the real nature of the other two. In a binary logic the *cogito* and the *sum* may both stand as arguments; in Frege's terminology, the *ergo* can only be part of a function.[7]

7. Only a triadic system such as that suggested by C. S. Peirce can render the three as equivalent 'values.' In Peirce's system the *sum* will be the object; the *cogito*, the representamen; the *ergo*, the interpretant—all necessary 'parts' of a discursive space, with no one of them being epistemologically (far less, ontologically) privileged in relation to the others. This does not mean that no form of knowledge is possible but rather that that of classical (or "modern,"

Without the syntax the function provides, however, the others are non-sensical; indeed, we may say they exist (for us) only in virtue of the discursive *ergo*. The notion of a thought prior to syntax, or of known and knowable objects prior to it, is thus a matter of discourse (not so much the 'fact' of such objects as the 'style' of their perception). Each is the result of a particular elaboration of the discursive space thus conceived and practiced as lying between them. That is not to say that material objects and events are illusions but simply that they are ineluctably part 'fiction'. We cannot but agree with Charles S. Peirce when he remarks: "We have *direct experience of things in themselves.* Nothing can be more completely false than that we can experience only our own ideas." But his emphasis is on the opposition between experience and knowledge, observing that while we do so experience externals, our knowledge of such "things in themselves is entirely *relative,*" even though both experience and knowledge are "of that which is, independently of being represented." "At the same time," he immediately adds, however, "no proposition can relate, or even thoroughly pretend to relate, to any object otherwise than as that object is represented."[8] In the *Tractatus,* Wittgenstein wrote rather similarly: "The possibility of describing the world by means of Newtonian Mechanics tells us nothing about the world: but what does tell us something about it is the precise *way* in which it is possible to describe it by these means."[9]

Modern European analytico-referential discourses ignore all this. They assume the absolute reality of their referential and conceptual elements, rather than stressing that they are *their* elements.[10] They presuppose not only the division of thought and being but also the division of thought and 'its' expression. Indeed, the concept of a separate space of mediation may be considered a means of warding off all the difficulties posed by a practice (such as that of Hegel, for example) that would refuse such a separation: a means of warding them off and of avoiding having to confront certain consequences—among them the principal and insoluble difficulty

---

if one prefers) discourse is inadequate and distorted. It proposes a quite different concept from that of the truth at which the disputes aroused by logical positivism seek to arrive; these last still suppose a substantive division of the kind that results, for example, in arguments striving to justify a claim of real relationship between theoretical concepts and concrete actuality. See, e.g., Raimo Tuomela, *Theoretical Concepts* (Vienna, 1973). Claims of this sort strike me as insoluble in their own terms—as the incessant arguments pro and con indicate sufficiently.

8. Peirce, *Collected Papers,* 6.95 (1903).

9. Wittgenstein, *Tractatus,* §6.342.

10. This problem has recently received lengthy treatment in Thomas Nagel, *The View from Nowhere* (New York, 1986). By and large, the author admits to finding himself stumped by a difficulty whose solution can surely not simply be to include a kind of moderate self-awareness in theorizing; the presumption of individual primacy is a fundamental and traditional barrier within all such discussion.

(for this discursive class) of knowledge of the Other. After the failure of logical atomism, with its picture theory (or model theory, to be more precise) of correspondence between logical and factual chains, analytical philosophy has inscribed these divisions in its premises.[11] But I would suggest that the original failure springs from the assumption of this difference, of these divisions, which still mark the dominant discourses of our modernity.[12]

At the outset of the *Tractatus*, Wittgenstein made these assumptions clear: "The aim of this book is to set a limit to thought, or rather—not to thought, but to the expression of thoughts: for in order to be able to set a limit to thought, we should have to find both sides of the limit thinkable (i.e., we should have to be able to think what cannot be thought). It will therefore only be in language that the limit can be set, and what lies on the other side of the limit will simply be nonsense."[13] This "nonsense," Wittgenstein argued, appears as such only when we try to speak of 'it' in language: language can only *show* it, can indicate it as the sign of a somewhere that is outside language itself; language cannot express such "nonsense" as the content of some proposition. There is, wrote Wittgenstein, a "totality" of the world that exists in thought (therefore) but that is inexpressible.

Russell answers this by affirming that to speak of the inexpressibility of this totality is to presuppose its existence, for it would be otherwise meaningless to speak of its "inexpressibility"—(or of anything else about it, come to that). He responds, then, that such a totality is a fiction and that all there is is the mass of atomic facts, corresponding to the mass of elementary (atomic) propositions.[14]

Russell's retort can be made concerning thought itself. Indeed, Wittgenstein comes very close to doing so in the *Tractatus* (§§ 5.542, 5.5421, 5.634). Thought must also be a discursive fiction (or partly so), for it too can exist only as a public concept (one, as Peirce remarked, dependent

11. Wittgenstein himself implied the 'failure' of the model theory in the *Tractatus*, noting that there was no way at all of knowing that propositions do in fact work as that theory would have them do. Without such assurance, the reliability of the representation essential to logical atomism was entirely undermined: "Propositions can represent the whole of reality, but they cannot represent what they must have in common with reality in order to be able to represent it—logical form. In order to be able to represent logical form, we should have to be able to station ourselves with propositions somewhere outside logic, that is to say outside the world" (*Tractatus*, §4.12).

12. The assumption of the divisions here indicated is exemplified in arguments deployed by John Searle against Jacques Derrida; see Derrida, "Signature Event Context," and Searle, "Reiterating the Difference: A Reply to Derrida," both in *Glyph: Johns Hopkins Textual Studies 1* (Baltimore, Md., 1977), pp. 172–208; and Derrida, "Limited Inc abc . . .," in *Glyph: Johns Hopkins Textual Studies 2* (Baltimore, Md., 1977), pp. 162–254. To read this debate is to watch shadowboxers: one has the impression that no real contact is ever made.

13. *Tractatus*, preface, p. 3.

14. Bertrand Russell, introduction to *Tractatus*, pp. xxi– xxii.

upon "Community") insofar as it is expressed. It may here be objected, I am aware, that such a view implies the neglect of the entire semantic process (then considered as the rendering in language of some *other*). And indeed, if what is called thought is nothing but a discursive product, it becomes somewhat difficult to speak of some meaning as the representation of some external. The matter will return later, but a reply proposed by this discourse itself may be suggested right away—a reply related quite precisely to the notion of thought.

Unless we equate Frege's *Vorstellung*, the individual's image of what appears exterior, with thought (but then we would have to allow that all animals *think*), we have to place thought at the level of what Frege called "sense" (*Sinn*). Now sense is a matter of more or less abstract generality held in common by all those who share a given linguistic or other sign system. This must be so by definition; otherwise, all expression would be incomprehensible. But sense, as Frege and others have observed, is *already* an expressive ordering of signs and is not possible without such ordering: "I do not deny that even without symbols the perception of a thing can gather about itself [*um sich sammeln*] a group of memory-images [*Erinnerungsbilder*]; but we could not pursue these further: a new perception would let these images sink into darkness and allow others to emerge. But if we produce the symbol of an idea which a perception has called to mind, we create in this way a firm, new focus about which ideas gather."[15]

Sense can be public, communal, collective, only by communication. All sense is dialogic (the result of dialogue, if one wishes, but also always caught in present and future dialogue); all sense is discursive (in the meaning being given to that term here); and, ipso facto, this dialogic discourse is what is called thought. It follows that the semantic process lies in the actual production of propositions, not in what those propositions might be supposed to stand for.

This notion of thought and discourse enables us to avoid two presuppositions of analytico-referential discourse that have led to the establishing of a particular ideology of representation and power. For we must understand that to ask what a given sign-system is an ordering *of*, what it stands *for*, depends upon these two prior assumptions: (1) that of intentionality, of *vouloir-dire* (to be discovered in the subject enunciating a given proposition), and (2) that of referential truth (to be found in the predicate of the proposition). To be able to ask about a proposition's *meaning* in these terms implies that these two assumptions have in fact been occulted; if not, we could no longer ask the question in at all the same way. It would instantly become apparent that meaning (as "other") is formally

15. Gottlob Frege, "On the Scientific Justification of a Conceptual Notation," in *Notation*, pp. 83–84.

produced by and within discourse, and that its nature is the result of that formal production.

The notion of the inexpressible in Wittgenstein prevents the assimilation of thought to its expression and maintains the conception of language as the expression of something *other*. Only this permits Wittgenstein to affirm that "the *truth* of the thoughts that are here set forth seems to [him] unassailable and definitive."[16] The separation in question supposes, then, that there is a place (that of thought) independent of expression, whence the truth or falsity of expressed propositions may be judged. The concept of such truth is essential to analytico-referential discourse. One may say that it is *the one function conceived as absolutely essential to that discourse.*

In light of that necessity, it is easy to see why neoclassical scientific discourse formed the model for all analytico-referential discourses. While for their truth those others (nonscientific, in the eyes of those inhabiting that discursive class) were obliged to suppose some *other*, attainable through thought, the discourses of the natural sciences—and they alone—were bound on one side by something that appeared genuinely and distinctly *other*. Thus they established the seemingly certain status that truth possessed for those discourses. They appeared bound (at least once the Cartesian analytical order had been accepted) by their reference to a series of facts—events, situations—whose order was not produced out of discourse. Scientific discourse could even imply doubt as to its *knowledge* of factual series (recognizing that its "laws" were in some sense inventions, conceptual artifacts), but external reality nonetheless offered itself as a guarantee of truth at the point of observation, at the 'moment' when discourse and facts converged. That is to say, the data treated by the discourses of the natural sciences was taken as beyond discursive control prior to the latter's elaboration, even though these discourses could be understood as *existing* prior to their inclusion of any particular datum as referent. The types of event dealt with in other discourses could always be conceived as based in and as a product of discourse: they are not taken as 'bound' in such a way. That, indeed, was Giambattista Vico's objection to the classical ideal of knowledge as corresponding to the natural sciences, affirming that the only true human knowledge must necessarily be limited to that of the systems we have produced ourselves.[17]

16. *Tractatus,* preface, p. 5. Quite different considerations marked Wittgenstein's later work, though it represented a natural progression, precisely to the extent, e.g., that the logical space explored in the *Tractatus* would subsequently appear nongeneralizable.

17. Giambattista Vico, *The New Science,* 3d ed. (1744), revised translation by Thomas G. Bergin and Max H. Fisch (Ithaca, 1968), p. 96, §331: "The world of civil society has certainly been made by men, and . . . its principles are therefore to be found within the modifications of our own human mind. Whoever reflects on this cannot but marvel that the philosophers should have bent all their energies to the study of the world of nature,

When we speak of an inductive system, we are, speaking, it would seem, in fact of the occulting of the operative awareness (in discourse itself) that we are working with a particular ordering of the process of knowing. Galileo, Descartes, Bacon, and Hobbes, for example, were all well aware, as their writings made constantly clear, that deductive scientific knowledge was the imposition of a logical conceptual order upon things otherwise unknowable, and that what we call phenomena were but objects adjusted to a particular order of reason. Bacon's idea of a constant play between "particulars," "axioms," "works," and discourse is most enlightening in this respect. But all of them were clear that the discourse of analysis and reference, based upon a precise truth function, answered a clearly stated and specific demand: a demand for *a technical usefulness whose aim was the amelioration of human life and special power for those producing such usefulness.* That was what Bacon called this science's *legitimacy:* a "legitimate" discourse was one operating according to *true laws* and producing *useful events* in the world.[18]

Later, the natural sciences found it necessary to suppress (the expression of) this awareness, its traces in discourse; otherwise, no true ("objective") knowledge of reality could be presumed. In a way, the claim of induction sought to satisfy this very grave problem. Its claim was that there could be a reason that took its origin not in conceptual a prioris but in unmediated natural objects. It became necessary to demonstrate that perceptions had some identity with things (a clearly impossible task, since it had to assume beforehand that there was an immediate knowledge of things already) and that these perceptions in their turn could somehow enter immediately into the reasoning process. Sixteenth-century logic had deemed it necessary to cut short the infinite multiplication of signifying levels that the scholastics had increasingly found themselves having to introduce into the concept of meaning, eventually reducing the levels to the three we have seen, but the problem was not really solved. If one must assume a division of activities such as were expressed through the *cogito* ("world," "language," "mind," for example), how could that division be made whole without once again falling into a "bad infinity"?

Later Cartesianism and empiricism set themselves this task, and from Newton's *Opticks* through Lavoisier's *Elementary Treatise* and down to present-day popularizers of science, induction was assumed the only genuine basis for the scientific effort. Indeed, Einstein's objection to

which, since God made it, He alone knows; and that they should have neglected the study of the world of nations, or civil world, which, since men had made it, men could come to know."

18. For Bacon (and, to some extent, Hobbes), see my *Discourse of Modernism,* esp. pp. 198–225; for Descartes, "The *concevoir* Motif"; and for Galileo, "Espaces de la pensée discursive."

quantum physics—to the effect that "God does not play with dice"—
reflected the same attitude.[19] Yet the inductive method does little more
than remove the awareness of manipulation. J. L. Austin correctly noted
that this kind of knowledge required some solid foundation. And there is
in fact no fundamental difference, in regard to the demand for a sure
foundation, between "clear and distinct ideas," "real objects," and the kind
of compromise indicated by the logical positivists' phrase "sensible data"
(or "phenomena," if one emphasizes the mental side of the equation). All
correspond to the need for "correctibility," descended from the "problem
of origin" and reflecting the demand for foundations—for Benveniste's
anchor (yet again). Austin's response was that there could be no such
unique place of certainty, and that to go in search of it was to try to grasp
a will-o'-the-wisp.[20] One can say in this sense that contemporary empiricism, idealism, and logical positivism, for example, are all tarred with the
same epistemological and ideological brush (which does not, however, per-

19. Albert Einstein, in a letter of September 7, 1944, to Max Born, in *Born-Einstein Letters*
(London, 1971), quoted in Ronald W. Clark, *Einstein: The Life and Times* (New York, 1972),
p. 421: "You believe in the God who plays dice, and I in complete law and order in a world
which objectively exists, and which I, in a wildly speculative way, am trying to capture. I
firmly *believe*, but I hope that someone will discover a more realistic way, or rather a more
tangible basis than it has been my lot to do." See also Neils Bohr, "Discussion with Einstein
on Epistemological Problems in Atomic Physics," in *Albert Einstein: Philosopher-Scientist*, ed.
Paul Arthur Schilpp (La Salle, Ill., 1969), esp. I: 211–18. This attitude remained Einstein's
until the end of his life, and his project of discovering a unified field theory ("theory which
describes exhaustively physical reality, including four dimensional space, by a field") sought
to satisfy it. To do this he had to deny the logico-theoretical implications of such concepts as
complementarity and indeterminacy, and to speak of them as of a theoretical surrender. He
could thus pen such a criticism as follows: for "the present-day generation of physicists . . .
the conviction prevails that the experimentally assured duality of nature (corpuscular and
wave structure) can be realized only by such a weakening of the concept of reality [i.e., "that
the state of a system cannot be specified directly"]" (*Relativity: The Special and the General
Theory. A Popular Exposition*, tr. Robert W. Lawson [1916; rpt. New York, 1961], Appendix 5,
"Relativity and the Problem of Space" [1952], p. 157). It seems to me, though the understanding of the mathematics is closed to me, that Heisenberg's use of "duality," for example,
makes that concept depend upon a particular type of theoretical exposition, a kind of limit
case of his own discourse. Einstein wanted to treat that limit case as irreducibly representative of some reality: or at least potentially so. He never accepted the thought that discourse
and reality might in some way be 'co-productions.' Yet nature's dualism is experimentally
assured only because we establish scientific experiments capable of provoking certain events
and certain situations in nature. It is the type of experiment elaborated that results in our
ability to describe a phenomenon according to two different sets of parameters. Heisenberg
thus replied to Einstein that in such a case it is the experimental situation that is double, not
nature, and that we are therefore justified in speaking of a dualism in our interaction with
the world but *not* in speaking of a dualism of the world itself. The world would be a kind of
'open' field, open to the reception (as it were) of experimental *laws*. To call that a theoretical
surrender is to maintain an absolutist and totalizing view of knowledge and fully explains
the search for an exhaustive theory of reality. The requirement corresponds to that scientific
"hegemony" decried by Evelyn Fox-Keller.
20. John L. Austin, *Sense and Sensibilia*, ed. G. J. Warnock (London, 1962), pp. 104–6.

mit us to argue, with Derrida, that the tarring occurred at the time of Plato).

Both Cassirer and Susanne Langer, among innumerable others, have shown that the concept of an external nature can never refer to an *unmediated* nature. It is always the highly discriminated *ground* (as Peirce called it) of our more particular knowledge, set for us by our past and present collectivity in its language(s), conceptual habits, social customs, and so on. The concept is itself the result of a series of 'previous' deductions. One must thus argue that knowledge, as a total accumulation of 'things known' at any given time and place, is the result of a constant dialectic, exchange, between the *ground* made present as the result of innumerable past deductions (for example as nature) and the continuum of present deductions (so called). This continuum is actually, as has already been suggested, the production of propositions in discourse—in 'systems' that obtain, through their very production, their meaning. In this sense, the (be)getting of knowledge is always deductive, and to speak of induction as *the* form of all true scientific knowledge—as the Enlightenment and the nineteenth century did—is only a means of hiding the fact that what we understand as objective truth is neither more nor less the result of collective human representation (that of the enunciator of any given scientific discourse) than was previous knowledge, however scorned as scholastic, animistic, or anything else. This is very far indeed, though, from any claim that knowledge altogether invents its objects; to argue *that* is merely to adopt an opposite pole within analytico-referential discourse.

There would seem to be no such thing as "objective induction" as analytico-referential science understood it. Peirce's concept of *abduction* or *retroduction* holds out more fruitful possibilities: a hypothesis that may account, by means of provisional laws, for some of a series of evolving facts, itself participating in an evolving semiosis. 'Facts,' here, are understood as communal and habitual experience of events, processes, situations.[21] The reality provided by this evolving accumulation may be provisional in one sense, but its stability is nonetheless long term and communally effective. We derive information or cognitions, writes Peirce, "by induction and hypothesis from previous cognitions which are less general, less distinct, and of which we have a less lively consciousness." These have themselves been derived from even more murky ones. The series is infinite in that it has no specific moment of "beginning *in time*." Thus the real, what we are used to calling reality, is our present (sociocultural) environment as the provisional 'final' product of understanding

---

21. On this matter, see, e.g., Maryann Ayim, "Language Universals and Scientific Hypotheses: The Children of Retroduction," and esp. (in respect to the points just made) my response, "Peirce and Chomsky on Abduction: A Reply," plus a short reaction by Ayim that completes the exchange, *Canadian Journal of Research in Semiotics*, 7 (Winter 1979–80), 89–108. There is, of course, no shortage of commentary on Peirce's concept of retroduction.

accumulated over time. The real "is that which, sooner or later, information and reasoning would finally result in, and which is therefore independent of the vagaries of me and you. Thus, the very origin of the conception of reality shows that this conception essentially involves the notion of a COMMUNITY, without definite limits, and capable of an indefinite increase of knowledge."[22] Such a view is quite close to the Fregean notion of "sense" and may perhaps be understood as a generalized version of a similar concept. Indeed, Peirce might almost have been foreseeing, here, the Fregean opposition between the actual and the objective. As he had written just before this passage, the real would be that imaginary "ideal" at the beginning of any series of induction and hypothesis (yet again, Benveniste's anchor). But, Peirce reminds us, for us "it does not exist *as such.*" Its ontological status has nothing to do with the retroductive logic that alone provides *our* reality. Indeed, we have no way of grasping the real in that sense, as Frege's "actual." What we can know is the "objective," as a communal consensus.

The emphasis on the supposed impersonality (that is, "objectivity" in its commonsensical meaning) of induction was one of the many neoclassical, or modernist, occultations permitting the concealment of the personal, individualist, origins of true knowledge (proceeding from the privilege granted to the enunciating subject, the Hobbesian private fiat). This subject was conceived as providing an exact, objective description of things. Yet, that said, we must also recognize that the discourse of the natural sciences was the first to see that this was not the way to cope with the 'power structure' of utterance; that the idea of induction was obstructing its own ideal, the search for truth. Such, I think, despite the references so far made to Wittgenstein's early text—indeed using this as its 'positivist' starting point—is the import of the *Tractatus.* The *activity of meaning* produced by that text (a matter to which I will return) is the acknowledgment of this obstruction, of the general invalidity to which I referred before. The *Tractatus,* one may say, *shows* that obstacle at work.

Apparently starting from the premise of a logic of the excluded middle, Wittgenstein concluded that the propositional series of such a logic is tautological, that nothing meaningful (true) can be said, only "*shown,*" and that for such a discourse the existence of logical structures is itself the only possible "truth." They "*say*" nothing. Toward the beginning of this text, Wittgenstein advanced a proposition containing in germ much of the *Philosophical Investigations* of 1953: "In a proposition a situation is, as it were, constructed by way of experiment [Im Satz wird eine Schlage probeweise zusammengestellt]" (*Tractatus,* § 4.031). The extension of that

<hr>

22. Peirce, "Some Consequences of Four Incapacities" (1868), in *Chronological Edition,* II:239. All previous reprintings of this text mistakenly give the last phrase as "a definite increase of knowledge."

principle must clearly assert that *all* such discourse is a construction of experimental situations, that it can produce meaning only within a particular "language game." The same principle must naturally apply to the *Tractatus* itself.

Neoclassical or modernist discourse, however, as we have seen, always held that it somehow enabled us to obtain knowledge of a reality standing outside it, and that with respect to this reality the knowledge conveyed by a given proposition (asserted) had to be either true or false. Whatever the precise modalities accorded this knowledge, the binary equation has, since its Cartesian (re)establishment, been fundamental to our discourse and our concept of truth. By and large, it remains so for us, today, despite the discomforters who have appeared from time to time along the way. These characteristics, along with the notion of a "right" ("legitimate," "correct") language as following a progressive, syntagmatic order (of asserted propositions), remain the a prioris of our discourse. Our observation of this fact and the observation itself have become clichés. The condition of our discourse as a general (social) system individually ordered by the originator of each utterance—which thus becomes each time a new contractual imposition of that subject's intention, meaning, will, power, and so forth—is also a truism. It could, of course, be a *true*-ism nowhere but in that discourse, for it is there that these truths are established, that they constitute themselves.

That the discourse *works*, that it is public, that it assures are doubtless some of the reasons why such a truism can stand. It shows at once in discourse, for example, the opposition between necessity and freedom, entrapment and will, coexisting at (and with) ease. To use such terms is to make senseless propositions, inasmuch as they refer us to the real existence of something outside discourse (unspeakable *by* discourse). They have nonetheless been, and remain, the terms of traditional humanist criticism, which thought thus to be attaining some truth beyond its code. Yet even if such concepts could be more than 'mere' forms of discourse, there would be no way of knowing them as such; either they are discursive forms, or they lie within that area which, for the *Tractatus*, must remain silent.

Of this neoclassical view, the early Wittgenstein was at once typical and at the same time most virulently critical. "A proposition," he wrote, "must restrict reality to two alternatives: yes or no." Or again: "In itself, a proposition is neither probable nor improbable. Either an event occurs or it does not: there is no middle way" (*Tractatus*, §§ 4.023, 5.153). Here we have the triple assumption of the structural identity between propositions and reality, of referential adequacy, and of the *tertium non datur. How* a proposition does this is, for the Wittgenstein of the *Tractatus*, a matter of the well-known distinction between *showing* and *saying:* "A proposition

shows how things stand *if* it is true. And it *says that* they do so stand."[23]
Here we are in the midst of Frege's concept of truth value (*Wahrheitswert*),
whose ambiguity in terms of any traditional logic of the excluded middle
was demonstrated long since by Bertrand Russell.[24]

A proposition, then, is an assertion concerning the nonpropositional
reality of a logical relationship. But if a proposition is a "construction of
experimental situations," the question of demonstrable truth becomes
more than simply problematic, for what can possibly *show* us that we are
beyond the point of experiment, so to speak, and into that of experience?
Some will answer: a calculus of probabilities. Such a response already
changes the concept of meaning and truth. Indeed, it brings us quite
close to Peirce's idea of truth and fact as communal accord—provided it
is not simply Laplace's calculus of Cartesian common sense. They actually
refer to the same set of ideas, but the Laplacean view (referential truth on
the basis of statistical proportion) emphasizes the *object* within the Peircean triad, while Peirce's idea (true meaning as a communal accretion of
information predictably effective in the production of what Bacon called
"works") emphasizes the *interpretant*.

An insuperable difficulty proceeds from the nature of Wittgenstein's
showing. For within the reality to be "shown," the experimental construction needs to be included as an operation, especially in the case of one
discourse's practice upon another, where meaning and structures (to use
these terms for the present) necessarily intermingle—the case, for instance, where discursive criticism is concerned, whatever the material
through which the discourse being analyzed produces its meanings. In
this case, the experimental *evidence* provided can be only a function of the
discursive experiment performed. The traditional concept of truth then
becomes irrelevant and can be seen as no more than a particular functional element necessary for what we may call the stabilization of a specific
type of discourse.

Wittgenstein underscored the paradox of the *Tractatus*'s enterprise in
just these terms. On the one hand, he affirmed that tautologies (and
contradictions) lack sense and are to be separately considered from propositions that "show what they say": to them the notion of truth condition
(*Wahrheitsbedingung*) cannot apply. Either (the case of tautologies) they are
unconditionally true, or (the case of contradictions) they are true under no
conditions (*Tractatus*, §§ 4.461, 4611, 462, 463). On the other hand, he

23. *Tractatus*, §4.022. Cf. §4.121: "Propositions cannot represent logical form: it is mir-
rored in them. What finds its reflection in language, language cannot represent. What
expresses *itself* in language, *we* cannot express by means of language. Propositions *show* the
logical form of reality. They display it."

24. Russell, "The Logical and Arithmetical Doctrines of Frege," in his *Principles of Mathematics*, pp. 502–22. See Chapter 1, above.

argued that (elementary) propositions contain their own extension, so that all such propositional extensions are necessarily tautological (*Tractatus*, §§5.124, 134; 5.3). He further argued that one cannot make a proposition concerning an elementary proposition (one that is not therefore its simple extension), since that very impossibility is one of the marks of its elementariness (*Tractatus*, §§4.21–221). It follows from this series of assertions that there is no nonelementary proposition that is not tautological (*Tractatus*, §§6.1– 6.126).

With these elements as background, we may now go considerably further. An elementary proposition, we saw Wittgenstein insist, is either true or false. It could be true or false referentially—in relation, that is, to some known outside itself—but that is impossible, since that known (and Wittgenstein agrees with Peirce on this), insofar as it could be known to be known, would be another proposition. In that case, the first one was not elementary. The question of referentiality can therefore never be applied to the truth of an elementary proposition. Alternatively (and therefore necessarily), an elementary proposition is true or false by virtue of a formal definition concerning its logical construction—and that of all other such propositions common to its logical space or language game. But that, too, makes it tautological. The *Tractatus* avoids the difficulty by making the elementary proposition itself, in its formal ordering, the ultimate known. Truth, then, may have sense (within a logical construct), but it has no meaning. The movement is the same as we saw (in Chapter 1) followed by Frege, who found himself finally obliged (in "The Thought") to make truth either a mere statement about the efficacy of human action or an axiom: "An elementary proposition is a truth function of itself."[25]

The proposition of neoclassical discourse (and others, no doubt, but not necessarily of all discursive classes) ascribes a name to the expression of something. That naming marks the ascription of meaningfulness. For while a name may be arbitrary insofar as its predicate is concerned, it is very far from arbitrary as to the system permitting the ascription. It is taken as having meaning *through* the concept. This name (let us call it *proper*, since it is taken as denoting its conceptual referent *truly* if the proposition can be verifiably asserted as true about what is denoted about the name) signals the fixing of a knowledge, of a *savoir* (a "form" of knowing, as opposed to any particular *connaissance* within such *savoir*). Gilles Deleuze has written in this respect that "the proper name is guaranteed by the permanence of a *savoir*."[26] He is far from alone in such a claim, but the formula is strictly reversible, for *that* particular knowledge

25. *Tractatus*, §5; Frege, "The Thought," pp. 291–93.
26. Gilles Deleuze, *Logique du sens* (Paris, 1969), p. 11.

(*any* form of knowledge) is sealed and certified by the proper names that compose it.

The Discourse of Criticism and the Uncertainty Principle

One of the first discursive types to *practice* the problem to be posed by Wittgenstein was, as I have already remarked, the very epitome of the neoclassical discourse of truth, the type that provided the model for all others within the class of analytico-referential discourse. The discourse of neoclassical Newtonian physics had begun to discover that its (discursively) unmarked creation of its own objects risked turning it into a solipsism. It was certainly no accident that it was a physical scientist and chemist, C. S. Peirce, who first attempted to develop a coherent ternary semiotic—or that his work did not become at all widely known until the 1930s, when Werner Heisenberg, Niels Bohr, and the Copenhagen School had already started to build the experimental and constructive nature of discourse into the nonbinary propositions of quantum mechanics by means of the principles of uncertainty and complementarity.[27] Here, for the first time, the very model of a neoclassical, veridical discourse sought to elaborate in its very operation a function other than that of 'truth,' as it had until then been defined. (Of course, they still sought a single hegemonic mode of science, remaining very far from Evelyn Fox-Keller's ideal of diverse conceptions and strategies.)

Heisenberg's analysis of the meaning (and sense) of physical truth, Wittgenstein's similar analysis of logic and the notion of truth, and perhaps Derrida's of language all tried to avoid assumptions of logical apodicity on the one hand, and of any taint of apriorism with respect to nondiscursive events on the other. Derrida has observed, as we have already seen Wittgenstein do, that discourse should assume no objective 'essence' as lying *before* the naming of which I was just speaking (shades here, perhaps, of the transfer of a Sartrean ontology to the domain of epistemology—to this matter I return in Chapter 5). The fixing of any permanent meaningfulness would have lain before language, so to speak; it would have been the "origin" of such use, as the making of grammar and the possibility of sense. Neoclassical discourse presupposes *meaning* as what it speaks about. But that is clearly a presupposition relating to the very possibility of this discursive class; it cannot lie outside it as though it

27. I am aware that Heisenberg and the others were theorists. I am using the term "experimental" in the same sense here as before: as shorthand (drawn from Wittgenstein) to indicate one of the "defining" elements and indeed forms of analytico-referential discourse.

were some other origin, some primary essence, a secure anchor in the actual. A proposition asserting *that* meaning is sense-less. The logical positivists dismissed it as "metaphysics." For Wittgenstein, it pertained to that of which we cannot speak and about which we must remain silent.

It follows that the only 'meaning' possible in the donation of a name, in the invention of knowledge, becomes that of the *act* itself: of the activity of forming and uttering a discourse, at least to the extent that such an act is part of a coherent total socio-cultural environment. This we will call "sense," retaining the word "meaning" for Frege's *Bedeutung:* ordinarily translated as "denotation" and designating the exterior event taken as (intentionally) referred to by a given proposition and assumed to determine the concepts of truth, reality, objectivity, and so on. The production of "sense" is thus common to *all and any* discursive activity; the production of "meaning" is specific to the analytico-referential.

Wittgenstein pointed out that in naming, all we do is "put a piece in its place on the board." To do so, we must already know the rules of the game: in Wittgenstein's analogy, we do not even know where to put the piece or how to move it unless we know its potentialities vis-à-vis the other pieces and their possible moves.[28] The rules governing naming are already part of discursive use. This difficulty arose with particular acuity in the domain of quantum mechanics. Coming out of an area (the natural sciences) exemplary for neoclassical discourses the problems it was forced to confront and its attempts to resolve them reveal a striking resemblance to the trajectory followed by Wittgenstein between the *Tractatus* and the *Investigations*. Quantum mechanics had to reopen a number of epistemological questions latent in Western philosophy at least since Descartes. Though it has arrived at no satisfactory solution, its responses, however incomplete, show a certain likeness to the notion of "semiosis" found in Peirce (itself revealing some resemblance to a Hegelian dialectic—though that remains a largely unexplored relationship).

It first became apparent that such names as "momentum" and "position" had no very precise meaning at all outside the language game of modernist physics. The situation as it appeared under the experimental conditions that quantum mechanical discourse sought to perform could not be 'described' without 'new' names. Yet such names could not be given, nor even seen to be necessary, outside the experimental elaboration in question. There was no meaning, only a production of discursive *sense*. With respect to an entirely similar matter, Heisenberg wrote: "The most important new result of nuclear physics was the recognition of the possibility of applying quite different types of natural laws [drawn from

28. Ludwig Wittgenstein, *Philosophical Investigations*, tr. G. E. M. Anscombe (1953; rpt. Oxford, 1972), I , §§49–64 pp. 24–31.

different 'scientific systems complete in themselves'], without contradiction, to one and the same physical event."[29] (Here, we do seem close at least to an intention of Fox-Keller's ideal.)

It speedily became clear, too, that the "event" itself possessed so complex a status in respect to discourse that it could not be, in any neoclassical or modernist understanding of the term, a matter of "description" at all. Wittgenstein observed that "naming is a preparation for description,"[30] but in the end it must perhaps be argued that what is *described* is really the process of giving names, the *act* of knowing. As Heisenberg has put it: "The demand to 'describe what happens' in the quantum-theoretical process between two successive observations is a contradiction *in adjecto*, since the word 'describe' refers to the use of classical concepts, while these concepts cannot be applied in the space between the observations; they can only be applied at the points of observation." The discourse of quantum physics applied, he proposed, to this "space between": "Natural science does not simply describe and explain nature; it is a part of the interplay between nature and ourselves; it describes nature as exposed to our method of questioning."[31]

An exactly similar argument had been advanced by Wittgenstein in the *Tractatus,* speaking (precisely) of the limits of a specific theoretical scientific discourse. To no one's surprise, perhaps, his comments were addressed to Newtonian mechanics as imposing "a unified form on the description of the world":

> Let us imagine a white surface with irregular black spots on it. We then say that whatever kind of picture these make, I can always approximate as closely as I wish to the description of it by covering the surface with a sufficiently fine square mesh, and then saying of every square whether it is black or white. In this way I shall have imposed a unified form on the description of the surface. The form is optional, since I could have achieved the same result by using a net with a triangular or hexagonal mesh. Possibly the use of a triangular mesh would have made the description simpler: that is to say, it might be that we could describe the surface more accurately with a coarse triangular mesh than with a fine mesh (or conversely), and so on. The different nets correspond to different systems for describing the world.

The use of the phrase "more accurately," here, clearly begs Wittgenstein's own question, since only the particular net itself could allow such a judgment, but the principal point was Heisenberg's: "Laws", Wittgenstein thus concluded, "like the principle of sufficient reason, etc, are about the

29. Werner Heisenberg, *Philosophical Problems of Nuclear Science* (New York, 1952), p. 24.
30. Wittgenstein, *Philosophical Investigations*, I, §49, p. 24.
31. Werner Heisenberg, *Physics and Philosophy: The Revolution in Modern Science* (1958; rpt. New York, 1962), pp. 145, 81.

net and not about what the net describes."[32]

The problem posed is therefore that of going beyond the model that forced us to make use of the idea of such a fixed place as "nature": that is, of the net taken as concrete actuality. It was in response to this problem that Heisenberg inserted into his discourse the notion of *potentia,* by which a name was provided for the simultaneous and symmetrical *invention* of discourse *and* its produced sense (*invenire* = to find and to come into existence): "The seemingly contradictory pictures yielded in the interpretation of experiments in atomic physics initially had the effect of placing the concept of 'possibility,' of merely 'potential reality,' at the heart of the theoretical interpretation. The conflict between the material particles of Newtonian physics and the force-field of the Faraday-Maxwell physics was thereby resolved; both are possible manifestations of the same physical reality."[33]

The manifestation in question is the *production* of a given experimental discourse as well as of something else, of a *sense* resulting from an activity within a space whose 'limits' are described by an epistemology of language on the one hand and by analysis of objects/events producible in accordance with a particular experimental order on the other: the sense is that of a discourse seeking to make its space a plenitude, to spread itself 'to the limit,' to fill all the meshes of its net. The element *potentia,* defined as an "objective tendency or possibility" ("objective" clearly having Frege's meaning here), marks the 'subject' and 'object' of discourse as *essentially* interactive and suggests the impossibility of a general descriptive system, of any generalizable "Grand Theory." The experimental realization of this *potentia* is a discursive production of sense, the realization of certain given experiential possibilities, by an act still called (productive) "observation":

> It is then on the one hand *not* simply the thing-in-itself in the external world, *nor* on the other hand is it simply the transcendental ego; it bridges both the external world and the transcendental subjectivity of the knower. As Heisenberg wrote in the *Martin Heidegger Festschrift* (1959), "the search for the natural laws of the [ultimate structure of matter] entails the use of general principles of which it is not clear whether they apply to the empirical behavior of the world, or to *a priori* forms of our thought, or to the way in which we speak.[34]

32. *Tractatus,* §§6.341, 6.35.

33. Werner Heisenberg, *Across the Frontiers,* tr. Peter Heath (New York, 1974), p. 83. The "physical reality" in question here is of course the Peircean Firstness, unknowable as such, but an ineluctable "anchor" for any and all genuine (triadic) meaning and knowledge. It is Frege's "actual," not his "objective."

34. Patrick A. Heelan, *Quantum Mechanics and Objectivity: A Study of the Physical Philosophy of Werner Heisenberg* (The Hague, 1965), p. 151. The Heisenberg citation is from "Grundlegende Voraussetzungen in der Physik des Elementarteilchen," in *Martin Heidegger zum siebzigsten Geburtstag: Festschrift* (Pfullingen, 1959), p. 291.

This lack of clarity corresponds to an awareness that the divisions of neoclassical discourse, here specified by Heisenberg, were no longer pertinent. A logic of the *tertium non datur* is impossible here. There will be, rather, a logic of 'indecision' absorbing that of the true/false binarism and corresponding to a concept of "coexistent potentialities." One recalls Wittgenstein's warning: "Don't regard a hesitant assertion as an assertion of hesitancy."[35] The concept of uncertainty or indeterminacy does not signify acausality in any simple sense, or (even less) Derrida's notorious "undecidability," but indicates a transformation in the manner of speaking about and understanding that which has been called knowledge.

Heisenberg's problematic of the frontier between events, their elaboration, and the propositions about them—finally asserting that the activity of quantum-theoretical discourse is one of *making sense*—is strictly analogous, it would appear, to Deleuze's treatment of sense in a more general context. Here, sense was taken as at once the expressed of a proposition *and* the attribute of a state of things: it marked the frontier (though I would add that Deleuze's "state of things" is considerably more neoclassical than Heisenberg's "objective tendency"). Asserting this, Deleuze wrote a veritable paraphrase of Heisenberg: "*Sense is* inseparably *what is expressible or expressed by a proposition, and the attribute of a state of things.* It turns one side toward things, the other side toward propositions. But it is no more one with the proposition expressing it than it is with the state of things designated by the proposition. It is precisely the frontier between propositions and things."[36]

The uncertainty principle that leads Heisenberg to *potentia* overthrows the notion of a simply dichotomous sign. Here the modernist alternative true/untrue simply does not hold. Furthermore, what would have been the "signifying discourse" is no longer unitary, is no longer the discrete place

35. Heisenberg, *Physics and Philosophy,* pp. 180, 185; Wittgenstein, *Philosophical Investigations,* II x, p. 192. See on this question, Carl Friedrich von Weizsäcker (from whom Heisenberg developed his idea of "coexistent potentialities"): "If the physical world picture dissects the living relationship of I and the world—which both, active and suffering at once, become what they are only in interaction with their opposite poles—into the schematic confrontation of subject and object, then that is itself basically a productive recasting of reality. But while it is generally only a question of leaving out and thinking away parts of experience, modern physics itself produces its own experience as it were by an act of violence. The experiment, which itself brings to birth the state of reality which it shows us, is an especially eloquent material manifestation of the mind which only knows as it creates" (*The World View of Physics,* tr. Marjorie Grene [London, 1952], p. 57). "Indecision" ("undecidability") is the word for this *only from within* the analytico-referential, whatever deconstruction criticism may claim.

36. Deleuze, *Logique,* p. 34. It is surely not by chance that the same passage in *Alice through the Looking-Glass,* where Alice is always unable to fix the position of a "large bright thing," has been taken to signal both the elusive frontier of sense (see Deleuze, *Logique,* p. 56) and the impossibility of asserting processive substance in quantum mechanics; the discursive mechanism is the same. See Martin Gardner, ed., *The Annotated Alice* (New York, 1960), p. 253 n.9.

of the Cartesian *cogito;* the reference of discourse and the process of discourse are situated together (as it were) in a field of sense the modality of whose 'precise' and diverse implications are set at any one production by the play between it and other fields in contact with it. 'Truth' is no longer absolute or even subject to a probability calculus; it is subsumed under some kind of contextuality that can be 'defined' only by its practice. We are then very close indeed to a Peircean (or Bakhtinian) discourse—a matter I wish to approach gradually.

It will doubtless be objected that the fact of science is not the same as the fact whose study and interpretation have been supposed those of criticism (literary or other).[37] Paul de Man, for example, has commented that literary language "is the only form of language free from the fallacy of unmediated expression." It is the only form of language whose text "implicitly or explicitly signifies its own rhetorical mode and prefigures its own misunderstanding as the correlative of its rhetorical nature."[38] In fact, this view of literature is entirely traditional and bears witness to a certain privilege granted to literary discourse in our environment.[39] The literary has been taken as that exemplary *use* of language that renders the blindness of language itself functional, the fact that it hides what it claims to reveal: reference or intention, thing or concept. As a definition of the literary it may be doubtful, but even if it is partial (and equally applicable to other types of discourse), this view places literary criticism in the peculiar position of being necessarily queried (as a supposed objective discourse, saying something *about* something else) by the very discourse it wishes to explicate. On this point, science may have its say as well—as Michel Serres has written:

Criticism is something like a physics. A phenomenon exists: the work. To be dissected in such a way [Wittgenstein's net]. It happens to be already constructed and not wild like the immediacy of the sensible that we must expurgate in order to experiment with it. Constructed and highly complex, saturated with laws. . . . You say someone is on the work's side, disturbing the phenomenon, disturbing the laboratory. Indeed, and physics knows it, and never ceases taking it into account, for it is a science of the relations between the observer and the observed, of dialogue and communication. How is it that in order to establish itself as a science, a certain discourse, where the human is in question, effaces a presence that the exact sciences, precisely, have raised up in the heart of their discourse, where the world is in question?[40]

37. I have approached this question in one section of my "Société, discours, littérature." It will be discussed at greater length in my *Discourse and Society.*

38. Paul de Man, *Blindness and Insight: Essays in the Rhetoric of Contemporary Criticism* (New York, 1971), pp. 17, 136.

39. This is argued at length and in detail in my *Meaning of Literature.*

40. Michel Serres, *Jouvences sur Jules Verne* (Paris, 1974), p. 74 (my translation).

Without wishing to attach more than a simply indicative import to such a remark, I suggest that this is to repeat Vico's question—but reversed. In the Italian philosopher's enlightened era, the sciences had not yet made the discovery underscored here by Serres—who places the ball squarely back in the court of nonscientific discourse and has sought to do for it (in *Hermès,* for example) quite precisely what Heisenberg wanted to do for quantum physics: "If the observational process is itself subject to quantum-theoretical laws, it must be possible to represent its result in the mathematical scheme of that theory."[41] But if the experiment is included in a lawful representation that simultaneously represents the observational process, and if the experimental process in turn necessarily and always transforms the observation, then the laws and discourse accounting for them must be in some kind of 'dialectical,' ongoing relationship. And we must remember something else: the sensible is not "wild" but is itself always "saturated," "theory-laden" (as it has been called); it is this field called "nature," already mentioned. There, too, "someone is on the work's side": the "we" who are the ongoing result of 'impersonal' and constant epistemological choices.

The consequent dilemma has contributed to crisis not only in some sciences but in other discursive areas: one result is the attempt to escape it by means of a comfortably detached *errance* justified as a questing practice of "desire," or else by means of certain rather suspect political choices (I return to these questions in Chapters 8 and 9).

Bacon sought to replace such a discourse with one of utility and power; the operation of a certain kind of truth proved essential to it. We can no longer return to that. He and his contemporaries may have succeeded, but that discourse's limits seem to have been reached, and we must find and elaborate some other: perhaps some discourse where knowledge is not a power founded upon truth and vice versa (in all possible permutations— which analytico-referential discourses, including Marxism and Freudianism, succeeded in elaborating). We may be better equipped now, because and not in spite of analytico-referentiality, to return to the human—not to the human as object of knowledge (to which Michel Foucault referred at the end of *Les mots et les choses*) but to the human as cause/effect and circuit for all meaningfulness, to the social as the 'space' where habits (as the Peircean notion of laws in constant process of formation but provisionally 'halted') are continually created. Here the traditional notions of discrete atom, atomism, and endless divisibility become either inapplicable or

41. Werner Heisenberg, "Remarks on the Origin of the Relations of Uncertainty," in *The Uncertainty Principle and Foundations of Quantum Mechanics: A Fifty Years' Survey,* ed. William C. Price and Seymour S. Chissick (London, 1977), p. 6. The previous reference is to Michel Serres, *Hermès,* 5 vols. (Paris, 1968–80).

meaningless. We now know that elementary particles exist only as a continual movement and exchange of energy.

Contemporary criticism is, I think, entirely marked by the series of problems suggested here: the end of a discursive class, the return of its occultations, the need for some more effective discourse, the emergence of new forms, and so on. Today's outpouring of critical theory and practice is perhaps the result of this dilemma. Criticism has often been accused, in certain of its manifestations, of being unnecessarily hermetic, of using a language that one critic maliciously referred to as "Bulgarian," of escaping into a realm beyond comprehension. As to the last, I have sufficiently remarked that this concept of "comprehension" refers quite precisely to participation in a specific discursive class: concepts 'useful' for *our* 'needs' remain to be found. I realize, of course, that these concepts also belong to the analytico-referential, but to be able to practice other 'concepts' would presuppose that we were already 'elsewhere.' Who will grant a modern Bacon the right to say (as the original did) that s/he has discovered the right path but cannot well communicate a discourse whose operative laws are entirely different from those to whom s/he sought to communicate them? And who, unless the future were already established out of such laws, would be able to know? We confront here the difficulty of Wittgenstein's lion, whose talking we would not understand.

As to the first two accusations, criticism finds itself today rather in the position of quantum mechanics some six decades ago. Having finally become aware that all discourse occurs, so to speak, in the space of the Cartesian *ergo,* which forms an artificial link between the thinking and the (thing) thought, it faces the difficulty of having to discover a voice capable of speaking the new without destroying itself (a matter confronted again in Chapter 7). One might well adapt as motto Heisenberg's response to the demand to "describe what happens": we need (initially at least) to find 'concepts' that operate "in the space between the observation," 'concepts' corresponding to ongoing process: theirs and that of their 'references.'

All this implies that critics are not altogether correct when they grant a certain privilege to literary discourse—always, as in the beginning (during the seventeenth century), lagging behind the discourses that provide its models. It has long since been observed (I have only been reemphasizing it) that the scientific fact, to the extent that it can be known in a system of relations, is a product of the discourse that envelops, that develops, it. Furthermore, the uncertainty principle suggests that any fact is given as such only for the period covered by a (provisional) stability of the triadic relationship object/proposition/(experimental) activity, into which the 'fact' can be inserted (a view identical to that expressed by the Peircean "habit"). Though the particular relationship may be taken as an exact statement of the configuration of a given moment, a change in any part of it will change the configuration—without, for all that, changing the 'precision' of the relationship. 'Truth,' then, will lie in the repeatability of its transformations, *as well as* in the fact of their unceasingly changing progression.

Since Peirce, since Bakhtin, and even more since the philosophical (and logical)[42] elaborations of quantum mechanics, we are aware that sign systems give us a 'truth' consisting in the ever increasing extension of their own relationships. The difficulty frequently appears to be that the 'truth' they provide still tends to become the very same Truth of analysis and reference so derided by certain practitioners of that "structuralism" and/or semiology that thought to question it. There is a considerable distance between their theoretical assertions and their practice. Very often this practice is directly opposed to what these discourses *wish to conceive* as their premises (the neoclassical elements here being emphasized through love of the pleonasm). The question this provokes is whether all discourse is condemned to come up against its own aporias, or whether some discourse could be practiced that always showed and undermined them.

All and any discourse obviously has to confront the dilemma of how to "say," without discourse's coming apart, once it 'knows' its own construction. But the dilemma would appear to be posed, as I suggested, especially acutely to a criticism of discourse, for its own 'object' is constructed as it is itself. Such discursive criticism always takes an elaborated discourse *as such* as its object.[43] Questions here might include these: What is the status of the elaborated discourse with which our own constructed discourse is dealing? In what way can such an elaboration be the *object* of critical discourse? How far, and in what sense, can it be regarded as a separate 'entity' having some 'truth value' of its own? According to the discursive characteristics we have so far been exploring, truth, object, and subject in any traditional understanding of the terms simply do not apply.

Such questions—constantly asked as they may be—are the wrong ones. They correspond to a different discursive class: the neoclassical, modernist class of analysis and reference. The concept of truth in that discourse played the role of a sort of measure of value. It was (shall we say) the most elementary discursive function. To questions of that kind we can use Heisenberg's answer, with respect to the need for 'concepts' reflecting ongoing process.[44] In the discourse of synchrony, of field, of triadicity,

42. I am thinking here of the attempts made by von Weizsäcker and others to discover a ternary logic, a logic of the "included third (middle)," or *tertium datur.*

43. For the most part, only literary critics have asserted that this is what they do. Most others (setting aside such as Peirce, Bakhtin, Heisenberg, Bohr, Serres) claim to be dealing with a nondiscursive object. In any *meaningful* way, there is no such thing.

44. The term "concept," as Locke discussed it in his *Essay concerning Human Understanding* and as it had been traditionally used, corresponded in many ways to Frege's *Sinn:* it is the

of dialogism (to signal just a few characteristic indices from a variety of attempts at such discourses), truth function becomes irrelevant, inoperant. We do, however, need some operative function that will allow the discourse suggested by the theory to *work* in a form sufficiently stable to permit the elaboration of relationships that hold together, whatever the specificity of the discursive *type* in question—and one that does not immediately falsify its theoretical premise. The analytico-referential idea of truth was a particular operative function for and within a particular discursive class. It cannot perform in a different class. We would have to consider a dynamic (discursive) circuit composed of the discourse at trial (*probeweise*), the critical discourse in process, and the interactive operation itself. That relationship would, furthermore, be constantly evolving, because each of the elements would constantly be acting upon all the others—once again we are close not only to Heisenberg but to Peirce and Bakhtin.[45]

This is simple to say, considerably less easy to do, as many have discovered. The result of any such interplay risks being unreadable, or merely anarchic—partly because such a discourse could not seek, in any traditional way, to adduce meanings based upon the opposition of truth and falsehood; partly because of the quite simple fact that we are *used* to the binary discourse of truth. It provides the rules of all our behavior. This other discourse would try rather to establish *process,* to perform discourse (and therefore the social in general) as a constant order of transformations. It would show, for example, that thought cannot merely fix information as knowledge but is necessarily a constant functioning of the operation of knowing; it would show that *that* knowing is the transformation of relations.

This appears to be the necessary 'conclusion' of all I have been saying so far (and it does not take us very far). But there remains a further matter: if it is clear that truth-functional discourse has rather lost its effectiveness as far as knowing is concerned ("rather" may be the operative term here), that discourse nonetheless benefits from an enormous inertial force. Once the truth function was available, it was available to everyone.

---

abstraction enabling a private *Vorstellung* to be translated into communal understanding. In analytico-referential discourse it serves the function of 'explaining' and justifying the passage from material sensation to communicate rationality; in some sense, *concept* guarantees the *value* of something said (and thought) *about* something else. It is an operator within the *cogito-ergo-sum* system, enabling one element to pass into another. Another discursive class would therefore have to redefine "concept" or invent a new operator.

45. In literary criticism this would dispense with certain discussions and choices. For example, we would no longer have to consider a possible 'opposition' between text-oriented criticism and reader-oriented criticism; they both belong within analysis and reference. The first emphasizes the literary text as the *factual object* of critical discourse (whatever it then seeks to do with it); the second emphasizes the fact that criticism is making a *proposition* about such a text.

Once obtained, it did not require any changing or even any adjustment. Indeed, *its* definition as truth could not allow any change. This habitual, consensual aspect of the truth function is exceedingly important: it may well be what most sustains it.

Discourse, then, is not only a matter of obtaining, processing, and communicating 'knowledge.' It is also a far from neutral practice serving to sustain a particular customary social environment. If the familiar discourse produces more disadvantages in its action than advantages, then some other practice needs to be developed, or to develop itself. And a vast number of questions require resolution:

> Can there be some single function (such as that of truth in analytico-referential discourse) that will simultaneously prescribe and describe our discursive practice as mediated expression?
>
> If so, can we nonetheless give it form, as practice, in conjunction with a habitual, social, communal exchange between, say, writer and reader, speaker and listener, individual and group? That is to say, can such a discursive mode function as a means of social exchange, or are we forced to use at least two forms of discourse, corresponding, for example,to the nonliterary and the literary in our tradition, a commonsensical discourse and a self-consciously rhetorical one?
>
> Should not speaking about interpretation in fact be incorporated into all discursive production?
>
> How can you preach your practice *and* practice your preach?
>
> Must we not, whatever the difficulty, inscribe the productivity of meaning in all discursive (and therefore social) practice, if we are to avoid exchanges always based upon a false telling, inasmuch as it pretends to transparent objectivity and to expressing the "view from nowhere" (as false as the hiding of lies in Houyhnhnmland by asserting the nonexistence of whatever is not)?

What follows can be only a restricted attempt to answer some of these questions in a particular domain: the limited one of that criticism acknowledging its own discursitvity (in the sense of its marking in its own elaboration that it produces meaningfulness, and that it opposes this to what is represented by the discourse of analysis and reference).[46]

We may begin, I think, by returning to the concept of *potentia*. We need not, however, understand the potentiality of sense as an assumption of subjectivity (as many assert), or as a simple falling back into some confused and naive hermeneutic circle. But neither are we obliged to seek an objectivity of the interpretive practice in some authorial intention, however subtly we may conceive that. Such an intention, like textual structure or other *object* of distinct analysis, may be "objective" in a particular sense:

46. This limitation for the present; my *Discourse and Society* will take up the questions across a much broader spectrum.

it may provide the "meaning" of a text. But it is objective and meaningful according to the criteria of a discourse dependent upon the true/false dichotomy, of a discourse whose assumptions have already been shown to be of dubious general applicability. According to the distinction made earlier, such an intention in fact provides *only* a "meaning," while "sense" is to be situated in the actual production of the "intention" itself—the way in which discourse produces what it then calls "meanings." It is certainly no accident that E. D. Hirsch writes now of "validation" instead of his earlier "verification"; the more obviously dubious proposition of outright (absolute) truth has been replaced by that of a sort of tentative truth.[47] It still remains, quite naturally, a truth in his and others' eyes. But objectivity, in regard to sense in discourse, is a red herring. Sense is production and productive. It cannot be taken as set once and for all.

If words and linguistic forms in general—indeed, broadly speaking, all elements of all semiotic systems—attain significance only in terms of the criteria governing their use within a given class of discourse and between discursive types within that class, then there can be no such thing as a transcendental meaning or a concept corresponding to some a priori image or model. Either would be an extrapolation from the *use* in question. In classical discourse the picture "takes us in," as Wittgenstein put it, just because we assume it to be separate from the words relating it; because we take it as corresponding to a thought or sensation that language "interprets." Wittgenstein suggested, however, not that we could reverse the order of relation in such a way that language would precede concepts but rather that *we have no way of dealing with* a question concerning such priority.[48] Such questions are sense-less. They demand an *explanation* of a certain kind, and such an explanation is impossible, since the instrument of the explanation is at the same time the 'object' to be explained. As soon as we use the terms "object of explanation" and "explanation," we are already within the realm of the very same a prioris, where we want to invent new ones.

That is not, of course, to deny that there are events requiring explanation. It simply emphasizes how such events are already 'added' by and to explanation. In our familiar discourse, however, the relation explanation/object does not allow such play, such 'give and take.' Logical positivism hardly resolves the matter by saying that the object in question is in fact the measure taken. Even less do such methods as those of semiology resolve the question when they make use of Russell-like language hierar-

---

47. Hirsch, *Validity in Interpretation*. This volume is exemplary of a viewpoint that strikes me, obviously, as untenable. Except most generally, however, it cannot be criticized in the terms I am seeking to use here, for it functions within a quite different set of a prioris. Within them it is perfectly coherent—which is why it is exemplary.

48. Wittgenstein, *Philosophical Investigations*, II vii, p. 184.

chies to convince themselves of having achieved more certain explanations because they have sought to clarify their limits.

If emphasis is placed upon *practice* and *use,* the difficulty may be avoided. Discursive use is such that thought and language become simultaneous: the two faces of the elaboration of *a* sense (of sense in general). The use of the notion of "logical space" or "language games" in Wittgenstein, or of "discourse" elsewhere, corresponds to this idea. It then makes no difference whether we consider, for instance, the sense of a text as that 'intended' by its author, or as proceeding in some way from the text itself, or, again, as the result of a "reading-relationship"; discursively, the three are resolutely identifiable one with another. We need rather to consider the discursive 'network' as a constant practice of sense.

Here the distinction made by Frege between the *objective* and the *actual* may come in handy: a distinction not to be equated entirely, perhaps, with the more celebrated one between *Sinn* and *Bedeutung,* sense and reference or (as it is on occasion translated) meaning. Heisenberg adopted that distinction, and his commentator, Patrick Heelan, has clarified the issue by showing that the objective refers to "the *public objectivity of a concept.* [Heisenberg] eventually came to contrast 'objective' with 'real' or 'actual' (*wirklich*). A wave function, he says, is 'objective' but not 'real'; for *real* or *actual* implies an empirical content while *objective* does not. The logical consequence, from which Heisenberg does not shy, is that quantum mechanics is a science of immanent acts and objects; it no longer 'describes nature but our knowledge of nature,' as he wrote."[49] The *actual* is what is referred to by the *Bedeutung* of a proposition; what is *objective* is its sense. It is objective because *sense* is of necessity *public;* it is shared, communal, consensual. It is controlled by the "rules of the game," by habit, by the (actual) *use* of discourse. Neither of these could correspond, for example, simply to the intentionality of an author, or to any 'absolute' structures of textuality or of mind (such as the "semiotic" or "logical square," the "deep structure" of transformational generative grammar, or the narrative order of reason). They can correspond only to the dwelling-within a particular class of discourse—and to the use, practice, of a given type inside that class.

Within these domains, "author" will represent a kind of locus for the organization of forms. An author, if you will, has a certain "responsibility" for a text but uses relations, categories, forms already present.[50] These

49. Heelan, *Quantum Mechanics and Objectivity,* p. 150. The Heisenberg quotation is from *The Physicist's Conception of Nature,* tr. Arnold J. Pomerans (London, 1958), p. 25. For the reference to Frege, see *Foundations,* p. 35, §26.

50. *Responsibility* refers here to the discursive mark of "the awareness within discourse of the individual's 'enunciative responsibility' " (Reiss, *Discourse of Modernism,* p. 34); it indicates the 'discourse's' internally indicated awareness of organizing its elements and 'objects.'

precede the author, and we do not get at *them* through that authorial figure but at *it* through them. The (literary) critic or historian works upon the text within that field or network, not upon the wielder of the pen. And when the historian reads a text within a complete discursive field, the sense is provided by the circulation of all discourses characterizing an "episteme." This circulation is "anchored" in the society to which it gives form and meaning and for which in turn it provides an anchor (both rather mobile); the whole is what I refer to as the "sociocultural environment."

For the critic, literary or otherwise, *Bedeutung* can no doubt be set aside. There is indeed an actual, but it can be only the physical existence of the signs carrying the discourse at trial, the material through which it is manifested. Certainly that will be part of the sense. but we may ignore it for the present. What the critic has to deal with is the sense, objective in that it is a public 'grammar' of a given type and class of discourse. But how may the critic accede to that sense, given that it is doubtless multiple (and multiplying) even with respect to its possible 'reduction' within any individual textual context that may be at trial in the critical discourse?

In quantum theory, Heisenberg remarked, we are concerned "with the consequences of the fact that every measurement in the atomic field requires an act of intervention."[51] This act of intervention, as we know, affects (even *ef*fects) the activity being measured: it produces it in a geometrical sense, or extends it in a logical one. The act of intervention changes the measurement being made, that measurement which, in the neoclassical concept, corresponded to the presence of a fixed and/or precisely repeatable event that was "available for the making." In quantum theory the *availability* must be erased, because there is no longer "something already there" whose measurement is unique, true, and permanent. The "something" in question *is* the measurement that will be *produced*. (Contrary to what some would believe, the "something" is not, thereby, a fiction or an illusion: our real world is an *actual* product of such interaction.) This production is a particular mark, an indication of a possibility in the activity being measured, as well as a practice of the (discursive) measuring activity. This is the space in which the uncertainty relationships perform, the space of *potentia*.[52]

---

51. Heisenberg, *Across the Frontiers*, p. 19.

52. The indeterminacy relations, as a mathematical formalism, are applicable only to certain pairs of conjugate observables— position/moment, time/energy—and one can know, e.g., the position and energy of a particle to any degree of accuracy because these are not such a pair. I thank Lewis Pyenson for this commentary, but I would suggest that it does not resolve the difficulty concerning the general relationship between the activity to be measured and the activity of measuring; at the most, limits are placed around the difficulty within a certain discursive type. In particular, it does not resolve the case of discourses dealing with other social, communal discourses (i.e., all discourses outside the natural

Is this not quite similar to what occurs in the activity of criticism? The immediate "reason" why measured and measuring activities form a kind of coproduction is that in the quantum-theoretical discourse the material of their activities is the same, and it functions within the same space/time/mass spectrum: the subatomic particles being measured and the subatomic particles doing the measuring. The discourse of criticism in its relation with the discourse criticized operates at the same level (there can be no "metadiscourse"). Each uses the same discursive elements, whether semantic or semiotic. The production of the critical discourse is its sense, a sense depending upon the production of the discourse criticized. It cannot, therefore, be a description, an "interpretation" of the criticized discourse, measured by some supposedly extradiscursive standard (such as "truth" "intentionality," or the like). For that standard would relate to *sense* (namable only 'elsewhere,' in a different discursive space) in just the same way as the measurement "available for the making" would relate to the production provided by quantum mechanics simply as the discursive realization of an objective potential.

Following Peirce, I may propose that we will be dealing with a constant relation between a 'fact,' a proposition relating to that 'fact,' and the activity 'resulting' from these two (the relation being the genuinely triadic one of object-representamen-interpretant, in which we can speak neither of separate elements nor of cause and effect). That relation provides the only practice able to be called *truth,* and that truth then consists in this relation's stability with respect to a given field (phaneron). The truth thus produced is not singular; it is not opposed to some falsity. It is a concept of truth as a stable mode of transformations—not of 'facts,' not of propositions, not of produced activity in whatever form, but of the dynamic relation itself.

In Peirce's terminology the criticized discourse (the discourse at trial) is the object, the critical discourse the representamen, the sense the interpretant. No 'one' of these may be separated out of the triadic relationship in question. The relationship marks a permanent 'crisis' to the degree that its stability lies in its constant motion. Each element in the trial is in what Peirce called a "genuine" relationship with each and all of the others, both singly and communally (and therefore always improperly named, as Welby observed in a similar context, by the adjectives "each" and "all" and by the nouns "element" and "others"), and also, in the discursive process, constantly moving. The entire configuration is *'momentarily'* meaningful (though *that* cannot of course be "measured"), but the element, sense, that

---

sciences, which, having raised the problem and provided a terminology, could only "resolve" it for their own particular case).

was there an interpretant becomes a representamen in a subsequent configuration by the very fact of having been *said*. "The object of representation," wrote Peirce, "can be nothing but a representation." There is, as he acknowledged, "an infinite regression" in all this, precisely because nowhere may the process, in itself and as such, be stopped: "The interpretant is nothing but another representation to which the torch of truth is handed along; and as representation, it has its interpretant again." What does 'stop' it, as we saw, is the momentarily or provisionally fixed habit of a community.[53]

This provisional stoppage will perhaps produce what Peirce called the *immediate* object and interpretant, while the movement itself produces what he referred to as the *dynamic* object and interpretant.[54] There is something more than slightly akin here to the measured configuration of quantum mechanics: it is repeatable but cannot be given as a once-and-for-all identity (whence no doubt the extraordinary and seemingly endless proliferation of so-called 'elementary' particles—anticipated, as we saw, by Peirce).

The movement corresponds in one way to the regressive naming of names discussed by Deleuze, but it goes further and escapes regression[55] because the discourse at trial, out of which a given (triadic) object was brought into relation with the representamen of the critical discourse, continues to furnish objects for successive representamina. Successive interpretants are thus constantly being yielded, and we are faced with graspable, intelligible actualizations (in each triad); these, however, are constantly overtaken and outstripped—but never entirely so, as Peirce added in the passage about "regression" (note 53), for there is always a residue. As he put it, the clothing of a representation, its *sense*, is never entirely stripped off but merely exchanged for something "more diaphanous." This is the movement underlying that more general movement within the entire sociocultural environment of which Bakhtin spoke: "This is the order that the actual generative process of language follows: *social intercourse is generated* (stemming from the basis); *in it verbal communication and interaction are generated; and in the latter, forms of speech performances are generated; finally, this generative process is reflected in the change of language forms.*"[56] I obviously disagree with Bakhtin's hierarchy, as set forth here, which proceeds from an aprioristic use of the infra/superstructure division, but the bond he proposed establishing between the

53. Peirce, *Collected Papers*, 1.339.

54. Peirce discussed these in his 1906 *Monist* paper, "Prolegomena to an Apology for Pragmaticism," ibid., 4.530–72.

55. See Deleuze's discussion of the infinite regression of sense underscored by Lewis Carroll in his paradox "What the Tortoise Said to Achilles" (*Logique*, pp. 27, 41–44).

56. Vološinov [Bakhtin], *Marxism*, p. 96.

various semiotic levels emphasizes the importance of what is at stake. When one speaks of the constant outstripping of sense (without forgetting that retrievable "pockets" of it are constantly left along the way), one is clearly no longer thinking only of a mere literary or even discursive criticism. It is indeed the entire sociocultural environment, the very mode of human life itself, that is in question.

That said, however, there yet remains a final serious question as to the extent to which certain questions fundamental to the epistemology of quantum physics, or physics in general, may be made use of with respect to other types of discourse: does not their very use place us back in a variant of the analytico-referential scientific model and thus force us back into the same discursive class? The matter is one, I suppose, of finding the possible analogies between certain 'concepts' permitting the ordering they deal with. David Bohm, one of the strongest critics of the "absolutist" stance of such quantum theorists as Heisenberg and Bohr, made the point that a given ordering can apply only at certain specified levels and within certain limits, and that any physical discourse must learn to note those specifications (see note 52 and Heisenberg's own concept of "closed theories"). He remarked of scientific discourse in general that "the test of reproducibility enables us to tell why we have *not yet* included all of the significant causes. But there exists no test which could prove that we have included all of those causes."[57] At the very 'outset' of analytico-referential discourse, Bacon similarly implied how the quest for complete objective knowledge of the world required the necessity of exhausting all possible examples of an experimental phenomenon, while he acknowledged the impossibility of ever doing so.

The reproduction of which Bohm spoke (referring to the 'nether end' of that same discursive class) occurs only within the limits of a particular "theoretical discourse," within a closed system. The point indicated by the discourse of quantum mechanics is that there is a certain set of natural conditions ("background," in Bohm's terms) such that no causality is deducible *at the level at which it operates*. However, in this discourse it has been possible to specify with mathematical exactitude the background conditions in question and to apply them as the end point of the idea of causality. In Wittgensteinian terms, one may say that quantum mechanics has defined the boundaries of its language game. Bohm then argued that with this knowledge it should be possible to go behind (or "below") these background conditions to a "sub-quantum" level, where a new set of laws entirely could be envisaged as operating. Thus the "potential" nature of quantum-mechanical discourse itself would be delimited—in favor of the

57. David Bohm, *Causality and Chance in Modern Physics* (1957; rpt. Philadelphia, 1971), p. 9.

need to do the same for what Peirce might call a subsequent representation, a further interpretant taking up "the torch of truth." The quantum level would provide that momentary halt of which I have several times spoken, while leading directly into the next moment in the discursive series.

Now, it seems to me, we are at a point of manifest difference between the discourses of the natural sciences and others. For example, the background of the literary critical discourse is the existence and the form of the literary text itself. If one supposes, as one must unavoidably do, that this discourse is absorbed in a whole network of discourses, all by definition interdependent and interactive, then the "background" is unavailable to specification in any precise sense whatsoever—not least because the critical discourse is itself part of the network (as discursive production, this is true of natural-scientific discourses as well). I am suggesting that *critical* discourse is that discourse which discloses the fact of this network and makes it function in its own practice. It is, in the sense just mentioned, the discourse of the end point itself (and therefore not "Kantian," for it must view itself not as posing absolute terms to forms of knowledge, but as defined by a historical context). It would *show* the limits of all other discourse within a given sociocultural environment (hence, we should not speak of a specifically *literary* criticism, or undertake one). By doing so, it might serve to define the limits of their possible and various applicabilities. It would set forth the functions and interrelations obtaining between the discourses of a class and the eventual definition of classes, making possible in turn the self-critical critical discourse that itself provides the control for the use of those others.

This is not, therefore, a descent into some skeptical subjectivity or relativism—quite the contrary. Once again, we should not be taken in by the red herring of some opposition between objectivity and subjectivity, or between absolute and relative; these are oppositions brought from another discourse. The elements of discourse, both semiotic and semantic, can be and are being specified. But neither must those specifications be confused with criticism, though it must make use of them, must produce them. Those specifications belong in a different arena, an arena whose *problem* is not the producing of sense but the identification of the elements making such production possible, elements whose permanence will eventually be erased by that production, for they, too, are a momentary stoppage. They refer to an already given process; they reproduce a knowledge "from the past" and are only (but necessarily) useful to the degree that they can enter into the triadic relation of meaningful discursive production about the sociocultural environment.

This argues that we must also begin to describe the general conditions of existence of different types of discourse within a given discursive class.

And such a description can be undertaken only within the limits of definability constantly to be shown by the critical discourse on the one hand, and within the definition able to be given of the epistemic class itself on the other. This last definition cannot be aprioristic but can be given only by a close study of the types that, hypothetically (in Peirce's sense), seem at first to be members of that class. There you would have something like Foucault's archeology of discourses, showing the place and the limits of such practices. It is essential, because it alone can show the point of departure for any future projection. That is the place of discursive *criticism*.

In *our* present, therefore, there was first a querying of the nature of meaning, truth, intention, subjectivity, and the rest—of all those elements, in sum, essential to the binary discourse of analysis and reference set in place in the European seventeenth century. Then there had to be a historical description of the way in which those elements actually came into place and actually functioned. Discourse must go on to perform the production of a discursive replacement for the epistemological and social function of that analytico-referential class of discourse—still, currently, dominant.

The criticism of which I am now speaking is perhaps always at this point: on the edge of sense, shall we say?

While literary history, sociology, psychoanalysis, and so on, may be possible *within* the classical episteme of analysis and reference, they are not exploratory. They must deal with meanings and with meaningfulness already *given* by the general class of discourse. In that sense, they merely reproduce already given knowledge. They are secretly tautological (which fact does not prevent the analysis of a discourse—it prevents any escape from the constraints permitting such an analysis). Hirsch is right, then, when he writes that the meaning of a text stays always the same; within its class of discourse, indeed it will. 'Beyond' this, possibly, is that archeology already mentioned, which will place each type of discourse in its functional position within the entire network composing the overall dominant class. Beside these two activities, in a space that in a way absorbs them both, lies criticism. Not a naive criticism that is the pronouncement and development of opinion (whether one wishes to call it, revealingly, "educated" or not), the more or less apparent imposition of a dominant (or subordinate) ideology, a make-work, but a genuine criticism (in Peirce's sense of the word genuine)—neither literary nor historical (these being also a part of the "white mythology")[58] but a genuine criticism as constant triadic process, the discourse of *crisis:*

58. Jacques Derrida, "La mythologie blanche," in *Marges de la philosophie* (Paris, 1972), pp. 247–324.

κρίσις . . . a separating, putting apart: *hence* a picking out, choosing 2. a deciding, determining; a judgement, sentence. 3. a trial. II. a dispute, quarrel. III. the event, issue, decision [Liddell & Scott, *Abridged Greek-English Lexicon*]

Crisis . . . 1. *Pathol.* The point in the progress of a disease when an important development or change takes place which is decisive of recovery or death; the turning-point of a disease for better or worse; also applied to any marked or sudden variation occurring in the progress of a disease and to the phenomena accompanying it. . . .
   3. *transf.* and *fig.* A vitally important or decisive stage in the progress of anything; a turning-point; also, a state of affairs in which a decisive change for better or worse is imminent; now applied *esp.* to times of difficulty, insecurity, and suspense in politics or commerce. . . .
   4. Judgement, decision. *Obs.* . . .
   5. A point by which to judge; a criterion, token, sign. *Obs.* . . . [*Oxford English Dictionary*]

To this I will return especially in the final chapter. Let me conclude the present point with a metaphor. For the critical discourse, the criticized (*any* given semiotic system) will be a kind of irreversible flow within which sense (potentially a saturation) will offer momentary pockets of reversibility: *sense* will be a "divergence" in the critical discourse which will always eventually return to the stable flow of the text in process.[59] 'Each' produced sense will give rise to others but will 'return' to the discourse whence it came, the stable object of its relation. Yet that 'stability' itself is also provisional, or course, depending—in regard to a text—on its insertion into what we call a "tradition." The tradition provides a particular 'aura' of meaning. Discursive criticism, like the sociocultural environment within, for, and by which it functions, will always operate as a production toward some other future.

That future, it goes without saying, is not merely one of discourse, even if one wishes to define the term as broadly as I have sought to do, and even if one acknowledges that our environment is human only to the extent to which it can be made meaningful. Society and history (however defined) are not accessible *merely* by the application of an analysis of meaning. Thus the danger in all this is of making a plunge into idealistic vacancy and, even more, of ahistoricity (the trap, by and large, into which "deconstruction" has fallen).

Of these perils, we must indeed be aware, though the first is less problematic than the second. Alice Jardine has some wise words about silly accusations of "idealism"—hinting that these may be the dogmatic

59. Michel Serres, *La naissance de la physique dans le texte de Lucrèce: Fleuves et turbulences* (Paris, 1977).

mouthings of thoughtless ideologues—in speaking about her attempt to elaborate the notion of "gynesis":

> It is too easy to put gynesis down to "idealism" as somehow opposed to feminism, a true "materialism." As long as we do not explore the boundaries of and possible common spaces between modernity and feminism; as long as we do not recognize new kinds of artificial, symbolic constructions of the subject, representation, and (especially) experience, we will be engaging in what are ultimately conservative and dated polemics, not radical theory and practice. It becomes particularly tempting at times of extreme political crisis to abandon this challenge of our century and revert to a "natural view of things": reality is what I see, hear, and touch. Nothing could be more reactionary—or pointless—in postmodern culture.[60]

This applies *pari passu* to the arguments made up to this point about truth and meaning, subject and object, and all the rest, folded (as it were) into a search for new conditions and meanings of all those terms—or, rather, those practices of a particular discursive class. The difficulty is exactly that confronted three and a half centuries ago by Bacon: a new instauration requires new ways of speaking and understanding; those new ways of speaking and understanding will be strictly incomprehensible to the old ways (and easily dismissed as idealistic nonsense).

To avoid the danger of ahistoricity, we must try to find the means to set the kinds of analyses implied or explored in the foregoing chapters in contact with the concrete environment of which they are a part. For the present, the emphasis is on questions of the nature of meaning, subject, language, and so forth—on the side of discourse, that is to say. This is inevitable to the degree that the concrete itself will first of all have to enter in terms of the essaying of unfamiliar discursive articulations. Throughout the rest of this book, in fact, the questions are explored entirely in terms of the discernible limits of current speaking.

60. Alice A. Jardine, *Gynesis: Configurations of Woman and Modernity* (Ithaca, 1985), p. 155. By "gynesis" Jardine means a discourse articulating together and making 'useful' the (negative) 'self'-undermining of (post)modernity and the (positive) establishment of *'the'* feminine, against the masculine values of the dominant discourse of analysis and reference. (Ultimately, of course, it is not enough merely to voice the protest.)

CHAPTER FOUR

Carnival's Illusionary Place
and the Process of Order

Antiquity deserveth that reverence, that men should make a stand thereupon and discover what is the best way; but when the discovery is well taken, then to make a progression.
—Sir Francis Bacon, *The Advancement of Learning*

Reason wills that we shou'd think again, and not form our Conclusions or fix our foot till we can honestly say, that we have without Prejudice or Prepossession view'd the matter in Debate on all sides, seen it in every light, have no bias to encline us either way, but are only determin'd by Truth it self, shining brightly in our eyes, and not permitting us to resist the force and Evidence it carries. This I'm sure is what Rational Creatures ought to do, what's then the Reason that they do't not?
—Mary Astell, *A Serious Proposal*

The previous chapters have suggested that some kind of nondualistic rational order appears to offer a way out of the aporias and impasses of analytico-referential, instrumental reason. Before exploring this suggestion further, we need to confront one set of ideas frequently urged as just such a response to these dilemmas: the notion of "otherness" or alterity. In political theory it often takes the form of utopianism; in philosophy and psychology it seeks to alter the perceived relationship between Self and Other, between Mind and World; in (some) feminist theory it becomes the confrontation between male order and female generosity (Julia Kristeva's symbolic versus semiotic); in deconstruction and its fellow travelers it is "phallogocentrism" against the dispersion of Writing. In all areas it reproduces the nostalgic desire for a generous uncontaminated Eden confronting discontent with the restricting order of fallen civil society.

I mention these several different spheres of discussion because the notion of otherness has acquired a widespread and disproportionate attractiveness. One of its most generally used embodiments is the idea of "carnival," and that idea may provide us with as useful an approach to the problem as any other. For this notion of "carnival" has indeed become a snare—not so much, doubtless, as an object of historical knowledge, or as providing certain tools (however vague and imprecise they may be) for the

[135]

study of the literary or the historical text, but to the degree to which it has been set up precisely as a general "postmodernist" form of functioning. This is as much the case, we will see, in the political and social arena as it is in that of 'pure' ideas.

I think, for example (and deliberately simplistically), of the "flower children" of the 1960s, or of the political carnival of May 1968 (as it was quickly thought of)—indeed, one may reflect upon the entire phenomenon of "counterculture." Carnival is a snare quite exactly for our modernity, yearning for some kind of certainty. The idea may well function under such circumstances as a challenge, the very mark of an interrogation brought against a particular social and discursive order. But when it is proffered as a "solution" to an epistemic and social, political and conceptual crisis, then carnival is removed from a position by definition limitrophe and placed, anarchically, in the very center of an order that it could never do other than contest. For behind the notion of carnival, as it has come to be frequently used, lies some such general idea as the *Other* of our culture. In this case, that Other is offered as a way out of some fundamental crisis being experienced by contemporary Western civilization.

The problem has been created at least partly by the attempt to transpose a historically situated idea into some other 'place' and into a different history, as though it were one among certain universal concepts and practices. These are used as if they were not bound to endlessly changing discursive and social contexts, not caught within realms of meaning corresponding to different circumstances. When Bakhtin fell upon the notion of "carnival," however, and applied it to texts and contexts from Ovid and imperial Rome to Dostoevsky and Czarist Russia via Rabelais and Valois France, he took care each time to indicate a different *sense*. In each case he observed that the term "carnival" pointed to a particular kind of activity and behavior acquiring its specifiable characteristics in virtue of the forms taken by the dominant discourse of *that* environment. So, he wrote, one can follow the trajectory from the medieval and Renaissance carnival, through the grotesquerie of Romanticism, to Dostoevsky's dialogic novel (whether or not we agree with that analysis is less important than the effort to historicize it). Carnivalesque elements—especially in the form of the grotesque—served the Romantics, for example, as "the expression of a subjective, individualistic world outlook very different from the carnival folk concept of previous ages." For the Romantics, Bakhtin continued, the great carnival of times long past (itself no doubt nothing but an Edenic nostalgia for a life lived in the *other* of our supposedly fragmented monologic discourses) had become something altogether different: "as it were, an individual carnival, marked by a vivid sense of isolation. The carnival spirit was transposed into a subjective, idealistic philosophy. It ceased to be the concrete (one might say bodily) experience of one, inexhaustible being, as it was in the Middle Ages and the Renaissance."[1]

So vast a difference surely means we should admit that we are in fact no longer talking about the same thing. But can we make such an admission? When we read those who have written on the matter of carnival, festival, or feast, it almost appears that we cannot; it is as though some profound yearning or nostalgia were blocking any access to history and change, as if carnival were the shadowing, ghostly figure of some *other*, some 'elsewhere'—neither some *thing* nor something recognizably similar or the *same* but a nostalgia for some unified, holistic past forever lost. "The festival in fact," Roger Caillois argued, "manifests itself as a re-enactment of the first age of the universe, the *Urzeit*." Among primitive societies, he added, "the festival is Chaos rediscovered and newly created."[2] We need not be concerned here with whether or not Caillois was correct—and in any case, *we* could never know. But the word "as" (*comme*) of the first citation plays an important role, because it clearly shows that the "re-enactment" (*actualisation*) in question is entirely fictive, that "festival" acquires a *sense* only to the extent that it is a part of our familiar order.

Festival (carnival) would thus show the limit of the system of meaning habitual to the society to which it is 'opposed,' yet festival is incorporated within that society as one element of its own practices. We may therefore doubt the extent to which the one is questioned by the other, whether we are thinking just of the system of meaning or of society itself. Caillois will go so far as to propose, in his comparison of war and festival, that both are manifestations serving to *define* nations (*MS*, pp. 172, 177–78). Festival, like the everyday that is opposed to it, has its own laws, its own system of right: "You *must* gorge yourself entirely [on dancing, singing, eating, drinking], to the point of exhaustion or illness. That is *the very law* of festival. . . . destruction and waste, as forms of excess, are *by right* the very essence of festival" (*MS*, pp. 97–98; my emphasis). That is why Caillois can speak of "the order of chaos" (*MS*, p. 127; French, p. 162; the passage is ambiguous), much as others have spoken of the "order of disorder," implying that the disorder is only that of a logical space beyond the borders of our own.

A confusion lies in all this, however. At times of carnival, Caillois informs us, "you need to act [*il importe d'agir*] contrary to the rules. Everything must be [*tout doit être*] done upside down" (*MS*, p. 114). Now that

1. Mikhail Bakhtin, *Rabelais and His World*, tr. Hélène Iswolsky (Cambridge, Mass., 1968), pp. 36–37.

2. Roger Caillois, *L'homme et le sacré, augmentée de trois appendices sur le sexe, le jeu, la guerre dans leurs rapports avec le sacré* (Paris, 1963), pp. 130, 134. The English translation is taken from *Man and the Sacred*, tr. Meyer Barash (Glencoe, Ill., 1959), pp. 103, 112 (cited in the text as *MS*); I have on occasion brought the English closer to the French original, published in 1950 (though an abbreviated edition appeared in 1939).

kind of assertion means that carnival emphatically cannot be conceived outside the order of our familiar discourses. Quite evidently, the rules here are those of the everyday and of the dominant discourse regulating it. We might simply say that the use of this vocabulary shows the conceptual limits of Caillois's own thinking—except that we find it everywhere, including in Bakhtin, our more common contemporary source of these arguments. It is no doubt not accidental that Bakhtin never provided anything like a *definition* of carnival but left us instead with an accumulation of related terms: laughter, parody, obscenity, physicality, the grotesque. All may be subsumed under such notions as inversion and overturning, transgression and disobedience, and depend upon such notions as totality and wholeness, unity and undividedness.

It is as though a practice were thought to exist, generally available to our social process, that afforded the means of putting into question the very lawfulness of our habitual environment—in some kind of potentially complete and permanent way. Carnival is then upheld as a utopian other *in which we can in fact abide.* Our judicial system, for example, is defined as an adversarial one, as though such a definition served to distinguish it from other processes in our society. Yet quite clearly, our entire sociocultural environment, our political, economic, social, and cultural relations, are entirely adversarial. Truth, justice, power (whether bad or good) are inevitably defined in terms of oppositions, of contrary forces. There is nothing new or astonishing in that kind of pronouncement: feminist thinkers identify its values with the masculine nature of our dominant discourse, and it is clear in any case that its violence is endemic to what we may call the practice of authoritarian liberalism (see Chapter 6, note 32). In nostalgic opposition to that conflictual process, the idea of carnival—of a collective, unifying, balanced process—has been established as its pertinent *other.* (An older version—and a more formalized one—may be found in the *Gemeinschaft* that Ferdinand Tönnies sought to oppose to the modern *Gesellschaft.*)

Festival or carnival may thus be understood as a concept useful, and even perhaps necessary, to our ability to think *our* cultural reality, neither more nor less. It may in some way provide access, however imperfect, to the otherwise unthinkable. Yet the idea of carnival can really remain only a handy means of disputing the dominant forms of discourse (and of ideology). That marks its *own* limit as well, of course: as contestation, it could never, *itself,* replace what it is disputing and challenging; as such, it could never become the dominant discourse. Furthermore, as dispute, it will *always* be recuperated and absorbed by its adversary: it will be the Roman or medieval festival with its precise dates and its prescribed 'deviations' (providing the "order of disorder" with another meaning); it will be the labor holidays consecrated in the official calendars of capitalist and

Communist states alike; it will be the Belgian Banque Lambert's offer of a prize in a cultural competition described in the program of a performance of Bertolt Brecht's *Threepenny Opera,* which itself equates capitalist financial practice with general theft and criminality;[3] it will be Roland Barthes enshrined in the Collège de France, or even the popular Feast of Saint John transformed into the official National Day of Quebec (whose implications are only confirmed by the Parti Québecois's creation within that provincial government of a Directeur-Général des Festivals).[4]

Such recuperation is always, therefore, the sign of a failure, of a return to the supposedly challenged past, of an impulse that is fundamentally conservative, reactionary in the strictest meaning of the word—the very concept itself of contestation will thus have been absorbed and enfolded in familiarity and habit. One might think, here, of the return to order after the days of May 1968 in France, of the progressively more libertarian and/or totalitarian swing in both West and East after the optimistic ferment of the 1960s and early 1970s. But this same nostalgia for 'wholeness' is equally apparent in other areas where modernist conceptions of the individual and society have been criticized. So, too, is its manner of recuperation.

At the wider level of concern, one need only consider the remarkable turn either to the rather mild forms of religiosity manifest in the stance of diverse intellectuals previously on the left (especially in France; in the United States the trajectory has seemed rather toward the libertarian faith of the 'New Right') or to the extreme forms of evangelical fundamentalism increasingly, and frighteningly, manifest in the political arena itself in the United States. Both of these seem predicated upon a quasi-Rousseauesque notion of socialization as a Fall from Edenic grace and of religion as an offer of (political and cultural) redemption. Hegel long since, perhaps, had the last word on this kind of venture:

The life of God and divine cognition may well be spoken of as a disporting of Love with itself [elsewhere he speaks of the "Bacchanalian revel"]; but this idea sinks into mere edification, and even insipidity, if it lacks the seriousness, the suffering, the patience, and the labour of the negative. *In itself,* that life is indeed one of untroubled equality and unity with itself, for which otherness and alienation, and the overcoming of alienation, are not serious matters. But this *in-itself* is abstract universality, in which the nature of the divine life *to be*

---

3. The performance in question, furthermore, was supported by the Caltex Foundation! I owe this anecdote to Emile Copfermann, *Le théâtre populaire, pourquoi?* (Paris, 1969), p. 103.

4. This official's existence was mentioned by the Quebec sociologist Marcel Rioux during the 1979 colloquium at which most of the material of this chapter was presented. With the disappearance from government of the Parti Québecois, that post may well have gone as well.

for itself, and so too the self-movement of the form, are altogether left out of account.[5]

In other words, such demagogues as Pat Robertson, Jerry Falwell, and the rest are busy elaborating abstract myths that serve not only as concealing receptacles for despair but as simplifying mystifications of real sociocultural praxis in all its complexity.

A similar phenomenon is at work, it would appear, in *some* feminist and/or psychoanalytic views of the socialization of the individual as a fall from *its own* wholeness (the Platonic myth of the undivided complete being is seemingly tenacious). Thus Jacques Lacan's "Imaginary," Julia Kristeva's "semiotic chora," and Hélène Cixous's "Mother" are all presented as primal or primitive moments of existence, located in earliest childhood (though the function is phylogenetic no less than ontogenetic: see, for example, Jacques Derrida's *archi-écriture*). These names are given to a purported condition within which no distinction has yet been established between self and world, inside and outside, same and other, individual and collective, signifier and signified, *cogito* and *sum.* The eventual passage into the "Symbolic" order of the "Father" and of alienated language is a *fall* into social order.[6]

In his last writings, Roland Barthes (to return to my scapegoat) sought to inscribe within his discourse the contestation of which I have been speaking as an effective tactic to escape such recuperation. He started by arguing that language is "fascist" in some essential way: it "forces one to speak" in terms of *its* order, of its system. That this has been asserted by many others (most notably, perhaps, by Michel Foucault, whose response was very different) is of small importance. What is relevant in the present context is the conclusion Barthes drew: "In speech, then, servility and power are inescapably intermingled. If we call freedom not only the capacity to escape power but also and especially the capacity to subjugate no one, then freedom can exist only outside language. Unfortunately, human language has no exterior: there is no exit. We can get out of it only at the price of the impossible."[7]

He went on to mention Kierkegaard and Nietzsche, before continuing: "But for us, who are neither knights of faith nor supermen, the only remaining alternative is, if I may say so, to cheat with speech, to cheat speech. This salutary trickery, this evasion, this grand imposture [*leurre,* i.e., that lure or *snare* of which I spoke before] which allows us to under-

5. G. W. F. Hegel, *Phenomenology of Spirit,* tr. A. V. Miller (Oxford, 1977), p. 10. I return to some of these issues, esp. in Chapters 6, 8, and 9.

6. See, too, Chapter 2, nn.2 and 17, above, and their associated text. The appeal of, and to, Rousseau is both implicit and explicit.

7. Roland Barthes, *Leçon* (Paris, 1978), pp. 14, 15; English translation, "Inaugural Lecture, Collège de France," in *A Barthes Reader,* ed. Susan Sontag (New York, 1982), pp. 461–62.

stand speech *outside the bounds of power,* in the splendor of a permanent revolution of language, I for one call *literature.*"[8] At bottom, Barthes was saying little more than that the very idea of permanent revolution (whether Trotskyite or Maoist, no doubt) is a confession of impotence. It would therefore be something almost worse than the return to an already challenged past, for what he presented here was something like a false impression of effectiveness, actually going nowhere.

One might be tempted to suggest that the results were speedily visible in France, especially in that general sense of decline so profoundly experienced by the intelligentsia after May 1968—an event with all the appearance of a political carnival, and all its inability to establish any definitive transformation. Claude Lefort described the failure in these terms:

> Furthermore, the seething excitement of May scarcely matters, nor the oratorical and provocative play, nor the cult of old illusions: beyond them hover the constants of a critique and a demand. The critique questioned the "organization's viewpoint," beneath which our world tends to be ordered, the squaring of every sector of the social arena, the labeling of individuals, an entire system of discrimination among disciplines and expertises, of aptitudinal measurement, of exclusion of deviants from the norm, of work quantification, of the programming of forms of knowledge and what is known. And so it attacked the ruling representation of Science, whence the Organization draws its legitimacy. To this was opposed a demand that no formula at all could explain entirely, but which acquired its sense through an unwonted double assertion: of the *I*, in response to bureaucratic anonymity, and of the collective, in response to the atomization of individuals. This demand was manifested in the practice of brute speech and brute communication [*l'exercice d'une parole sauvage et d'une communication sauvage*], and in taking control of a space everywhere partitioned and disciplined [*surveillé*].

Lefort went on to show just exactly how people had let themselves be caught in this snare of a discourse "in (permanent?) revolution": "In that sense, this was a political critique and a political demand. Afterward, people stuck on them the label of cultural revolution, through inability to understand just what politics implies."[9]

8. Barthes, "Inaugural Lecture," p. 462.

9. Claude Lefort, "Maintenant," *Libre,* no. 1 (1977), 16 (my translation). It is by no means indifferent to all this that as early as the end of 1968 the *New Left Review* brought out a special issue, "Festival of the Oppressed, France 1968," containing essays by Ernest Mandel, Jean-Marie Vincent, André Gorz, and André Glucksmann, as well as Lenin's 1908 essay "The Student Movement and the Present Political Situation." In the introduction, Perry Anderson (in the name of the entire editorial committee) confirmed much of what I have been suggesting here. "The Revolution," he wrote, "was not finally achieved. Indeed, the State apparatus was not only not broken, but in some ways emerged strengthened from its ordeal." Only until late 1968 was it still possible to assert that the May events nonetheless

Such an analysis makes an occasion like that of May 1968 fulfill quite precisely the terms Caillois set forth with regard to festival, which, he wrote, plays out "a crisis, climax, or moment of precipitation and overwhelming presence" (*MS*, p. 163). That commentary provokes two further remarks right away. First of all, as carnival, the occasion at hand "represents" (the word is Caillois's) a *permitted* crisis, and one therefore always and already under control ("tamed," if we stay with Lefort's "*sauvage*"), contained *within* the dominant order. Second, carnival may well *mark* a moment of crisis but cannot permanently remain a representation of it—whence, precisely, the baffled disappointment in France after the May outburst. A profound misunderstanding is involved in all this, I think: one cannot live in crisis, in "permanent revolution." Caillois has long since spoken to this question. Although carnival might have a role to play in the social order as the very confirmation of that order, "on the day when its energy was liberated in a sinister paroxysm, disproportionate in grandeur and power to the relative fragility of life, then the equilibrium would definitively be broken in favor of destruction. This excess of seriousness in the festival would make it fatal not only for humans, but perhaps also for itself" (*MS*, p. 180).

Quite clearly, to go from contestation to construction is a difficult matter. One needs the right tools; one needs to see the proper place to set the foundations (those corresponding to what we might call, could we but know them, the 'requirements' of the cultural conjuncture in which we live); one must be able to understand what we might call the play of surrounding circumstance, correctly excavate the hole for those foundations, and make use, finally, of good materials. The construction can never be achieved by throwing the stones all over the place higgledy-piggledy, by merely "turning a world upside down." One cannot build a house by simply upending architectural norms, and practices enabling the construction of a new order of society and culture never came from simply conflictual conditions; they bring nothing but total collapse. Order does not come from anarchy—and the social, the discursive are

---

showed that "imperialism is vulnerable everywhere"; such a comment today would strike us as far less plausible. One of the indications that it might not succeed, the introduction argued, was the lack of "effective political slogans. . . . In one sense, there was a plethora of slogans: picturesque inscriptions which expressed the carnivalesque and millenarian dimensions of the revolution, its vital *élan*. Without this impulse towards carnival there would have been no revolution: the same impulse made itself felt in Petrograd with revolutionary fêtes and theatre in the street" (*New Left Review*, no. 52 [November–December 1968], 1, 6). So it did, let us add, in 1789 and the years following in France. What this suggests—and it is one of the arguments of the present book—is that although the limits may thus be shown (by "carnival," by turning familiar elements upside down, by referring to their Other, by showing the bounds of habitual sense), without some new model allowing them to be 'surpassed,' no passage into a new sphere of action is possible.

necessarily and by definition ordered. But that is not to say, either, that one is forced to think of such order in terms of the imposition of a Subject, in terms of a conflict between individuals supposedly in full possession of their own will, intention, rights, and so forth.

What is all this about? The fact is that the notion of carnival has not been used simply to describe a particular kind of historical or textual event. It has frequently been thought of as a *practice* affording some kind of functional answer to the feeling of crisis undermining all theoretical and practical activities in the West over the last few decades. I do not think the *fact* of something like a "crisis" is in doubt—particularly in social and economic conditions. Certainly there are places where it seems more evident than in others: one might think of Italy and a general level of disorder, of Britain's gradual change to "Third World" status, of the increasingly accepted effects of worldwide terrorism. In cultural practices, one may think of various essentially contestatory developments in art, in music, in the novel and the theater. In the discursive practice of knowledge, the enormous outpouring of critical theories comes to mind. All these appear to offer not a way of 'going forward' but rather a process of turning in circles.

There has been in our modern history at least one other moment of such felt general crisis (quite different, I think, from the more punctual critical moments marked by the French and American Revolutions, or, later, the October Revolution—which, I would suggest, were all pieces of the *same* process occurring later). From the beginning of the European seventeenth century, it was not that people finally realized something was no longer 'working' but that people at last began to find a solution to what had been felt as a crisis for at least half a century.

What was the problem? According to Descartes, it was that thinkers and doers inhabited a multiplicity of discourses, frequently obscure, often self-contradictory, expressing without rhyme or reason opinions, truths, beliefs, appeals to authority, and so forth. According to Galileo, it was that science deferred to opinion or authority, failed to take aim on reality, was useless for human life. According to Bacon, it was that all ideas were muddled up together, that thought took no heed of what might be useful, that thinkers did not wish for real knowledge but allowed themselves to be distracted by "idols," by an insufficient distinction between the different levels of thought, practice, action, and so on.[10] All three were complaining of inhabiting a condition that we might (after all I have just been saying) be tempted to refer to as "carnival," a lack of "reason" out of which these thinkers would be able to forge the *Other* of *their* true Reason.

10. For Descartes, see Parts 1 and 2 of the *Discours de la méthode*. Galileo's and Bacon's comments are far more scattered; let me refer (yet again) to chap. 6 of my *Discourse of Modernism* for Bacon, and my "Espaces de la pensée discursive" for Galileo.

All of this marked a reaction to the decline of the old feudal system, to a crisis in the European economy provoked in part by new theories concerning the circulation of wealth and goods, by the questioning of theological teachings on the matter (the principle names here being those of Bernardo Davanzati, Jean Bodin and, more or less incorrectly, Thomas Gresham),[11] and in part by the massive influx of gold brought by Spain from the Americas; reaction, too, to the shaking of relations between states on the one hand and within states on the other (between 1550 and 1650, civil war was endemic, and scarcely a nation in Europe was not at war, or almost, with every other at some time during the period), to the gradual progress of a new science, to a new conception of technicity (in mechanics, in medicine, in mining), to the comprehensive questioning of old authorities. "Reaction" is perhaps the wrong word. All these things together constituted the situation to which such as Bacon, Galileo, Hobbes, and Descartes sought a response. They marked a mutation; eventually a new realm of meaning (discursive class) was established that understood the "disordered state" of the preceding centuries to be but the phantasm (as Hobbes might call it) of its own unreason, a kind of carnival of which Rabelais—Bakhtin's Rabelais—would be the epitome.

The theoretical arguments of a Bacon, a Galileo, or a Descartes correspond to the political activities of a Richelieu, later ratified in Jean-Baptiste Colbert's political and economic achievements, at a time when the English Revolution—involving its brief reconstitution of a relatively absolutist monarchy and its final establishment of a "constitutional" one—seemed to be discovering a quite different response to the same crisis: a supposed balance between equal individuals, each in full possession of *him*self and *his* property. The questions all these matters raise can scarcely be examined here: I mention them simply as indications of a particular kind of solution to felt crisis on the one hand, and of elements essential to the modernist crisis on the other. But one must add immediately that the fragmentation and multiplicity confronted by the thinkers just mentioned is obviously not the same as ours: apart from the fact that authoritarian liberalism itself is part of what is now in serious question, that new instauration also presupposed an idea of Truth that is itself now null and void. I merely wished to propose the moment of this particular mutation and the reactions it provoked (which were, obviously, a part *of* it) as a practical and historical example of certain potentialities in the confrontation with a complete change of discourse, with the passage into another realm of meaning.

11. Copernicus is significant, as well; see, e.g., Timothy J. Reiss and Roger H. Hinderliter, "Money and Value in the Sixteenth Century: The *Monete Cudende Ratio* of Copernicus [with a translation by T. J. R.]," *Journal of the History of Ideas*, 40 (April–June 1979), 293–313.

Carnival (the ability to *conceive* otherness and *practice* apparent difference) functions, then, as a kind of momentary contestation. That implies that once the contested practices have disappeared or become subordinate, or once the contestation itself has been recuperated by those practices, then it will lose its meaning, its sense; it will become but a dysfunction. This may well be our present situation, at a time when the contested practices have been so since at least the end of the nineteenth century. Those practices were first described and established during a massive transformation in the sociocultural environment, of which the names just mentioned are merely symptomatic—though they also set forth precise goals and a well-defined vision of society and its aims in response to a blockage they sought to describe in ever more precise terms.

For pleasure—but also because the case, though exceptional, is still quite representative—I would like to make use of a particular reading of *King Lear.* I do not wish to present it as "definitive" (whatever that might conceivably be), nor would I ask the reader even to 'believe' it. I propose it merely as the form taken by certain questions at a particular moment in time: given the decline of a particular social and discursive order, with what can one replace it? Can it be replaced by an order formulated only through contestation? Or can one attempt to restore the old order? The reply to this apocryphal series of questions, not actually posed but nonetheless raised in the play, is a categorical and abrupt negative to the second two and an ambiguous irresolution of the first (for there can be no individual response by fiat).

Old King Lear, considering he is near death, feels that in order to avoid strife between his daughters and sons-in-law after his death, he should undertake now to divide his kingdom, assuming he will still remain king "in name" and thus in a position to assure the smooth running of such a division. To this end, he demands that his daughters exchange an avowal of love for their share of the kingdom. Now the oath (of love) in question takes the form of a declaration of loyalty between a vassal and a feudal suzerain, whereas the idea of exchange introduced by Lear—thinking thereby to guarantee both the future of the kingdom and his own—introduces an entirely different contractual order. What he fails to understand is that in thus yielding his real power to his daughters, he simultaneously yields up his suzerainty, thus rendering the act of allegiance entirely null and void. Wanting to guarantee some kind of equilibrium, he actually introduces a fundamental instability, for everything will now depend upon a respect for speech exchanged between equals. Lear does not see that in dispossessing himself of suzerainty, he erases the very *fact* of the feudal system of obligation and meaning. That is as much as to say that the king mixes together two different realms of meaning.

In the system we may call "feudal" for reasons of brevity, words have use value: by naming, they act. The value of an utterance may be thought of as dwelling in the fact that it has a kind of "intrinsic" relation with what is uttered: everything is in everything, and speech resumes that state of affairs (I am, of course, claiming this not as "sufficient" for a feudal system but simply as one element within its discursive class).[12] Cordelia, Kent, and the Fool are all representatives of this realm of meaning. Goneril, Regan, and Edmund are situated elsewhere: to them the only utility in words is to be found in the particular needs of a specific instance of exchange; they use words only to the end of profit and acquisition of wealth. To Goneril and Regan, their declaration of love is exchanged only for their share of the kingdom; Lear's later request for shelter and honorable treatment requires, in their view, a new contract, and all he then has is the household with which he circulates. Little by little, Lear comes to realize his error, his confusion; when he recognizes that he has quit one realm of meaning without having the wherewithal to establish a new one, he goes mad and withdraws into an entirely private world.

While this conflict indeed shatters the old order, it does not at all succeed in establishing a new one, based on a system of rational exchange in place of a feudal hierarchy. The (implied) "new" order appears to be branded with a mark of criminality, fundamentally conflictual and strife-ridden. In the play it is defeated by an expedient borrowed from the old order: judicial combat, a process predicated precisely upon the assumption that act, speech, and meaning are somehow bound in an absolute whole. Won by Edgar over Edmund, that combat puts things back, it might appear, in their place. But it does so entirely ambiguously, for the old system once overthrown can never be reestablished (as Edgar himself remarks), while the potentially new has been undone from within—through excess, through the fact that the endless desire for acquisition and possession must always rule the relationship among the very holders of this discourse (Hobbes's state of nature and the continual search for "power after power"): whence the death of Cornwall and the two sisters, whence the very existence of the letter making possible that judicial combat whose result is Edmund's death.[13]

In answer to the foregoing series of questions, *King Lear* suggests that contestation is never sufficient; that an order once shattered can never be reestablished; and finally—in the terms of the conflicts played out in the tragedy—that a system for the provision of meaningfulness (which

12. See chap. 2 of Reiss, *The Discourse of Modernism*, pp. 55–107, for a longer discussion of this effect.

13. The complete reading is to be found in my *Tragedy and Truth*, pp. 183–203, chap. 7, "The Lear of the Future." I repeat it here because it is evidently easier to exemplify the elements of a past transformation than those of a present one still under way.

renders action itself possible), a dominant discursive class to 'replace' the lost system, will not be found within a conflictual site and process as such.

The response proposed by philosophers, scientists, political theorists and practitioners was quite different and in fact displaced the question. It did indeed accept that risk of simplemindedness, about which it may be said that "neither a merely ethical reaction nor an esthetic rejection serve to liberate. At times when the code, in its imperialist form [what Barthes referred to as "fascist"], has taken mastery over all positive modes of utterance, and where the serious appears to turn into 'stupidity,' only abstinence would in fact be 'admirable' . . . whether leading to silence, or forcing one into the invention of some new speech, new because it accepts the simplemindedness of believing it has never been said, new because it accepts the simplemindedness of assuming its own stupidity."[14] In this passage Françoise Gaillard was praising Barthes's project (wrongly, in my opinion). But what someone like Vico admired in Bacon was just precisely that he had taken the risk of abject failure. The Lord Chancellor had taken the risk, that is to say, of not taking up once again the old habitual analyses of power relations—of not reworking yet again earlier solutions to problems of knowledge, being in society, state relationships, and so forth—but rather of rethinking them from some entirely 'new' angle. It is from the viewpoint of such a displacement that we should perhaps rethink the opposition established by Hobbes between socialized humanity and that kind of brute beast of the state of nature, the brutal being (to use his own terms) in a constant state of war; that we should rethink the idea of a contract based on the passage from a primordial and continual conflict among beings always in search of power and property, and on the voluntary cession of everyone's right to such power in favor of a single sovereign authority. For the two terms of this 'equation,' looked at closely, are radically incommensurable. They are, however, comprehensible as a way of understanding the confrontation between two quite different realms of meaning.

That Bacon, Hobbes, Descartes, and others were quite conscious of this seems not to be in doubt. Descartes, for example, retraced his life in the *Discourse de la méthode* so as to emphasize just how much the discovery of *method* represented in his eyes a definitive *rupture*. Similarly, Bacon wrote in an early text the following revealing passage, fictively addressed by the philosopher of a new method and logic to a Parisian academy:

But suppose you were minded to give up all you have been taught and have believed; suppose, in return for the assurance of the truth of my view, you were prepared to abandon your favorite views and arguments; I should still

14. Françoise Gaillard, "Qui a peur de la bêtise?" in *Prétexte Roland Barthes* (Paris, 1978), p. 274 (my translation).

be at a loss, for I do not know how to convince you of a thing so novel and unexpected. *The difficulty is that the usual rules of argument do not apply since we are not agreed on first principles. Even the hope of a basis of discussion is precluded, since I cast doubt on the forms of proof now in use and mean to attack them. In the present mental climate I cannot safely entrust the truth to you.* Your understandings must be prepared before they can be instructed; your minds need healing before they can be exercised; the site must be cleared before it can be built upon.[15]

The Baconian texts preceding the *New Organon* (and even that one) are almost entirely given over, one might say, to establishing a new discourse: a new discourse permitting, quite precisely, the discovery (or indeed the creation) of "a new face of bodies, another universe or theatre of things," as he wrote in 1620—all in all, one might say, a new kind of truth.[16]

Indeed—and the characteristics of this discourse are now quite familiar: the idea of referential truth and internal logical coherence (an idea repeated in our own day by Frege, Russell, Wittgenstein in the *Tractatus*, and others); the occultation of the enunciating subject, hidden site for the imposition of knowledge, authority, and power; the alienated capitalization of discourse, by means of a passage leading from a clearly marked *I* of enunciation avowedly producing knowledge and power (what I earlier called the "responsibility" of enunciation), through its surreptitious replacement by a supposedly collective *we* (as occurs in Descartes's *Discours de la méthode*, that exemplary text), to conclude in a discursive practice purporting to be at once transparent to the truths it communicates and an ordered system whose coherence is alone responsible for the "value" of those truths. It is a discourse which, through the occultation of the enunciating subject and the cession of 'its' responsibility for speech to a purported 'collectivity,' will allow, among other consequences, the hypostatization of the concept of contract; of reason as that "good sense" which, according to Descartes, "is the best distributed thing in the world";[17] of the *self* as site of a Will whose power equals God's, as Descartes (once again) put it in his 1649 *Passions de l'âme*. All these elements are among those characterizing a realm of meaning, a discursive class whose products will be hypostatized to become themselves objects of analysis (the most celebrated nowadays being, perhaps, that human figure whose "disappearance" was foretold by Michel Foucault at the end of *Les mots et les choses*). They are thus proper and particular to a specific moment in the history of society and culture: a moment that, for us, cannot but be exemplary (it is, after all, our 'past').

15. Bacon, *Redargutio Philosophiarum*, in *Works*, VII:63–64 (my emphasis).
16. Bacon, *Parasceve*, in *Works*, VIII:357.
17. René Descartes, *Discourse on the Method*, in *The Philosophical Writings of Descartes*, tr. John Cottingham, Robert Stoothoff, and Dugald Murdoch (Cambridge, 1985), I:111.

All that constituted an ordered response to a crisis marked by confusion of thought, by the overthrow of the European economy, by the dissolution of state relations and (frequently) the apparent decay of nations themselves, by rapid transformations in class relations, by widespread and overwhelming violence, and the rest. The old feudal and religious order of the Middle Ages was already disappearing, confronted by a massive series of challenges—of which the "carnivalesque" nature of such texts as Rabelais's (as read by Bakhtin) was merely a minor sign. No doubt carnival (or something *like* "carnival") did become generalized—in the form of that "sinister paroxysm" spoken of by Caillois (in a phrase reminiscent of Antonin Artaud writing on the plague)—but the practices it thought to contest had long since disappeared.

A new discursive order replaced that contestation. That order became ours: of positivist science; of so-called "modern" philosophy; of laissez-faire economic thinking and practice; of capitalist, imperialist, or authoritarian politics; of neoclassical, romantic, or modernist literature. After the moment of carnival, which by definition could not be permanently established (in disorder), that discourse in its various typical manifestations brought a clear response. It did not respond to carnival by seeking to make use of its elements or terms, nor did it reply to medieval discourses by trying to rework theirs. Rather, it marked the passage—as Bacon wrote in 1608 and Wittgenstein added some three and a half centuries later—into a new "logical space," into a new language-game. And like Bacon, Wittgenstein was to remark how such a space could not be thought from within another. That is a quite different kind of "leap" from the one criticized by Barthes with regard to Nietzsche and Kierkegaard.

Nonetheless, it was Barthes (following Foucault) who succeeded in situating, somewhat, the problem *for us*. "In fact, today," he wrote in 1971, "there is no language site outside bourgeois ideology: our language comes from it, remains closed up in it. The only possible rejoinder is neither confrontation nor destruction, but only theft: fragment the old text of culture, science, literature, and change its features according to formulae of disguise, as one disguises stolen goods."[18] And that is a practice Barthes himself sought to pursue through *Le plaisir du texte, Roland Barthes par lui-même, Fragments d'un discours amoureux* (whose considerable success in English translation as much as in its original may well make one think, for to what public 'anxiety' may it respond?), *Leçon*.

But he had long since been outdone, as far as his project went, by the old chancellor who, passing into a new discursive space, found himself obliged simply—and quite madly when one thinks about it, taking the risk

18. Roland Barthes, *Sade, Fourier, Loyola*, tr. Richard Miller (New York, 1976), p. 10.

clearly seen and assumed in turn by Vico—to say: "You will not understand me, because I am using entirely different logical rules." Or we might think of Wittgenstein, for a time risking silence and willing to his poor commentators the traditional but ridiculous task of explaining the existence of the *Tractatus* and of the *Investigations* by means of a single author who would have, in some sense, divided himself in two: the *Investigations* would, quite simply, be that attempt to pass into some *other* place whose possibility is simultaneously denied. Yet the 'place' of the latter text is already contained in the former (as we saw in Chapter 3); more precisely, the first provides the second's point of departure. Indeed, neither Bacon nor Descartes nor anyone else ever produced the new from nothing, any more than from mere contestation, that *other* of our discourse that we have been calling "carnival." It may well be that Marx undertook an analysis parallel to Bacon's earlier one: both a questioning and a using of elements provided by the previous dominant discourse. That does not mean that the *same* work is to be done; it does mean that it may be taken as exemplary of critical reflection. It cannot be a matter of starting over from zero (as Marx and Bacon asserted they were doing) but rather of understanding how people managed, at a particular historical moment, to *avoid* starting over from zero.[19]

No doubt that all remains quite vague and hesitant. If I refer back to Bacon and his contemporaries, it can only be as a kind of pretext—just as he referred back to the Pre-Socratics. What we need, that is to say, is emphatically *not* an elaboration of some such notion as that of "carnival." Carnival and what it means are not here in question, for carnival does not actually exist—not, at least, in the sense some have sought to ascribe to it. It is a no-place, and the belief that it could actually be realized is slightly perilous: a descent toward some kind of utopian anarchy. Deprived of the object of its challenge, it is strictly a non-sense (Wittgenstein's *sinnlos,* that which can have no sense outside its language game, *as* an 'outside' of that game). It would be that myth of the originary Garden (most popular, precisely, during the Renaissance) in which Swift and Voltaire were entirely correct (in their time of Enlightened order) to see a place of retreat and flight: nostalgic recall of the shamanic *illud tempus* (as some historians

19. In *The Discourse of Modernism,* I suggested that there was a profound analogy in this respect between Machiavelli and Marx: Machiavelli made it possible to make "a particular conflictual and contractual political practice into a meaningful and inescapable class of analysis"; Marx made an analytical tool from the "socioeconomic fact of relations of production" (pp. 384–85; cf. pp. 100–101). Because in many ways such a parallel underlies the arguments of this book as well, it is worth mentioning a similar remark I have since come across in Ignazio Silone's *School for Dictators* (1938), tr. William Weaver (New York, 1963), p. 14: "In our own time, Marx—with different means and different intentions—fulfilled the same function as Machiavelli in the 1500s: he tried to clarify the real workings of the capitalistic society of his time. . . . For this reason, he has rightly been called the Machiavelli of the proletariat."

of religion call it), of some supposedly absolute and entire freedom and wholeness—a myth whose essential contradictions were quickly demonstrated by the theorists of natural right. Its aporias and outcome are perhaps sufficiently emblemized by the mystic ritualistic fire of the traditional Feast of Saint John transformed by the Parti Québecois (perfectly logically, we have seen) into the sacred flame of the nation; or, at a quite different level, by that carnival of permanent cultural revolution whose illusoriness was sufficiently demonstrated in China under Mao; or again, by the revolutionary explosion of the Soviets now reduced, if you will, to a yearly military parade on the first of May.

Some new order is to be found elsewhere; it is yet to be constructed, from its own place, by reference to needs (if that is the word) that no longer correspond to earlier ones. Put in such general and abstract terms, what we are dealing with so far, however, can be little other than the weak call to order of demagoguery. And speaking of that one would do well to keep in mind Descartes's old assertion:

> This example convinced me that it would be unreasonable for an individual to plan to reform a State by changing it from the foundations up and overturning it in order to set it up again; or again for him to plan to reform the body of the sciences or the established order of teaching them in schools. But regarding the opinions to which I had hitherto given credence, I thought that I could not do better than undertake to get rid of them, all at one go, in order to replace them afterwards with better ones, or with the same ones, once I had squared them with the standards of reason.[20]

Indeed, the establishment in question will no longer occur from a single place, nor a single discourse. An appeal for the time being, therefore, to work—and perhaps to silence, though such silence can be only a (Wittgensteinian?) provisional disengagement, a moment in which to catch breath. It corresponds, maybe, to Julia Kristeva's "thetic" instance of passage from her semiotic to the symbolic, where a *new* ordering might be produced.[21] And, as I observed in Chapter 3, that requires other kinds of active gestures. Kristeva herself has put it rather well: "We must therefore attack the very premises of this rationality and this society, as well as the notion of a complete historical cycle, and dismantle them patiently and meticulously, starting with language and working right up to culture and institutions. This ruthless and irreverent dismantling of the workings of discourse, thought, and existence is therefore the work of a dissident.

<hr>

20. Descartes, *Discourse*, I.117.

21. Julia Kristeva, *La révolution du langage poétique* esp. pp. 41–43 ("Le thétique: Rupture et/ou frontière"), and also pp. 43–61, 108–16, 155–63. In her recent individualist psychological writing, melancholia and depression fulfill this moment of *le thétique*.

Such dissidence requires ceaseless analysis, vigilance, and will to sub-version. . . . True dissidence today is perhaps simply what it has always been: *thought*."[22]

This notion of thought, of *thinking* as a process critical of its own past, in interaction with its contextual present and productive of some chang-ing future, is quite akin (not surprisingly) to the Peircean identification of semiotic process discussed earlier. For such thought cannot be, as Kristeva rightly adds, either a guardianship of the laws (a welcoming acceptance of Barthes's "fascism" of language) or simply an endlessly iterated attempt at their dissolution (as Barthes undertook with a gradually increasing sense of despair, and as Derrida and his followers continue to rehearse). It must be a reworking both of its own processes and of those that led to its present situation as *a particular kind of discursive practice,* and it must equally be a reworking of the "environmental praxes" with which those processes constantly interact (I mean all the diverse praxes, directly or indirectly meaningful, by which we recognize that we belong within a specific sociocultural environment and which appear to us, by and large, as composing a coherent totality, however 'internally' varied and various it may be). Of course, such thought does not rework praxes 'before' they rework it. Thought is not itself primary (*pace* Kristeva). The environment, in all its processes, is just such a continuous flow as that referred to metaphorically in the last pages of the preceding chapter. That is just why thought cannot be either a guardian or a dissolvent: either is a renunci-ation of its necessarily critical task—which is not simply a response to something called "crisis" (which it may be at some rare moments) but a constant involvement in an environment that is by definition in move-ment. The question, obviously, concerns the way to make that involvement *work* as a way of moving 'forward' an environment whose structures, categories, issues, and developing interests acquire *sense* through and in that very thought.

22. Julia Kristeva, "A New Type of Intellectual: The Dissident," in Moi, *Kristeva Reader,* pp. 299. Many of these matters return in later chapters. Kristeva's own most recent work seems, however, to turn ever more about and upon itself, and it is therefore hardly surpris-ing that she has taken to speaking in terms of "the eternal return of historical and mental cycles"; in *Soleil noir,* p. 265, that phrase begins the final paragraph.

The Matter of Signs: Language and Society in Sartre's Argument

> We can best help you to prevent war not by repeating your methods but by finding new words and creating new methods.
> —Virginia Woolf, *Three Guineas*

> Give voice to each individual form of the unconscious, to every desire and need. Call into play the identity and/or the language of the individual and the group. Become the analyst of every kind of speech and institution considered socially impossible. Proclaim that we reveal the Impossible.
> —Julia Kristeva, "A New Type of Intellectual: The Dissident"

The connections between language and thought, between the subject and community, between "self" and "other"; questions of social and political continuity and change, of the private and the public, of comprehension and analysis, as well as the idea of a juster social order, preoccupied Jean-Paul Sartre throughout his life. His discussions of these various topics (and his efforts to put some of his conclusions into practice) have remained the subject of sharp debate. What follows, therefore, uses Sartre's work to prolong the debate commenced in the preceding chapters, at the same time seeking to draw away somewhat from their more or less strictly individualist terms.

Like the earlier ones, this chapter will certainly raise more questions than it settles. Indeed, I make no further claim than to be setting forth a few elements not so much of some Sartrean "theory" about a philosophy of language or concerning the relations between language and society (for I do not think one exists) as of a lifelong preoccupation with these latter questions. They form an integral part of Sartre's work, and though one objective will be to show (once again) their fundamental ambiguities and the reasons for them, what follows would be of small interest were it not that many of their elements may lead us into potentially fruitful paths.

It may well be that those ambiguities proceed form Sartre's very position as an attacker of the dominant forms of power—whether political, philosophical, or cultural; from his frontal attack on neoclassical or modernist forms of thought and action. For he epitomizes one of Kristeva's four types of "dissident": he is the first of the four, "the rebel who attacks political power. He transforms the dialectic of law-and-desire into a war waged between *Power and Resentment*. His paranoia, however, means that he still remains within the limits of the old master-slave couple."[1] Caught more or less entirely within the very discursive processes he seeks to query and undermine, Sartre can think of Western cultural and political order only in terms of something like its *other*, though not entirely *perceived* as such (a path followed by the *Tel Quel* collective itself, we may add, turning at first to the "festival" of 1968, then to Mao's China, now to a U.S.A. viewed, at once strangely and condescendingly, as benefiting/ suffering from never having internalized a highly verbalized [logocentric?] European rationality—as though it were a literal manifestation of Kristeva's semiotic chora).[2] To commit oneself to—or be caught up in— that kind of analysis is necessarily to repeat that environment's own self-understanding.

Ambiguities and snares ineluctably surround the important elements of Sartre's preoccupation with language and society which I wish to set forth. My aim is not the rather trivial (and pedantic) one of criticizing Sartre's participation in the now familiar discussion of the human use of signs, even though such a criticism would be by no means so simple as some appear to believe. I wish only to bring these elements together; to use them to suggest ways of going beyond them. To this end, I think it will be seen, the ambiguities themselves become fundamentally important.

Do I need to add I have no intention of deforming Sartre's thoughts about language by pretending he was some kind of linguist? Certainly, he proposed an occasional "analysis"—for example, of the semantic aspect of verbal units. Where prose was concerned, he most often applied such

1. Kristeva, "A New Type of Intellectual," p. 295. The reference to "law-and-desire" is also to what is in actuality often thought of as that choice between guardianship and dissolution mentioned at the end of the last chapter: two of her three forms of dissidence appear to speak directly to the latter. The second is the psychoanalytic play with, and upon the imaginary (semiotic) and thus its refusal of "an all-embracing rationality" (a claim that strikes me as very dubious). The third is that of playful experimentation with identity and law, with and in language (doubtless she has Derrida, Barthes, and Philippe Sollers in mind here). Sartre, or any other male, has no clear access to the fourth form: "And sexual difference, women: isn't that another form of dissidence?" (p. 296).

2. For the reference to Kristeva, see Chapter 2, n.39. The assertion that Sartre is uncritically within a "logocentric" metaphysics of presence is clearly untenable, and this chapter seeks to show not only the profound ambiguities in Sartre's adherence to it but also (and chiefly) his gradual working out of something that appears notably different. Here I agree fully with Rhiannon Goldthorpe's remark: "The 'soi' of the *pour-soi* is never, *pace* Derrida, fully present to itself. . . . For Sartre, the body as subject is not a basis for the stability of the self, but an uneasy vacillation between subjectivity and objectivity, fluctuating between instrumentality, resistance and complicity. In its lack of self-coincidence, consciousness invalidates the laws of identity" (*Sartre: Literature and Theory* [Cambridge, 1984], p. 199). Parts of Goldthorpe's book cover some of the same ground as this chapter (see esp. pp. 39–61, 159–97), and our agreement is strong.

"analyses" to a criticism of certain verbal usages or what he asserted to be persistent confusions.[3] Where poetry was in question, he tended to use "semantic analysis" to show how the poet used words as "images," as significant sonorities or rhythms themselves endowed with an ontological status similar to that of any other material entity: a concept that always remained rather vague (and to which I will come back). Words such as "proposed," "most often," "tended to" and the quotation marks with the term "analysis" are necessary to indicate just how much—at least for most of his working life—Sartre's reaction to language at this level (that which Saussurean linguistics thinks of as the level of the signifier) remained largely impressionistic. It is almost as if Sartre adopted on his own account the criticism of "abstract objectivism in the study of language" advanced by Mikhail Bakhtin in 1929. According to this criticism, the word, as a fixed, stable entity present in an equally fixed and stable linguistic system, was nothing but an abstraction invented in order to provide a purportedly scientific linguistics with a material object similar to the objects studied by the natural sciences.[4]

What always concerned Sartre, in fact, was not so much the grammatical, syntaxic, semantic, or lexical aspects of language as such but what people *did* in the social or psychological practice of discourse (natural language being thus only one aspect of a much larger whole). What he was interested in, so far as language was at all a consideration, were such questions as the manner of its actual use, the play between its use and social relations in a larger context, its role within the production of a human history of which it is simultaneously the product. At that level, there can be little question but that Sartre was interested from the very outset of his career in matters of language practice. Roquentin's difficulty in *La nausée,* for example, could well be characterized by a series of questions: how does one grasp and *speak about* the world? how place oneself

3. This aspect was criticized very early on by Jean Paulhan in a rather slight and facile essay, "Jean-Paul Sartre n'est pas en bons termes avec les mots," *La Table Ronde,* 35 (November 1950), 9–20. If we are to believe Paulhan, it is not so much the meaning of words that floats, or is multiple, but rather our ideas about what they indicate. In his view the indicial relationship between word and object is entirely unproblematic; it simply requires deciding upon, once and for all. As a good 'Cartesian,' Paulhan saw linguistic matters as involving only the relating of a series of stable points. Sartre, drawing initially upon Husserlian and Heideggerian sources, even in so seemingly accessible a text as *Qu'est-ce que la littérature?* (though we will see that it is far less accessible than has been thought), had from the outset shifted the question of language not only away from such positivist illusions but into a far broader and more complex arena: social, political, and philosophical. (Let me add that Paulhan's 'Cartesianism' is definitely of the vulgar variety here. Descartes, had he cared, would have been appalled by so simplistic a view of language.)

4. Vološinov [Bakhtin], *Marxism,* esp. pp. 52–61, 67–71, where this view of language as a "system of self-identical linguistic norms" is submitted to an exhaustive critique. See also Chapter 2, above.

discursively with respect to other people? how communicate?[5] I realize that the term "discourse" has many, often only vague, meanings. Here, it is used as throughout this volume: *grosso modo*, in that sense derived from Michel Foucault, of an ordered practice of language and other signifying materials and processes; a systematic way of organizing propositions; a network of forms of control, ideologies, ways of seeing; a particular kind of creation of the very 'objects' capable of entering into the forms of knowledge that constitute all discourse.

In presenting this 'definition' I am well aware (the point will be of considerable importance, provoking a basic ambiguity in Sartre's thinking on the matter) that it tends to contradict Sartre's initial and long-maintained opinion that discourse, after all, grasps something that is always *already there*—whether object, phenomenon, or concept, and whether we consider the conventional language of prose or the "Cratylic" language of poetry.[6] Certainly, this *being-already-there* is only "there" insofar as it composes the material of one specific mediation among an entire set or network of mediations between the individual act and socioeconomic reality. But that is just where our initial ambiguity is to be found: language, outside the individual and marking the point where and the particular way in which that individual enters the social order, 'belongs' to everyone and comes from everyone, at the same time as it is the best means for individual expression. This is the familiar paradox of having to express the "self" in a language that is "other" and belongs to the "other." That, precisely, was Roquentin's dilemma. As Benjamin Suhl has put it, "The dilemma of language that constantly preoccupied Sartre is, after all, that of expressing our own unique experience in a language capable of expressing it to the Other."[7]

To the extent that language is always and already present—*before* individual experience, as it were—it is a material phenomenon to be confronted almost as an obstacle to be overcome. In that sense language is essentially recalcitrant, characterized by the resistance common to all matter. Sartre could thus speak, for example, of "outdated" or "lapsed signs" (*signes périmés*) for which a meaning has to be *reinvented*. On the other hand, insofar as reinvention is at all possible, language is not *simply* an obstacle. It is marked by intention, and it is the mark of an intention: I confront a system that opposes certain limits to expression, and doubtless to thought as well, but within that system I am entirely free (this, surely,

5. Rhiannon Goldthorpe has discussed this aspect of *La nausée* in association with texts from around the same period (*Sartre*, pp. 39–61).

6. Gérard Genette has examined this last matter in a surprisingly simpleminded essay, "Sens et signification: La théorie sartrienne du langage poétique," in *L'analyse du discourse / Discourse Analysis*, ed. Pierre R. Léon and Henri Mitterand (Montreal, 1976), pp. 193–99.

7. Benjamin Suhl, *Sartre: Un philosophe, critique littéraire*, tr. Jean-Paul Cottereau (Paris, 1971), p. 42.

is Wittgenstein's language game). From this point of view, the relation of the user of signs to the signifying system s/he is obliged to use is entirely similar to the child's relation to the social system initially experienced within the family.[8]

We may perhaps add that for Sartre this relation holds true for a whole series of seemingly diverse levels of being and acting and that it stretches in all directions. In the distant (and mythical) origins of language, the word as image/thing would have preceded the word as communicative instrument (this is itself one form taken by the "holistic," communal Other discussed in the preceding chapter). Next, following a dictum common to both Descartes and Freud, ontogenesis would recapitulate phylogenesis: in the growth of the individual the child would grasp and use words as some sort of material entity before considering them as "the collective means of communication."[9] Finally, in the everyday use I make of language, I must find a way through the screenlike obstacle of words as they are given so as to express myself, nonetheless, in those very words.

Discourse, the actual way of using this language, will therefore (for Sartre) always start with an intention—in the phenomenological sense of an *élan* of "pure consciousness" toward the exterior. From the outset Sartre situates himself in terms of a conception of language and the individual that will later cause many difficulties: "The efficacy and timelessness of the *cogito* is precisely due to its revealing a kind of existence defined as an unmediated presence to oneself. The word interposes itself between my love and myself, between my cowardice, my courage and myself, not between my understanding and my consciousness of understanding. For consciousness of understanding is the law of understanding's very being. That is what I will call the silence of consciousness."[10] For Sartre, thought as "consciousness," as "understanding," precedes any and all discourse.[11] Discourse may be essential inasmuch as it expresses my social being, my interpersonal life—indeed, as it actually makes that being and life possible, and is responsible for its forms. Nonetheless, I can always withdraw from the seal of discourse: "I know what I wish [will, *veux*] to express, because I *am* it in an unmediated way [*sans intermédiaire*].

8. On this question, see Fredric Jameson, *Marxism and Form: Twentieth-Century Dialectical Theories of Literature* (Princeton, N.J., 1971), pp. 216–19. The literature on this subject is evidently quite massive, not to mention Sartre's own *Les mots*.

9. Jean-Paul Sartre, "L'écrivain et sa langue" (1965), in *Situations IX: Mélanges* (Paris, 1972), p. 42. All translations from Sartre's writings are my own.

10. Jean-Paul Sartre, "Aller et retour," in *Situations I: Essais critiques* (Paris, 1947), p. 235.

11. It is the case that in *L'idiot de la famille: Gustave Flaubert de 1821 à 1857*, 3 vols. (Paris, 1971–72), Sartre no longer seems to hold this view: Gustave's consciousness is born already "alienated" in and by language (and see Sandro Briosi, *Sartre critico* [Bologna, 1981], pp. 136–80, esp. 156–59). But the very idea of such alienation of course presupposes that "something" was already there (at least potentially) to be alienated. I do not intend to suggest that the matter is at all unambiguous, even at this early stage (see, e.g., n. 2 above).

Language can resist me, can lead me astray, but I will never actually be taken in by it unless I want to be. For I have the possibility of always coming back to what I am, to the emptiness, the silence that I am, through which, for all that, there is a language and there is a world"[12]

All discourse will therefore be the social expression of an individual consciousness that exists prior to being 'set' in language. Here we may perhaps view Sartre as a successor to the two strains of linguistics criticized by Bakhtin: on the one hand, that of "abstract objectivism," whose most celebrated representative was Ferdinand de Saussure and whose *pseudos proton* was the idea of speech as rigorously individual; on the other hand, that of "idealistic subjectivism," whose original falsehood lay in the idea that this same speech might be entirely explained "in terms of the individual psychic life of the speaker."[13] Actually, of course, the difference between the two was only one of strategy, the epistemological foundations remaining the same, and the question was presented as that of knowing whether the point where individual consciousness enters the social might be studied 'objectively' or not. The first answers no, the second yes.

Clearly enough, Sartre would tend to take the side of the second strain, whose principal representatives when Bakhtin was writing were Karl Vossler and Leo Spitzer, and whose implications (at least where the study of written texts is concerned) have since been pursued by such as Roman Ingarden and, more recently, Wolfgang Iser. Clearly, too, if one assumes that individual consciousness precedes its 'setting' into language, then one can never get beyond the idea that expression is always a kind of conflict between the part and the whole, an imposition of the individual upon the social (or vice versa), a seizure of the world and the *other* by a willful subject through its enunciation. The expression of the writer's "commitment, " for example—the enunciation of the writer's social, cultural, political *situation*—will therefore always be in some way counterfeit, for it cannot but be perceived as coming after some originary separation, *écart*, that the subject is always prepared to reestablish (see, for example, the second Sartre quotation two paragraphs above). We may well feel that not only during childhood (as he wrote in *Les mots*) did Sartre conceive of the writer as a heroic knight-errant with the sacred duty of telling the world the truths about itself.

The idea that consciousness precedes the circulation of signs, in some absolute and timeless way, will flaw all Sartre's work in this area. Only hesitatingly and doubtfully, as I will try to show, does he appear to draw closer to Bakhtin's position, who wrote at one point, for instance, that *"the individual consciousness is a socio-ideological fact."*[14] The opposition

12. Sartre, "Aller et retour," p. 236.
13. Vološinov [Bakhtin], *Marxism*, pp. 61, 82.
14. Ibid., p. 12.

between these two views, the need to adjust a quasi-Cartesian view of the individual subject to the idea that the 'subject,' its experiences and activities, are essentially embedded in the social, created a contradiction impossible to resolve when put in such confrontational terms.

Bakhtin 'resolved' the difficulty by arguing that consciousness comes into existence only through the circulation of signs (concepts of priority or posteriority being entirely misleading). Consciousness exists only as participating in that social circulation of signs (the "environment," in the sense earlier given to the word, is essential not simply to the forms of consciousness and to our understanding of it but to its very nature): "*Consciousness itself can arise and become a viable fact only in the material embodiment of signs.* The understanding of a sign is, after all, an act of reference between the sign apprehended and other, already known signs; in other words, understanding is a response to a sign with signs. . . . Signs emerge, after all, only in the process of interaction between one individual consciousness and another. And the individual consciousness itself is filled with signs. Consciousness becomes consciousness only once it has been filled with ideological (semiotic) content, consequently, only in the process of social interaction."[15] Without knowing it, Bakhtin was repeating the concept forming the very foundation of C. S. Peirce's work, as well as Victoria Welby's. For them, too, consciousness and thought were entirely a matter and a product of signs, which are in their turn and by definition entirely social and communal.[16]

15. Vološinov [Bakhtin], *Marxism*, p. 11.

16. The idea that the subject is in some way a *product* of the sociocultural environment, or at least ineluctably produced *with it*, is essential to the thinking not only of those just mentioned but also to the school of Vygotsky, Alexander Luria, and their colleagues: Lev Semenovich Vygotsky, *Mind in Society: The Development of Higher Psychological Processes*, ed. Michael Cole et al. (Cambridge, Mass., 1978); *Thought and Language*, tr., rev., and ed. Alex Kozulin (Cambridge, Mass., 1986); *The Psychology of Art*, tr. Scripta Technica (Cambridge, Mass., 1971). See also James V. Wertsch, *Vygotsky and the Social Formation of Mind* (Cambridge, Mass., 1985). In a similar tradition, see V. N. Vološinov [M. M. Bakhtin], *Freudianism: A Marxist Critique*, tr. I. R. Titunik, ed. I. R. Titunik with Neal R. Bruss (New York, 1976). Discussing Freudian versions of individual creativity, Lucien Goldmann also denied the primacy of the subject: "On the other hand, if, as we believe, the creative process is situated essentially at the level of the Superego—even allowing that its energy comes from the Id—" then of course the entire evaluation and understanding of the created work will be transformed. Like Vygotsky and the others, Goldmann did not deny the existence of libidinal energies (Vygotsky's "lower" psychological processes) but merely asserted that "that element is only a *secondary* dimension of important works, situated on the level of what we call their material, their richness, and not on that of their meaning." When that element predominates, Goldmann suggested, far less interesting—because less *meaningful*—works are produced: *Situation de la critique racinienne* (Paris, 1971), pp. 12–13. Here, he came close to the Hegelian critique of Romantic literature on the grounds of its individualistic fragmentation. Many useful discussions of the subject as creature of discourse and the sociocultural environment have been appearing in relation to semiotics, psychoanalysis, and feminism. For brief expositions, see Kaja Silverman, *The Subject of Semiotics* (New York, 1983), esp. pp. 126–236; Jardine, *Gynesis*, esp. pp. 105–17; and Catherine Belsey, *Critical Practice*

The ambiguities in Sartre's thinking about language in his earlier work were indeed due to his seeing society as a place of 'semiotic' exchange (though that is certainly not the adjective he used), while simultaneously removing individual consciousness from it (though he did try to reintegrate the latter by means of a notion of the "interiorization of exteriority" and the "exteriorization of interiority"—both of which presuppose, however, that initial separation). For Sartre, the material that linguistic signs are is one of those historical phenomena into whose practice every individual must seek to enter. The individual's *use* of language is the mark of a *project* aimed at some future that will, indeed, have been changed in some essential way by this project itself but which nonetheless remains forever cut off, as it were, from its origin.[17] Nonetheless, the mediation that *serves* to bring into existence that project is at once part of the project *and* of the changed and changing history resulting from it.

That is what we need to examine here, and from the earliest texts. For Sartre's consideration of language in its relation to the individual and society has its own history, We can already see that we cannot rely on any single Sartrean text to criticize a given aspect of his thinking about discourse. We cannot, for example merely dismiss a so-called "Sartrean theory" of poetic language on the grounds that its author simply rediscovered a Cratylism long since dismissed as an invalid flummery.[18] Sartre was far too aware that linguistic phenomena cannot be treated in so facile a

---

(London, 1980), esp. pp. 52–124. On the modern analytico-referential constitution of the subject, see Reiss, *Discourse of Modernism*, pp. 58–75; and, more recently, Catherine Belsey, *The Subject of Tragedy: Identity and Difference in Renaissance Drama* (London, 1985). For a completely different notion of the self, or its very absence (in our sense), see esp. Albrecht Dihle, *The Theory of Will in Classical Antiquity* (Berkeley, Calif., 1982); and Michel Foucault, *Histoire de la sexualité* (Paris, 1984), vol. II: *L'usage des plaisirs*; and vol. III: *Le souci de soi*. With regard to the Middle Ages, see Aron I. Gurevich, *Categories of Medieval Culture*, tr. G. L. Campbell (London, 1985), pp. 42–91, 288–311.

17. In his *Idiot de la famille*, as Sandro Briosi pointed out to me, Sartre sought to situate this "Origin" in prenatal life and thus to make it almost "natural," as though it had nothing at all to do with consciousness (Vygotsky's lower processes again?). But that contrivance solves nothing; where one situates the moment of passage from consciousness-in-itself to consciousness-in-society ("for-others") matters little, as long as one continues to envisage something like consciousness existing in itself (even if one implies obscurely and ambiguously that such existence lies somehow 'before' the *cogito*). In fact, one merely obfuscates an already complicated dilemma.

18. I have in mind esp. Genette's "Sens et signification," but I think, too, of Robert Champigny's study "Langage et littérature selon Sartre," *Revue d'Esthétique*, 19 (April–June 1966), 131–48. *Situations II: Qu'est-ce que la littérature?* (Paris, 1948), was discussed there as though Sartre had published nothing before or since. Kristeva has recently reasserted some such view of "poetry" as this, claiming it to be the expression of the melancholic's inability to symbolize; using instead "melodies, rhythms, semantic polyvalences" thus assures "an uncertain but adequate grasp of the Thing [primary chora]" (*Soleil noir*, pp. 24, 109–15). Subsequent analyses of Hans Holbein, Gérard de Nerval, Dostoevsky, and Marguerite Duras aim to prove this claim.

manner, that they are sufficiently complex as to make nonsense of any nondynamic or merely bipolar model one might try to use to account fully for them.

That said, we need perhaps to observe a further anomaly concerning Sartre's thinking on language: the fact that linguists and philosophers of language have paid scant attention to his ideas on the matter. One result has been that only literary critics, by and large, have discussed the question, and they have all given preference (not altogether surprisingly) to the polemical *Qu'est-ce que la littérature?* With this text as virtually its only reference point, opinion has remained divided between those who agree entirely with Sartre's apparent acceptance of a traditional division between a referential language of prose and a poetic language using words as objects or "direct" images, and those who emphasize one or the other of these. One critic may have decided that the dilemmas of a referential language have been resolved and no longer require discussion (Paulhan). Another has concluded that Sartre's ideas on poetry evidence a naive and muddled Cratylism long since rejected (Genette). Yet another has argued that Sartre simply manipulated words in some inadmissible manner so as to maintain his polemical position (Champigny).[19] It is certainly the case that in *this* text Sartre does seem to make a sharp division between poetry's language/thing and prose's referential language. The division may be readily understood as a consequence of the broader contradiction between an idea of the word as an object of appropriation, an object *pursued, aimed at* by consciousness; and a perception of the word as the space of a (potentially) transparent mediation, the fundamental (and communal, social) *expression* of that same consciousness. Already in this text, however, we can see various forms of interference tending to invalidate so simple an opposition.

And there remains yet another consideration to be taken into account with respect to the criticisms just mentioned: the situation of *Qu'est-ce que la littérature?* itself. That is a question—twofold, in fact—at which it is worth our while to pause a moment (and in view of Sartre's own constant attention to this concept of "situation," we owe it to him in any case). The text needs to be considered first within the synchronic context of its actual publication and then within the diachronic context furnished by Sartre's own work, though the two clearly overlap and can be separated to some extent only artificially.

The first consideration serves to remind us that Sartre always had a keen sensitivity regarding his audience and that we need to think for whom the polemic was written. There can be only one clear answer: "the reader of the *Temps moderne*." That is, a well-informed reader, broadly

19. This criticism cannot be applied to Goldthorpe's admirable *Sartre*.

but not expertly interested in the matter at hand and having socialist or Marxist political and social opinions. Such a (possibly militant) reader is likely not to believe, at first shot, that poetry can have any social or economic efficacy, and Sartre will therefore need to distinguish carefully and with some precision between effective writing and ineffective writing. Because both evidently use the medium of language, he will have to make his initial distinctions at that level. I will come back to this matter shortly.

We must also be attentive to the "diachronic" axis however. In this regard, we cannot but view the text (published as *Situations II*, in the series of which there would be ten before Sartre's death in 1980) as only a single part of a much larger work whose development implies a rereading of previously published texts. Sartre frequently came back to themes and preoccupations explored in earlier writings, and we may have some difficulty understanding René Girard's criticism of those who supposedly fail to see the "epistemological breaks" in the philosopher's work. In his view, Sartre's work was characterized by a continual series of such breaks, though within some sort of continuity, and he asserts that for those critics who perceive only an uninterrupted development, "any real break, any true adventure is absent."[20]

I admit to some difficulty in understanding why a development cannot itself be an "adventure." I would rather see the relationship between the works neither as an uninterrupted development nor as a series of breaks within an overall continuity (a claim that seems to beg some questions, at the least, while having and eating its cake at once); what is to be followed is the story of some 'dialectical' relation, of a constant rereading of these writings in the light of one another. We may then be enabled to understand how *Situations II* comes to Sartre's thinking on language, as it were, from 'without.' It offers a kind of accompaniment and commentary. This text may in fact be understood as an elaborate critique of concepts of language that seek to define it once and for all (in Saussure, let us say, or the Wittgenstein of the *Tractatus*, the Russell of the *Inquiry into Meaning and Truth*, the researches of the Vienna Circle, or Charles K. Ogden and I. A. Richard's *Meaning of Meaning*) and simultaneously as a criticism of the linguistic abuse resulting from such established divisions and certitudes. I therefore use this diachronic axis to throw some light on the synchronic.

Sartre's last texts on the subject of language (I am thinking of "L'écrivain et sa langue" and, especially, the third lecture published in his *Plaidoyer pour les intellectuels*) emphasize clearly that language perceived as an instrument of communication (in the two functional forms into which

20. René Girard, "A propos de Jean-Paul Sartre: Rupture et création littéraire," in *Les chemins actuel de la critique*, ed. Georges Poulet (Paris, 1968), pp. 223–41; this quotation, p. 229.

Situations II had divided it) is simply one aspect of a far broader phenomenon. Toward the end of his life Sartre seemed to be drawing ever closer to the concept of a constant semiotic circulation, in respect to which I have already mentioned such names as those of Peirce, Welby, and Bakhtin. We will then no longer be preoccupied merely with the instrumentality of language but will need to examine the discursive (meaningful) nature of society as a whole. From this viewpoint, to divide language into two distinct and quite separate functions would be to alienate oneself from the social arena. Using the distinction made by Sartre in *Saint-Genet*, which served only to clarify the one already offered in *Situations II* four years earlier, we may insist that language should not be understood as endowed with *either* a (material, imagelike) sense *or* an (expressive, communicative) meaning. The 'two' must work together. To use language as though a choice must be made between the 'two' will be sign of a poor writer, whether in poetry or in prose: "The contemporary writer," said Sartre even later, in 1965, "the poet who professes to be a prosewriter . . . has taken *common* language as her/his material."[21]

In terms that Sartre made use of from the outset (I think of what I said with respect to the relation between individual consciousness and language), we may say that *sense* belongs to language as we find it: it is language as *matter,* as a kind of resistance that can and must be organized through *meanings.* Such meanings are the enunciating subject's "project." But that *project* can be effective, can *work,* only insofar as we take account of the limits due on the one hand to the very materiality of signs and on the other to the fact that language is not only the mark, trace, index of the *other* but the very place of my presence to that *other*—and of its to me. One could say that just as light is both wave and particle, so language is both a circuit of ever renewed meanings and a materiality already given, a resistant *matter.*[22]

That is to say that the "poetic" project of acting as though language exists only in and through its materiality (a materiality, furthermore, belonging to a nonhuman world—the world of "nausea") is a flight from the social world, a flight out of history. Sartre took the case of Jean Genet as exemplary of an *effective* use of such language that is, however, essentially destructive. He argued that to use language in this way (to be forced to do so, in Genet's case) is to turn away from the human, and that was all he wanted or needed to demonstrate in *Qu'est-ce que la littérature?* The word,

---

21. Jean-Paul Sartre, *Plaidoyer pour les intellectuels* (Paris, 1972), p. 87.

22. This comes close to Bakhtin's idea that every utterance develops a *theme* (always unique and dependent upon a social context whose parameters can never be entirely captured, an idea not unlike the Vienna Circle's *protocol*) and a *meaning: "Theme is reaction by the consciousness in its generative process to the generative process of existence.* Meaning *is the technical apparatus for the implementation of theme*" (*Marxism*, p. 100).

"poetry," as he used it in that text, was aimed less at a certain kind of literary writing than at a certain refusal of the world resulting from a resolutely traditional discursive division (recalling again those nostalgic appeals to Otherness already discussed). Even understood in such a light, however, poetry could sometimes act with a particular and peculiar kind of efficacy—though only on unique occasions and in specific situations.

Genet's case was certainly rather special because society itself had taken from him the use of its language, thus repeating perhaps a parallel social gesture aimed long since at François Villon. Such writers, Sartre argued in *Saint-Genet,* must seek elsewhere if they are to find a voice, and the result will of necessity be a kind of insult thrown in the face of the society responsible for the exclusion. Sartre asserted this to be the case as well for Arthur Rimbaud's poetry and that of the poets of the "négritude" movement. Such poetry works not because it seeks some material sense in language but because in the violent confrontation between reader and writer discourse bursts with new meanings. Yet its principal meaning is in the very confrontation itself. The black poet, Sartre wrote, chose to use poetry because prose (however complicated it may be, as we will see) was proffered as the language of white oppression. The case may be more general, but it is otherwise identical to Genet's. In the black writer's poem the white reader saw his situation in history thrown completely upside down: the "sense" of language, its materiality as "outdated signs," was *used* by the poet or—more precisely, perhaps—through the subsequent act of reading was constrained by that use so that language became *other.* The reader was forced to perceive language as if alienated from it, and it from her/him. In a word, the white reader, Sartre argued, was forced into the same situation vis-à-vis that black poetry as its poets found themselves vis-à-vis the common language of the white oppressor.[23]

Whether or not we may agree with these claims is, for the present purpose, beside the point. Sartre's preface to Léopold Senghor's anthology, published in 1948 (the same year as *Situations II*), should have served notice to those who mock what they call Sartre's theory of poetry that that so-called theory had a particular role to play in his overall philosophical arguments. It pillories any idea of language that would allow the writer to turn away from history and refuse to act in some humanly effective way: that is, to act in order to change human relationships for the better (the detail of that melioration is not my present subject). The theory does not so much define poetry as denounce a certain conception of writing. In the case of certain specific poets (Genet, Villon, Rimbaud, and Senghor and his colleagues), the *fact* of poetic language may have a role to play and

23. Jean-Paul Sartre, "Orphée noir," preface to *Anthologie de la nouvelle poésie nègre et malgache de langue française,* ed. Léopold Sédar Senghor (1948; rpt. Paris, 1969), pp. ix–xliv. On "Orphée noir," see esp. Goldthorpe, *Sartre,* pp. 176–84.

a meaning in the ongoing formation of social relationships, as attempting abrupt and revolutionary confrontation, but its play with the materiality of language is unhelpful to the steady unrolling of society, is a deliberate flight from it. It is in this sense that it differs radically from what Sartre calls "prose."

Poetic language *escapes* from the limits of the necessary exchange that is society. What the poets of négritude do is *show* those limits. Now, in a given logical or discursive space (a familiar, habitual site of exchange), as Wittgenstein put it, one may *show* those limits, but they cannot be said; in order to *say* them, one must be *within* the system allowing such saying to occur (the familiar moves of pieces on a chessboard). Limits cannot be characterized as being within; they are, to come back to the arguments of my previous chapter, the line where "carnival" begins—the line *of* carnival. Even when it works effectively in that sense, therefore, poetic language cannot participate in the development of a social exchange whose elements are already in place. That is why Genet attempts to use discourse as a form of "murder" (*assassinat*), says Sartre; of common language and its role and of the society dependent upon it.

It is thus just because poetic language is, so to speak, "marginal," that it is useless for social development (except, of course, in the extreme and unique sense just discussed). It is worth adding that Sartre never deviated from this idea. In a 1965 interview, for example, published under the title "L'écrivain et sa langue" (The writer and his/her language), he remarked that "in prose there is a reciprocity (between writer and reader); in poetry, I think the other only serves as revealer."[24] Poetry's utility was therefore situated elsewhere. The critics' mistake, it seems to me, was to view Sartre's discussion of "prose" as though he merely wished to establish some conflictual relationship with "poetry." That was not at all the case. But there was no need to wait for four years and the appearance of *Saint-Genet* to make this supposed opposition ambiguous, and even less to put off doing so for twenty-five years, until the three volumes of the *Idiot de la famille* were in print. Five years earlier in *L'être et le néant*, Sartre had written enough about language to warn us that the apparent opposition of *Qu'est-ce que la littérature?* needed to be understood in its "situation."

The informed reader (of *Temps modernes*, for example) should not have been unaware that in Sartre's view, and in a very broad sense, language—discourse—is itself *the very situation* of humanity. Any distinction at all that one might have to make within this general reality, in order to account for some particular and specific situation, should never blind us to this overall context. It will suffice, I think, to quote two passages from *L'être et le néant*, to which writers on Sartre and language have been insufficiently attentive

24. Sartre, *Situations IX*, p. 58.

(ordinarily considering, as they have, a purely "literary" context): "Language is not a phenomenon added on to being-for-others: it *is* originally being-for-others; that is, it *is* the fact that a subjectivity experiences itself as an object of the *Other*. In a universe of pure objects, language could in no circumstance be 'invented,' since it assumes at its origin a relation with another subject. And in the intersubjectivity of the for-others, there is no need to invent it, for it is already given in the recognition of the *Other*." Language, Sartre went on, is therefore neither an instinct nor an invention of the (enunciating) subject, because "it is a part of the *human condition*. It is originally the experience a for-oneself may have of its being-for-others. Later on, it is the outstripping of this experience and its utilization toward possibilities that are my possibilities: that is, toward my possibilities of being this or that for the *Other*. Language is therefore not distinct from the recognition of the *Other's* existence. The *Other's* upsurge opposite me as a look makes language surge up as the condition of my being."[25] And he adds that anything one may say of the body may equally well be said of human language. Such an assertion prefigures the experience recounted in *Les mots* (1964), the situation summarized in his "Autoportrait à soixante-dix ans" (Self-portrait at seventy; 1975), according to which he will be "at home" (*chez lui*) in language.[26]

In *Qu'est-ce que la littérature?* the distinction prose/poetry has to be understood as working in terms of this totalizing vision. The prose writer will be the person who fully accepts that situation; the poet will be the one who rejects it: "The speaker is in situation in language, invested and possessed by words. They prolong his senses. He maneuvers them from within. He feels them like his body. . . . The poet is outside language. He sees words in reverse."[27] Moreover, despite his assertion that the prose writer is a person who makes meanings (*QL*, p. 16), Sartre insisted, at least at the beginning of this text, upon the thought that prose is entirely situated in that intersubjective process that *is* language and society. Prose always awaits the reader for its meaning to be completed. And that 'completion' is a prolonging that would, strictly speaking, be infinite: "No

25. Jean-Paul Sartre, *L'être et le néant: Essai d'ontologie phénomènologique* (Paris, 1943), pp. 440, 441.
26. See Jean-Paul Sartre, *Situations X: Politique et autobiographie* (Paris, 1976), pp. 133–226.
27. Sartre, *Situations II*, p. 19; henceforth *Qu'est-ce que la littérature?* is cited as *QL*. The masculine here is Sartre's. I sought to avoid the bias in the earlier translations (since it concerned only the agreement of possessive adjectives with the noun they qualified), but it was impossible to do so here. In *QL*, Sartre's sexism became thoroughly overt: he constantly used male/female images to underline the relation between the writer and *his* public, the one as powerful and violent, the other as passive and—as a typical phrase has— requiring to be "ravished and fecundated." Equally typically, he could write: "The concrete public would be a tremendous feminine questioning, the waiting of a whole society which the writer would have to seduce and satisfy." I am indebted to Kathryn Kirkpatrick for this observation and for the examples.

prose writer, even the most lucid, understands *altogether* what he means to say; he says too much or not enough, each sentence is a wager, an accepted risk . . . no one . . . can understand a word to its very bottom" (*QL,* p. 48 n.5).

With this word "understand," we are brought back to the very ground opened up by *L'être et le néant:* language as the place where interhuman relationships occur, where they are defined and made. One cannot "understand" to any last degree, because that understanding depends upon relationships that are by definition endless. One might better say that understanding *is* those relationships. And relationships are possible because a given assertion, or utterance, is marked by a secure and in some sense *exhaustible* foundation of meaning: an utterance will project relationships that are inexhaustible, but it will nonetheless be endowed with something like a central core.[28] Writing's efficacy will therefore always depend upon, *be,* simultaneously a coercion and a constraint, an opening and a 'readiness' requiring the *other*'s activity: "The operation of writing implies that of reading as its dialectical correlative, and these two conjunct acts require two distinct agents. Out of this combined effort of author and reader will surge up that concrete and imaginary object that is the work of the mind. There is no art save for and by others" (*QL,* p. 55). Or again: "To write is to appeal to the reader that he bring about the objective existence of the unveiling I have undertaken, by means of language" (*QL,* p. 59), as Sartre writes, expressing views not at all dissimilar to those of someone like Roman Ingarden.

Unfortunately, we remain confronted at the same time by that fundamental ambiguity already mentioned: the existence of an individual consciousness somehow aloof from or to one side of this exchange, of a consciousness that in some way *precedes* 'its' use of language and *uses* words to express some phenomenon's 'presence' to that consciousness (this being a different problem, of course, from the one of that consciousness's 'presence to itself,' of which Rhiannon Goldthorpe has written with authority: see note 2). The "core of sense" that could have been nothing but a sort of stable reference point tends therefore to become *the subject's intention to speak truly.* That is how Sartre can write of words in prose: "It is not first a question of knowing whether they are pleasing or unpleasing in them-

---

28. In *Saint-Genet* (Paris, 1952), Sartre gradually complicated this presence of a somehow 'superficial' meaning (*signification*), using the opposition *sens/signification* (sense/meaning), although it is to be found in *QL*—and even to a degree, perhaps, from the beginning of his writing. "Sense," here, is not the same as that exhaustible meaning but a kind of matter/image to which even the concept of understanding cannot be unambiguously applied. It incorporates a notion of depth opposed to the 'surface' of "meaning," and it functions by analogy to the depth of consciousness. On the opposition *sens/signification*, see Goldthorpe, *Sartre,* esp. pp. 42–43.

selves, but whether they indicate *correctly* a certain thing in the world or a certain notion" (*QL*, p. 26; my emphasis). The concept, the rule of order signaled by the word "correctly" (*correctement*), clearly inflects the concept of "understanding" in a particular direction.

The circuit of exchange has been broken. The enunciating subject (individual consciousness) becomes possessed of certain thoughts that it will seek to *insert* in a process in which it does not itself fully participate. That is why we find ourselves confronting the strange idea that a thought, once thought, will remain always the same as it was—*is*, therefore—and that "a few words thrown in haste upon paper will suffice" to rediscover an idea just as it was: a thought *is* (a thing). Consequently, "to speak is to act" so as to put into operation or knowledge such and such a *particular* thought (*QL*, pp. 28–29). Sartre will then come close to being constrained to establish the writer not as provoker of a development toward some future but as conserver of some past condition.

For if the concrete expression of a thought is to become one of the chief intentions of the writer, then some value judgment will be issued upon that thought in terms of "good sense" (*bon sens*): "Do you have anything to say?"—that is, "anything worthwhile communicating." And that judgment, concludes Sartre, can be made only in terms of a "transcendent system of values" (*QL*, p. 28). Now it is clear from the mode of the question that such a system cannot be prospective; it clearly precedes the communication indicated. So it must be an already existent and generally accepted system. Accepted by whom? Who is fit to make such a judgment? Who can even request that it be made in these terms? The reader, one must suppose, of the *Temps modernes* or, more generally, an elite of those who write utterances that *do* satisfy this requirement, an elite of literary people. Such a system seems to represent, then, a step back from what we have already seen in *L'être et le néant* and later texts, for this system breaks entirely the intersubjective circuit of exchanges.

It is almost as though polemical requirements have caused a rift in Sartre's prospective thinking, have forced him, for the present, to bet on the side of the individual consciousness. Why? Possibly just to facilitate the argument that a writer can act directly upon the other in some fairly straightforward way. The fact remains that here we find once again all the elements of neoclassical, analytico-referential discourse: the individual and its thought preceding its setting into speech; the idea of verbal transparency—"since words are transparent and our look passes through them" (*QL*, p. 32); the idea of a discourse whose action is somehow secret and deceitful—a fine style "influences [the reader] imperceptibly, and you think you are yielding to arguments when [in fact] you are seduced by a charm you do not perceive" (*QL*, p. 33). This sentence, too, resumes notions of the subject's presence (in its personal style: *charme*) and of verbal transparency (*qu'on ne voit pas*).[29] Prose would thus be a commentary *upon* the social and the moral. The kind and "value" of the commentary may vary, but the basic condition will not change. Discourse (here, written), which has been the very place of the communal and intersubjective exchange, seems to have become a "parasitic" element of superstructure (*QL*, pp. 110–12).

The writer has thus become for the moment the user of particular forms (already given) of language, someone aloof, someone who is no longer within the movement of history but who comments upon it, who can select "his" situation and make "him"self in terms of that choice. One feels that Sartre does not 'want,' so to speak, to follow such a path. It results from the basic contradiction we have mentioned, which can be indicated in another fashion. 'Existentialist' thinking (if I may be forgiven the simplifying generalization) presupposed an individualism according to which humans create themselves—in relation to the other's presence, certainly, but according to personal choices on the one hand and in terms of a human nature and human relations whose *idea* does not change on the other. Marxist thinking presupposes that society's history and the individual's history form one another simultaneously and mutually, and that the writer cannot—any more than anyone else—be on one side of this formation. Whence, now, a certain number of contradictions and incoherences (almost) with respect to such relations as those of language and society, writing and writer. This last, writes Sartre, for example, is "plunged deep into his [class] surroundings" and "cannot judge them from without" (*QL*, p. 155). In that case, how on earth can there be any kind of "commentary"?

Still, Sartre was fully aware of the contradictions, and he managed to find a way out: it was not that the first analysis (that is, that the prose writer is that person who constantly shakes the circuit of intersubjective exchange and thereby provokes its development toward a "better" future) was incorrect; it was rather that *the contradiction needed situating within society as it was currently established.* His analysis was *not* prospective but merely descriptive and hence not only useful but essential for an eventually prospective analysis. If one understands literature as a participant in such an ideal circuit of exchange, then indeed it "is, in its very essence, the subjectivity of a society in permanent revolution" (*QL*, p. 195). Unfortunately, however, such a society does not yet exist, and the writer must therefore remain in that isolated situation just discussed: the writer, then, will remain a "guide," a kind of director of

---

29. On these discursive elements as neoclassical, modernist, or analytico-referential, see Reiss, *Discourse of Modernism*; also, more particularly, Reiss, *The Meaning of Literature*. Some treatment is to be found in a number of published essays; see esp. my "Power, Poetry, and the Resemblance of Nature," pp. 215–47, 269–73.

conscience for the reader (*QL*, p. 331).

An ambiguity nonetheless comes to complicate the initial contradiction—even as we begin to see how that contradiction itself can be ascribed to a particular historical moment. Sartre had appeared to argue that the relation language/intersubjectivity was ontologically founded, that it was an aspect of the human in its essence. The difficulty was that by stressing individual consciousness as foundational to all intersubjective relationships, he had undermined the possible primacy of intersubjectivity. He thus argues now that the relation between those two 'foundations' (the word itself is clearly wrong here) is an evolving one: society will evolve from the first condition toward the second. It is almost as though Sartre wanted to explain a conceptual contradiction by concretizing it in social reality: he 'relativized' two statements about the nature of society, each of which was supposed to summarize a permanent condition; in doing so, he came close to arguing that conceptual orders themselves function only within the history of a particular sociocultural environment.

But this argument, as it appears in *Situations II*, provokes another contradiction. Sartre had said that under *current* social conditions, the writer must be the person to lead the reader by the hand toward a new society. At the same time, however, he wrote that the writer must do this in a language no longer even capable of accounting for those present social conditions, to say nothing of future ones. Failing to articulate consciousness and society together, and signaling this inability in the form of an actual chronological gap between a time of individualism and one of collectivism, Sartre appears almost to introduce the possibility of a whole series of such "gaps." He will write, for example, that on the one side is "historical and psychological reality," on the other "the verbal apparatus [which] we have at our disposal" in order to speak (*QL*, p. 337). Now, the particular "realities" that became "most important" during the interwar years, for instance, escape the available "apparatus," which is capable only of expressing some past reality. And Sartre can then assert that the crisis of language (discourse, rather) "marking the literature" of that era was due to that gap.

Had he been able to avoid the initial contradiction, I think a quite different solution might have been found at this point. For in fact, of course, the discursive crisis *follows* nothing; at precisely the same time there was a social, political, and economic crisis. "History" in its entirely, if you will, was in a state of feverish tension. Why need we ascribe priority to one or the other of the areas mentioned? Clearly because the introduction of gaps, spaces, *écarts,* leaves room for the necessary (?) reintroduction of an order of cause and effect. Actually, as we can see, the priority attributed to consciousness (however complicated Sartre had made it) never ceased to pose an enormous problem.

Had he adopted straight out a position similar to Peirce's, Welby's, or Bakhtin's, Sartre would no longer have had to confront such a difficulty. In this instance, for example, if it were said that discourse 'precedes' consciousness and form, if it were acknowledged that discourse is not some superstructural 'addition' but is precisely the meaningful process permitting the articulation of history and society, then the notion of "crisis"—or, rather, of the inexpressibility of the changes supposedly symptomatic of crisis—would disappear. One could perceive the entire process as but a moment within a single development of which discourse is at once the expression and the organization. One might add that this perception does away with the opposition between base and superstructure which is essential to a rather simple Marxism and which explains both Sartre's choices here and certain ambiguities in this regard to be found in Bakhtin's published works.

Thenceforth, I think, Sartre goes off in an unsatisfactory direction—at least until some twenty-five years later and his last interviews. Indeed, one may well wonder whether the dialogue form was not itself responsible for a certain return to the idea of discourse and society as a kind of 'semiotic' or discursive circuit: dialogue signaling a sort of break with the visually and monologically oriented culture of the West established in the seventeenth century. Be that as it may, it seems clear that Sartre took the consequences of his contradiction even further in the *Critique de la raison dialectique* of 1960. In that work he conceived of "History" as first of all "this swarming of individual destinies": "the historical dialectic rests upon individual praxis insofar as this is already dialectical."[30] Such sentences serve notice that what remains important is that individual psychology (consciousness) precedes all social exchange (whatever definition this "consciousness" is given). Where language in particular is concerned, that implies in turn that social mediation is always seen initially as apart from, as a stranger to, the self who is conscious of it. Between *I* and language is all the distance to be found between *I* and all matter. Yet such a statement is in profound contradiction to that other statement according to which consciousness can manifest itself only as a dialectical partner in intersubjectivity through and in language—a relationship that is *essential*.

Here, it seems to me, Sartre was taking up yet again a neoclassical motif. It is a matter of a particular "occultation," of a particular contradiction subsisting from the very 'origins' of the discourse of possessive individualism. In Hobbes, for example, we can also find the idea that the truly human comes into existence at the same time as society itself, that humans and society 'invent' one another together, that before society

---

30. Jean-Paul Sartre, *Critique de la raison dialectique, I: Théorie des ensembles pratiques* (Paris, 1960), p. 165.

there was nothing but "brutish" monsters. Nonetheless, it was humans who established—by means of a "fiat" in every way resembling the original divine Fiat of Genesis—society. In this dual and seemingly contradictory articulation there is a kind of deceit (Sartre might well call it a "stylistic effect") whose result is to conceal the imposition of the Subject, of an originating utterance, in favor of a kind of community, a social exchange that would in theory always have been there. The contract introduced by fiat created a society of individuals under the rule of a single sovereign authority, but the idea of distributive justice fundamental to the very notion of the contract and of individual rights which supposedly directed the brutish humans toward its necessity depends upon a *prior* idea of law for which civil association is itself requisite. The gesture, whatever the difference of terms, was identical to this later one of Sartre's.[31]

Again, this contradiction—this paradox and tension—no longer exists either in Peirce or in Bakhtin. For them, consciousness and thinking are themselves signs and sign processes. Society, too, is conceivable only as a meaningful functioning of signs and by means of signs—that is, events and practices that have meaningfulness for consciousness and thinking so understood. Consciousness and society are therefore essentially mutually formative: "The only possible objective definition of consciousness is a sociological one," wrote Bakhtin, and "the logic of consciousness is the logic of ideological communication, of the semiotic interaction of a social group."[32]

For the Sartre of the *Critique de la raison dialectique*, language was less a space of exchange, a mediation, than a reference point used by two

31. The same problem remains apparent in the second volume of the *Critique: Critique de la raison dialectique, II (inachevé): L'intelligibilité de l'histoire*, ed. Arlette Elkaïm-Sartre (Paris, 1985). Here Sartre was trying to overcome the theoretical confrontation between individualist subjectivity and society conceived as a "totalization" within the process of some universal (quasi-Hegelian or Marxist) History. He sought to do so by starting his analysis not from some such construct as History, but from an examination of the actual struggles of groups in a particular sociocultural and political environment. The trouble was that such struggles were still thought of as first of all an affair of individuals or of groups conceived as individuals. The image of a wrestling match, with which Sartre begins, is extraordinarily revealing: the two wrestlers, although in a situation of "antagonistic reciprocity," seem to form an "indissoluble" whole. This whole is readily understood as an illusion, however: "There is, if you will, a single movement of these two bodies, but the movement is the result of *two* enterprises running counter to each other" (p. 13). This metaphor for struggles within society underscores their dependence upon the conscious project of some individual subject (its "enterprise"), a project no less predominant in Sartre's much longer analysis of boxing that follows. To be sure, the whole purpose of the volume was to confront just that difficulty. But Sartre went on to view the successes and impasses of Soviet totalitarian Communism almost entirely in terms of individual leaders, and that suggests serious problems in the analysis that may help explain why Sartre neither completed nor published *Critique II*. See also Introduction, n. 16, and Chapter 6, pp. 198–200—as well as Aronson's *Sartre's Second Critique*.

32. Vološinov [Bakhtin], *Marxism*, p. 13.

consciousnesses for the purpose of communicating: "Speech does not consist in sending a word into someone's brain through the ear, but in using sounds to send one's interlocutor to that word, as a common and exterior property."[33] Words are presented to us as more or less stubborn things, as objects whose surface returns the echo of a sound emitted by the Other like some kind of underwater sonar. So the word remains, as I have already suggested, essentially conservative. Matters work as though discourse were not in continual motion, as though in fact there were *no* exchange between speaker and listener, writer and reader, but simply a dubious imposition of the former—"dubious" because the imposition occurs by means of an intentional reference to a word separated from, outside the site of, both 'participants.' To change the meaning and context of words would therefore always imply a power play on the part of an enunciating subject, unfortunate but essential if the consciousness revealing itself is to achieve *its* project.

Here, too, Bakhtin takes a position diametrically opposite that occupied by Sartre. Words, argued the Russian, change quite naturally and ordinarily in the dialogical exchange of society. In this sense, something like 'polysemy' is the mark of a society's vitality, not of a loss of ability to cope with its own "crises." The word, he wrote, "is the most sensitive *index of social changes,* and what is more, of changes still in the process of growth, still without definitive shape and not as yet accommodated into already regularized and fully defined ideological systems."[34]

Granting primacy to the individual consciousness, to its confrontation with the dense materiality of words, their *matter,* results in Sartre's finding himself forced to situate elsewhere, somehow, the possibility of social communication—elsewhere, that is, than in the intentional use of words. Yet because consciousnesses are primary, and because intentional meaning corresponds to the particular project of a "total system of interiority" specific to each consciousness, any social communication proves difficult to conceive, to say the least. Sartre will therefore come up with the notion of "a fundamental communication," "a reciprocal recognition and a permanent communicative project." This appears to be an Idea, of which each utterance will be a particular manifestation: "such and such a person's present project to particularize that general communication."[35] It must surely be the low point to which Sartre was brought by the series of contradictions, paradoxes, and ambiguities just traced. Language (discourse) appears here in some astonishing manner as a kind of last resort, a makeshift, or a surplus it would be best to do without. Language, once given as a tool and instrument, participates in communication and

33. Sartre, *Critique I,* p. 18.
34. Vološinov [Bakhtin], *Marxism,* p. 19.
35. *Critique I,* pp. 180–81.

all social exchange, but the communal 'circuit,'—the exchange of meanings and actions—is now *tributary* to consciousness and so distorted from the outset.

In a rather more complicated form, all the elements of the linguistics Bakhtin criticized are to be found here; fixedness of language; separation of language from the individual using it; displacement to a 'different' level of consciousness and thought, which precede it and determine its use. It is almost as if Sartre had been trying to get around the Saussurean impasse resulting from his rejection of speech, and the Vosslerian aporia consequent upon Vossler's separation of language from the consciousness that was nonetheless taken as controlling it. Sartre's attempt to get around these difficulties did not come at all from considerations about language: speech was nothing but a specific manifestation of a "permanent communicative project." At this point, he seems to have constructed some sort of transcendental triangle of meaning: language, the system of reference for any communicative project; Speech, the Idea of interhuman communication; speech, the particularization of that Idea by means of material furnished by language and reflecting a "total system of interiority."

That Sartre set himself to building this weighty, pseudo-Hegelian system—almost the travesty of an attempt to put some sort of dialectic into the very models criticized by Bakhtin—resulted directly from the initial contradiction. All genuine dialectic must surely be excluded from any relationship set up between consciousness and a semiotic system of which it is supposed to *make use* and which is conceived of as in some way *confronting* that consciousness. The various elements remain always separated: individual thought, common language, individual speech. Up to this point, *mutatis mutandis*, this remained Sartre's system—however much broader and more complicated he sought to make it. Repeating it, he had nonetheless tried to respond to Bakhtin's basic criticism in respect to the concept of speech as individual act: "Indeed, if this were so, neither the sum total of these individual acts nor any abstract features common to all such individual acts (the 'normatively identical forms') could possibly engender a social product."[36] Each act would be nothing but a rigorously individualist slicing-up of a social whole.

Now in the act of communicating, what is primary for any listener (or reader) is discourse itself as semiotic practice (as ongoing production of interpretable meanings). Further, in the dialogue that defines any and all communicative acts, the speaker, enunciator, is in a similar situation: there is no 'origin' in consciousness as some kind of precedent—nor even separate—entity, because consciousness is always already engaged in, committed to, that dialogue. We must perforce accept Peirce's, Welby's,

36. Vološinov [Bakhtin], *Marxism*, p. 93.

Bakhtin's notion that for the human organism *qua* human there is no consciousness before signs, no thinking without signs whose functioning is by definition social. (That each interlocutor may have the experience of 'being individual' may well be the case, but that experience has to be understood, expressed to oneself as to others, thought, 'known,' in terms provided by available discourses.)

If one were to start with such a hypothesis, one could avoid from the outset the Sartrean paradoxes discussed above. One would not, for example, have to undertake the arduous task of putting thought into words, because between thought and discourse the distinction would simply be that of a part to the whole. Linguistic, discursive reality is not the totality of what the *Critique* calls "a permanent, collective, institutional communication," is not an Idea situated in some transcendental beyond the matter of language.[37] Discursive reality is the very use of that matter. Reality is discourse understood as a production of meanings and an organization of social relations. Such material organization is society and thought in a given place and time. Language is not some inert matter from which to draw some practice. "Language" exists only as discourse, only *as* those practices. Nor can the "human" be separated from them.

After the *Critique*, Sartre wrote what was—to a degree—its autobiographical echo, *Les mots*. In commenting upon the latter volume in the interview published as "L'écrivain et sa langue," he seems to retrace his steps somewhat; the contradictions do not disappear, but he tries to adjust them to one another, to take them by the horns. Words themselves seem to gain somewhat over the enunciating subject's power or that of thought. To invent new ideas or perceptions, for example, is also and at the same time to search for the means to express them: "It's a little like working in the dark; you don't really know what you're doing."[38] As Joseph Halpern wrote concerning *L'idiot de la famille:* "Ideas are still preferred to words, but meanings are no longer thought to be so easily controlled."[39] The darkening of the individual, intentional consciousness is due to a change of stress: "Every deeper plumbing of object and of self takes place from the basis of a constant *praxis* whose instrument and mediation is language."[40]

Sartre goes so far as to say that there is no distinguishing between word and idea: "The notion is not capable of being broken, of being separated from the word expressing it. The idea of thought without word makes no

37. Sartre, *Critique I*, p. 181.
38. Sartre, *Situations IX*, p. 49.
39. Joseph Halpern, *Critical Fictions: The Literary Criticism of Jean-Paul Sartre* (New Haven, Conn., 1976), p. 163.
40. Sartre, *Situations IX*, p. 53.

sense to me."[41] (He might have had the grace to say "no longer makes sense"!) If such is the case, and because words now (and always, in fact) are part of a common—even communal—place, then the primacy of the individual consciousness is disappearing. If consciousness had been an intentionality making itself present by means of "its" thoughts, then the moment when all and every thought, the process of thinking itself, is conceived as an integral part of the social arena rings the knell of such a consciousness.

It is almost as though an experiment conducted right through the *Critique* had ended in failure (at least from the viewpoint of considerations on language) and as though Sartre were starting afresh, using the other half of his contradiction. He now begins to argue there is no Being *before* the 'semiotic' relationship (although that is not his term): language and the human itself are always "in the midst" (*au milieu.*)[42] From the point of view of what is written, he now insists that the activity of reading is the "same" as that of writing: the one is strictly necessary to the other. Here we come back to some of the passages quoted earlier from *Qu'est-ce que la littérature?* In fact, Sartre seems to approach Bakhtin's idea, for example, that the novel is only a particular manifestation of an ideological field, the product of a specific semiotic context, revealing the stability or transformation of the infrastructure as a kind of "performance" but unable to *say* either—just because it is a part of that structure, and to 'say' it in the novel would be nothing but a further manifestation of that stability or change. The novel always participates, in its singular form, in the totality of sign circulation (as do, of necessity, the critical discourses seeking to speak 'about' it).[43]

What does Sartre now say about this? That I, as writer, am "part of a totalization in progress, I am the product of this totalization and, because of that, I express it entirely. But I can only express it by making myself a totalizing agent [*en me faisant totalisateur*], that is, by grasping the world head on in a practical unveiling. That is what explains how Racine produced his society (his era, its institutions, his family, his class, etc.), by producing in his works unveiled intersubjectivity." The writer's material therefore "is the world's unity constantly queried afresh by the double movement of interiorization and exteriorization or, if you prefer, by the impossibility of the part's being other than something determining the whole and blending into the whole that it denies by that determination . . . which nonetheless is made possible by the whole."[44]

41. Ibid., p. 73.
42. Ibid. p. 52–53.
43. Vološinov [Bakhtin], *Marxism*, p. 18.
44. Sartre, *Plaidoyer*, pp. 99, 101.

In "L'écrivain et sa langue," Sartre embarks upon a 'definition' of the relationship between writing and reading which one might almost believe elaborated straight out of Peirce. Indeed, Sartre's "triple mediation" recalls fairly exactly the American philosopher's triadic semiosis: "Meaning is a mediation between human and thing, that is, between signifier and signified—and inversely, between signified and signifier. The signified is a mediation between the signifier and meaning [*la signification*], meaning and the signifier. And all that can occur only through the reader, as mediation first of all between signified and signifier, and then between meaning and signifier." In Peirce, Sartre's "signifier" here would be called the interpretant; meaning would be the representamen; the signified would be the object. And the whole is in so permanent, constant, and stable a relationship that no element can even be conceived of without the others. In Peirce, the reader would be a new interpretant, and a new circuit would be always being added to the 'first.' Sartrian *praxis* is here in process of becoming Peirce's *semiosis*.[45] It echoes the 'ideal' described by Kristeva (in the epigraph to this chapter) and the aspirations already urged, as we have several times seen, by Cournot, Peirce himself, Welby, and many others. Goldthorpe has argued quite convincingly that it was Sartre's own 'conclusion' as well: "The themes of Sartre's work are dramatised in the very process of our reading. We are not the recipients of a mastered body of knowledge. And as we are also invited to disclose the mobile relations between and within his own texts, and between his own texts and those of others, the process of reflecting upon our reading of Sartre can never be complete."[46] This chapter has sought, of course, to adopt just such a process.

It follows that Sartre can now speak afresh of communicative polysemy with the same confidence as Bakhtin; such polysemy being the mark not of a crisis or a complete lack of 'security' but of a vital social development. The very early criticism put forward by Paulhan asserted that this polysemy, mistrusted by Sartre, was unimportant because in practice , meaning could be sufficiently singularly fixed. At the time, Sartre would have wished (it would appear) to have been able to say something rather similar. Now, the case is quite different.[47] Such a view is not only the mark of a bourgeoisie that always imposes *its* meanings, fixing, sealing, and control-

---

45. Sartre, *Situations IX*, pp. 56–57. For Peirce, see above, esp. Chapter 1. Sartre had earlier defined the "signifier" as the consciousness whence the intention to mean is elaborated. *Now*, this 'intention' (and the word is improper, as the quotation suggests) comes from a *praxis* always already in process. This returns us, of course, to the notion that the subject (of intention) *does not precede* but is simultaneous with the social praxis it embodies (see n. 16). Such a notion, set forth with greater clarity, might well have helped provide the beginning of a solution to the problems confronted in *Critique II* (see n. 31).

46. Goldthorpe, *Sartre*, p. 202.

47. Sartre, *Plaidoyer*, pp. 107–8.

ling them; it is also in utter bad faith, for it is in fact to alienate language from oneself—since it will 'belong' to the Other, who will seize upon it and possess it totally. At the same time, and for the reasons now seen, such a gesture is to alienate oneself from the dynamics of society itself, since discourse is fundamentally embedded in those dynamics, as they in it. To act thus would be to refuse a practice essential to being human: one's always partly new recomposing of a semiotic space that is (nonetheless) always already composed.

It is only participation in the production of society's meanings—events, actions, objects, and the rest—that can confirm my responsible (in the earlier sense of "enunciating responsibility") adhesion to the human, and my integration in a particular historical moment. That articulation of discursive function and social practice, essentially dialectic, is what one needs constantly to essay. Sartre, one is sorely tempted to say, succeeded.

The Trouble with Literary Criticism

The philosophers have only interpreted *the world, in various ways; the point is to* change *it.*

—Karl Marx, *Theses on Feuerbach*

I am somewhat painfully conscious of disability . . . [that being] the condition of expression which is only adapted to discuss the received scheme of ideas on these subjects.

—Victoria Lady Welby, *Other Dimensions*

Sartre's treatment of language and literature from the perspective of a thought seeking (eventually) to embed them in the sociocultural environment was in some ways almost marginal to his more general political, ethical, psychological, and epistemological concerns. I wish now to discuss a pair of writers who, likewise situating themselves in a generally 'Marxist' context, try to understand literature and language as fundamental within that environment. More precisely, I wish to discuss forms of critical work for which the social and political dimensions are *essential*. It seems evident that whatever problems there may be in this attempt will be most urgent for writers within a Marxist tradition.

Indeed, a rather remarkable uneasiness pervades many such works of avowedly Marxist literary criticism, as though the critic is conscious of some vague guilt at dealing with superstructural artifacts while the real work of transforming society goes on somewhere else: in the actual "struggles of men and women to free themselves from certain forms of exploitation and oppression," as Terry Eagleton (one of the most uncomfortable of these critics) has put it.[1] The first task of such criticism, therefore, has often seemed to be that of justifying or even excusing itself: by arguing, for example, that literature provides an opening upon ideologies, upon "the ideas, values and feelings by which men [*sic*] experience their societies at various times," in ways and in specifiable areas that "are available to us only in literature" (*MLC*, p. viii). The two books this chap-

---

1. Terry Eagleton, *Marxism and Literary Criticism* (London, 1976), p. vii (hereafter cited as *MLC*).

ter primarily considers present the reader with diametrically opposite responses to this challenge, as do the two *oeuvres,* by and large, of which they are a part.[2]

In Eagleton's *Criticism and Ideology* the 'shame' takes the form of an apology for its "inadequacies," for its "inconclusiveness," for the "parasitic" nature of its participation in the international debate of which general Marxist theory is composed.[3] It almost appears as though an "adequate" criticism would at once be "conclusive" (the previous chapters have already sufficiently queried that notion) and incorporated *as* production rather than as a commentary *upon* such production (there, too, earlier chapters have had their say). Clearly, at this point, Eagleton has not yet worked himself away from an essentially positivistic criticism.[4]

Such uneasiness, then, is doubly remarkable. In the first place, it proceeds transparently from a not altogether critical acceptance of a base-superstructure division, which means that one must in fact take a human productive activity (literature, and even more, its criticism) to be quite distinct from what are assumed to be the most 'basic' modes of human production. Eagleton's *Criticism and Ideology* sufficiently indicates the paradoxes into which such a division must lead—and they are 'liberal' paradoxes before being taken over by a certain kind of Marxism: one of them is immediately apparent in my first quotation, from *Marxism and Literary Criticism.* The notion of humans "experiencing their societies" runs the danger of suggesting a kind of passive reception by humans of a history that is going on elsewhere, as though the reality of society in some way pursued its development independently of those experiencing it (we saw Sartre confronting this very peril). "Understanding," writes Eagleton, "contributes to our liberation" (*MLC,* p. viii), but one is seriously tempted to ask, "Liberation from what?" if active social forces are somehow 'over there,' while we are 'over here.' In his *Marxism and Literature,* Raymond Williams addresses this kind of problem at length and with perspicacity.[5]

The uneasiness is remarkable in the second place because it tends to re-endow literary criticism with that very superiority which appeared

2. This essay was originally published as a long critical review. I have made no attempt here to incorporate subsequent work by its two prolific subjects; the issues justifying its inclusion are sufficiently indicated by the volumes discussed.

3. Terry Eagleton, *Criticism and Ideology: A Study in Marxist Literary Theory* (London, 1976), p. 7 (henceforth cited as *CI*).

4. To some degree Eagleton has sought to escape this "positivism" in such work as his *Walter Benjamin, or Towards a Revolutionary Criticism* (London, 1981), but by and large, his subsequent writing—even his most recent and rather idiosyncratic book on Shakespeare—has not really done so.

5. Raymond Williams, *Marxism and Literature* (Oxford, 1977) (henceforth *ML*). This was the problem Sartre spent a lifetime confronting (see, e.g., Chapter 5, n. 31, above, and accompanying text).

to have been dispelled as a result of the base-superstructure division. The kind of argument Eagleton proposes obviously concludes by simultaneously endowing both literature and its "scientific" analysis, supposedly provided by criticism, with a kind of shamefaced privilege: "Literature, one might argue, is the most revealing mode of experiential access to ideology that we possess," writes Eagleton (*CI*, p. 101), in an odd kind of reification of literary texts, as though they provided an object of observation whose very reading could itself avoid what he means by "ideology." Quite evidently, he is repeating a familiar commonplace of our criticism, differently expressed but identically felt, in the following assertion by Jonathan Culler, in which the language and ideology are only seemingly antithetical: "Though [literature] is clearly a form of communication, it is cut off from the immediate pragmatic purposes which simplify other sign situations. The potential complexity of signifying processes works freely in literature. Moreover, the difficulty of saying precisely what is communicated is here accompanied by the fact that signification is indubitably taking place. . . . Literature forces one to face the problem of the indeterminacy of meaning, which is a central if paradoxical property of semiotic systems."[6] And for that exact reason, one may add, it cannot be limited only to literature.

Culler's claim and Eagleton's are both versions of thoughts expressed one hundred years earlier by Matthew Arnold and Hippolyte Taine, the view of literature as the reflector and ennobler of nature and society. Or they are T. S. Eliot's ideal of the "classic" as the lively memory of imperial form borne down to us across the ages by Augustan Virgil. These are all but modernized versions of Alexander Pope's "nature still, but nature methodiz'd" or of the more generalized Enlightenment concept of literature as the reflection and the bearer of society's real ethical knowledge: seven versions, we might say, of Joseph Addison's notion of literature as the "treasure-house" of knowledge for the wit, for the educated, leisured, relatively wealthy purveyor of a dominant culture.[7] More reasons, no doubt, for unease.

All of these strike one as parallel explications of a single phenomenon. Referring to one type of discourse, they all express a particular, singular understanding of what knowing is. They do so in ostensibly different terms, but they refer unquestionably to the same dominant discursive class, to a single practice of knowledge.

6. Jonathan Culler, *The Pursuit of Signs: Semiotics, Literature, Deconstruction* (Ithaca, 1981), p. 35. The matter is pursued at greater length in my review of this volume and Culler's later *On Deconstruction: Theory and Criticism after Structuralism* (Ithaca, 1982): "On Exposition," *Canadian Review of Comparative Literature*, 12 (September 1985), 422–32.
7. All these issues are explored in my *Meaning of Literature*.

Williams, once again, takes sharp aim at the kind of claim upon which these assertions rely. In his earlier writings, up to and including his admirable *The Country and the City*,[8] a similar uneasiness was to a degree 'exorcized' by autobiography: these writings were "deeply anchored in the experience of an historical individual," as Eagleton remarks (*CI*, p. 22), though for the latter that tends to invalidate such writings as any exemplar of generalizable practice. *Marxism and Literature* deals at length with the question of the base-superstructure division (and its concomitant "scientific" privilege, both of which Williams correctly identifies as part of the debris of a "bourgeois" dualism that Marx and Engels constantly sought to jettison) and that of the subject's relation to sociohistorical process and practice, to which relates the first of the paradoxes mentioned as problematic for Eagleton.[9] In this work, autobiography is no longer a form of exorcism or a way to avoid a perhaps more vital engagement with Marxism; it has become a means of freeing Marxist criticism from a mechanical dualism and from confusions directly due to attempts to escape that dualism—by a mere complicating of the relationships between what continued to be seen as two fundamentally separate levels of activity.

Of *The Country and the City*, so sympathetic a critic as Evan Watkins was able to remark that Williams had succeeded in transforming the kind of ambivalence visible in a Georg Lukács, for example, and in proceeding from an equivocal acceptance of the dualistic model, by introducing a third term enabling him to produce "a dialectical action involving three distinct, though integrally related moments: the creative act of the individual; the critical and revolutionary awareness of the actual, shifting social relationships through which that act comes into existence; and a realization of a new form of community made possible."[10] Whether or not we find such a suggestion at all convincing in its detail strikes me as of less interest than its obvious affinity with the kind of triadic process that Peirce posited and that Chapter 3 has already tried to 'extend' toward discursive criticism. The first "moment" advanced by Watkins is Peirce's representamen (a "reaction" to actual, social relationships); the second is his object (the 'referential' field to which the individual creative act reacts); the third is his interpretant, produced from that exchange and ready to become itself the representamen and/or object of subsequent triadic process—or even, perhaps, a provisionally halted habit ("final interpretant"): here, of course, a new social and cultural formation.

At the end of *Marxism and Literature,* Williams makes Watkins's interpretation (and to some degree, my further gloss) explicit:

8. Raymond Williams, *The Country and the City* (1973; rpt. St. Albans, 1975).
9. For the former, *ML* passim; for the latter, *ML*, pp. 128–35, 192–98, 206–12.
10. Evan Watkins, *The Critical Act: Criticism and Community* (New Haven, Conn., 1978), p. 153.

Creative practice is thus of many kinds. It is already, and actively, our practical consciousness [consciousness as inherent in, produced from, and constantly related with material activity and production]. When it becomes struggle—the active struggle for new consciousness through new relationships that is the ineradicable emphasis of the Marxist sense of self-creation—it can take many forms. It can be the long and difficult remaking of an inherited (determined) practical consciousness: a process often described as development but in practice a struggle at the roots of the mind—not casting off an ideology, or learning phrases about it, but confronting a hegemony in the fibres of the self and in the hard practical substance of effective and continuing relationships. It can be more evident practice: the reproduction and illustration of hitherto excluded and subordinate models; the embodiment and performance of known but excluded and subordinated experiences and relationships; the articulation and formation of latent, momentary, and newly possible consciousness.

Within real pressures and limits, such practice is always difficult and uneven. It is the special function of theory, in exploring and defining the nature and variation of practice, to develop a general consciousness within what is repeatedly experienced as a special and often relatively isolated consciousness. For creativity and social self-creation are both known and unknown events, and it is still from grasping the known that the unknown—the next step, the next work—is conceived. [*ML*, p. 212]

Wanting to express the same practice, Eagleton remarks that a Marxist criticism, which "analyses literature in terms of the historical conditions which produce it," must at the same time "be aware of its own historical conditions" (*MLC*, p. vi). The difficulty is that Marxism must needs see such awareness as itself an ongoing production of what Williams calls "practical consciousness" and that it must therefore be inscribed in the very production of the critical text. Historical materialism cannot simply contain—as Eagleton asserts, using a recognizably Althusserian turn of phrase—"a scientific theory of the genesis, structure and decline of ideologies" (*CI*, p. 16), as though such "ideologies" were in some sense self-contained and discrete objects, separated from the distanced and aperspectival science capable of understanding them (a matter to which I return in Chapter 9).

It is therefore distinctly revealing that Eagleton should criticize as a fundamental misunderstanding Williams's rejection of the base-superstructure equation on the grounds that it does not correspond to lived experience: "No one, surely, ever took the base/superstructure distinction to be a matter of *experience*."[11] The point is that orthodox Marxism *acts* as

11. *CL*, p. 22. Williams's rejection of the base-superstructure distinction to which Eagleton is here referring can be found in his introduction to *From Culture to Revolution*, ed. Terry Eagleton and Brian Wicker (London, 1968), p. 28. A more elaborate and nuanced presentation of Williams's arguments on the matter is his "Base and Superstructure in Marxist

though it were. And a further point, surely, is that once the conceptualization is available, it *should* in fact become a matter of experience. That it
does not and has not done so is evidence of an error in the analysis—one
that Marx tried to take into account, for example, in the rejected introduction to the *Grundrisse* (1857) and the much earlier *Economic and Political
Manuscripts of 1844* (from which Williams frequently quotes in *Marxism
and Literature)* and that Engels increasingly attempted to parry.[12] Eagleton's weakness is that he strives to maintain division as foundational while
recognizing the paradoxes into which it perforce conducts him. That is
tantamount to ignoring the error. The reason such conceptualization
should, if 'correct' (that is, functionally, practically effective and productive), become a matter of experience is that it would have become
an element of practical consciousness, which itself inheres in the material
activities of society. That is precisely what Williams's work has been
striving toward.

These introductory remarks indicate, therefore, that the fundamental
urge of *Criticism and Ideology* on the one hand is quite different from that
of *Marxism and Literature* on the other; indeed, the difference holds for the
total projects of their respective authors as evidenced in their published
work to date. Eagleton wants to show us what a Marxist literary criticism
is and how it should set about its "task": *Criticism and Ideology* is essentially
prescriptive. Using a technique familiar to us from earlier works,
Williams's project in *Marxism and Literature* is first of all to situate Marxist
literary criticism both its own tradition and the broader Western tradition
within which Marxism distinguishes itself as a fundamental turning
point.[13] To do this, he begins with an analysis of some of the major
general concepts involved—"culture," "language," "literature,"
"ideology"—which are brought into Marxism from the broader tradition.
From here he can advance to a review and a critique of many of Marxism's essential concepts—"base and superstructure," "determination,"

Cultural Theory," originally published in *New Left Review,* no. 82 (November–December,
1973) and reprinted in his *Problems in Materialism and Culture: Selected Essays* (London, 1980),
pp. 31–49.
  12. Karl Marx, *Grundrisse: Foundations of the Critique of Political Economy (Rough Draft),* tr.
Martin Nicolaus (Harmondsworth, 1973), esp. pp. 109–11. The *Economic and Political Manuscripts of 1844* are readily available in Karl Marx, *Early Writings,* tr. Rodney Livingstone and
Gregor Benton (Harmondsworth, 1975), pp. 279–400.
  13. I think here of such writings as Raymond Williams, *Culture and Society, 1780–1950*
(London, 1958); *The Long Revolution* (London, 1961); *Modern Tragedy* (London, 1966);
Drama from Ibsen to Brecht (London, 1968); and *The Country and the City.* Since then, Williams
has broadened his field of inquiry to culture and society in a very wide sense, and has
become increasingly more theoretical—at the same time as he becomes increasingly familiar
as a novelist.

"productive forces," and so on—showing to what extent they break with the tradition, to what extent they mark a radical production of emergent elements and structures taken from the tradition, and to what extent they remain caught within its hegemony. He can then go on to the second part of his project, which is an effort to offer a radical alternative direction within Marxism to the mechanistic models still very familiar both in English-language and Continental Marxisms.

Emergent structures of practical consciousness, remarks Williams at one point (contrasting them, following Antonio Gramsci, to the dominant and the residual), depend on "finding new forms or adaptations of form" (*ML*, p. 126). That is really what *Marxism and Literature* is all about, and that is why its author combines an analysis of the central concepts as constituted with an inquiry into the practical process of their establishment (by examining the development of the terms used to embody them, of the social developments accompanying them, of the conceptual contradictions and the actual discussions to which they give rise, and so on). Williams's project, therefore, is to provide a kind of *exemplum* of the creative process of which he speaks in the concluding remarks quoted above (*ML*, p. 212).

The first difficulty for a Marxist criticism of the kind Eagleton seeks to prescribe is that our culture has endowed literature certainly since the second half of the seventeenth century (though Williams places it in the eighteenth), with a privileged status that the orthodox (or any other) Marxist cannot accept and remain intellectually honest—partly because literature, both as object produced (for its author) and as object consumed (for its reader) becomes simply another fetishized and alienated commodity, partly because all superstructural systems ("environments," as Mikhail Bakhtin has called them) must inherently be at the same level, and partly because such privilege is the mark of literature as the (alienated) possession of the class that owns the means of production.

Eagleton, of course, takes due note of this, both when he criticizes Williams for not sufficiently acknowledging, in his *Culture and Society,* the fact that culture is itself an ideological term (which strikes me as an odd commentary upon a work that set out precisely to show the growth, meaning, and implications of that concept between 1780 and 1950, though it is the case that neither there nor indeed until *Marxism and Literature* did Williams use the analysis to question his own critical project), and when he remarks that what is "at stake" is the "ideological significance" of "Literature"—though he proceeds to define the last, in the traditional terms of analytico-referential discourse, as "that process whereby certain historical texts are severed from their social functions, defined as 'literary,' bound and ranked together to constitute a series of 'literary traditions' and interrogated to yield a set of ideologically presupposed responses" (*CI*, p. 57). That particular definition is itself ideologically defined: there appear to be few societies without "literature" of some kind, but there may well be any number of different roles served by those literatures, depending on their overall sociocultural environment. Our Enlightenment tended to conceive of literature in the terms Eagleton uses to define it (whether overtly, consciously, or not), but one should avoid even the hint that such definition is at all generalizable.

Now while Eagleton does acknowledge the problem, he does not incorporate that acknowledgment in his own practice, as his constant and undefined use of the term "aesthetic" suggests. Because he accepts the basic dualistic model, he reinscribes into his own project many of the same presuppositions that underlie the bourgeois literary criticism whose support of "the dominant aesthetic and ideological formations" (however contradictory) he starts by criticizing (*CI*, p. 13). That is, he reproduces "in an altered form," as Williams remarks of earlier Marxist views of culture, "the separation of 'culture' from material social life, which had been the dominant tendency in idealist cultural thought" (*ML*, p. 19). The consequence of such a view is to miss "the concept of culture as a constitutive social process."

Eagleton does not, therefore, pose any genuine question as regards "literature." His initial project, he does assert, is aimed at its criticism: "to pose the question of under what conditions, and for what ends, a literary criticism comes about" (*CI*, p. 17). This is indeed a "branch" of criticism, and the question is important. But posed in such a manner, it avoids its own 'ground.' For it is not simply literary *criticism* but also literature that "comes about." To be sure, it is not just a matter of "the existential fact of the text" inasmuch as one can even conceive of such a notion, but neither is it merely, as Eagleton asserts, that criticisms "produce the literary text as their object, as the text for-criticism" (*CI*, p. 17). Clearly, it is that what one means by literature far surpasses the arena of any technical criticism that may seek to produce it and that is logically posterior to it. In fact, a professional and semiprofessional criticism in the modernist sense of the term emerged *at the same time* as did a particular concept of what literature is and does. The first question should be put to that simultaneous emergence—as it is by Williams. Eagleton, however, sees literature as a constant process, some of which "needs" criticism, some of which does not (*CI*, p. 17).

That view makes for a serious ambiguity. If the material base is always fundamental (see *MLC*, pp. 3–5; *CI* passim), then literature is at one level in the superstructure, while its criticism belongs at another level. Moreover, such an idea also means that the superstructural system (or process) of literature is in some sense permanent and independent of changing material conditions,[14] while that of criticism is subject to varying "ideological" determinants, which *do* change as the base develops. Literary criticism can thus be equated with the writing of history, with psychoanalysis, with the study of political economy and of falling bodies and so on (*CI*, pp. 17–18). Literature as the object of such criticism, however, has then to be equated with the *objects* of history (societies and their development, say), the objects of psychoanalysis (the human psyche and its functioning), the objects of the natural sciences (nature and its laws). Furthermore, the privilege of literature, to a great degree, has consisted in its supposed ability itself to engage all those 'objects' in some way or other (Addison's "treasure house").

This, with a certain number of complicating clauses, is the view Eagleton adopts in practice. And yet it is clear that the 'objects' in question (including what we call "nature") become a part of practical consciousness simultaneously with their study—not to mention that they become a part of the material base in diverse ways, the most obvious of which is the conception and production of experimental tools and instruments of technique. These in turn profoundly alter material social activity, both as commodity to be produced and as means of production, and change the practical consciousness thoroughly embedded in the whole process. In the present instance the same could easily be shown to be true of communication tools and techniques, including the printed material commonly called literature.

Criticism, writes Eagleton, needs to be inserted into its ideological history. But so too does literature. I have argued elsewhere that " 'Shakespeare' is the outcome of the historical development of a class of discourse [a particular hegemony] as well as but before being a particular set of texts written at a particular time and place, now available for interpretation."[15] It is not simply, I repeat, that literary criticism "becomes a crucial ideological instrument" (*CI*, p. 19); it is that literature does so as well.[16] Actually, of course, this last statement is itself a dubious proposition (as Eagleton sometimes recognizes), for it has no genuine meaning unless one has accepted the dualism already mentioned. Indeed, it is not enough to note that literature is included in the material base as a particular mode of production, even if one endows it with its very own acronym, "LMP" (e.g., *CI*, pp. 51–53). It is a visible form of practical consciousness that is incorporated through and through in material practice.

14. This, of course, was a problem for Marx, expressed in the introduction to the *Grundrisse*, that Eagleton does not in the least resolve (*MLC*, pp. 10–13).

15. Timothy J. Reiss, "The Environment of Literature and the Imperatives of Criticism: The End of a Discipline," *Europa*, 4, no. 1 (1981), 43.

16. Cf. *ML*, pp. 45–54.

The problem, that is, lies in the very notion of ideologies as superstructural, however complex (once again) their relations may be said to be. The dualism such a notion sets up is inescapable. So too, apparently, is the privilege thus produced: "The aesthetic is for a number of reasons a peculiarly effective ideological medium [cf. *ML,* pp. 158–64]: it is graphic, immediate and economical, working at instinctual and emotional depths yet playing too on the very surfaces of perception, entwining itself with the stuff of spontaneous experience and the roots of language and gesture" (*CI,* p. 20). With regard to the discursive class dominant from the seventeenth to the twentieth century, all this may be said to be "true." That is why such loaded terms as "graphic," "immediate," "economical," "instinctual and emotional depths," "surfaces of perception," "spontaneous expression," and "roots of language" appear unquestionably meaningful. For us, Eagleton's intended readers, they are. But they are meaningful because every one of these terms refers to a set of concepts developed in and by the "neoclassical," "modernist," "analytico-referential" model, by the bourgeois hegemony, if you prefer: self and other, inside and outside, depth and surface, nature (spontaneity, instinct, and emotion) and culture (language and order), immediate and mediate. The dualism on which they rest is readily apparent. They are precisely the elements composing the concept and practice of possessive individualism, of the control of the other, of culture as a particular kind of progress.[17] They organize a "world view" depending upon a continuous expansion of a domain controlled by the individual, by means of an activity at once spontaneous and ordered, taken as the common characteristic of humankind (though within this culture the emphasis—and more—is always placed on *man*kind) and organized by a rationality equally general, equally common, always and everywhere the same.[18]

Eagleton correctly remarks that the "aesthetic" for these reasons can "proffer itself as ideologically innocent" (*CI,* p. 20), in spite of its being-in ideology, for it does indeed correspond to a seemingly immediate human experience. The trouble, of course, is that such "real experience" is itself a part of the dominant ideology. What Eagleton thus fails to consider is that that experience, to say nothing of the account rendered of it ("aesthetic" or other), is also very far from innocent. Contrary to what he appears to assume, that account of human experience—and doubtless the experience as well—grew with the growth of that literature (I am not suggesting that the one *caused* the other, in any simple sense, but that they are a part of the ongoing process of what we recognize as "our" socio-

17. The reference here is to Crawford Brough Macpherson, *The Political Theory of Possessive Individualism: Hobbes to Locke* (Oxford, 1962).

18. Williams takes up these matters in *ML;* with respect to the "aesthetic," see esp. pp. 151–57, 159–62.

cultural environment). For in the sense Eagleton ascribes to the term "innocent," *no* experience can be conceived of that would be in any way "pure" and "spontaneous." As Williams and others have correctly observed, experience is practical consciousness, and that is always producing and being produced within the material activity of society.[19]

The various notions with which Eagleton here surrounds the "aesthetic" seem to correspond to that level of "General Ideology (GI)" in which literature (with "Aesthetic" and "Authorial Ideologies": "AI" and "AuI") is to be situated; again the dangerous consequences of the division are only too apparent. Clearly, literature and the aesthetic in general are conceived of as in some way separate from the "real social form which provides [their] material matrix." This form is the "*ultimate* signifier of literature, as it is the ultimate signified" (*CI*, p. 72). Saying this, Eagleton finds himself obliged to bring in a quite familiar notion of mediation, though he describes it as a mediation through, in, and of complex ideological formations, with "fiction" as "the term we would give to the fullest self-rendering of ideology" (*CI*, p. 77). This attempt either to render the notion of mediation more complex or to incorporate it somehow in the "formations" (and thereby to imply that it is not really a 'mediation' at all) is really little more than a means of concealing the divisions that have been introduced between the "material matrix," "ideological formations," "literary text," "Authorial Ideology," "General Ideology," and the rest. Nor is it any way out of them to assert, for example, that "AuI, then, is always GI as lived, worked, and represented from a particular overdetermined standpoint within it." (*CI*, p. 59).

Williams observes that the concept of "overdetermination" has been introduced in order "to avoid the isolation of autonomous *categories* but at the same time to emphasize relatively autonomous yet of course interactive practices" (*ML*, p. 88). For such purposes, it is a more useful concept than the more merely linear causal one of "determination" but can in turn be readily "abstracted to a *structure* (symptom), which then, if in complex ways, 'develops' (forms, holds, breaks down) by the laws of its internal structural relations." It is just because Eagleton wishes to set in place (necessary) "categories for a materialist criticism" (*CI*, pp. 44–63), I would suggest, that he confronts just such a situation. Once again, Williams may be given the last word: "Any categorical objectification of determined or overdetermined structures is a repetition of the basic error of 'economism' at a more serious level, since it now offers to subsume (at times with a

---

19. I think here of, e.g., Lucien Goldmann's concept of "world view" (explored with what still seems to me convincing assurance in his *Le dieu caché* of 1955), of Antonio Gramsci's concept of "hegemony," or of Williams's own concept of "structures of feeling" as presented in *ML*, pp. 128–35 (though I think the phrase may actually come from Goldmann).

certain arrogance) all lived, practical, and unevenly formed, and formative experience" (*ML*, pp. 88–89).

That is what happens to Eagleton. It is why he finds himself forced to repeat a variant of the concept of literature and the aesthetic as reflection, representation, or reproduction of reality. Of course, he himself states that this is a misconception, but to assert that "the text strikes us with the immediacy of a physical gesture," not providing us with the image of an "actual state of affairs" but rather revealing "the *nature* of the environment which could motivate such behaviour" (*CI*, p. 75), is hardly to avoid the mirror concept (however "fractured" and "fissured" the mirror may be). The text, avers Eagleton, "destructures ideology . . . in order to process and recast it in aesthetic production" (*CI*, pp. 98–99). Literature, that is, *defamiliarizes* ideology and makes it more "accessible" to consciousness. At the same time, criticism will "show the text as it cannot know itself" (*CI*, p. 43). For criticism too is essentially a matter of (distinctly privileged) defamiliarization: "The function of criticism is to refuse the spontaneous presence of the work—to deny that 'naturalness' in order to make its real determinants appear" (*CI*, p. 101). Once again, after one has got past the difference in language, how is this argument to be distinguished from what we saw in Jonathan Culler, or from the claims made by T. S. Eliot or F. R. Leavis? How dissimilar is it from Arnold, Taine, Pope, Addison, Samuel Johnson, or even John Dryden, for the matter of that, who long since spoke of the need to discriminate between the fundamental rules governing all literary texts and the superstructural determinants that vary according to the specific cultural conditions in which a given work is produced?[20]

Indeed, Williams is able to show at length how these concepts are simply repetitions, in a more 'radical' form, of the separations inherent in liberal bourgeois concepts of knowledge and of the responses provided within the world view they produced (*ML*, pp. 95–100, 191–92). For it is ultimately an evasion to say of Joyce, for example, that the internal contradictions of his art are "a *production*, not a reflection, of the ideological formation into which Joyce as historical subject was ambivalently inserted—a production which, by putting that ideology to work, expresses its framing limits" (*CI*, p. 155). One might fruitfully compare this claim with Georg Lukács's comparison of Joyce with Thomas Mann: the second, says Lukács, expresses a "dynamic and developmental" view of the world, to which a dialectic of individual and society, of intellect and praxis, is

---

20. The reference here is to *The Grounds of Criticism in Tragedy* (1679), where Dryden argues that the rules of tragedy should be copied from the Ancients, "those things only excepted which religion, customs of countries, idioms of language, etc., have altered in the superstructures": *Selected Criticism*, ed. James Kinsley and George Parfitt (Oxford, 1970), p. 165. See, too, my *Tragedy and Truth*, pp. 6–7.

fundamental, while the first echoes the "static and sensational" decaying individualism of late "bourgeois capitalism." Or we might compare it with Umberto Eco's very different but revealing exploration of *Finnegans Wake,* in which that novel's techniques and intentions are interestingly linked (and in considerable detail) with some implications of relativity theory.[21]

Such inquiries are more or less complex repetitions of what criticism in our time has always done (and by "our time," I mean the period since the late seventeenth century). Nor are they very different from what Eagleton is requiring—at least as regards their epistemological assumptions. For no criticism ever maintained that art was a pure reflection of anything; that is precisely why criticism was "necessary" (a "need" Eagleton repeats: *CI,* p.17). And do we need reminding that modern criticism and modern literature were coeval? Eagleton's argument about Joyce intends to show how that author's work may be taken as *exposing* the limits of an ideology. It does so because criticism *shows* it to do so. Reflection at a double remove still remains reflection.

For Eagleton as for so many of his predecessors, then, literary criticism endures essentially as a form of truthful knowledge, able to abstract both literature and itself from "ideological" determinants. Criticism is the *science* that will reveal the hidden ideological and aesthetic determinants of literature. In theory, criticism is also bound to and by these constraints; in practice, its self-awareness releases it from them. To a considerable degree, Eagleton has taken over Louis Althusser's concept of ideology as a (false) system of "image and representation" (*CI,* p. 107; a matter on which he congratulates Matthew Arnold!), and, like him, has opposed it to "science" as the true system of knowledge, enabling in its turn a correct social praxis.

Quite evidently, part of the difficulty here is that this concept of ideology is itself the ideology of a particular "episteme." It is itself the mark of a particular hegemony and scarcely helps one escape from it. Indeed, to assert that ideologies are systems of representation, or even sets of potentially affective mythologies that might come to permeate lived sociocultural experience (*CI,* pp. 108–9), is to come close to affirming that ideologies exist only within a hegemonic system in which the concept of representation on the one hand and of concealed dominance on the other are primary compositional elements. Awareness of this fundamental nature of ideology would then allow the critic to assert its profound, if complex, relationship with literature (not at all dissimilarly 'defined,' after all), and to assume that such distanced awareness makes the critic's own practice in some way "innocent," denials to the contrary (*CI,* p. 17). In

21. Georg Lukács, "The Ideology of Modernism," in *Realism in Our Time: Literature and the Class Struggle,* tr. John and Necke Mander (New York, 1971), pp. 17–46; Umberto Eco, *Opera aperta* (Milan, 1962).

accepting the Althusserian division between ideology (concerned with *practice*) and science (concerned with *knowledge*), Eagleton is able mutely to propose that a science of literary criticism (*his,* at least) can be ideology-free.[22]

Indeed, a further major dilemma confronted by Eagleton, and by a significant part of Marxist literary criticism as a whole, is that in hoping to break with "its ideological prehistory" (*CI,* p. 43), it acts as though it were placing *itself* outside or beyond practice, as though it could innocently fill in those 'holes' in the literary text that reveal the latter's relationship with the various supposed levels of ideology and, through them, with the modes of "real" production (*CI,* pp. 44–63). The function of criticism, Eagleton writes therefore, "is to install itself in the very incompleteness of the work in order to *theorise* it—to explain the ideological necessity of those *'not-saids'* which constitute the very principle of its identity (*CI,* p. 89). Showing the text as it cannot know itself, making "its object . . . the unconsciousness of the work" (*CI,* p. 89), criticism *makes* the text into a mirror of ideologies—or, more exactly, into a screen placed before them, which is simply to reverse the metaphor. At the same time, it gives criticism something to do: it has the task of silvering the screen so that it will tell us something. Literature may be a privileged form of communication, but criticism is both privileged *and* scientific: "It is not [the critic's] fault that he has to be so arrogant," wrote I. A. Richards, "His claim to be heard as an expert depends upon the truth of these assumptions."[23] Eagleton's theoretization aims to place literary criticism in the domain of science, 'across from' ideology, as it were, just as ideology itself is 'across from' the "material matrix."

The literary text is taken as a practice providing access to ideologies because, as a practice, it is replete with their presence: a presence, we have seen Eagleton insist, marked by absences in the text. The literary critical text, therefore, is the science able to provide knowledge of the meaning of those absences. It is small wonder that Eagleton is unable to define his much-used term "aesthetic." Doubtless it indicates an absence in his own text: in order to speak of literature as a privileged type of discourse (the one providing us with "the most revealing mode of experiential access to

22. Louis Althusser's best-known writing on this subject is "Idéologie et appareils idéologiques d'état (Notes pour une recherche)," in his *Positions (1964–1975)* (Paris, 1976), pp. 67–125. Actually, from Eagleton's point of view a more interesting and subtle distinction, especially with regard to the literary (novel) text, is that suggested by Lukács between narration and description, already latent in his early *Theory of the Novel,* tr. Anna Bostock (Cambridge, Mass., 1971), and more specifically explored in *Realism in Our Time.* See, too, "Art and Objective Truth," in Georg Lukács, *Writer and Critic and Other Essays,* ed. and tr. Arthur D. Kahn (1970; rpt. New York, 1971), pp. 25–60. The matter of the ideology/science opposition receives further attention below in Chapter 9, esp. pp. 267–69.
23. Richards, *Principles of Literary Criticism,* p. 37.

ideology"), he is forced willy-nilly into practicing an essentially liberal criticism, however ostensibly radical its form. In its own practice it ignores the fact that like 'culture,' the "aesthetic" is a category within a particular hegemony.

Like others before him, therefore (I think, for example, of Pierre Macherey, Jeremy Hawthorn, or Herbert Marcuse), in his attempts to achieve "rigorous" formulations and to avoid the "hypostatization" of the diverse ideologies as sets related only extrinsically to one another (*CI*, p. 54), Eagleton hypostatizes criticism itself: it becomes the 'scientific meta-discourse' (furnishing, in Marcuse's case, a "social conscience" for bourgeois capitalism) so beloved of a diversity of contemporary positivisms.[24] That is probably why, in his chapter concerned with the practical analysis of literary texts (*CI*, pp. 102–61), he is determined to show that the "major fiction," "the finest achievements of nineteenth-century realism" in England (*CI*, p. 125)—the novels of Jane Austen, the Brontës, Charles Dickens, George Eliot, and Thomas Hardy—were produced just because those authors were "ambiguously placed within the social formation."[25] Their art (and for analogous reasons, later that of Henry James, Joseph Conrad, T. S. Eliot, Ezra Pound, James Joyce, D. H. Lawrence, and W. B. Yeats) produced ideological conflicts in the text that reveal their ambiguous situation in a developing and conflictual class situation. Their art corresponds, he argues, to "the historical self-division of bourgeois society" (*CI*, p. 129).

The problem in that kind of assertion is that Eagleton has earlier (in his first chapter) characterized literature *generally* by its internal absences and contradictions, and it is hard not to see the one as a hypostatization of the other. Has he not simply generalized a particular interpretation of nineteenth-century fiction (the familiar "greats," let it be noted in passing) into a definition of the aesthetic as a whole? The answer appears to be yes. When he comes, then, to the question of value (*CI*, pp. 162–87), he suggests that the Marxist must inevitably view as the "greatest literature" those texts that analysis shows to reveal the contradictions "between the forces and social relations of material production" (*CI*, p. 175). Now while it may be correct to view class society as essentially conflictual, that particular contradiction marks a moment of very specific transformation: that of a general change in modes of production. Eagleton seems to be

24. Pierre Macherey, *Pour une théorie de la production littéraire* (Paris, 1966); Jeremy Hawthorn, *Identity and Relationship: A Contribution to Marxist Theory of Literary Criticism* (London, 1973); Herbert Marcuse, *The Aesthetic Dimension: Toward a Critique of Marxist Aesthetics* (Boston, 1978).

25. Once again, here, one might do well to think of Georg Lukács's analyses of Walter Scott and Balzac: esp. for the former, see *The Historical Novel*, tr. Hannah and Stanley Mitchell (London, 1962); for the latter, chapters in *Studies in European Realism* (New York, 1964).

inscribing it as a permanent condition of human societies and, simultaneously, as *the* characteristic of "major" literature. He has characterized literature, that is to say, in terms of a particular hegemony, while dealing with it as though it were a relatively invariant form of access to ideologies—sometimes "needing" criticism, sometimes not (which would of course be the case even if a notion of conflict were taken as broader than that of a specific transformative moment).

Eagleton is certainly right in asserting a concept of value to be essential. It is in any case unavoidable. As Evan Watkins has remarked: "characterization and evaluation are inseparable," and they refer in some way— especially evaluation—to the extent to which the work produces a choice and permits the clarification and development of social and personal relationships. One might well prefer to Eagleton's idea of a value judgment based on a rather static concept of class conflict the formulation proposed by Watkins: "Genuine critical value judgments thus become reciprocal. Just as Faulkner [in *Absalom, Absalom!*] can judge Shreve only to the extent that Shreve's creation is allowed to judge Faulkner in return, so it is that the critic also allows the poem to judge him" (Watkins is referring here to analyses of his own that precede the remark).[26] Eagleton's value judgment becomes, rather, "great is the literary work that reveals class conflict": that is to say, it is an essentially abstract evaluation of a work in terms of an avowed tradition, not a practical judgment in terms of its role in present practical consciousness. Eagleton's "judgment" depends on a particular hegemonic moment from which his whole argument would like to recoil but seeks to escape in vain. Value, as Watkins and Williams have it, is a matter of fruitfulness in moving "practical consciousness," not a matter of judging "major" and "minor" texts (in a style confirming Richards's dictum about the critic's unavoidable arrogance). Eagleton does on one occasion approach the former idea, in a phrase tending, however, to contradict his own actual practice. A materialist aesthetics, he writes, must grasp "form as the structure of ceaseless self-production, and so not as 'structure' but as 'structuration' " (*CI*, p. 184). As Watkins puts it, form should be conceived as the dialectical "activity of mediation between personal and social."[27]

To some extent, Eagleton's book wants to respond to the 'mechanical materialism' of much orthodox Marxist criticism, to a simplistic economism that views the economic base as entirely determining all other human activities and that tends to view it (theoretically) as an object, not an activity. Eagleton himself makes this point by means of a reference to Williams's objection to such an understanding (*MLC*, p. 54). In reply, he

26. Watkins, *Critical Act*, chap. 8, "Criticism and Community: On Literary Value," pp. 213–36; these quotations from pp. 213, 217.
27. Ibid., p. 185.

makes much use of such notions as "overdetermination" to indicate that ideological processes are not in simple one-to-one relation with the base and with each other; "historical materialism" to argue that the base is a process, not an object; "mediation" to assert that the text is not a mere "reflection" of an objectified base. These notions and arguments enable him to introduce a rather more sophisticated version of what is essentially the same conceptualization: the literary text does not reflect the real base but allows us access to the ideologies that are in a highly mediated, over-determined relation to that base. Williams has an easy time taking this kind of attempt apart. He shows the very idea of separated and linearly produced effects (and Eagleton's model, though Williams does not refer to it, remains fundamentally of such a kind, whatever complexities he may have sought to introduce) to be a generalization of capitalist modes of production. To take over such ideas in any form is therefore to repeat the claims of "bourgeois" ideology (*ML*, 92–94).

That is no doubt why Eagleton is able to remark, apparently without asking any fundamental question, that "even those only slightly ac-quainted with Marxist criticism know that it calls on the writer to commit his art to the cause of the proletariat" (*MLC*, p. 37). To be sure, his reference is ironic, and he is rejecting simplistic versions of this view as Stalinist, inevitably accompanied by the Proletkult excesses of Andrei Zhdanov, the Soviet Writers Union, and socialist realism. Yet he merely generalizes the same kind of appeal, referring the critical "task" to "the struggles of men and women to free themselves from certain forms of exploitation and oppression" (*MCL*, p. vii). Indeed, the rarity with which Eagleton avoids writing only in masculine terms might also give one pause in this respect—not that revolutionary leftist politics is exactly renowned for its gender awareness.

Eagleton's appeal to the people's struggle is doubtless a rousing call, but it remains extremely vague, because the nature of the "oppression" against which that struggle is supposed to be taking place remains de-fined in terms similar to those which, in the *Grundrisse,* provoked Marx's comment that the pianomaker is a productive worker while the pianist is not, "since his labour is not labour which reproduces capital" (Williams, *ML*, p. 93).[28] This is not simply a question of "updating" (Williams); rather, the analysis of productive labor as work on raw materials to pro-duce commodities to reproduce capital in point of fact reproduces cap-italism's own analysis of itself. At the same time (and the remark is by no means an irrelevance), that very analysis excludes from consideration the vast majority of workers in advanced industrial countries and actually

---

28. The reference is to Marx, *Grundrisse*, p. 305.

helps the alignment of forces in such countries.[29] No wonder that in the area of literature and criticism we find it so very difficult to avoid repeating the tradition.

The remarks with which Lucien Goldmann began his talk at the February 1969 Stockholm Conference on Czechoslovakia are apposite here: "I am rather afraid that, when we speak of contemporary economic events, of social events, and particularly of political events, we tend to use ancient categories which emerged in a world now in process of disappearing, categories and words of which even the relative validity existed only within such a world. This is true, not only for reactionary thought, but also, and particularly so, for socialist and even for Marxist thought."[30] One can of course avoid the difficulty by speaking of "service *industries*," of the "entertainment" or "culture" industry, of "professional unions" (to whose thoroughgoing difference from industrial workers' unions anyone associated with them can readily attest), or, as Goldmann himself does in the text just mentioned, of "self-management," of "specialist technicians," and of "qualified workers" who replace the older type of industrial worker. Then, too, one can call "proletariat" all those who do not own the means of production. By such (metaphorical) means one can hope to apply a nineteenth-century analysis of the conditions of early industrialism to the advanced industrial nations of the late twentieth century—in which it is quite clear, however, that the relation of owner to producer, of oppressor to oppressed, and so forth, is utterly different. It is in this regard that Williams, following Gramsci's lead and analysis, introduces the concept of hegemony (*ML,* p. 111–14). A totally transformed materiality requires, and already implies, a new hegemony. Such is our contemporary situation.

Eagleton (in *MLC* and implicitly in *CI*) adopts the now familiar criticisms of "socialist realism" in order to observe that the struggle for 'the liberation of the proletariat' is not thereby furthered. The question that Western Marxists must ask themselves, however, is just this: "What is the meaning of such a concept as 'freeing the proletariat from oppression?' " When Marx and Engels undertook their analysis—and it was their point—the industrial proletariat, especially in England, was in a clear numerical majority, and its material and spiritual oppression by a powerful owning minority was equally clear. Under such circumstances a call for the proletariat to free itself from that oppression was evidently meaningful. It was indeed (and the reminder is surely unnecessary) just the lack of

---

29. Roger L. Taylor is one of the few to have pursued this kind of argument relentlessly to its logical conclusion: that art is a bourgeois form of representation and that it works against the interests of the masses (*Art, an Enemy of the People* [Atlantic Highlands, N.J., 1978]). A similar impulse has led Robert Pattison to try to renew the concept of literacy in his *On Literacy: The Politics of the Word from Homer to the Age of Rock* (New York, 1982).

30. Lucien Goldmann, "Eppur si muove," in his *Power and Humanism*, ed. and tr. Brian Trench and Tom Wengraf (Nottingham, 1974), p. 39.

such circumstances that made them argue the impossibility of socialist revolution in Russia, for example.

That situation no longer exists; in the West it is obvious that the industrial proletariat (that was) now has access to material and spiritual wealth—even, to some extent, access to the means of production—to a degree undreamed of in the nineteenth century. In its class relationships the Soviet Union now finds itself approximately in the situation of the industrial West some fifty or more years ago; the signs are perhaps to be perceived in intellectual protest and ethnic unrest. The signs of the present situation in the West are to be seen, for example, in the fact that all the ridings of a 'working-class' area such as Birmingham can vote massively for a fundamentally reactionary conservative government, or, more recently, in the complete collapse of the so-called "Democratic alliance" in the United States and the resulting blue-collar vote not only in favor of Ronald Reagan but on behalf of a Republican Senate.[31]

None of this, I need hardly say, is to argue that the internal conflicts have been resolved, with the comforting effect of evacuating the question of social and political conflict. It is to say that emergent structures of feeling are slowly consolidating themselves and that a new analysis of the social facts implied by and brought with them has become imperative. It is to say that the internal conflicts of Western nations in the twentieth century are not those of nineteenth-century Britain, France, Germany, or India. The great risk of accepting uncritically the Marxist analysis of social conditions is that one may thereby ignore a more urgent peril.

One may suggest that insofar as the Marxist analysis is correct in its detail, it applies today to the relation between the industrialized nations and the Third World, though no doubt "correct," here, is the wrong word for "applicable." What I am arguing, therefore, is not that we can rid ourselves of our social conflicts by exporting those conflicts to "them" (as was effectively done under imperialism and colonialism) but that it is simply inappropriate to seek to apply the Marxist analysis uncritically to

31. The reference is to the election of the first Thatcher government in the 1978 British elections, and to the overwhelming defeat of Jimmy Carter in the U.S. elections two years later. Since then, Margaret Thatcher's reelection in 1983, Ronald Reagan's unprecedented sweep in 1984, Helmut Kohl's and Jacques Chirac's elections all seem to confirm the point being made here. Though one can obviously not entirely elide local conditions, these events do offer evidence of retrenchment and an inability to escape old habitual and familiar schemes of thought and action. Indeed, one has an overwhelming impression of a general fear before the unfamiliar and a despair of dealing with it. The all too familiar consequence is a retreat to self-interest and defense. This has been recently manifested in the serious erosion of freedom of expression in both England and the U.S., first in the Law Lords' decision to forbid reporting all media discussion about Peter Wright's *Spycatcher* (with its "revelation" of collusion between M.I.5 and the Tory Party to overthrow the then Labor government), and second in the almost simultaneous ruling by the FCC (both occurred in July 1987) to do away with the fairness doctrine of equal media time (made possible by a prior presidential veto of a congressional attempt to make the doctrine legally binding).

the internal relations of modern industrialism, even though such an application appears satisfying to many would-be 'revolutionaries.' Indeed, their inability to do anything about the situation thus analyzed needs explaining, as does the fact that supposedly revolutionary attempts are infallibly recuperated by the discourse of order (see, obviously, Chapter 4). Why were the potentially insurrectionary events of 1968 merely subsumed under the continuing Leviathan?

I may propose that it is at least partly because the analysis in question is precisely (as I have already remarked) industrialism's analysis of itself, which is why nothing new can be produced from it. The analysis follows the logic of the discourse of order (I will not try to make this generalization more specific here, though earlier and subsequent chapters provide it with meaning). What is essential, therefore, is not a retrospective analysis of this kind but a prospective one—though by definition any analysis must make use of predetermining elements in order, for example, to distinguish the residual from the emergent. In their time, a prospective analysis is just what historical and dialectical materialism were.

The principal and most obviously perilous dilemma of the present and immediate future lies less simply *within* the industrialized nations (between an industrial proletariat and an industrial ruling class), or between the industrialized West and the industrialized 'communist' nations, than it does between advanced capitalism and the more primitive capitalism of the Third World. That is the locus of the first urgent task needing resolution. But mere 'resolution' is not enough, for the unavoidable danger under the present circumstances is that 'resolution' of that conflict can only reinstall worldwide more of the same, can only confirm the hegemony to which Marx and Engels were already addressing themselves. That is to say, while the Marxist analysis may well be applicable in detail only to Industrialism/Third World relations, to deal only with that and no more is to risk replaying in a different dimension the history of the past century.

For to perform such an analysis, though absolutely necessary, is also simply to transport industrial capitalism's self-analysis to a new level, that of external (as opposed to internal) sociopolitical and economic relations. It is not for nothing that the frontispiece of Hobbes's *Leviathan* pictured the State as one man made up of many humans (Sartre's group as individual). Hobbes's authoritarian Leviathan, Montesquieu's liberal monarchy with its mediating legislator as the interpreter of universal law, Rousseau's general will, Hegel's Idea of the State were all (different) transferences of individualism to the level of relations between states (I have elsewhere suggested that all may be called versions of "authoritarian liberalism"). Bacon argued that war was the sport of nations: it strengthened the sinews of their "bodies," kept them in good health and always prepared for the constant struggle characteristic of relations between states. Hugo Grotius's arguments concerning war and peace served to justify an always adversarial and conflictual relationship between nations. Hobbes was to view the contract as a means of overcoming the continuous state of conflict—characteristic of the "state of nature"—between individuals, but that state of conflict remained essential to the relations between nations, as Bacon and Grotius had already assumed.

Indeed, one could almost say that if the violence between individuals became on the one hand the covert violence of relations of production as far as the internal conditions of a given society were concerned (theoretically both justified and concealed by John Locke's arguments concerning the 'equality' of property rights—though not of actual ownership, of course), on the other it could remain overt by being both subsumed under and 'sublimated into' the external conflictual relations of an individual state in its external struggles with equally individualized rivals. This is hardly the place for a thoroughgoing analysis.[32] The important point I wish to make is that the kind of relationship of which I am speaking is clearly built into the analytico-referential discursive class in its application to and practice in the political and economic domains. An analysis must indeed be undertaken in its terms but always accompanied by the awareness that such an analysis will not provide the way out of the difficulty. It will inevitably reveal the detail of a historical repetition, albeit in a new

32. Some aspects of such an analysis have been explored in my *Discourse of Modernism,* are further commented on in this volume, and are a longer-term goal of current research. My repeated use of the phrase "authoritarian liberalism" is intended in all seriousness to indicate the kind of political authority hegemonous in the West since the late seventeenth century, however superficially diverse its forms. It goes back no doubt to Antiquity, but its modern appearance is due to two things: the perception of a real Europe-wide political and social crisis throughout the sixteenth and into the seventeenth century (see, e.g., Chapter 4, pp. 143–44), and a theoretical combination of concepts of natural rights and state sovereignty, whose details were gradually elaborated during those two centuries. Both Machiavelli and Jean Bodin (among many others) thought of civil society as forged from an earlier condition of violent conflict and as requiring a strong centralized sovereign authority. This view was shared, with variants, by such as Thomas Hooker and Bacon, Cardin Le Bret and Richelieu, Giovanni Botero and Hugo Grotius, many of whom were at the same time evolving a theory of individualist natural rights. The strands came together in Hobbes (see, e.g., Chapter 4, pp. 147–48, and Chapter 5, pp. 171–72) and in Locke (though Spinoza and Leibniz would not have dissented unduly). Hobbes's view of civil society as created by every individual's ceding of its natural power to a single sovereign authority was constitutive. The authority was "liberal" because it was then held to guarantee to all the individuals (in theory) the continued enjoyment of such natural rights as did not absolutely impede those of others. Nor did it matter whether the sovereign was an individual (Hobbes), some collective embodiment of a "general will" (Locke, Montesquieu, Rousseau), or the state itself (Hegel). The underlying structure of power relations was in each case the same: it assumed that individuals were somehow free but subordinate and subject to a collective control whose form maintained their liberties. At the end of the seventeenth century, a prominant English statesman, the marquess of Halifax, could thus sum up the matter in his "Anatomy of an Equivalent": "There can be no government without a Supreme Power; that power is not always in the same hands, it is in different shapes and dresses, but still, wherever it is lodged, it must be unlimited. . . . Where this Supreme Power is mixed, or divided, the shape only

dimension. It will reveal just why such a condition can produce nothing new. It will serve to show limits.

New forms of discourse, new forms of conceptualization, become essential. Their development cannot come from any individual fiat, but they may proceed from an initial recognition of limits and of the bankruptcy of certain kinds of action. Literature is part of what was the dominant discourse of three and a half centuries (at least); it was established as such. As currently conceived it can be considered only part of an obsolescent hegemony. To call for the elaboration of what I refer to as a new "discourse" (by which I mean a hegemony concerning *all* forms of meaningful social process) is not to deny that such a discourse must make use of emergent forms, of elements present in analytico-referential discourse. Raymond Williams makes the timely reminder that to take heed of this "aesthetic" and of "literature" as categories produced out of the eighteenth century should not result in facile dismissal, for both categories contain "elements which cannot be surrendered, either to historical reaction or to a confused projective generalization" (*ML*, p. 145).

That is assuredly the case. It is also the case, however, that we could not dismiss them if we wanted to; they are a part of what Williams calls our "structures of feeling" (*ML*, pp. 128–35), whose "presence" is not merely a theoretical but a practical fact. The question must arise, however, as to how far emergent elements of such structures (and by "elements" I do not

---

differeth, the argument is still the same." And yet the ultimate purpose of such governmental authority, he insisted, was to take care of the "rights inherent in men's persons in their single capacities." That sovereignty, he had written in his slightly earlier "Character of a Trimmer," must further "all kind of right which may remain in the body of the People," protect "the common good of mankind," and uphold those individual liberties which are "the foundation of all virtue," that liberty which, as he unsurprisingly described it, "is the mistress of mankind," for which (for whom?) every man's "reasonable desire . . . ought not to be restrained" (George Savile, Marquess of Halifax, *Complete Works*, ed J. P. Kenyon [Harmondsworth, 1969], pp. 135, 59–62). Sartre, we have seen, substantially echoed such a view. So too had Kant, who conceived of individual and society as in a conflict brought under control only by social laws whose irresistible force ordered individual freedoms: in his view, these laws were in fact embedded in the mind as the "categorical imperative" of social duty (see, e.g., Chapter 7, pp. 236–38). In Freud's later psychoanalytic system, the superego performed a similar role. The phrase "authoritarian liberalism" enables one to see the links between what might otherwise be thought of as quite different political systems. Maurice Merleau-Ponty's 1947 "defense" of Stalinism may help reveal the underlying similarity of assumption; see *Humanism and Terror: An Essay on the Communist Problem*, tr. John O'Neill (Boston, 1969). One might call Merleau-Ponty's defense "fundamentalist," for its argument rests (precisely) on the party's need to uphold the rights of the many to the detriment of those of a few, whose freedoms (it was claimed) would impede the rights of the majority absolutely. And one would do well to consider the implications of readings of Rousseau's political thought that go from revolutionary liberalism to totalitarianism. My point is that analytico-referential political discourse (authoritarian liberalism) runs, but controls, that whole gamut. The late seventeenth century, it would seem, had already glimpsed that inclusiveness.

mean to imply discontinuities) can be grasped meaningfully in their *pres-entness* without their necessarily being objectified. The determination of a radical break is therefore not to be seen as a practical fact but rather as a matter of practice. It makes use of emergent forms, but its impulse is to break with the practical hegemony. It must emphasize the break simply because an emphasis on the elements already present within the hegemony tends, as an objective fact, to lead straight back into it. That is Williams's point regarding "orthodox" Marxist criticism as a whole, and mine concerning Eagleton's argument in particular.

In some sense, Williams's *Marxism and Literature* may be understood as offering a complete critique of the kind of position taken by a writer such as Eagleton. So there is a particular poignancy, a special irony in the latter's remark: "It is a curious feature of Williams's intellectual career that, working by his own devious, eclectic and idiosyncratic route, he has consistently pre-empted important theoretical developments" (*CI*, p. 35). The publication of this plaintive comment in 1976 appeared to forecast the "almost wholly theoretical" book (*ML*, p. 6) that Raymond Williams, his teacher, published just a year later. And in that book, Williams began by setting forth, in his familiar historical style, both the novelty and the limitations of those early Marxist analyses that were to become the orthodoxy of later generations, limitations still entirely applicable to an attempt such as Eagleton's.

One further example will suffice, just because it concerns the key concept of culture (and, with it, of the aesthetic and the literary). Williams remarks upon Marxism's analysis of "civil society" as a specific historical form: "bourgeois society as created by the capitalist mode of production" (*ML*, p. 18). Such an analysis implied the view that the enabling concepts of civil society were the marks of what Michel Foucault called a particular *episteme* (a term I think we may now equate, at some level, with *hegemony)*. Williams adds, however, that that analysis "was still largely constrained within the assumptions which had produced the concept [of 'civil society' and, within it, of 'civilization']: that of a progressive secular development, most obviously; but also that of a broadly linear development"—for the Marxist analysis, from feudalism to capitalism to socialism, each at first progressive and each except the last reactionary in its late stages (*ML*, p. 18). He notes, too, that Marxism's rejection of "idealist historiography" (which saw history as the rational "overcoming of ignorance and superstition") and its inclusion of "materialist history" as an emphasis on " 'man making himself' through producing his own means of life" were entirely new. But again he adds that the stress laid upon material history and the "discovery of the 'scientific laws' of society" led to the separation of the cultural from the material and to an emphasis on the "secondary, 'superstructural' " status of culture: "Thus the full possibilities of the concept of culture as a constitutive social process, creating specific and different 'ways of life,' which could have been remarkably deepened by the emphasis on a material social process, were for a long time missed, and were often in practice superseded by an abstracting unilinear universalism" (*ML*, pp. 18–19). Williams justly remarks that this situation still exists (*ML*, p. 20). I have been arguing that a powerful statement such as Terry Eagleton's is forceful evidence of it and, for precisely that reason, requires refutation.

One can observe in many writings of Marx and Engels, particularly in some of the latter's late remarks on or about literature, just the view Williams is here urging. Indeed, Eagleton quotes a letter from Engels to Joseph Bloch of September 21, 1890:

> According to the materialist conception of history, the determining element in history is *ultimately* the production and reproduction in real life. More than this neither Marx nor I have ever asserted. If therefore somebody twists this into the statement that the economic element is the *only* determining one, he transforms it into a meaningless, abstract and absurd phrase. The economic situation is the basis, but the various elements of the superstructure—political forms of the class struggle and its consequences, constitutions established by the victorious class after a successful battle, etc.—forms of law—and then even the reflexes of all these actual struggles in the brains of the combatants: political, legal, and philosophical theories, religious ideas and their further development into systems of dogma—also exercise their influence upon the course of the historical struggles and in many cases preponderate in determining their *form*. [*MLC*, p. 9]

It was essentially Leninism, and the extension of some of its yet more reductive elements by Stalinism, that put an end to that kind of expansiveness. The political requirements of a specific moment and national context demanded that linearity and hierarchical concepts be emphasized: both from the top down (the party as intellect and head of the national revolution) and from the bottom up (change in material production as the basis of the revolutionary process). That required the subordination of every other kind of worker in the first case, and of every other kind of production in the second. That Western Marxists have failed, until extremely recently (if even now), to see such a view as the necessary particular consequences of a specific conjuncture and preferred to generalize it (with an equally reductive reaction as one of its frequent consequences) was no doubt partly the result of the wishful thinking that followed the Bolshevik revolution's success, and partly the result of the fact that such assumptions were indeed but a variant of the hegemonic concepts of advanced capitalism (as Williams observes). While opposing the implications of that capitalism at one level, Western Marxists did not actually contradict them or it, nor did they imply any fundamental questioning of its a prioris. It is just that that explains why Soviet Leninist-Stalinism has led to forms of state capitalism and imperialism that certain parts of the Third World aptly characterize as similar to those of advanced Western industrialism.

Eagleton's argument, expelling all "expansiveness" as "non-Marxist, revisionist, neo-Hegelian, or bourgeois," tends to place him in the camp of a restrictive and reductionist Marxist criticism. The comment is Williams's, regarding the views expressed by an earlier English Marxist criticism (*ML*, p. 3), but it could well be interpreted as a response to Eagleton's comments on Williams himself (*CI*, pp. 21–42). Raymond Williams's desire is to turn the more expansive arguments of Marxism toward a production of the emergent.

How Can 'New Meaning' Be Thought?

If a lion could talk we could not understand him.
—Ludwig Wittgenstein, *Philosophical Investigations*

Here sitting on the world . . . she could not shake herself free from the sense that everything this morning was happening for the first time, perhaps for the last time.
—Virginia Woolf, *To the Lighthouse*

The question of emerging structures and the development of some new sociocultural environment is the principal preoccupation of these final three chapters. Like the preceding ones, they concern forms of conceptualization, but all three strive to link those forms with the realities of their environment. This chapter focuses once again on problems of language and mind. From structural linguistics and anthropology I take the idea of (psychological and biological) innateness to show, first, that those very ideas are not some eternal and ubiquitous verity but a product of our environment and, second, the possible consequences of that showing with regard to the transformations whose present process and need I have been exploring.

Those consequences, of course, go far beyond linguistics and anthropology to engage the entire sociocultural environment. Like previous chapters, this one seeks to make that engagement entirely clear, to indicate some of the profound ways in which these concerns and debates are ineluctably bound up in one another, regardless of the ostensible domain of their particular type of discourse. For while it may be a familiar truism to assert that no human activity is foreign to any other, the assumptions being increasingly adduced here as to the overall coherence of such activities within the social and historical environment and the mutual interdependence of all human practice inevitably mean that no single sphere of activity can be indifferent or irrelevant to all others. Indeed, in what follows, I often have cause to emphasize that much of the failure of modernist assumptions is due to the assertion of such separation and indifference.

My assumptions carry with them the further corollary that the attempt to find solutions to a critical blockage in any one sphere is at least potentially enabling in relation to the overall environment, though that is of course not a claim that such "solutions" can simply be transferred from one domain to another. Rather is it a claim that what we are after is to understand what are the historical, social, and cultural conditions of human functioning within a particular environment and to recognize that the discovery of constraint and contradiction within one type of discourse cannot but affect our understanding of the dominant discursive class ruling the entire environment. It is in that light that I undertake the following exploration of the supposed basic mental structures of language, of some arguments about mind and its transformation or development, and expand those to the broader question of social and cultural change. To that end, Chomsky, Lévi-Strauss, a science fiction novel by Ian Watson, a poem and a novel by Raymond Roussel are little more than convenient pretexts, leading from a modernist (classical) notion of mind toward an interactive idea of mind and environment.

Replying to a question put to him by a television interviewer in 1978, Noam Chomsky remarked that there is no way in which his postulate of an innate universal grammar common to all humans can be experimentally tested in the laboratory: "In the case of humans, we cannot design artificial, contrived environments and see what happens to an infant in them"[1] The possibility of such an experimental situation is one that has constantly intrigued, indeed haunted, the linguist, and he has elsewhere been more specific as to the aim of such experiments. A scientist, he has written, would be able to test certain assumptions about the allegedly fundamental structures of universal grammar, for example, "by exposing children to invented systems violating the proposed conditions and determining how or whether they manage to acquire those systems. If acquisition of such systems is possible but qualitatively different from acquisition of natural language—if, say, it has the property of scientific discovery—then [the scientist] will take this as confirmatory evidence for his theory" that the assumed elements of universal grammar are likely to be the truly *objective* elements that do indeed compose such a system. Chomsky adds that if one could find or invent a language that violated "the innate linguistic universals postulated in universal grammar" but was nevertheless "learnable by humans exactly in the manner of attested

1. *The Listener,* April 6, 1978, p. 435: conversation with Bryan Magee in the eleventh program of the *Men of Ideas* series, produced by BBC Television, 1977–78. See also Noam Chomsky, *Language and Mind,* enlarged ed. (New York, 1972), p. 82 (henceforth cited as *LM*).

human languages," then, of course, universal grammar would have to be rejected.[2]

The goals of such experiments would be to discover whether humans are indeed "programmed" by a genetically inscribed and species-specific innate grammar that orders a kind of rich creativity in the world and, at the same time, "to discover something about the limits of our science-forming abilities." The alternative, suggests Chomsky (quite wrongly, I think), would be the discovery that humans are "plastic organisms without extensive preprogramming." Under such circumstances, "the state that our mind achieves would, in fact, be a reflection of the environment, which means that it would be extraordinarily impoverished," because an enormous gap clearly lies between individual experience and individual knowledge.[3]

The profound error in this alternative proceeds from its originating assumption of a radical discontinuity between the mind and the world on the one hand and of binarism on the other (the one a referential a priori, the other a logical presupposition). Separated from the world, the human mind must either contain its own controls, rendering it capable of resisting the outside's menacing importunities—of repulsing the *other*—or be at its entire mercy (we have seen this fear expressed before, in Frege, in Saussure, in Benveniste). Nor is there any kind of conjoining possible, such as might provide the idea of some middle way. (I will return to this matter.)

Depending upon such assumptions, the structural linguist must therefore argue for the former, the presence of an innate system of controls, on the grounds that in fact "a small amount of rather degenerate experience allows a great leap into a rich cognitive system—essentially uniform in a

2. Noam Chomsky, *Reflections on Language* (New York, 1975), pp. 208, 209–10. The idea of such experiments has of course haunted the West at least since the Enlightenment. Behind Rousseau's *Emile* (a thought experiment not dissimilar in its implications to the one I use here) is the memory of his *Essai sur l'origine des langues,* of Etienne de Condillac's statue, and John Locke's blank sheet of paper—all of them thought to be provided with the possibility of concrete experimental verification by the "wild children" who appeared from time to time from the woods of Europe. The most famous of these cases has received a lucid and engaging exposition by Roger Shattuck in *The Forbidden Experiment: The Story of the Wild Boy of Aveyron* (New York, 1980). A now celebrated book dealing precisely with the problem of creating a socially communicative mind in children through providing forms of expression in largely controllable experimental conditions was Bruno Bettelheim's *The Empty Fortress: Infantile Autism and the Birth of the Self* (New York, 1967). Bettelheim, of course, is concerned not with verifying any hypothesis similar to Chomsky's but with 'awakening' children into the social environment normal to the experimenters. Chomsky is right: such experiments must necessarily be left to the imagination—or to such fictions as Rousseau's, B. F. Skinner's *Walden Two,* or the one this chapter examines. In the real world, only the hospitals of Nazi concentration camps (or perhaps the Gulag) could have undertaken such experiments (but did not do so, as far as I know).

3. *Listener,* p. 436.

community and, in fact, roughly uniform for the species."[4] Chomsky's experimental goal, then, would be to find evidence confirming a hypothesis whose implications would be far reaching indeed. Politically, for example (and as we will see), Chomsky asserts that the concept of the unlimited malleability of the human species, of the human as nothing more than the ever changing product of an ongoing and manipulable history, is an enabling concept for the worst kind of ideological manipulation (whether from the left or from the right). The notion of a genetically inscribed set of rules, making possible the generation of infinite but well-ordered ideas, processes, and actions, assures on the contrary both human creativity and the ultimate resistance of the organism to such manipulation.

Ian Watson's novel *The Embedding* puts many of these propositions and their implications to a fictional test. It does so in a quite complex way, on the basis of linguistic concepts and problems drawn avowedly from Chomsky; anthropological concepts and problems drawn more or less explicitly from Claude Lévi-Strauss; and a sociopolitical problematic of confrontation whose obvious reference is to revolutionary Marxism, whether this is presented through an anthropologist's experience with the Frelimo guerillas in Mozambique or his later experience (as recounted in the novel) with Brazilian revolutionaries in the Amazon jungle.[5] All three aspects of the novel deal with frontiers: between a familiar language felt to be stultifying of any new development and some new language that might make available new possibilities of thought and action; between advanced industrial civilization and other societies (whether embodied in the "Xemahoa" discovered by anthropologist Pierre Darriand in the depths of the Amazon jungle or in the "Sp'thra," the "Signal Traders," who come from space to trade information with Earth); between the "Empire" of the great world powers and the aspirations of the peoples of the Third World.

All three aspects are viewed as but different angles taken from a single dilemma: one that concerns the attempted achievement of what the Sp'thra call some form of "Totality" (p. 114), what the Xemahoa speak of as the "full language of man" (p. 87), and what the guerillas refer to simply as a proper "sharing of wealth" or "Socialism for all" (pp. 85, 86). The outcome is catastrophe for all—because the means forbid the ends, because all try to use force on the basis of insufficient understanding, because all seek shortcuts where only development over time can achieve the goal. Would you be willing to lose a little time now, asks Chris Sole, the

4. *Listener,* p. 435.
5. All references to this novel, indicated simply by page number in my text, are to Ian Watson, *The Embedding* (London, 1975). The first edition was published in 1973, and there is an American edition by Bantam (New York, 1977), whose pagination is entirely different.

linguist, of the negotiator from space, Ph'theri, "if it saved *all* time for the Sp'thra?" (p. 117). The extraterrestrials accept and will be destroyed for having done so.

In a hospital somewhere in England, Chris Sole has been secretly engaged upon Chomsky's impossible experiment. No doubt it provides little but informed suggestion in response to Chomsky's wish to determine the validity of the concept of a universal grammar, since it is a fiction (is it more so, one wonders, than the concept?). It makes entirely convincing, however, the impossibility of experimental exploration of the frontiers mentioned—not simply on moral grounds (though these are clear enough) but on scientific ones, for the experiment's success would be incomprehensible to the experimenter. S/he would have created the language of Wittgenstein's lion, or have demonstrated what our 'normality' would classify as a passage into 'madness.' And if the experimenter *could* understand the new language created by—or, at least, in—the experiment, through having herself or himself imbued the concepts that made it possible, there would be no return to the concepts of our 'normalcy'; the experimenters would themselves be incomprehensible. That is indeed what happens to linguist Chris Sole at the end of the novel, and either he will eventually return to normal from his voyage into some other conceptual order, or, as the hospital's director puts it, his mind will be considered "cracked" (p. 184).

The difficulty with Sole's experimental technique (with its very assumptions) is that he wishes to make possible a change in humanity as a whole on the basis of an individual fiat. He would set aside the historical development of humanity, the slow process of evolution, in order to produce an immediate transformation. He forgets that the means to an action inevitably inflect the outcome of that action, its shape and its meaning, its form and the kind of action it enables. His experiment is founded on the contradiction implied by Chomsky: he wishes to code into a human mind—into the minds of his four child guinea pigs—a new process of conceptualization and a new language to accompany it (necessarily). His underlying assumption is that of "unlimited malleability." Yet he assumes that a single universal grammar is common to all humans and will therefore provide a firm defensive control. "Ever since Chomsky's pioneer work," he explains, "we all assume that the plan for language is programmed into the mind at birth. The basic plan of language reflects our biological awareness of the world that has evolved us, you see. So we're teaching three artificial languages as probes at the frontiers of mind" (p. 31). And he asserts with even more precision:

A permanent form isn't practical for every single word—we only need remember the basic meaning. So you've got one level of information—that's the actual words we use, on the surface of the mind. The other permanent level, deep down, contains highly abstract concepts—idea associations linked together network-style. In between these two levels comes the mind's plan for making sentences out of ideas. This plan contains the rules of what we call Universal Grammar—we say it's universal, as this plan is part of the basic structure of mind and the same rules can translate ideas into any human language whatever. [Pp. 33–34]

Chris Sole's experiment aims at manipulating not simply the surface and not simply the plan of universal grammar. It assumes a two-way relation between that plan and the concepts underlying it. It assumes that it can create a new order of conceptualization—in effect, a new mind. It may be the case, as in so much experimentation (fictional or real), that the goals of his manipulation are in themselves initially praiseworthy: to study the possibility of changing human capacities (assuming them to be intrinsically bound up with what I have called "classes of discourse") under conditions in which the effects of the actual use of present human conceptual capacities are taken to be essentially vicious. Sole wants to change the nature of human conceptualization, the scope of human action, the foundations of social processes. The fundamentally selfish, greedy, brutish, and shortsighted reasons for the catastrophic outcome certainly seem ultimately to justify the linguist's desire. But the blame for disaster lies also with him; his own techniques must confront similar criticisms. For the goal necessarily entails just those coercive kinds of techniques, and that is why Chomsky views such an attempt as misguided from the outset. Such experimental methods, he argues, could not "get us anywhere towards modifying these capacities," because the faculties in question are "biologically given."[6]

Still, as we will see, the main deficiency lies neither in Sole's manipulation nor in Chomsky's biological determinism—both of which are doubtless at fault. It comes, rather, from the originating instance of that kind of thinking: the idea that mind is discrete, entirely separate and divided from the world and all other minds. That notion undermines the entire way of seeing that remains here in question, lying still within analytico-referential discourse. For even if one could conceive of the change implicit in Chomsky's and Watson's hope as potentially evolutionary, it could never be undertaken by mere individual fiat. This fact suggests another way in which Sole's effort is misguided, as *The Embedding* amply shows: the suffocating manipulation to which Sole has to submit "his" children (the notion of *possession* plays an obviously important role here—the children are "his," they are "the children of my mind": pp. 11, 179) contradicts the free creative expansion that remains his ostensible goal. In this it echoes

6. *Listener*, p. 436.

the fundamental and quite generalized contradiction characteristic of the dominant discursive class of the West over the past three centuries. For the operative model of analytico-referential discourse assumed an unlimited expansion, while inscribing some kind of knowable totality as its achievable aim. It functions on the basis of an opposition between movement and stasis, between process and entropy—or between history and utopia. Throughout the period of dominance of analytico-referential discourse, this tension seems to have been ineluctable. The second half of the nineteenth century reveals the beginning of its collapse, perhaps of its making possible—after about three centuries—the passage into something new: the consequence of a self-determined discursive evolution.[7]

Such self-expansion can occur, of course, only within a broad interactive context (of which it is one element), within a Peircean "phaneron," if you will. And this conduces to an ongoing but slow and gradual development. As Walter Benjamin put it: "During long periods of history, the mode of human sense perception changes with humanity's entire mode of existence. The manner in which human sense perception is organized, the medium in which it is accomplished, is determined not only by nature but by historical circumstances as well."[8] Historically, there have been moments of apparently much swifter transformation: for example, in the period between the European mid-sixteenth and mid-seventeenth centuries (when a long period of more gradual development had finally been brought to a kind of crisis). But in both situations the development of mind, the transformation of its capacities, the changing of the world and society, of the forms of language and the functioning of sign systems, are entirely and *genuinely* (to use Peirce's word for the inseparable nature of the 'elements' of these processes) interdependent and correlative. Chomsky and his fictional avatar, Sole (whose name is certainly not accidental), can envisage only separate spheres. The result will be catastrophe.

In *The Embedding*, when the new language and its accompanying altered conceptualization finally "takes," the organism that was Vidya (the

---

7. Reiss, *The Discourse of Modernism*, pp. 159–62, 171–73, 359–60, 373. In *The Embedding* a U.S. government memo asserts that in consequence of having chosen "the technological path . . . man must elect to expand outwards by means of his technology—or else collapse. No steady-state is conceivable or desirable once expansion has begun. The steady-state may be dreamt of or fantasized about [utopia]—but it is merely a pipe-dream which will not work in practice, and which would have disastrous cultural and psychological repercussions, if any sustained effort was made to make it work" (p. 147). A later memo (pp. 160–61) cancels out this expansiveness and exchanges it for the short-term gains of maintaining the status quo and the present ordering of world power, whose consequences are indeed disastrous for many of the novel's protagonists. But then, so have been the colonialism, imperialism, and economic monopolization justified in the first memo. The process/stasis opposition is discussed in Chapter 9, pp. 267–77 and n. 29.

8. Walter Benjamin, "The Work of Art in the Age of Mechanical Reproduction," in his *Illuminations*, ed. Hannah Arendt, tr. Harry Zohn (1968; rpt. New York, 1969), p. 222.

first of the children in whom the experiment 'succeeds') destroys itself, taking the 'imperialist' scientist with it. The child *might have been able* to pass into some new logical space, but not by the possessive force of coercive techniques drawn from within the old. That kind of action is in all ways analogous to the torturing of the guerilla woman, Iza, by the Brazilian police: the electronic devices and the drug used as techniques to force Sole's four children into some new mode of conceptualization are matched by the electrical probes and the tapir whip used to force the terrorist to confess (pp. 121–24, 126). In his argument with the Sp'thra, Sole admits as much, implying that he has not yet found techniques enabling passage into a new and unfamiliar logic and action: "This idea of getting outside of the reality you're already part of—it's illogical. . . . Reality determines how you view things. There's no such thing as a perfect external observer. Nobody can move outside themselves or conceive of something outside the scope of the concepts they're using. We're all embedded in what you call 'This-Reality'—" (p. 100). Such a protest denies his own experiment any validity, of course. When he then quotes Wittgenstein's conclusion to the *Tractatus*, "Whereof we cannot speak, thereof we must keep silent," only to be taunted by the alien, he instantly denies that such is human "philosophy at all." The ambiguity of these various assertions matches the contradiction inherent in his scientific method and project.

The explosive outcome of his experiment accords with Chomsky's assertion about the human organism's inability to learn a language that violates universal grammar (if the hypothesis is correct; actually, it merely does not falsify it), at least "under normal conditions of access and exposure to data," though it might be learned under other conditions.[9] The outcome's implications also correspond to the agreement between Sole and Ph'theri that the Sp'thra "can imprint a language directly into the brain . . . provided it conforms to . . . the rules of Universal Grammar" (p. 93). In both cases the concern is with fast, even forced, individual learning—not, it goes without saying, with some gradual or even rapid evolution of *society's* conceptual space.

Of this last a different fictional situation provides evidence: the 'primitive' tribal organization and conceptual patterns of the Xemahoa Indians. A different kind of scientist, too, confronts that evidence, far more passively and from within; he becomes a participant rather than an observer from without. This is the cultural anthropologist Pierre Darriand, ambiguous friend to Chris Sole, lover of Sole's wife and father of her son. But we will return later to this alternative approach to a different reality.

9. Chomsky, *Reflections on Language*, p. 29.

The Embedding clearly suggests that an imposed and artificial creation of the different conditions necessary to some altered state of conceptualization is itself *reactionary*. It forces a naturally (and self-protectively) resistant human organism into an apparently unnatural posture (Vidya going 'mad' in an apparent dysfunctioning of the organism itself, if it is not a case of Wittgenstein's lion). Sole's action is no different from that of the Americans and the Russians at the end, who force the Brazilians—and much of the Third World—to accept their "Empire" (p. 73), as together they destroy the alien Sp'thra and put the lid on Third World political aspirations. By force, Sole breaks open a perhaps necessary "prison" of reason without having anything known to put in its place; his experiments are, in fact, a case of "let's see what will happen if . . ."and his theoretical 'grounding' a case of taking a hypothesis—imprinted universal grammar—for a fact:

> Reason—rationality—is a concentration camp, where the sets of concepts for surviving in a chaotic universe form vast, though finite, rows of huts, separated into blocks by electric fences, which the searchlights of Attention rove over, picking out now one group of huts, now another. . . .
> Vidya's concentration camp had bulged at the seams. The fences fell over from sheer pressure of bodies. The outermost fence—the boundary beyond which lay the inarticulable—had snapped too. And this was unfortunate—for the concentration camp is the survival strategy of the species. [P. 182]

This aspect of the matter corresponds to Chomsky's concept of the rules of universal grammar as a kind of defense mechanism against the otherwise limitless malleability of the human organism. Yet these prisonlike rules can also be misused—as Pierre Darriand puts it: the Amazon flood, the direct consequence of economic acquisitiveness and colonial greed, is going to wash away the Xemahoa "into the concentration camps of priests" (p. 85). It is a *particular kind* of reason that functions in such a way. Darriand's real-life counterpart, Lévi-Strauss, concludes *his* story of anthropological researches in Brazil with the plea that humankind continue at least to contemplate the "tenuous arch linking us to the inaccessible," for such contemplation will afford us the privilege "of arresting the process, of controlling the impulse which forces us to block up the cracks in the wall of necessity one by one and to complete our work at the same time as we shut ourselves up within our prison." The image with which the anthropologist hints at the possibility of some alternative startlingly recalls Wittgenstein's now familiar lion: perhaps we may grasp that other essence of humanity, he suggests, "below the threshold of thought and over and above society . . . in the brief glance . . . that, through some involuntary understanding, one can sometimes exchange with a cat."[10]

The Janus-faced nature of logical space, the ambiguity of these detentive rules of conceptualization, was equally emphasized by Michel Foucault in his commentary on Raymond Roussel's language. Roussel is an author whose importance in *The Embedding* is overwhelming; he provides, among other things, its basic concept of an alternative form of conceptualization, in a poem that puts familiar logic to flight (p. 9).[11] Foucault remarked of Roussel's verbal pyrotechnics: "These prisons, these human machines, these coded tortures, all this lattice-work of words, of secrets, and of signs, have issued miraculously from a single linguistic fact: a series of identical words says two different things. The exiguousness of our language which, cast out in two different directions, is suddenly brought face to face with itself and forced to cross over its own path."[12]

The mind is a most delicate affair that must be gentled and not forced. The prison of reason may be beneficial or malevolent. The discipline of language is always two-faced. Equilibrium is all, and while evolutionary development is possible—as the Xemahoa, no less than the Sp'thra, reveal—abruptly forced change leads only to cataclysm. Sole sees this quite early in the case of Vidya: "Abruptly a spasm twitched across the boy's face. Like a skater coming to grief on thin ice, the tight surface of sanity cracked and he fell through into chaos. His lips parted in a scream" (p. 38).[13] Even under more favorable circumstances, Darriand notes the dangers of his attempts to enter a new form of conceptual ordering: "Yet there had been a terrible danger. He still sweated at the thought of it" (p. 78). This precariousness of the mind and its thinking, in all its manifestations, was earlier picked up in not dissimilar terms by Claude Lévi-Strauss: "No contact with savage Indian tribes has ever daunted me more than the morning I spent with an old lady swathed in woollies, who compared herself to a rotten herring encased in a block of ice: apparently intact, but threatened with disintegration as soon as her protective envelope should melt" (*TT*, p. 20).

10. Claude Lévi-Strauss, *Tristes Tropiques,* tr. John and Doreen Weightman (New York, 1975), pp. 414–15, hereafter cited as *TT*; I have sometimes silently brought this translation closer to the French original (Paris, 1955). Lévi-Strauss may of course have "obtained" his feline image from Baudelaire; my reference here is to incommensurable rationalities.

11. Raymond Roussel, *Nouvelles impressions d'Afrique,* suivies de *L'âme de Victor Hugo* (Paris, 1963), pp. 7–85.

12. Michel Foucault, *Raymond Roussel* (Paris, 1963), p. 22.

13. Part of the problem comes from the fact that this kind of experiment is falsified from the start because the 'patient,' victim, or "subject" (strange noun to use) has already been separated from its full environment. The experimental conditions presuppose division: of mind from the world, individual from collectivity, of the individual from its genuine "ecosystem."

The mind's equilibrium, its skating on thin ice, its implicit echoing both of the physical world (the need to maintain the ecological balance of the jungle for the Xemahoas' survival—a theme running through *The Embedding*) and of civilization itself is made clear at the novel's end by the icy disintegration of the spaceship "in the icebox of space" (pp. 171–77). The final catastrophe also marks the disintegration of an Amazonian civilization and perhaps of much of the Third World at the same time. It has a parallel at the end of Ian Watson's later *The Jonah Kit* in the whales' autogenocide under the pressure of 'scientific' experimentalism, and again in the mob-murder of the "shaman" at the end of the same author's *Martian Inca*.[14]

Fragments of mind, fragments of civilization, fragments of people meet. But far from "coming together, recognizing their affinity, and being almost fused one with the other"—like the Europe and Brazil of Lévi-Strauss's teacher, Georges Dumas (*TT*, p. 20)—they end in complete destruction as a result of fear, ignorance, plain conservatism, or the naked imposition of force. In Watson's world the civilization of the dominant analytico-referential discourse is like the rotten herring of Lévi-Strauss's old woman in her shawls. So it is, however, in Lévi-Strauss's own world (no less than in that of his successor, Pierre Darriand): "I know that, slowly and gradually, experiences such as these were starting to ooze out like some treacherous water from a humanity saturated with its own numbers and with the ever-increasing complexity of its problems" (*TT*, p. 29).[15]

As flood, bomb, and drug destroy all at the end of *The Embedding*, again we find the old woman of civilization—a body rotting and swelling from within, protected by the thin icelike covering of precarious culture—like Vidya's brain, about to burst, with death and disease, with otherness and insanity. Or it is like the experimental minds kept in the "blank aquarium" of Sole's hospital laboratory (p. 8), like the Xemahoa Indians inhabiting "the blur of a dirty aquarium tank" (p. 125), like the minds kept on ice in the globe that is the aliens' spaceship. Roussel's *"maître,"* Martial Canterel, as one among the seven wonders of his isolated and lonely estate (called "Locus Solus"), had similarly carried out experiments on mind and body

14. Ian Watson, *The Jonah Kit* (1975; rpt. London, 1977); *The Martian Inca* (1977; rpt. London, 1978).

15. The phrase I have translated here as "treacherous water" is *eau perfide* in the French original (p. 18). The Weightmans translate it as "insidious leakage," while the earlier American translation simply has "pus": Claude Lévi-Strauss, *Tristes Tropiques*, tr. John Russell (1961; rpt. New York, 1972), p. 31. I have preferred the literal equivalent because of the evident connection with the ice metaphor. Elsewhere, Lévi-Strauss has written of our modern culture since the time of Descartes as a "virus" within the body of "flesh and blood" civilizations: *Anthropologie structurale deux* (Paris, 1973), p. 333. I have made the comments I think such views deserve in my *Discourse of Modernism* (pp. 42, 379), but their application to the implications explored by Watson is apparent.

in an aquarium where swim the dancer, Faustine, and a naked cat.[16] The precarious glass walls of the aquarium, like the ice, create a metaphor emphasizing the dangers of trying to cross frontiers, of breaking down necessary barriers, of striving to implant unfamiliar capacities. Darriand records: "At times I'm afraid— scared to my marrow. . . . It's a different universe of concepts here. A different dimension. A political crime is being committed against them" (pp. 46–47).

Yet again, the danger of crossing the forbidden boundaries has been nicely described by Lévi-Strauss, commenting on the impact left on the Amazonian tribes by early European travelers:

> Although the civilizations which they were the first to observe had developed along different lines from ours, they had nevertheless reached the full development and perfection of which their natures were capable [a description we may doubt], whereas the societies we are able to study today—in conditions which it may well be illusory to compare with those of four centuries ago—are no more than debilitated communities and mutilated social forms . . . they have been shattered by the development of European civilization, that phenomenon which, for a widespread and innocent section of humanity, has amounted to a monstrous and incomprehensible cataclysm. It would be wrong for us Europeans to forget that this cataclysm is a second aspect of our civilization, no less true and irrefutable than the one we know. [*TT*, p. 326]

The ambiguous contradiction again makes its presence felt, on a broader—cultural and social—scale this time. But its consequences are not in the least ambiguous: "The visitor camping with the Indians in the bush for the first time, is filled with anguish and pity at the sight of human beings so totally bereft; some relentless cataclysm seems to have crushed them against the ground in a hostile land, leaving them naked and shivering by their flickering fires" (*TT*, p. 293). The play having been mentioned in an earlier chapter, one is irresistibly reminded here of Lear's, "Poor naked wretches, whereso'er you are,/That bide the pelting of this pitiless storm" (*King Lear*, III. iv). And yet the pitiless storm does not prevent human contact: one still hears, writes Lévi-Strauss, "whisperings and chuckles," the embracings of couples seeming to seek "a lost unity" (*TT*, p. 293).[17] That unity is just exactly what the Xemahoa are seeking to

16. Raymond Roussel, *Locus Solus* (1914; rpt. Paris, 1974), pp. 65–115.

17. I cannot help wondering whether Lévi-Strauss's commentary may not be the recall of the Fool's opposite reflection in *King Lear*, concerning the world turned upside down and the urge for too swift or too careless a satisfaction of desire (sexual, especially, but not only) necessarily leading to disaster (*King Lear*, III.ii). Indeed, Lévi-Strauss's "nostalgie d'une unité perdue" also suggests a certain futility. I mention this "intertext" here simply because the question of the relationship between fact and fiction (in this instance, the anthropologist's judgment on 'reality' as some version of Shakespeare), already raised in the margins of Chapter 1 and generally implicit in the very idea of "discourse," will shortly come up again.

discover through their Bruxo, the shaman who, Darriand writes to Sole, "will hold a giant embedded statement of all the coded myths of the tribe in his present consciousness. . . . Soon, he may achieve total consciousness of Being. Soon, the total scheme underlying symbolic thought may be clear to him" (p. 75). He is about to be crushed however, like Lévi-Strauss's Nambikwara, under the weight of alien civilizations: "The whole weight of American imperialist technology. The Brazilian military dictatorship. Imposing their will on this jungle from afar, while the Indians within it are trapped as casually as flies are trapped on a fly-strip, whilst the making of the meal goes on—the great feasting of the giants on the Amazon's wealth: the meal of spectacular consumption" (p. 75).

Darriand's continuing description of the Xemahoa tribe throughout *The Embedding* carries implications similar to those explored in *Tristes Tropiques*. New meaning, new cultural forms, new political order, new concepts, and new actions must somehow develop organically, and from within a collectivity, out of some kind of 'historical' necessity. Just so had both the Sp'thra and the Xemahoa evolved until confronted by an order seeking to impose its own norms upon them: Sole, apparently innocently, thinks to himself while bargaining with Ph'theri, whose techniques he finds unfamiliar, that "bargaining is a competition, not a free exchange of gifts" (p. 102). And by his offer to the Sp'thra of a Xemahoa brain in return for a knowledge of interstellar travel and a "Tide Reader" (a member of another alien race, whose ability to read the tides of space "is an inherited part of their reality, coded into their nervous systems": p. 99), he achieves just such a spectacular consumption as that of which Darriand accuses the Americans and the Brazilians (p. 117). So too, of course, do the Sp'thra themselves, since they are hoping to save "all time."

In fact, all are guilty of trying to find the same kind of shortcut, of urging a rupture rather than a development. Chomsky argues that universal grammar is presumably species-specific, just as Ph'theri has told Sole that the Sp'thra had to carry a Tide Reader with them because the Sp'thra themselves cannot have access to the system of logic enabling the former to read the tides (p. 99), and just as Kayapi, Darriand's native informant, seems continually to doubt that the anthropologist can learn what he calls Xemahoa A, let alone the fully embedded language of the Bruxo, Xemahoa B. But the Sp'thra, the Signal Traders, wish to go beyond that species-specific reality into the "Totality . . . outside of This-Reality" (p. 114), into what they call "true reality." That is why they are pursuing the beings they call the "Change Speakers" (pp. 113–16), who are able to "shift across realities" and "modulate all the reality tangents," who "change-speak" their way through realities (reminding us of Augustin Cournot's and Victoria Welby's multiplicitous language, mentioned in Chapter 1). The relation to 'our' reality is parallel to that of transfinite to infinite numbers. The Sp'thra have been hoping to get outside their reality into some "parareality" by superimposing "the reality-programmes of all languages." Then, says Ph'theri, they will be able to overcome "the Bereft Love [they] feel for the Change Speakers": a bereavement perhaps not unlike that from which Lévi-Strauss sees the Nambikwara as suffering. For they too have lost their earlier and more 'perfect' embedding in reality. Sole offers the Sp'thra a shortcut.

This utopian ideal of some kind of "unclosing" of language, earlier dreamed of by Augustin Cournot and Victoria Welby in moments of wildness (but a familiar seventeenth-century dream as well, from Descartes to Cyrano de Bergerac, from Dalgarno to Wilkins to Leibniz), has more recently been expressed in a perhaps more humorous and whimsical mood by David Lodge. In his novel *Small World*, a Japanese translator, Akira Sakazaki, relaxing by driving a hundred golf balls into a netted range, sees in this exercise an allegory of language as "the net that holds thought trapped within a particular culture" (or, as Chomsky perceives it, within a particular species). But Sakazaki then thinks: "If one could only strike the ball with sufficient force, with perfect timing, it would perhaps break through the netting, continue on its course, never to fall to earth, but go into orbit around the world." [18] Language in orbit would, however, become inaccessible save as the sounding board for interpretive signals: something our contemporaries might call a metalanguage. Or else it would necessarily take the place of the former language and itself be reinscribed within the particular culture formulating it, becoming the very language we had thought to eradicate, 'limited' and culture-bound. A language that leaped beyond the bounds of a particular culture would no longer be a language at all. Even Chomsky's prelinguistic "deep structure" is caught in the bounds of the human. Nonetheless, as we will see, this humorous thought about the nature of language may be instructive: at the least, it removes the constraint of dependency upon individual minds *qua* individual.

In Watson's novel the Xemahoa have also got beyond this stage. The Bruxo, writes Darriand, hopes to achieve "a total statement of reality, to be able to control and manipulate that reality" (p. 75). Like the Tide Readers who read the tides of space, the Xemahoa read the jungle. For them, nature is a "glossary" (pp. 64–65). Their intricate kinship relations (pp. 43–44), their myths (e.g., pp. 44, 49–54), their language, their social life in the forest are all comprehended in a single logical system: "The intricacy of the links that held the mental and social life of these people together! Links between tree and soil and fungus; shit and sperm and

18. David Lodge, *Small World: An Academic Romance* (1984; rpt. Harmondsworth, 1985), p. 141.

laughter. Between floodwater and language, myth and incest. Where was the boundary between reality and myth? Between ecology and metaphor? Which elements could safely be left out of the picture? The eating of a handful of soil? The spilling of sperm on the soil? The counting by significant feathers (in whatever way these were 'significant')? The tree that the maka-i grew on?" (p. 80).

The system corresponds to a reality and a form of conceptualization quite different from Darriand's, though he does succeed in partly understanding it: "Today the jungle seemed to be one vast beating brain" (p. 79). It is the jungle that provides "the tools of Xemahoa thinking" (p. 79), much as the tides of space provide those of the Tide Readers. These tools furnish a system of information entirely analogous to that of language: "For what was nature, what was the whole physical world, except information chemically and physically coded—and he who held access to the information symbols in their totality held direct access to reality, held the magician's legendary powers in his grasp. Even this did not seem totally impossible to Pierre, in the aftermath of his experience—though Logic and Reason fought against this fantastic dream" (p. 81). Darriand had earlier noted this difference and difficulty of understanding in his letter to Sole, where he commented that Xemahoa B "directs crippling blows at our straightforward logical vision of the world" (p. 74). And, of course, it possesses that one enormous difference from a Chomskyan notion of brain and language: its deep structures are envisaged *not* as embedded in the mind but as completely inextricable from the lived and living relationship between mind and world, language, culture, and society. It may remind us of Bakhtin's view of language and mind, to which I have already frequently alluded, and recall Benjamin's remark about language, nature, and historical circumstances—not to mention Peirce's foundational assumptions in this regard.

The similarity of the problematic confronted by the fictional French anthropologist has obvious affinities with the researches carried out by Lévi-Strauss on kinship and myth structures of "primitive" conceptualization. Pierre Darriand (too) arrives at partial understanding: "How intricate—and logical—this Indian culture is!" he thinks, as he works his way through the Xemahoa myths (p. 60). But he achieves his understanding of this quite alien culture, partial as it is, by using the drug "maka-i," under the tutelage of Kayapi: "When you meet maka-i . . . you are two men, three men, many men. Your mind is great with words. You speak the full language of man" (p. 87). And even Darriand expresses his doubts as to the value of such forms of apprenticeship, asking himself immediately: "But was Kayapi his evil genius or true guide?" The Bruxo is using the same means to arrive at his comprehension of totality: "He is killing himself in the process," writes Darriand to Sole (p. 75). The ambiguity here is that Darriand in fact is in the same situation in relation to Kayapi as are the children to Sole—save that the anthropologist has made the choice for himself. This ambiguity will return.

In his understanding of the oneness of the jungle and its denizens, Darriand feels he has attained "a *memory* of the dawn of understanding" (p. 77); is this Lévi-Strauss's "nostalgie d'une unité perdue"? It is as though the embedded wholeness the Bruxo appears to be achieving and the parareality sought by the Sp'thra were at some level of the mind beneath, beyond, or indeed indifferent to "universal grammar" in any narrow mentalist sense, and at some level that might not be species-specific. These are the terms in which Ph'theri talks of the Change Speakers and Darriand of the Xemahoa. Sole seems to feel that he is striving toward something similar in the experiments with his children. And he too wants to speed up the process by using a drug.

The connection among the three is explicit: "The Sp'thra found themselves confronted by something abnormal—something from outside of Nature. They built a universal thought machine to answer the challenge. The Xemahoa were faced by this unnatural flood and fought back in their own terms—not technological terms this time, but biological and conceptual ones" (p. 152). Or again: "the problem of the Sp'thra became [for Sole] a fantasy interpolation between the secluded solidity of Vidya's world and the equally secluded and solid reality of the Xemahoa people" (p. 156). But Vidya has already started seriously to break down, and the aquarium of the Xemahoa has already been spectacularly breached and left open. Kayapi's creation of new myths to enable the breach to be closed (pp. 157–59), the astronaut's idea that perhaps the frozen minds in the broken spacecraft might be "raised to a new life" by some yet-to-be-discovered technological means (p. 177), and Sole's co-worker's idea that the linguist might be able to provide useful information about what happened in Vidya's mind (and his own) when he "comes out of shock" (p. 184) are none of them given much hope. For unlike the suggestions of Bakhtin or Benjamin, Cournot or Welby, all are conceived in terms of individual and discrete minds confronting one another, society, and the world across some more or less unbridgeable distance. That was Sartre's dilemma, and it remains, still, Chomsky's.

The astronaut's prayer is ironically presented as the compassionate weeping of a pious man grieving over his niece's death, whom he hopes may one day be similarly brought back to life by the hoped-for technology (p. 177). Darriand dismisses Kayapi as "a vile opportunist, a dirty little village Hitler" (p. 162), thus answering his own earlier question about his informant. Sam Bax, the director of Sole's hospital, comments that the linguist may indeed be able to add something, "unless [his] mind is cracked as bad as the boy's" (p. 184). But if Sole had achieved some new form of conceptualization, he would be classified and dismissed as mad in any case. Thus the jungle missionaries scorn Roussel's poem, *Nouvelles impressions d'Afrique* (central both to Sole's experiment and to Darriand's attempts to understand the Xemahoa languages), as just so much "nonsense" (p. 25). Similarly, a "specialist in Abnormal Psychiatry from New York" asserts that the Sp'thra, with their partial understanding of and desire for the Change Speakers, "are collectively insane" (p. 115), a nice example of ethnocentric elitism, smugness, and self-satisfaction. Even the anthropologist himself talks of Xemahoa B ("in some ways . . . the *truest* language I have ever come across") as "a lunatic language, like Roussel's, only worse. The unaided mind has no hope of holding on to it" (p. 74). That, of course, is why experiment to change the use of language and the norms of conceptualization has to be coercive.[19]

Darriand is doubtless right about Kayapi, but the entire novel tends to suggest that the (natural?) impatience of the mind is an inevitable impediment to gradual evolution. It appears to propose that such an inbuilt contradiction is not only inescapable but disastrous, "cataclysmic," as Lévi-Strauss would have it. Sole's scientific effort, then (like Kayapi's new myth, or like the American and Russian economic and technological activities), reveals itself inevitably and objectively as a form of experimental fascism, whose means act against the very liberation they intended as their end and whose destructive consequences are identical to the flooding of the Xemahoa for commercial purposes and the murder for political reasons of the alien visitors. In every case, coercion leads to cataclysm.

As I suggested Watson's *Jonah Kit* and *Martian Inca* reach the same conclusion—as does his *Alien Embassy*, where human organisms are gradually "perfected" out of existence by learning successively "higher-order" languages. These humans are either maintained in a "chrysalis" state in liquid or are baked in clay (devices reminiscent of those used by Martial Canterel in Roussel's *Locus Solus*):

Important physical changes take place in the brain during the chrysalis phase, you see. The topology of thought grows more complex, more self-analytical. We all have an inborn program for learning human speech. But the channel width of language is still very narrow—even though there are a vast number of unused simple sounds, in every language, that could widen it. For example, the whole of the English vocabulary can be reduced to one-syllable words without robbing it of any subtlety—there are *so very many*

19. This blindness toward what is 'perceived' as *other*, as different (when it can be *perceived* at all) is to be seen at the level of the writing of the novel itself: where women are written of, they are either sex objects (Sole's *wife* and Pierre's *lover*, Eileen; the Xemahoa woman whom Kayapi *supplies* for Pierre), or police victims (Iza, the guerilla woman). Men are the only active ones, though in this novel that redounds to the credit of such women as appear, since the actions all tend toward evil.

unused combinations! The chrysalis phase takes the speech program one step further, by generating a potential for far denser, richer structures—with the language patterns of old as a sort of simpler, larval form. . . . What we're devising, and *using* . . . are higher-order languages that can express vastly more, tersely.[20]

This notion of the growth of (linguistic) mind, patterned on that of bodily growth from birth to death and involving a similar hope for some kind of immortal expansion, recalls Aldous Huxley's ironic *After Many a Summer* (1939), in which humans who live beyond three hundred years have developed into apes: humanity as the babyhood of primates (the association might lead us to reflect on Sole's experiments as directly parallel to vivisectionist experiments on animals). There, too, we find repeated the opposition of death to immortality, stasis to movement, utopia to process. Kant had long since sought to solve the problem in his *What is Enlightenment?* (1784), and precisely in response to individualist thinking, by making maturity of reason a *social* rather than an individual development, so that the problem of cataclysmic change would arise only when the individual sought individual imposition: society progresses, not any individual per se. Huxley's novel would be a *reductio ad absurdum;* Kant's reply was an attempt to get beyond individualism but in individualist terms, presenting society as itself the precise equivalent of a human—a matter whose implications we saw in the preceding chapter.

The explicit goal and means of the similar development depicted in Watson's *Alien Embassy* is genocide. The narrator remarks: "Bardo [the alien controlling authority] is about the . . . genocide of man, woman, human beings. Your Future Man will never exist. There'll always be something *beyond,* and beyond again. A dog never catches its tail" (*AE,* p. 285). It is with something similar in mind that Sole responds to his own guilty feelings about the children: "Isn't the saving of four such children a valid enough reason for this underworld's existence, whatever the outcome?" (p. 35). Perhaps, he adds, from within the "Aladdin's Cave" that is their hospital, they will "discover the Open Sesame for us poor mortals" (p. 12). With the same implications Lévi-Strauss had written: "The world began without man and will end without him" (*TT,* p. 413); and Michel Foucault would get into trouble for saying much the same some ten years later in his conclusion to *Les mots et les choses.*[21] The difference, however, is that both were speaking of some kind of natural conceptual and sociopolitical evolution. Not so the experimentalists of Ian Watson's world. Lila, the narrator of *Alien Embassy,* speaks from the position of Vidya in *The*

20. Ian Watson, *Alien Embassy* (New York, 1977), pp. 276–77 (henceforth *AE*).

21. Michel Foucault, *Les mots et les choses: Une archéologie des sciences humaines* (Paris, 1966), p. 398.

Embedding, and she is answered as Sole might answer him: "Just because a more conscious human being is emerging out of Old Humanity, is that murder?" (*AE*, p. 285). "How can extermination ever be benign?" Lila will later respond (*AE*, p. 303); the human race is gradually being reduced to nothing "so that it can disappear without a trace" (*AE*, p. 305), she adds, perhaps reminding us of Foucault's face of humanity traced in the sand, which the sea tides of history will erase—except that Lila is thinking of forced removal.

The pessimism doubtless goes beyond that of *The Embedding*—or, rather, it is a despair at the other end of the experiment. In the earlier novel, the changed "concept environment" (as it will later be termed: *AE*, p. 277) of Vidya destroys itself, and the past remains. In *Alien Embassy* the "higher beings" remain, by means and at the cost of destroying the past. That "past" takes the form of "lower"(human) beings, who are in a position similar to that of the Sp'thra relative to the Change Speakers, those superior beings who can modulate "their embedding in reality" at will, who can manipulate "what we know as reality" as they choose (pp. 113–14). " 'The problem,' Ph'theri said dismally, 'is what a two-dimensional being would face, trying to behave three-dimensionally: to the mocking laughter and love-taunts of superior three-dimensional beings' " (p. 101). The dilemma is Sole's when he confronts Vidya and his eventual passage into something beyond the familiar and habitual, or Darriand's when he seeks to understand the Xemahoa. So Sole thinks, as his mind "fuses" with Vidya's at the end: "Where was the third dimension, that kept reality spaced out? This world seemed two-dimensional now . . . [he was] trying to force something upon the world that could not be there in any rational universe—a dimension at right angles to this reality" (p. 181). Again, there is something here akin to the relation of infinite and transfinite, the second overcoming the unending regression of the first, transforming it into something else by providing boundaries that contain and surpass it. Darriand has earlier used the same metaphor: "How could a two-dimensional being who had been able to experience three dimensions set up a frontier post anywhere in his flat territory—and say beyond this point lies the Other? . . . In this three-dimensional flatland of ours, words flow forward and only hang fire of their meaning so pitiably short a time, while memories flow hindwards with such a pitiable feeble capacity to hold themselves in full present awareness" (p. 78).

In Sole's case certainly, but to a degree also in Darriand's, the experimental flaw is ineluctable, for it concerns the manipulation of the reality with which they are experimenting, the inevitable manhandling of the Other—as opposed to the elaboration of self-development and self-determination (of which the guerillas complain in political terms: p. 85). As Sole laments quite early, it is "so difficult to imagine the otherness of another person" (p. 6), so difficult to avoid what Ph'theri scorns as the solipsistic mirror awareness of the Other as "the signal of the Self" (p. 113). The lack of *that* imagination is why Sole also fails to comprehend the implications and possible consequences of manipulation and coercion, indeed of *any* relation with the Other, whether coercive or not. No doubt that is why he can be described as a mirror of himself: "Slide a mirror up against his nose and he wasn't split into two different faces, like most people, but a pair of identical twins" (p. 2). A similar problem of relation is explored between Darriand and the half-Xemahoa, Kayapi—the major difference being that whereas Sole tries to force Vidya into the mold of a form of conceptualization thought up by the linguist himself, the anthropologist finds it ready-made in a complete environment, into which he tries to work himself: an achievement accomplished instead, ironically, by Sole.

The question dealt with here, then, is one of a felt crisis: conceptual, political, economic, and social. Accompanying the assumption of crisis is the hypothesis that the only way out of it, beyond it (at least for Western culture), is not through some form of violent physical revolution but through a gradual and self-generating change of logical or discursive space. Such an idea, of course, is a contemporary repetition of the claims made (at the time) for the Great Instauration achieved during the seventeenth century, whose successes and failures provide the space of the present 'crisis'—which merely marks, if you will, the moment when that discursive space's limits have become visible.[22] The dilemma concerns the means (and purpose) of escaping from such discourse: the dilemma perhaps of Chomsky's, and certainly of Sole's forbidden experiment.

It is not irrelevant in this regard that the name Chris Sole, which opens the novel, echoes Roussel's *Locus Solus* (picking up the two central syllables), a novel relating an environment of altered sensibility (starting with a story about Africa), and of different conceptualization, in which are performed diverse experiments on the living—and the dead. This particular literary precedent is very shortly made explicit by the constant reference to the same author's embedded poem, *Nouvelles impressions d'Afrique*, which, remembers Sole, "became a sort of mistress for Pierre. . . . He wanted to master her, for the sake of logic and justice." He could not escape his fascination for the words of the poem, "yet the maze they formed forever defeated the unaided human mind. If Logic was so easily put to flight by a poem, what hope was there for the reform of the world itself by logic? This mistress was an elegant bitch, a Salomé who cared not a hoot for the Third World and the Poor" (p. 9; we may well recall at

---

22. This is the matter dealt with at length in my *Discourse of Modernism*, esp. pp. 21–54, 198–225, 351–85.

this point my comments in note 19 about the treatment of the women in this novel).

From the start, then, the poem contains and allows the development of the problem, for experiment is a matter of logic. Social and political revolution, whether from left or right, is a matter of logic. All attempts to overcome the immense void between the industrialized nations and the Third World still remain a matter of logic. And, it would seem, any imagined or imaginable evolution of humanity as a social species must also depend on an ingrained logic. For there can be no such thing as meaningless action within a sociocultural environment. Action as meaningful defines such an environment. And meaning is embedded in and derives from logic. Yet the dominant logic (discursive class) ruling our environment now shows innumerable flaws. We risk an unending repetition of the same—a system immensely successful as long as its expansiveness could follow its own logic, doomed to destruction as it simply confronts similar discrete spaces of expansion—as, for example, the Third World awakes to the same logic. Yet a new logic cannot be found by the "unaided human mind." Who, or what, is to aid it? And from what logical space?

That is the point. As was true for Bacon and his contemporaries, humanity may propose—and new discursive systems are doubtless the hypotheses of experiment—but only history and the collective development of society can dispose. Logic gives way to history, and that is why the experiment is forbidden: it cannot force evolution. Yet history develops logic(s). Hence the fascination of Roussel for Sole and Darriand: an invented and unfamiliar logic, the embedded poem provides an experimental matrix for the linguist and a real historical existence for the anthropologist in the language he calls Xemahoa B and in the very life of the tribe using it. Perhaps that is why the name, Chris Sole (a first—embedded?—reference to Roussel) is the first thing Sole's wife, Eileen, calls out (p. 1). The second reference to Roussel, explicit this time, appears in Darriand's letter from Brazil. It is not gratuitous to recall here that Levi-Strauss had gone to Brazil to unearth his first 'evidence' of the "savage mind," of structured "mythical thinking," and that he discovered a quite different organization of the conceptual environment—an ordering no less rational though apparently quite other than the analytical environment familiar to us, but not perhaps altogether dissimilar from what Darriand comes across. Indeed, the mounting floodwaters that are gradually drowning the world of the Xemahoa had already been similarly experienced by Lévi-Strauss:

Trees were growing in all directions, and flowers bloomed across waterfalls; it was impossible to say whether the river served to irrigate this fantastic garden, or whether it was about to be choked by a proliferation of plants and creepers, which seemed free to develop not only vertically, but through all spatial dimensions, as a result of the abolition of the usual distinctions between earth and water. There was no river any more, nor any river bank, but instead a maze of copses watered by the current, while the firm ground seemed to rise out of the very foam. This sympathy between the elements extended to living creatures. [*TT*, p. 330]

One would almost say that the anthropologist is recalling three letters on the relations of water, earth, and sky published by Cyrano de Bergerac in 1654,[23] more than the 'reality' of the Amazon basin—a note on the relation between reality and fiction (see note 17), on the bond between the mid-seventeenth and mid-twentieth centuries, that we may well bear in mind (and a reference that will recur).

The issue of distinguishing fact from fiction is the same one Frege sought to resolve in ordinary language by means of his concept of truth value (see Chapter 1), and it is endemic in any language of which the concept, with that of mind, relies upon a rigid and compartmentalized division between world, language, and mind, between sign and referent, between utterance and object, and so forth. In terms recalling Frege's dilemma and his attempted solution, Roland Barthes alluded to the difficulty when he remarked that in an utterance of a thing, our language "normally merges together its existence, the class to which it belongs, and the assertion of its particularity." Indeed, he added, "it is an altogether astounding phenomenon that language should not allow us to distinguish between the simple utterance of a thing and the assertion that it exists."[24]

The dispute between Frege and Russell, discussed earlier, had at its core just exactly that difficulty, and the need to distinguish between the 'truth' of an assertion and the 'truth' of what is asserted. At a time when a discursive class, a dominant logic, has been put into question, when other forms of discourse are being elaborated and new meaning is required, the issues of fact and fiction, of coherent truth and correspondent truth (in terms of analytico-referential discourse), and of how a new system of coherence may come into conjuncture with nondiscursive events, actions, and situations are clearly of fundamental importance.

The world entered by Lévi-Strauss, Cyrano de Bergerac, and Pierre Darriand is new and appears to require new forms of comprehension. Lévi-Strauss's primitive tribespeople not only occupy the same spatial environment as the jungle surroundings, in a kind of abolition of material distinctions; they also remind him that humanity occupies a kind of transfinite temporal realm as well. At one point, similarly, Darriand describes

23. Savinien Cyrano de Bergerac, *Lettres*, ed. Luciano Erba (Milan, 1965), pp. 29–39.
24. Roland Barthes, *Système de la mode* (Paris, 1967), pp. 99, chap. 7, §4.

certain peculiarities of the treatment of tense in the Xemahoa language, in which there is no future—in the sense of a temporal reference distinct from the present—but simply a present utterance that in fact already contains "the seeds of futurity," and indeed the past as well (pp. 50–51). We may well be reminded of Jorge Borges's "Tlönian" language in his story "Tlön, Uqbar, Orbis Tertius." In the West, thinks Darriand, "we have no direct experience of time," whereas the Xemahoa perceive time directly as always present all around them (p. 53). For his part, Lévi-Strauss is less pessimistic (if that is the word), having himself been brought to the experience of something analogous:

> As he moves about within his mental and historical framework, man takes along with him all the positions he has already occupied, and all those he will occupy. He is everywhere at one and the same time; he is a crowd surging forward abreast, and constantly recapitulating the whole series of previous stages. For we live in several worlds, each truer than the one it encloses, and itself false in relation to the one which encompasses it. Some are known to us through action; some are lived through in thought; but the seeming contradiction resulting from their coexistence is solved in the obligation we feel to grant a meaning to the nearest and to deny any to those furthest away; whereas the truth lies in a progressive dilating of the meaning, but in reverse order, up to the point at which it explodes. [*TT,* p. 412][25]

Such a commentary is just as applicable to Darriand's relation with the Xemahoa, to Sole's relation with Vidya, or to the Sp'thra's relation to the Change Speakers as is Roussel's poem. It is marked by the same mixture of past and present, of time and space, by the same idea of the presentness of 'past' and 'future,' not to mention by the importance of the opposition between an old and a new world, of the problematic relation between Self and Other, and of meaning in general.

25. One could multiply the number of affinities between *Tristes Tropiques* and *The Embedding* to an almost unlimited extent. Lévi-Strauss describes a *maté*-drinking ceremony on the Pantanal (*TT,* pp. 66–67) that is quite comparable to the Xemahoa maka-i ceremonies. The Nambikwara possess a poison, extracted from a tree with a peculiarly swollen trunk, whose application to an enemy is believed to induce a condition similar to that of the tree: the victim will swell up and die (*TT,* p. 291); the Xemahoa have maka-i, a drug extracted from fungus that grows on a tree whose trunk is an integral part of the tribe's myths of life and death, and whose application to a pregnant woman to help enable the birth of a "God-child" literally produces a child that has burst its bodily boundaries in a mass of hernias and whose brain is largely outside its skull (p. 144). Lévi-Strauss describes the Caduveo medicine man (*TT,* p. 176) in terms not dissimilar to those describing the Xemahoa's *bruxo* and shows how the Tupi-Kawahib chief, Taperahi, works himself into a fit (*TT,* pp. 359–60) much as does the *bruxo.* And so on. These analogies are not meaningless. Lévi-Strauss is also concerned with "the end of one civilization, the beginning of another, and the sudden discovery by our present-day world that it is perhaps beginning to prove too small for the people inhabiting it—these palpable truths" (*TT,* p. 22). Again, of course, this recalls the fact/fiction problem referred to throughout Shakespeare and Cyrano, Frege, Borges, and Roussel.

Yet if the Xemahoa do bear some relation to Lévi-Strauss's "savage mind" (the description of their complicated mythical system is worth remembering: pp. 49–52, 59–60, 157–59) or to Roussel's conceptions, they are also resolutely different. Their uniqueness perhaps underscores the debt the anthropologist owes to Roussel's fictions, no less than the debt Watson's fiction owes to certain inventions of science: it emphasizes the possible arbitrariness of all imagination and of all hypothesis—the role of fiction in that conceptual activity which Peirce, for example, saw as the single essential foundation stone of all and any truly "scientific" activity: hypothesis (ab- or retroduction).

Moreover, the Indians are unique in not practicing precisely that aspect of social relations which Lévi-Strauss views as universal:[26] "As far as kinship rules [among the Xemahoa] are concerned, there is a total lack of incest prohibition. Quite the opposite in fact. They are incestuous—in the widest cultural sense" (pp. 43–44). They are already 'elsewhere,' in terms of any familiar culture. They are some Other. Their exclusion from what Lévi- Strauss believes to be a universally valid cultural taboo (akin to the Chomskyan notion of a universal grammar, insofar as it offers the frame for a species-specific regulatory system) is matched only by their complete linguistic uniqueness: "There's a kind of linguistic fault-line that divides the Xemahoa from their neighbors. He [a Tupi interpreter] couldn't communicate with them in any of the dialects he tried"(p. 63). This utter uniqueness makes them a fiction akin to Roussel's, or even Lévi-Strauss's, something like the counterproof of Chomsky's imaginary experiment or the hopes entertained of the wild boy of Aveyron (and others). Occupying the category that would disprove what Chomsky hopes might be demonstrated by the forbidden experiment, they are menacing. But what could be done to them or through them (from our habitual logical space) is equally so. I have mentioned Darriand's fears, but Sole too feels that these potential discoveries are fraught with peril: he "shivered with morning misgivings. They often attacked him between waking up and getting to the Hospital" (p. 1).

The "Hospital," as I have already suggested, provides the reader with one hint of the kind of discursive imposition that may be in question. It is at the hospital that Sole is concerned with "trying to discover what the world really is, how the mind of Man sees the world!" (p. 3). At least, he is initially concerned with such a project—until Darriand's epistolary intrusion transforms him from linguist to social psychologist or conceptual projector. One is irresistibly reminded of the transformation undergone by Freud while studying with Jean-Martin Charcot at the Salpetrière in

26. See Claude Lévi-Strauss, *The Elementary Structures of Kinship* (1949), rev. ed., tr. James Harle Bell, John Richard von Sturmer, and Rodney Needham (Boston, 1969).

1885–86,[27] or by Lévi-Strauss under Georges Dumas at the Hôpital Sainte-Anne: from student of philosophy to anthropologist (*TT,* p. 20). Hospital or altered environment: Darriand recounts how his immersion in Xemahoa culture has left him somewhat "aimless"; Lévi-Strauss comments on "the mental disorder" experienced by anyone who is exposed to "abnormal living conditions over a prolonged period" (*TT,* p. 383). In each case, what is in question is a *passage* that suggests the possibility of changing to something else. The question then becomes one of proposing a logic, not so that a dominant order may impose it but so that a collective history may dispose.

Sole's initial project was simply to discover whether there exists an innate system in humans that controls language acquisition and the consequent conception of the world: to test Benjamin Whorf's hypothesis, if you will.[28] He wants to know whether it is correct, as Chomsky asserts, that the child "must possess, first, a linguistic theory that specifies the form of the grammar of a possible human language, and, second, a strategy for selecting a grammar of the appropriate form that is compatible with the primary linguistic data."[29] Actually, this is precisely what has been most severely tested, at least as to the assumption of the primary nature of such a grammar and such a strategy, in the work of Vygotsky and other Soviet psychologists and semioticians. Their working assumption (for which much validating evidence has already been provided) is that society is prior to the higher faculties of the individual, including language—and indeed the use of all semiotic systems.[30] Such a theory would seem to provide a more appropriate tool for understanding what one might refer to as socioindividual psychology in a culture no longer under the dominance of the analytico-referential.

We cannot yet speak of anything like that here, though. Earlier in the work just quoted, Chomsky hints at one grammatical system that might conceivably provide a test of falsifiability for his concept. He remarks that a highly embedded language is not humanly possible, because it defeats

27. The editors of the *Standard Edition* remark that Freud's account of his sojourn in Paris is that of the diversion of his "scientific interests from neurology to psychology" (I:3).

28. Benjamin Lee Whorf's writings remain for the most part scattered. The standard collection is still *Language, Thought and Reality: Selected Writings,* ed. John B. Carroll (Cambridge, Mass., 1956). This thesis is also the underlying argument of Piagetian developmental studies. See, e.g., Jean Piaget, *Le langage et la pensée chez l'enfant* (Paris, 1923), and many other writings.

29. Noam Chomsky, *Aspects of the Theory of Syntax* (1965; rpt. Cambridge, Mass., 1969), p. 25.

30. "The three themes that form the core of Vygotsky's theoretical framework," writes James Wertsch, "are (1) a reliance on a genetic or developmental method; (2) the claim that higher mental processes in the individual have their origin in social processes; and (3) the claim that mental processes can be understood only if we understand the tools and signs that mediate them" (*Vygotsky,* pp. 14–15). For Vygotsky's writings in English translation, see Chapter 5, n. 16.

human memory systems.[31] While human languages permit—indeed necessarily incorporate—a certain amount of embedding, a language entirely dependent on such processes (the example of Roussel's poem is *not* mentioned) would not be possible.[32] Surely only in fiction could such a language be imagined as entirely transforming conceptual space, given that some embedding is apparently integral to *all* natural languages. Darriand describes the euphoria and the fear of achieving such a comprehension in relation to the completely embedded system of Roussel's poem (p. 78). Roussel himself commented on the fact that the reader will ordinarily "extract" from the poem whatever data she or he can make coincide with her or his habitual logic, and only such data, though the poem itself is in part a deliberate (experimental) attempt to break with such logic.[33]

For his part, Chomsky argues that the child "approaches the [linguistic] data with the presumption that they are drawn from a language of a certain antecedently well-defined type, his problem being to determine which of the (humanly) possible languages is that of the community in which he is placed. Language learning would be impossible unless this were the case."[34] Such an argument is dubious in the extreme, for actually all that is required is a *capacity* for such learning, not a formal ordering process that such learning must follow (I will return to this matter shortly). Sole is trying to force the disappearance of such systems of logic (for his experiment to have any meaning at all, he must be assuming their existence); he is trying to deprive a Chomskyan child of any example of a language "possible" in terms of his supposedly innate model.

Because language and cognitive processes are essentially intermingled,[35] if Sole could succeed in imposing a new innate system (or one that will become so), then he would create not simply a new perceptual

31. Chomsky, *Aspects*, pp. 13–14.

32. Chomsky's initial proof that a "finite state grammar" is inadequate to English is the possibility of generating "embedded strings," which are at least potentially unlimited: Noam Chomsky, *Syntactic Structures* (1957; rpt. The Hague, 1966), pp. 20–23. As a device in the modern novel, embedding is not uncommon. A striking example occurs in *To the Lighthouse* at a point where the Ramsays are waiting for children and guests to return for dinner. Mrs. Ramsay's question "Did Nancy go with them?" gives way immediately to a long (parenthetical) narration of the outing upon which she had indeed gone, a narration itself containing embedded parentheses and thoughts. It lasts some eight pages, as a separate section (xiv) of the novel's first part, before leading to " 'Yes,' said Prue, in her considering way, answering her mother's question, 'I think Nancy did go with them' " (Woolf, *Lighthouse*, pp. 112–19).

33. Roussel, *Nouvelles impressions*, pp. 21–59. See also Raymond Roussel, *Comment j'ai écrit certains de mes livres* (Paris, 1963), pp. 11–35.

34. Chomsky, *Aspects*, p. 27.

35. Clearly, such a view is so widespread as not to need authority (any other view would be hard if not impossible to conceive), but I may as well indicate one from within the same linguistic framework: Noam Chomsky, *Current Issues in Linguistic Theory* (London, 1964), p. 27. Again, the assumption in Chomsky is that both language and cognition *originate* in the individual, though that individual is genetically defined as human. In a sense, one might say, its humanness starts with its individuality.

and conceptual system with the processes accompanying it but the potential for a new political order, a new social process, and so on. The dangers of this kind of mind manipulation are apparent (we know it as "brainwashing"), but the alternative of some form of self-evolution appears equally problematic, though in different ways. Chomsky has asserted that the attainment of an experimental coercion is impossible: the child may be able to learn different languages but cannot acquire a new system of rules for the formation of such languages, or of hypotheses to select between possibilities. While "children do learn a first language, the language that they learn is, in the traditional sense, an 'instituted language,' not an innately specified system" (*LM*, p. 22), and the learning of it is dependent upon and made possible by that innate specification; the genetic programming controls both the nature of possible human languages and their learning.

We saw Watson's aliens agree with Sole that any language can be learned with rapidity, "provided it conforms to the rules of Universal Grammar" (p. 93). All human languages, writes Chomsky, are differently but identifiably determined by the same innate mechanism: "Each natural language is a simple and highly systematic realization of a complex and intricate underlying form with highly special and unique properties."[36] This limitation, insofar as language, thought, and action are inextricably linked, implies that humanity is, in a quite concrete sense, locked into a continuous repetition of the same, whatever may be the instituted (and institutional) variants. For Chomsky, the only way out is to suppose some individual creative freedom at the surface level, as though there were no feedback, no interaction between what the scientist might be pleased to call the "two." The paradigm is not unlike that of some simplistic Marxism, supposing a kind of false superstructural freedom within a set forever laid down by forms of economic production (however much this itself may develop its own "objective" history to the exclusion of any subject).

The linguist does allow, however, that a nonhuman rational system might have a different innate ordering model and therefore different forms of conceptualization, of practice, and so on (Wittgenstein's lion again). This would mean, for instance, that a human child transported to such a civilization, say, on another planet (Sole's laboratory or the Sp'thras' relation to the Change Speakers being clear cases in point) either would not be able to acquire the language (not, at least, as it acquires a human one) or, if it did succeed in doing so, would invalidate the hypothesis of a universal grammar. At the same time, such a child would be unable to "think human," for its conceptual environment would be utterly different. The fact, that is to say, that "as far as we know, possession of human

36. *Current Issues*, p. 112.

language is associated with a specific type of mental organization, not simply a higher degree of intelligence" (*LM*, p. 70), implies a limit of some kind. In answer to a question put by the American, Tom Zwingler, as to what might be meant by the "mind's idea of all possible languages," Sole specifies all languages spoken by beings evolved on the same basis as ourselves. I can't vouch for languages that silicon salamanders elsewhere in the universe might have dreamt up!" (p. 36). And once again we are reminded of an analogous thought and a quite similar dilemma from that moment of parallel earlier development in the European seventeenth century.[37]

Yet there is surely no a priori reason why a species-specific mental organization should not evolve, change, and develop while still remaining species-specific (if indeed such a requirement is imperative), any more or less than do the economic, political, and social structures that it elaborates as it is elaborated by them. Human physical structures appear to have changed in the course of evolution, and there seems small reason to suppose that mental ones should not do so as well. Indeed, whether they might be said to evolve "by deliberation" or by "natural selection"—according to a Lamarckian or a Darwinian scenario—would be indifferent, because when we speak of a mental structure, we are speaking by definition of an organ whose very nature is one of autogeneration and constant self-reference, as it also—simultaneously—turns outward. At the conclusion of *The Descent of Man*, Darwin linked mental evolution, language, and human sociability in just such a way: "A great stride in the development will have followed, as soon as the half-art and half-instinct of language came into use; for the continued use of language will have reacted on the brain and produced an inherited effect; and this again will have reacted on the improvement of language."[38]

In a manner not dissimilar, Victoria Welby calls for just such a simultaneous development of language and mind in her own time. We need, she argues, a new kind of pluralistic language in order that "the cruel waste of the present day in the language-world will give place to a 'storing-up' of all our precious means of mutual speaking." And this will provide the widest possible kind of comprehension and development of meaning: "the power to master the many dialects of thought, and inter-

37. The battle between a salamander, breather and procreator of fire, and its opposite, the remora, represents a kind of high point in Cyrano de Bergerac's *Voyage dans le soleil*, whose principal preoccupation is with the possibility of a communicative language: see, Savinien Cyrano de Bergerac, *Histoire comique des état et empire de la lune et du soleil*, ed. Claude Mettra and Jean Suyeux (Paris, 1962), pp. 239–45, and my *Discourse of Modernism*, pp. 277–93.

38. Charles Darwin, *The Origin of Species by Means of Natural Selection or the Preservation of Favored Races in the Struggle for Life*, and *The Descent of Man, and Selection in Relation to Sex* (New York, n.d.), p. 912.

pret men to each other by learning their thought-tongues."[39] The form of her expression here is remarkably similar to what we have been seeing in Watson's novel. So, too, is Welby's ideal of what this might lead toward, for what she has in mind is nothing less than that self-developmental evolution of human mental powers: "We have not yet learnt that the true advance [in thought] is spiral, that is, must sweep back on itself to take up ancient things and set them in new light and on new quests in new directions." Only once we have learned this, she adds, will we find or create "new ways of speaking all our mind and reaching new mind thereby."[40]

Here perhaps we approach a useful evaluation of the relation between experiment and self-development, between subjective input and collective determination, between individualism and history, between what Charles Peirce might call the formulation of hypotheses and the formation of habit. Lévi-Strauss has put it in a usefully generalizable way:

> Incidentally, Marx's quality has nothing to do with whether or not he accurately foresaw certain historical developments [one may doubt this judgment, but Lévi-Strauss is referring to a Popperian judgment in terms of experimental falsifiability]. Following Rousseau . . . Marx established that social science is no more founded on the basis of events than physics is founded on sense data: the object is to construct a model and to study its properties and its different reactions in laboratory conditions in order later to apply observations to the interpretation of empirical happenings, which may be far removed from what had been forecast.
>
> At a different level of reality, Marxism seemed to me to proceed in the same manner as geology and psychoanalysis (taking the latter in the sense given it by its founder). All three demonstrate that understanding consists in reducing one type of reality to another; that the true reality is never the most obvious; and that the nature of truth is already indicated by the care it takes to remain elusive. For all cases, the same problem arises, the problem of the relationship between feeling and reason, and the aim is the same: [to achieve] a kind of *superrationalism,* which will integrate the first with the second, without sacrificing any of its properties. [*TT,* p. 57–58]

Wittgenstein said it more succinctly (though no doubt losing some of the nuances): "What a Copernicus or a Darwin really achieved was not the discovery of a true theory but of a fertile new point of view."[41]

Such views have of course become increasingly common. They help clarify the implications of the fact that Watson's fictional experiment is founded on Roussel's poem. In the first place, they suggest that the ex-

39. Welby, *What is Meaning?* pp. 60, 97.
40. Ibid., p. 16.
41. Wittgenstein, *Culture and Value,* p. 18 (note dated 1931).

periment will always be to a degree uninterpretable: as we have seen, the poem itself is at least partly concerned with the fact that the reader will necessarily seek to guide her or his interpretation by means of a linear analysis. In the second place, therefore, it (poem or experiment) will *always* be at least partly if not entirely falsified. Third, the 'falsification' is a matter of 'theory,' not of 'practice,' since its objective 'truth' will depend upon its subsequent utility and efficacy for transformed (and transforming) human action. Finally, again therefore, the whole matter is clearly politicized—both by Roussel and by Watson (as it was implicitly by Lévi-Strauss in the foregoing quotation). And the dangers are political as well.

Darriand notes that the relation of the non-Indian to the Xemahoa, like that of the reader to Roussel's poem, is "Caraiba," alien (p. 3) because of his or her inability to comprehend—just as the "barbarian" to the ancient Greeks was anyone who did not comprehend Greek. The present threat of destruction by outside forces makes the situation yet more ambiguous—a fear experienced by both sides. As Zwingler remarks: "We can't afford any loss of cultural confidence, can we? The world's in a pretty volatile state nowadays" (p. 73). The "human zoo," to which Darriand sarcastically suggests that his "quaint savages" should be taken for their own protection (p. 4), is precisely where Sole already has his children. And Sole is very well aware of the lost innocence and of the ambiguity of such alien imposition: "Now that Vidya, Vasilki, Rama, and Gulshen were learning their lessons in the Special Environments at the Hospital, Pierre's triggering of memories of that happy mood came with an accusing force" (p. 4).

Sole wants to make a potentially creative mental deep structure for construction of a natural grammar and the production of actually transformed verbal behavior and thought processes. He seeks to impose it "by stimulus conditions, schedules of reinforcement, establishment of habit structures, patterns of behavior, and so on." Chomsky continues this description of Skinnerian devices by adding: "Of course, one can design a restricted environment in which such control and such pattern can be demonstrated," but there is "no hope" in it (*LM*, p. 114). Sole, however, becomes concerned less with learning "about the range of human potentialities" (Chomsky comments that one might as well observe "humans in a prison or an army—or in many a schoolroom") than with *imposing* a new (*any* new) structure of thought upon the Other, the alien.

The concluding disaster suggests that indeed he might as well have been in a prison. Though the catastrophe remains ambiguous, Sole/Vidya (the two come together mentally in some way) seems to "expand" to some new dimension. The ambiguity is similar to that which marks the "destruction" of the Xemahoa culture. The drug maka-i "grows only after the ground's been covered with water" (p. 80), which implies that the entire area—not just one tree as before—might sprout with the fungus essential and sufficient, it would seem, to the Xemahoas' mythical, linguistic, and cultural organization. These ambiguities have to do, of course, with the difficulties of interpretation to which I just referred, and to the fact/fiction dilemma recalled earlier. They suggest, too, that there is some validity in Lévi-Strauss's remark about the passage from experiment to "superrationalism" and in Chomsky's observation that "the essential properties of the human mind will always escape such investigation" (*LM,* p. 114). Sole in fact shows that as in the case of subatomic physics, the mind's properties are inescapably altered by the very experiment that sought to 'know' them and that set out (it thought) to reveal them. But that is no more than to realize that mind and language cannot be separated out from their embedding in the sociocultural and natural environments.

Still, it may be said, at one level that is exactly what Sole *does* set out to show. But because he also alters his own mind, he is unable to communicate the results of his experiment. Thomas More, Francis Bacon, Cyrano de Bergerac, and others noted just the same difficulty at an analogous moment of transformation.[42] It is, yet again, Wittgenstein's lion, the difficulty of any kind of linguistic communication with a mind functioning in terms different from those familiar to us. It is in this sense that the notion of "bad language" is introduced—the "bad language" that others accuse Sole of teaching at the hospital (pp. 4–6). Their reaction is akin to that of Victoria Welby, who thinks of it as "mislocution," as a move away from good (more powerful, more effective, more meaningful) usage: "The phrase 'bad language' should gain a more general application, and include waste and misuse of words, abuse of speech, chaos in expression, degradation of painfully acquired and slowly rising standards of language."[43]

Sole interprets it in a more positive way, of course. For him, the phrase "bad language" denotes a language that does not match universal grammar, and the adjective "bad" simply indicates others' (inevitable) misunderstanding of his objectives and means to them. Chomsky has discussed the idea of "bad language" with Nelson Goodman (*LM,* p. 82), and in the context of his thinking, one would have to conclude that *any* language violating the postulated universal grammar is "bad"—not because it is simply sloppy or degraded but because it contradicts the very canons that order language (though that could hardly be apparent to the layperson, who would clearly understand it as misuse). Sole's attempt to justify his teaching by arguing that such language is therefore necessarily "bad" or "wrong" (regardless of which interpretation one puts on it) simply

42. See *Discourse of Modernism,* pp. 114–15, 214–15, 232–34.
43. Welby, *What Is Meaning?* pp. 140, 63.

because he is dealing with brain-damaged children (p. 5), clearly solves nothing. In the first place, such children would necessarily appear "brain-damaged," "mad," "insane," "lunatic," or in some classifiable way deviant. Just so were the wild children classified in the eighteenth century, and just so have aphasia and autism been classified in our own. In the second place, the "badness" of language is a way of marking irredeemable *difference,* not some mere slippage. In the third, neither in Welby nor in Chomsky nor in Watson is the particular adjective indifferent.

The fact remains that experimental imposition is a form of dogmatic fascism, since it seeks to control the Other to its own ends: a form of "Nazism," as it is accurately termed in *Alien Embassy* (*AE,* p. 303). In *The Embedding,* that position is Sole's rather than Darriand's. Politically, it is also that of the American president, who "had a firm faith in the possibility of managing people and events according to well-defined scripts drawn up by 'responsible' psychologists and sociologists . . . of orchestrating domestic and international events to make harmonious music" (p. 118). Yet the left-wing terrorists aim at nothing else either: "Of Marx or Christ. What did the choice matter to the Xemahoa! Whichever gained control over them, they would be destroyed," Darriand laments to himself (p. 86). "Soviets and Americans, we're both of us frontiersmen at heart," rejoices the American agent Amory Hirsch (p. 168).

This is a statement calling up a similar commentary by another novelist, one from the East this time. The narrator of Milan Kundera's *Unbearable Lightness of Being* relates that an American senator was to take the novel's heroine with his children to a skating rink and that he refers to this setting to express what happiness is: "stadium, grass, and children." She, however, cannot prevent a rather different thought: "At that moment an image of the senator standing on a reviewing stand in a Prague square flashed through Sabina's mind. The smile on his face was the smile Communist statesmen beamed from the height of their reviewing stand to the identically smiling citizens in the parade below."[44] Humanity has achieved a "bankrupt wealth" (p. 89), with which it papers over "the void in man" (p. 90). Left or right, it makes no difference, because in fact both use the same paradigm of control and the same patterns to impose their systematic models. Chomsky speaks directly to this dilemma:

The doctrine that the human mind is initially unstructured and plastic and that human nature is entirely a social product has often been associated with progressive and even revolutionary social thinking, while speculations with regard to human instinct have often had a conservative and pessimistic cast. One can easily see why reformers and revolutionaries should become radical

44. Milan Kundera, *The Unbearable Lightness of Being,* tr. Michael Henry Heim (1984; rpt. New York, 1985), p. 250.

environmentalists, and there is no doubt that concepts of immutable human nature can be and have been employed to erect barriers against social change and to defend established privilege.

But a deeper look will show that the concept of the "empty organism," plastic and unstructured, apart from being false, also serves naturally as the support for the most reactionary social doctrines. If people are, in fact, malleable and plastic beings with no essential psychological nature, then why should they not be controlled and coerced by those who claim authority, special knowledge, and a unique insight into what is best for those less enlightened? Empiricist doctrine can easily be molded into an ideology for the vanguard party that claims authority to lead the masses to a society that will be governed by the "red bureaucracy" of which Bakunin warned. And just as easily for the liberal technocrats or corporate managers who monopolize "vital decision-making" in the institutions of state capitalist democracy, beating the people with the people's stick, in Bakunin's trenchant phrase.[45]

In that sense, there is little difference indeed between Chris Sole and Skinner's T. E. Frazier, leader-director of *Walden Two;* or between Chris Sole and Amory Hirsch, the latter so contented with the reestablishment of undisputed American (and Soviet) power on Earth. It is really the dualistic 'alternative' that is in question, whether in Chomsky or elsewhere: *either* programmed *or* utterly malleable. Needless to say, either can be used for the political or social ends of the moment. It is not the one *or* the other that is inherently conservative or that can be used for reactionary objectives; it is the historical conjuncture that makes such concepts available for such use—in this case, certainly, that of the duality itself that is involved. So, the same problem *exactly* has been seen behind the key concept, the fundamental maxim of modern liberal political theory: "The ultimate *raison d'être* for the contract theory, all through its history, has been to reconcile the apparently conflicting claims of liberty and law."[46]

Kant long since pointed out that the ambiguous relation between law and liberty seemed to correspond to a spiritual contradiction within civilized humanity, whose consequence was that individual needs could not be satisfied by collective social organization. The philosopher of Königsberg spoke to the matter in the fourth and fifth propositions of his *Idee zu einer allgemeinen Geschichte in weltbürgerlicher Absicht,* remarking on humanity's fundamental *"unsocial sociability"* as "the cause of a law-governed social order," for this contradiction obliges humans to create laws that allow them to live in a situation they "cannot *bear* yet cannot *bear to leave.*" (The

45. Chomsky, *Reflections on Language,* p. 132. We have already glanced at the relation between 'free' reason and innate system, between 'liberty' and 'prison' (or "concentration camp"). Chomsky discussed the matter again in *Rules and Representations* (New York, 1980).

46. John Wiedhofft Gough, *The Social Contract: A Critical Study of Its Development,* 2d ed. (Oxford, 1957), p. 254. Similar arguments form the basis of Dennis Lloyd's *The Idea of Law* (Harmondsworth, 1964), and John Rawls's *A Theory of Justice* (Cambridge, Mass., 1971).

similarity of such a statement to the argument of Freud's *Civilization and Its Discontents* scarcely needs observing.) Human laws make human freedom possible; indeed, "the highest task which nature has set for humankind must therefore be that of establishing a society in which *freedom under external laws* would be combined to the greatest possible extent with irresistible force, in other words of establishing a perfectly *just civil constitution*."[47] Kant's utopian goal has yet to be achieved, and one of the matters being discussed here is precisely that no such constitution—perceived as a series of unresolvable contradictions, tensions, and ambiguities—is ever possible. His 'solution' indicates, too, just what may be the ultimate similarity, underlined by Watson as by Kundera, between 'East' and 'West,' and just why we may call that 'solution'—as I have—"authoritarian liberalism."

What we see in *The Embedding*, therefore, is that the depiction of these questions (at a lowlier level, to be sure) shows them indeed to be unresolvable from the grounds of their premise. Sole's means and ends are utterly incompatible. The terms of Chomsky's opposition are ultimately self-defeating. For the only way Sole's goal could be achieved (assuming its possibility in principle) would be by the self-development of the organism: not Vidya, therefore, but the Xemahoa; not Sole trying to impose an artificial system upon another but Darriand striving to work his own way into a new class of conceptualization, into a quite unfamiliar use of signs. Here, too, we may add, Kant foresaw one style of possible 'answer,' as I intimated before. That style remained individualistically oriented of course, but in his 1784 *Beantwortung der Frage: Was ist Aufklärung?* the argument that the growth to rational human "maturity" (itself embodied within the concept of *Enlightenment*) is a function of society and humankind as a whole, not just of the separate individual, represents perhaps a first faltering step away from the contradictory sphere within which the individual is opposed to the social, the self to the other, inside to outside, freedom to law and constraint, and the rest.[48] In political and social theory this view was to lead toward increasing emphasis upon the primacy of *social* order and process in any objective comprehension of human development or, rather, toward the understanding that the collective and the individual, conceptually 'separable' as they may be, are ineluctably

47. Immanuel Kant, *Political Writings*, ed. Hans Reiss, tr. H. B. Nisbet (Cambridge, 1970), pp. 44–46. I have elsewhere explored in a different context this relation between law and liberty, its traditional association with the nature of mind (in modern Western analysis), and the correspondent role played by the contract in the theory of political society; see "Science des rêves," esp. pp. 44–48, 56–58.

48. Immanuel Kant, "An Answer to the Question: 'What Is Enlightenment?,'" in *Political Writings*, pp. 54–60. On "authoritarian liberalism" and its implications, see Chapter 6, n. 32, above.

bound together—indeed, that the 'two' cannot fruitfully be thought of as separate arenas of knowledge and action.

The consequence of any other relation is disastrous: the nonfunctioning of Vidya, the destruction of the spaceship, the drowning of the Indians, and the subsequent destruction of the artificial lake—destruction as the necessary and inevitable consequence of any kind of manipulating imposition, whether conceptual, political, economic, or cultural (to take the four cases indicated in *The Embedding*). Does this mean that no kind of change is possible? That new meaning cannot only not be evolved, but not even thought? That we are therefore doomed to the kind of carefully conservative pessimism against which Chomsky warns? Again, I think not: the novel's discreet optimist in this sense is Pierre Darriand. He it is who first mentions Roussel's poetic creation (p. 3), who participates in wars of liberation as he studies the sociology of those same wars (p. 2), who strives to change his own conceptual space as he seeks to understand that of others—living, not artificial. In this sense *The Embedding* is a thought experiment that shows the consequences of *any* kind of manipulation, whether revolutionary or reactionary. It shows that *those* two poles meet in one, and that they are really the same thing. It is a fiction about scientific experimentalism, a fiction about the results of any manipulation of reality. As such it comes to reveal the manipulation undertaken by all experimentation in the name of scientific fictions; the question then becomes one of balance and of values.

Indeed, if we broaden the area of concern, as *The Embedding* urges us to do, then we can argue, for example, that just as Sole and Hirsch mirror each other in their violent manipulation, so too there is no such thing as a successful violent social revolution—if by that one means a successful redirecting and reordering of the energies and practices of an entire sociocultural environment. Of course, the phenomenon of violent social revolution—certainly any whose achievements are of the kind just suggested—is one of extreme rarity. Yet even more rare are those that *originate*—so rare indeed that one might almost say there has never been any such thing. The so-called "bourgeois revolution" of seventeenth-century England occurred at the end of a century-long political, economic, and social upheaval whose "theory" had been elaborated from the time of Thomas More and Machiavelli, of Bodin and La Boétie, of Bacon and Descartes. It was, one may say, borrowing a term from the topological studies of René Thom, the moment of "catastrophe" in a developing social and intellectual order, the moment when a quantitative development transformed itself into a qualitative change.[49]

49. The extremely slow and gradual nature of the change throughout the (very long) period of the so-called English Revolution, as well as the continued importance of a particular traditional heritage of political authority and social order, have been pointed out, e.g.,

Yet scarcely so much could be said of the revolutions of 1776, 1789, or 1917; however much each may have thoroughly changed the terms of political discourse in the countries immediately concerned, they appear rather to be parts of an urgent process of 'catching-up,' successive moments in the increasing homogenization of an enlarging cultural sphere. Once its revolution was over, France was ready to enter upon an era of industrial expansion and the concomitant alteration of social, economic, and cultural patterns—with which its neighbor Britain had been struggling for certainly more than half a century. The Soviet Union, once *its* revolution was over, could enter an advanced industrial phase, until then the prerogative of the "West," from which its predominantly feudal economic and sociocultural order had sealed it off. So far, other "revolutions" seem entirely compatible with such an interpretation.

One may suppose, indeed, that a comparable pattern will be seen within Third World countries as that same homogenization, in an increasingly worldwide sociocultural and economic order, progresses toward what Charles Peirce called the gradual fixation of habit. We may hope that this will lead not into some final cultural entropy but rather out of one pattern into another—toward, for instance, a resolution of the problem of the contract, because "freedom under the law" could no longer be ignored indefinitely by funneling self-interest against nonparticipating societies. It would have to be confronted from within, in a process we already see occurring: theoretically in the self-examination being undertaken both by Western Marxism and by traditional liberal thinking (currently finding a conservative and frequently reactionary outlet among the so-called "neo-Conservatives" and "neo-Liberals"); practically in the increasingly urgent economic and political confrontations and problems arising both within the Western 'democracies' and between them and the Third World (is terrorism a symptom of this?). We should be aware, then, that we must be speaking of a homogenization not simply in the narrow sense of customs, habits, and so on but in the broader sense of "episteme," "world view," "dominant discursive class," conceptual habits, and the like—of ways of deriving meaning from experience, of making experience meaningful. Raymond Williams has correctly remarked, in this respect, that "the historical process, in some of its main features, is now effectively international."[50]

Such a view seems to suggest that those cultures which have lived through the entire development are best placed to work out something

by Peter Laslett: *The World We Have Lost,* 2d ed. (New York, 1971), pp. 158–212. See also Charles Webster, *The Great Instauration: Science, Medicine, and Reform, 1626–1660* (London, 1975).

50. Williams, *The Country and the City,* p. 351.

radically new and to avoid Lenin's error of believing (in opposition to his mentors) that one can skip over levels of development. History has shown that he was objectively wrong, and that the price of force has been to make of the means necessary for effecting such a leap (the installation of the party as leader, judge, and sole lawgiver and executor) the very coercive formations he and his followers thought to avoid. Historically as well as theoretically (but the two should not be so separated), a process of more gradual development seems to have been essential. And the fact that change will have to be elaborated out of those advanced capitalist formations, the limits of whose functioning are now increasingly visible, is one of the broader implications of the failure of Sole's attempts to *force* a leap. Raymond Williams, again, has put the matter well:

> Independent development, which has to be bitterly fought for, then offers the only chance of any possible growth in the interest of the majority. And while it is true that if we add up all the developments, or the failures to develop, the global crisis is terrifying, it is a process that cannot be stopped in any one of its sectors. The decisive changes, indeed, if they are to come at all, will have to come from within the "metropolitan" countries, whose power now distorts the whole process and makes any genuine system of common interest and control impossible.[51]

True, Williams here argues that the only way out is one of violent revolution, on the grounds that forces of inertia and the power of those who dominate prevent the elaboration of any other means of changing direction. This may be. But change of direction implies a clear sense of direction, and that depends upon a thinking, upon activities and processes preceding any "revolution." And one would say that without them, no revolution can succeed; with them, no revolution is necessary, for their success would prevent violent revolution by achieving its goals beforehand. The exception would be (as already said) revolutions that are not rethinkings but means of catching up; history there has shown the necessity of the gun. But it has also shown that by and large the *same* system remains in place afterward as before, however the 'rankings' of the participants change.

Complete transformations of the kind we are here speaking about seem to occur only through a kind of collective redirecting of energies, by a gradual change in the structures of thought and action, composed both of such individual activities as Darriand's (or Roussel's) and such communal ones as those of a whole society in its ongoing dialectic of sign production, as Peirce and Bakhtin have it.

Such a view is neither Sole's nor Chomsky's. For both (and it is a common view) individuals are essentially discrete, each one repeating in each

<hr>

51. Ibid., p. 345.

generation the same language and concept acquisition, and therefore subject to the same limitations of understanding as their predecessors. Thus, writes Chomsky, "the same innate principles of mind that make possible the acquisition of knowledge and systems of belief might also impose limits on scientific understanding that exclude scientific knowledge of how knowledge and belief are acquired or used, though such an understanding might be attainable by an organism differently or more richly endowed."[52] For him, as for Sole—and the flaw is a dramatic one—although individuals may participate in a common human store of categories, thoughts, actions, genetic programs, and the like, they remain essentially individuals, each an island unto itself, both in space and in time. That is why, for Chomsky, each successive generation must be said to acquire its particular surface grammar from scratch and why, for instance, Peirce's 'explanation' of the fact that humans have 'true' knowledge in the face of a massive dearth of experience (to the effect that the mind is an involved part of nature and therefore shares its laws—an echo of what we have seen in both Lévi-Strauss and the fictional Xemahoa, and a pursuit of Peirce's argument concerning constant and "genuine" semiosis) is dismissed by the structural linguist as "entirely without force" (*LM*, p. 97).

For Chomsky, the individuality of the human ordering of a regulatory reason is precisely what guarantees any given individual's safety before the onslaught of the kind of manipulation practiced by Sole. He thus cites approvingly Rousseau's strictures against the social domination of other humans and the Cartesian argument from which they are derived: that humanity's distinction and the first sign of its essential freedom is its 'creative' use of language.[53] It is language, he writes, that "in its essential properties and the manner of its use, provides the basic criterion for determining that another organism is a being with a human mind and the human capacity for free thought and self-expression, and with the essential human need for freedom from the external constraints of repressive authority."[54] Chris Sole's monumental error is to believe that Skinnerian manipulation of language use can take humans away from past constraints into a new future—only to find that that way madness lies.[55] What Chomsky overlooks is that the supposed freedom in the creative use of language also permits Rousseau to argue in favor of men's oppression of women, and it is hard not to think of the upbringing of Emile and Sophie

52. Noam Chomsky, *Problems of Language and Freedom: The Russell Lectures* (New York, 1972), pp. 9–10.

53. Noam Chomsky, "Language and Freedom," in *For Reasons for State* (New York, 1973), pp. 387–408.

54. Ibid., p. 394.

55. For Chomsky's comments in this sense on Skinnerian behaviorism, see his "Psychology and Ideology," in *For Reasons of State*, pp. 318–69.

other than in terms of a "repressive authority" (this is, of course, to say not that Chomsky agrees with Rousseau but that *that* freedom produced *that* oppression).[56] Like Rousseau, Sole faces the dilemma of all liberal social reformers: how to 'guide' the collectivity into a collective future (shades of the Leninist party) when the view being promoted is by definition a minority one (since otherwise the future would be now) and when the thinking is resolutely individualist. That dilemma is simply added to the general one of how to convince others by convincing them of the wrongheadedness of their present way of thinking.

If the 'reformer' is also convinced that the wrongheadedness is ingrained in the way language is used and that such usage (*pace* Chomsky) is *not* genetically fixed, the dilemma is all the greater. But posed in such terms it is also insuperable. Hence the alternative: Darriand's discovery of such a language actually *in practice*—though of course threatened with an extinction that is the exact counterpart of the "birth" Sole is trying to provoke in his laboratory by means of his coercive manipulation of the four orphans, who are to be made into "his children" in the same way exactly as Friday was made into a servant by *naming* Crusoe "master."[57] And that coercion is in turn similar to the kind by which American might will extinguish the Xemahoa. The tribe's real praxis is a 'threat' in a way that Sole's laboratory-controlled experiment is not, until "madness" removes the "experiment" from the laboratory space at the end of the novel.

Chomsky himself posits (again following Rousseau and Descartes) the notion that a restrictive "system of formal constraints" is necessary to all "creative acts," to "historically evolving human nature," to "the possibility of self-perfection," and to all human "possibilities for freedom, diversity, and individual self-realization."[58] The mind, he remarks, becomes the image of a generative grammar.[59] Sole's error, then, is not the idea that some kind of leap may be necessary but the attempt to force a leap. He becomes guilty of some kind of "leftist imperialism" (though left or right makes no difference: we see Darriand and the Xemahoa submitted similarly to the assault of a right-wing imperialism, unable to allow the continued threat to the very idea of thinking on which its hegemony depends).

56. It may do so *inevitably*—as the practical result of its very theoretical structure. See, e.g., the last pages of my Introduction; Eisenstein, *Radical Future*; Mary Poovey, *The Proper Lady and the Woman Writer* (Chicago, 1984); and Reiss, "Revolution in Bounds: Wollstonecraft, Women, and Reason," in *Gendered Subjects: Theoretical Dialogues on Sex, Race, Class, and Culture,* ed. Linda Kauffman (Oxford, 1988).

57. For the naming of Friday in *Robinson Crusoe*, see my *Discourse of Modernism*, pp. 307–8. Darriand insists that *he* acts differently: Kayapi is not "my man Friday" (p. 42).

58. Chomsky, "Language and Freedom," p. 395.

59. Ibid., pp. 404–6.

Darriand, one might say, was fortunate: he found the Xemahoa practices already in existence—but then so had American power found the Sp'thra's. In both cases the response is the same: first a distortion of intention, then a falsification for short-term purposes, then destruction. The ideological misuse of signs, of facts, for political purposes is not far removed from the experimental manipulation of facts for 'scientific' purposes (of which Sole's unease shows him to be only too well aware). But then signs are signs and facts are facts only by a system of forms of knowledge in the first place, and Sole could argue in historically legitimized company that the ends justify the means—at least when he is not so blinded by anger as not to see that the American and Soviet destruction of the Sp'thra is not at all different from his own activities.

Whether or not the mind shares the laws of nature, as Lévi-Strauss, Peirce, the Xemahoa, and Pierre Darriand seem to agree, it does seem clear that language and mind are ineluctably social: a fact that does not in the least depend on the assumption that language is, for example, merely informative. On the contrary, the assumption that language is "characteristically informative, in fact or in intention" is, as Chomsky writes (with so many others) "quite wrong." It "can be used to inform or mislead, to clarify one's own thoughts or to display one's cleverness, or simply for play" (*LM*, p. 70). But Chomsky's assumption here remains the same as before—and as always: that of a discrete thinking being who *uses* a language whose composition and functioning it had previously to analyze and comprehend by means of the genetically inscribed possession of a deep structure programmed into the brain, and by the scanning of hypotheses concerning possible human languages.

For Chomsky, the human mind is discrete and essentially *bounded*. Within its bounds lies the imprint of a deep grammatical structure common to all humans *qua* humans. Within them, too, lie the means to generate (any and all) natural language from the elements of that structure. In fact, this theory is a refinement upon Descartes's idea of a common sense available to (within) all humanity. But the flaw in Chomsky's theory is the flaw John Locke pointed out in any theory of innate ideas: namely, that it assumes imprinted structures, when all it can really *mean* is that the human mind has a capacity for knowing such structures. Such a counterclaim of course weakens the mind's "selfness" and its boundedness. Nonetheless, there seems no theoretical need (as opposed, say, to an ideological one) to posit an awakening of knowledge already present in the mind.[60] The counterclaim also implies that *if* some deep generating gram-

60. Locke's remarks on this subject are to be found chiefly in Book I of the *Essay concerning Human Understanding* (1689). A most useful and intelligent summary is to be found in Rom Harré, *The Anticipation of Nature* (London, 1965), pp. 16–19. Chomsky may well have shown elsewhere that the idea of such a *capacity* for knowledge is only a "blank" term

matical structure common to all human languages does indeed exist (as not only Chomsky but also the Port-Royal and earlier grammarians assumed), we may as well, perhaps better, seek it in languages as in minds. In reducing languages (or minds) to their simplest denominator, we either lose them as language or come up with a logical or a semiotic square as the foundation for all thought (and narrative), a notion that is actually close to being trivial.

Furthermore, not only is the notion ultimately reductive, but we have in any case no conceivable way of testing for such an imprint. Indeed, if some kind of micro-neurosurgery could discover its trace, it would do so only in destroying it, just as the injection of Western elements (activities, diseases, ideas) into Amazonian societies destroyed them. But how can one explain, asks the Chomskyan, the speed and sophistication of language acquisition without positing some such innate grammatical structure? One could well counter such a question not only with the rather mild Lockean response but with a parallel question: how can one explain the equally impressive acquisition of knowledge not simply about the environment but about an *ordered* environment? (This is actually Peirce's question.) Is one constrained, à la Chomsky, to suppose an innate imprint of ordered-world possibilities? And if we assert that the human is human because of the singular identity of such imprints, then we have the considerable difficulty before us of explaining very different ways of ordering the world, attested and specifiable differences—or are these but changes rung up on a single profound structure?

Yet there is actually no need to posit an explanation for the speed and sophistication with which knowledge is acquired, other than that of mental capacity and the context of community. In fact, there is some evidence for such a reduced claim in the wild children who appeared to lose such a capacity once past a certain age; they acquired even rudimentary language only by dint of enormous cajolery. It is a currently accepted fact of child development that there is indeed a fading of ability if capacities are not properly exercised early on. This seems to speak against such an imprint, unless, of course, we assume that the imprint gradually fades away, like an old photograph. Doubtless that is possible—but what would be the purpose of such an assumption? The human mind, after all, has capacities for so great a variety of functions that we would appear then to be forced to posit an ordered imprint of some sort for every function, which would be to suppose that the mind does not nor cannot develop

---

without content—but that is just its point: one *can* go no further, for any experiment to provide evidence of content (let alone complex structures of order) would necessarily destroy the material in question (see below).

other than as a kind of geometrical projection and a tautological product of what it already always contains. It would, in fact, be a sort of machine functioning upon the kind of logic favored by the logical atomists. That is exactly the pattern supposed by the transformational generative grammarian.

Apart from the ethical objection that this amounts to a deprivation of hope, the objection that such a view of mind and of human development denies the experience of history appears virtually insuperable. Of course, one could also assert that the grammatical imprint must underlie all other forms (and possibilities) of knowledge acquisition, much as Piaget's child acquires ordered language before learning to order objects in the world (a view long since countered and made more complicated by Vygotsky). But that assertion must confront the problem of the variety of experience, of the fundamental differences in the ways humans relate to and know their environments, if the imprint is to be claimed as universal. Again, the assumption simply of a *capacity* seems more appropriate, more likely correct; it allows for the variety of experience, as it does for historical transformation, because it assumes the mind to be in an essentially interactive relation with the environment by which it is produced as it produces it. Ethically speaking, it provides a space for hope.

Furthermore, it does not forbid Sole's kind of experiment on the basis of some unstated morality (whether on the simplistic grounds that it is "fascist," on the aprioristic or religious grounds that it is immoral to tamper with the human mind or life in general—though we do so all the time—or on the humanistic grounds that it is wrong to cause possible pain to another: "do as you would be done by"). Rather, it forbids such experiments because they are useless. They would merely test for a capacity whose existence is taken as proven by history and human variety: a capacity they could not *test* because one of its principal features involves the temporal nature of the transformation, as it assumes that differences in experience are bound up in overall environments of an ecosystematic complexity so great that no laboratory could repeat them.

Even if the outcome of Sole's experiment in a nonfictional case were the same, it would not prove that an imprint had been erased and replaced by another, with which the mind lost its humanity and dissolved into the madness of all otherness or into monstrosity and alienness. It would simply show that too great a load had been placed upon the learning capacity, which, however great, is not necessarily infinite and at the very least needs time and normal environmental complexity: fish and reptiles did not acquire wings and feathers or primates become humans overnight. Dr. Moreau or Dr. Mengele may have fabricated monsters, but in either fiction or in fact that has nothing to do with humans and human society as a self-organizing process, as a negentropy that such experiments deny—indeed, by definition bring to an end.

So long as the problem is thought of as concerning such discrete thinking and speaking entities, then it is, it seems to me, insoluble (insofar as it concerns the possibility of a general transformation of conceptual space). In Chomsky's terms it leads but to an infinite regression: if we could explain how knowledge and belief were acquired or used in terms of an underlying deep structure of language, how could we explain the possibility of *that* explanation? The point is surely not that *individuals* use language (whatever the 'truth' of such a statement); it is that *communities* use language, that *communities* acquire knowledge, ways of functioning, habits of action, and so forth. The "correction" of understanding of which Chomsky speaks is better expressed by Bakhtin, for example, or by Lucien Goldmann: "every human fact [is] born of a rational need in a given era, but condemned to lose that rationality due to the very fact of the transformation of the social conditions which engendered it."[61] Such a concept must surely apply to language and the praxis it makes possible, perhaps even more than to other human capacities.

This communal aspect of language and conceptualization is not merely a matter of correction of hypotheses or even simply of acquisition of knowledge; it is essential to the very formation of knowledge, to the creation of concepts and objects, to the production of action. A minor example: Chomsky criticizes Bertrand Russell's analysis of naming—that is, giving a word to "any continuous portion of space-time which sufficiently interests us"[62]—by advancing (supposedly in contradiction) the argument that an artist can create an object by naming it as such, "say, a mobile, which need not meet the conditions of spatial continuity." Therefore, he writes, naming must involve "a consideration of the intentions of the person who produced the thing."[63] In the first place, we may note, this is a willful misunderstanding of Russell's argument, which has to do with a logical step in the acquisition of knowledge: here the correct analogy is not *our* conception of a namable thing, but that of Alexander Calder as a representative human. Second, once named, the mobile *does* meet the conditions of spatial continuity, for the 'empty' spaces in which its solid parts move have become a 'part' of it, essential to the concept *and* the object, "mobile." There is nothing outlandish or extraordinary about such a state of affairs; the juxtaposition in space of presence and absence, of

61. Lucien Goldmann, "Idéologie et marxisme," in his *Epistémologie et philosophie politique* (Paris, 1978), p. 117.
62. Bertrand Russell, *Human Knowledge: Its Scope and Limits* (New York, 1948), p. 89.
63. Chomsky, *Problems*, p. 14.

solidity and emptiness, of black and white, composes the single spatial continuity that is the very essence, for example, of Chinese calligraphy and its aesthetic, not to mention the more practical and familiar juxtaposition of the white and black lines ('empty' and 'full' space?) that form contemporary bar codes, labels to be read electronically.

All comprehension incorporates, though it by no means depends upon, oppositions: on the contrariety of black and white, of said and unsaid, presence and absence, structure and chaos, the marked and the unmarked, the spoken and the silent: "Voice is to silence, as writing (in the graphic sense) on white paper," as Roland Barthes put it.[64] One could well add the opposition between then and now, for naming composes its own time, just as it does its own space.[65] Our perceived world is composed in part of just such *découpages* and oppositions, some no doubt more 'arbitrary' than others. The error lies, as Lady Welby long since observed, in taking them for the be-all and end-all of any reason enabling knowledge and action. The naming of the mobile, like the naming of Crusoe's Friday, is in large part what makes the object 'possible,' just as quantum mechanical naming has made possible the hundred or so 'elementary' particles now taken to 'exist' within the conceptual model it provides. The intention of the individual doing the 'first' naming has something to do with such a .creation, no doubt, but what ultimately counts is 'community acceptability,' the social fixation of habit, and both Calder and Heisenberg would have been laughed out of court a mere fifty years earlier—or ignored, as Peirce's semiotics largely was.

When Marx, in the *Economic and Philosophic Manuscripts of 1844,* commented upon the invisible bond between humanity and nature—the latter standing as the former's "inorganic body"; when he remarked upon the fact that "plants, animals, stones, air, light, etc., constitute theoretically a part of human consciousness" and that "in the realm of practice they constitute a part of human life and human activity," he was noting precisely this interdependency of the so-called 'objective' and the so-called 'subjective.' Indeed, he was asserting the indissolubility of the human and the natural world, an indissolubility that is an essential conceptual element in what we call "society": "In creating a *world of objects* by his practical activity, in his *work upon* inorganic nature," added Marx, "man proves himself a conscious species-being." The humanness of humankind, its social nature, is at one very important, even fundamental, level evidenced only through this "objectification" (*Vergegenstandlichung*) by which nature

64. Roland Barthes, *Essais critiques III: L'obvie et L'obtus* (Paris, 1982), p. 225.
65. I have discussed this temporal aspect of naming (again reflecting on Russell) in *Discourse of Modernism*, pp. 284–87.

and humanity become bonded in society.[66] Thus conceived, "society is the complete unity of man with nature."[67]

This is not to romanticize or sentimentalize Marx; nor is it to overlook the obvious fact that what is first of all important about Marxism is its practical materialist account of society and history. But concepts of this earlier kind *do* form the *ground* for that subsequent analysis of human economic association. To say that is not to turn Marx into some half-baked representative of "communitas," a nostalgic searcher for some lost *Gemeinschaft*, or a believer in some forsaken wholeness of the human spirit (à la William Morris). On the contrary, it is to recognize the profoundly optimistic cast of the goals that were set *before* the materialist analysis of society and science of history, of the effort to understand the human technology of the world as a development both of humanity and that world. All thinking and all human action of whatever kind are then given as a constant evolution of the social relation. The very organs seemingly characteristic of human nature, insofar as they are *used*, are themselves subject to such development and the object of such creativity: an animal may hear sounds, but for it "the most beautiful music has *no* sense," for "music awakens only in man the sense of music." "The *forming* of the five senses," Marx goes on, "is a labour of the entire history of the world down to the present." At the same time, the development of humanity's capacities further develops the world itself as society.[68]

Such concepts are at the basis of the arguments we find in Peirce and Bakhtin to the effect that knowledge and action, human society and culture, are themselves a constant production of signs *out of* signs, a constant response of signs *to* signs. We may say that the cases of the mobile and quantum mechanics provide concrete examples, evidence of the acceptableness ('truth') of such assertions. Further, we should remind ourselves that Calder's or Heisenberg's activity is itself a *response* (what Peirce would call an *interpretant*); the "intention" of which Chomsky writes with regard to Calder would not have been *possible* fifty years earlier. If the works of both involve 'new' conceptions of space, of the relation between motion, substance, and extension, the one in the realm of art and the other in that of science (the two areas privileged by Marx in the *Manuscripts of 1844* as exemplifying human activities under given economic conditions of labor and production), then such a development clearly depends upon a collective, upon what Marx here terms a "social," development of some kind, upon some sort of "acceptability," forming itself (eventually) into what

66. *Economic and Philosophic Manuscripts of 1844*, in Karl Marx and Frederick Engels, *Collected Works* (Moscow, 1975–), III:275–77. Ernst Fischer has sought to apply this concept to the development of art forms: see, e.g., *The Necessity of Art: A Marxist Approach*, tr. Anna Bostock (1963; rpt. Harmondsworth, 1978), pp. 152–54.
67. Marx and Engels, *Collected Works*, III:298.
68. Marx and Engels, *Collected Works*, III:301–4.

Peirce called a "habit," the final interpretant. Here, needless to say, we return to the earlier comments on the contract and the general development of societies.

Such formations, such processes, are clearly a matter of social, not individual, conditions. And they are a matter of social conditions in constant evolution. The possibility of Roussel's *Nouvelles impressions*, of Darriand's discovery of a tribe whose embedded language system *he is able even to start to analyze*, of Sole's attempt to create a functioning embedded language, of Ian Watson's ability to write about both and, indeed, the very idea of a changing human logical space; the fact that *The Embedding* won the communal approval of two science fiction prizes, and that science fiction itself can now be taken "seriously" by scholars—all these things are evidence of just that kind of development in acceptability. The term "bad language," as Sole's experiment implies in response to some linguists, is a social judgment based upon a commonly accepted logical space, like "madness," "delinquency," "genius," or the "nonsense" of Marx (or Wittgenstein, for the matter of that). While society, in a given moment and place, must needs act within such a logical (or discursive) space, the latter may nevertheless come to reveal the limits of its effectiveness. When that happens, the space in question is obliged to transform itself—or rather, the social relations must transform themselves and the space of their functioning.

The question, then, is how such transformation can occur. Doubtless it is correct to affirm that experiments and manipulations of the kind attempted by Sole can lead only to disaster, to the cataclysm of which Lévi-Strauss speaks, or to the installation of some political entity as the totalizing manipulator of a history of whose 'legitimacy' it becomes the sole judge—whether the "Bardo" of Watson's *Alien Embassy*, the Soviet Communist Party, or even (at a less overt level and in a less absolutist manner) the traditional representatives of a certain liberal Whiggery, providing an accepted interpretation of human social development that was (and is) by no means without its constraints and its 'distortions' (as Reagan's America has come increasingly to show us). It seems clear that new meaning, new discourse, cannot be introduced by some kind of individualist fiat, as Bacon suggested for the Great Instauration, as Hobbes argued for the establishment of the new bourgeois civil society, and as Lenin invoked against Marx and Engels for the case of Russia (later defending it in his *"Left-Wing" Childishness* of 1918, his speech of October 1921 in honor of the fourth anniversary of the revolution, and the brief texts of 1923 published under the title, "On Our Revolution").[69]

69. Vladimir Ilyich Lenin, *Selected Works* (1963–65; rpt. Moscow, 1975–77), II:623–46; III:579–86, 705–8.

It *can* come from a gradual evolution of praxis, of which both basic mental structures and individual originations (Bacon's instauration, Calder's mobile, the origin and development of relativity or quantum mechanical theory) form an important part. Any revolutionary invocation of a fiat necessarily inscribes the invoker(s) of such a fiat as the sole authority, with all the associated constraints such authority involves. For it is not that the means come to obscure the ends; it is rather that the means dictate what the ends can and must be.

The Embedding is a thought experiment concerned with how one changes the how and the what of thinking itself. It bares the ground. It suggests what cannot be done, and with some complexity it implies many of the parameters that need to be accounted for and taken into consideration. It emphasizes the immediate relations between patterns of thought, forms of political action, the nature of social and cultural processes. Through its fiction of science, polity, and social ordering, the novel permits an approach to the real matter of sociocultural change by means of the opposition—perceived in these several spheres—between fact and fiction, self and other, individual and society, development and control.

The fact remains that no such change has so far been achieved in contemporary reality, though it is by no means enough—however easy and pleasing it may be—to assert that the failure is due to the replacement of genuine historical action by mere talk. The dismissal is facile. The action in question can have no goal or purpose without prior reason, and talk is necessary to understand just what barriers are being faced, just what constraints are being confronted. Only such awareness can expect to indicate the hope, the business, and the destination of change. My last two chapters, therefore, pursue the discussion into the areas where these questions of the relation between thought and action, theory and practice, individual and society, rupture and continuity have been most thoroughly and essentially raised: in Western Marxism and in recent European critical debate. The case is perhaps the more urgent because, despite the fact that these have addressed the issues in question with more precision and complexity than obtains in any other theoretical debate, they have still failed to reach any consensual certainty.

Social Context and
the Failure of Theory

But in some ages the world is more tattered and torn, than in other ages; and in some ages the world is patched and pieced, but seldom new and suitable; and it is oftener in a fool's coat than in a grave cassock.
　　　　　—Margaret Cavendish, Duchess of Newcastle, "Sociable Letters"

Revolution of necessity must borrow, from what it wants to destroy, the very image of what it wants to possess.
　　　　　—Roland Barthes, *Le degré zéro de l'écriture*

In the Tracks of Historical Materialism is in some sense, as its author Perry Anderson observes, a sequel to *Considerations on Western Marxism.*[1] Indeed, though Anderson does not expressly say so, the entire first chapter of the later book is more or less a summary of that earlier work, while in at least one case, *Tracks* is used to fill a lacuna in its predecessor: its omission of any discussion of Jürgen Habermas. These matters are of interest only insofar as *Tracks* represents itself as a discussion of aesthetic theory and (literary) criticism in the broader context of the critique of Western Marxism.

Now, while *Considerations* did discuss such thinkers as Lukács, Benjamin, Galvano Della Volpe, Theodor Adorno, Sartre, Goldmann, and others, it did not attend to them primarily in terms of aesthetic or literary theory. Its concern was rather to view them as successors to and within a Marxist tradition of holistic practical thinking about social order and change, and to follow them as they grew ever more distant from that tradition on the path to what Anderson sees as a disembodied and esoteric theoreticism. He called this development "the prolonged, winding detour of Western Marxism" and saw it as characterized chiefly by its speaking of

1. Perry Anderson, *In the Tracks of Historical Materialism* (Chicago, 1984), hereafter *THM*; and *Considerations on Western Marxism* (London, 1976). This chapter, originally a long review essay of the 1984 volume, brings together many of the issues referred to in earlier chapters and is tied directly to Chapter 9. I have left many of its "review" characteristics but have removed those most bound to the fact of its publication in a journal of scholarly literary criticism.

"its own enciphered language, at an increasingly remote distance from the class whose fortunes it formally sought to serve or articulate."[2]

That distance is of course the reason for the sense of unease I mentioned when writing of Eagleton and Williams (especially the former). In the process of falling into this remoteness, Anderson believes, Western Marxists failed to solve the key questions raised by Marx, Lenin, and Trotsky, including especially "the enigma of rationalism," the nature of "bourgeois democracy," the possibility of revolution without soviets, the character of imperialism, the real practice of internationalism, and the abolition "of bureaucratic privilege and oppression."[3] The preceding chapter has perhaps served to indicate the degree to which these essentially *political* questions may be bound up with more 'literary' and 'aesthetic' ones. The problem is to maintain the balance.

The questions are particularly appropriately raised in what is (here) fundamentally an epistemological and aesthetic series of studies, for they belong within a discipline (literary theory, criticism, and scholarship) that seems faced with a severe loss of confidence. I would argue that this loss at least partly reflects a far more general loss of confidence that inheres in our entire sociocultural environment. At the same time, however, it does have to be addressed within its own disciplinary context. Thus our primary preoccupations need now to be at least twofold: (1) to seek an understanding of the reasons for this loss of confidence, and (2) to place literary theory and practical criticism back in touch with the cultural and social history from which it has become too far divorced. Only in this way is it possible for literary critics to identify the history of their discipline as well as the history of the artifacts that are the objects of its study.

Lucien Goldmann (one of Anderson's failed theorists) once remarked upon the inseparability of all human social activity. He admonished such as Anderson (and all too many of those who are entrenched in their disciplines, whatever they may be) that "we have long since learned . . . that *every* mode of human thought and feeling is determined by mental structures which are closely related to the objective life of the particular society in which they develop." Some clearly have, equally clearly many have not, learned this lesson. One of Anderson's constant themes is the extent to which Western Marxism has itself moved away from such an assumption. More narrowly, we may be sure that literary theory and practice have only rarely understood it, let alone relied upon it. "The effort must be made to ground [the achievements and limitations of intellectual movements or of any critical practice] in the general categorical structure of the movement if we are to understand the factors making the achieve-

2. Anderson, *Considerations*, pp. 103, 32.
3. Ibid., p. 121.

ment possible and the limits inescapable."[4] The categorical structure is ineluctably grounded in concrete social reality. I believe that understanding arguments such as Anderson's may well help literary critics and theorists better to comprehend the aporias and contradictions of their own field, precisely with regard to the kind of argument set forth by Goldmann.

In the Tracks of Historical Materialism is itself centrally concerned with the series of large questions mentioned above. That is to say, Anderson's analysis takes them for granted. At the same time, he takes on questions and theorists whose significance to their field literary people will at once recognize and acknowledge. The three chapters making up this brief volume were originally delivered as the 1982 Wellek Lectures of the Program in Critical Theory (at the University of California, Irvine). Taking his cue from the end of René Wellek's own *Discriminations*,[5] which offered "A Map of Contemporary Criticism in Europe," Anderson avers that he is offering something similar for "historical materialism in North America and Western Europe"(*THM*, p. 9). Furthermore, he promises to speak of "critical theory" itself in an ambiguous manner by using the term to refer at once to a theory of society in general and to a narrower one of literature in particular. Indeed, if one starts with the latter, he remarks, the ambiguity is not simply *"permitted"* but actually imposed, for such theory is almost always in some way *evaluative* and tends therefore to "transgress the frontiers of the text towards the associated life beyond it" (*THM*, p. 9). The obvious retort of the pedant of literary criticism that while this may be true for Leavisian criticism, for example, it is certainly not the case for Formalism, New Criticism (overtly or professedly, at least), the strained scientism of some contemporary semiological 'criticism,' and others—is irrelevant to Anderson's point. For he intends to show how an avowedly socially oriented critical theory, arising out of Marxism, has in fact dissipated itself in an increasingly idealist theoreticism, moving away from that (supposedly inevitable) "transgression."

Marxist critical theory, almost alone among systems of thought concerned with society as a whole, was from the start deeply interested in aesthetic matters. The first chapter of Anderson's little book (*THM*, pp. 9–31) seems to imply that in some way this profound aesthetic interest itself diverted Western Marxism from its major goal, at least if one can associate theoreticism and aestheticism. In *Considerations*, Anderson showed how this diversion had indeed occurred in the work of Lukács, Adorno, and Marcuse, the last of whom viewed "aesthetics as the central

---

4. Lucien Goldmann, *The Philosophy of the Enlightenment: The Christian Burgess and the Enlightenment,* tr. Henry Maas (Cambridge, Mass., 1973), p. 15.
5. René Wellek, *Discriminations: Further Concepts of Criticism* (New Haven, Conn., 1970).

category of a free society."[6] The precise reference here is to Marcuse's *Eros and Civilization* and *An Essay on Liberation*.[7] By the time of his Wellek lectures, Anderson could well have added *The Aesthetic Dimension,* a work whose seemingly reactionary aesthetic claims are fairly astonishing.[8] Thus a discourse whose primary basis was so deeply embedded in the fate of a "popular practice seeking to transform" the world (*THM,* p. 14) that its own development and self-criticism as theory were always *in the first place* responsive to that practice gradually moved toward a divorce of theory and practice so profound that by the 1950s "there was scarcely a Marxist theoretician of any weight who was not the holder of a chair in the academy, rather than a post in the class struggle" (*THM,* p. 16). One is tempted to snipe at Anderson's own "post" or at the role in the class struggle played by the determinedly elitist *New Left Review* that he edits. Perhaps that would be unfair. It is yet another sign of the sense of unease mentioned before (Chapter 6).

A further mark of the dissociation of theory and practice was the theoreticians' turning toward non-Marxist intellectual traditions, writes Anderson: Lukács to Weber, Gramsci to Croce, Sartre to Heidegger, Althusser to Lacan, Della Volpe to Hjelmslev.[9] This was itself, urges the *New Left Review's* editor, "a function of the dislocation of the relationships that had once held between it [theory] and the practice of the workers' movement" (*THM,* p. 17). Those theorists simultaneously succumbed to overwhelming pessimism and produced only a brilliant series of analyses of *"cultural* processes—in the higher ranges of the superstructures" (*THM,* p. 17; one glimpses here more than a hint in Anderson of that "economism" for which Raymond Williams criticized Eagleton and others like him). Anderson had earlier stated this view in *Considerations,* arguing that the typical concerns of Western Marxism were those superstructural orders ranking "highest" in the hierarchy of distance from the economic infrastructure: "It was not the State or Law which provided the typical object of its research. It was culture that held the central focus of its attention"—and most especially "Art."[10] Art and Ideology became the privileged domains of these thinkers, as they distanced themselves in this way particularly from the generally Stalinized Communist parties of Western Europe (*THM,* p. 17).

More recently, in the 1970s and 1980s, Western Marxism has undergone startling changes. First, there has been an outpouring of works

6. Anderson, *Considerations,* p. 77.

7. Herbert Marcuse, *Eros and Civilization* (Boston, 1955); *An Essay on Liberation* (Boston, 1969).

8. I have briefly discussed these implications of Marcuse's aesthetics in "Environment of Literature," esp. pp. 43–44; see also Chapter 6, above.

9. *THM,* p. 6. Cf. Anderson, *Considerations,* pp. 56–58.

10. Anderson, *Considerations,* pp. 75–76.

concerned with concrete economic and political analysis accompanied, nonetheless, by some (mild) continuation of cultural analysis. Second, Anderson claims, the English-speaking world has taken a lead in critical theory, especially in the area of Marxist historiography (Maurice Dobb, Christopher Hill, Eric Hobsbawm, Edward P. Thompson, George Rudé, Rodney Hilton, Eugene Genovese, and Eric Foner are among those he mentions). Third, Marxist theory and its own history have come together, and in discussion across national boundaries (he notes the dispute between Althusser and Thompson—which actually started earlier between the same French thinker and John Lewis—and similar confrontations elsewhere). There are naturally omissions here (some of them perhaps inspired by personal feelings), but one serious one to which I will return) is Anderson's failure to mention *any* of the feminist historians working in this tradition. This is the more serious because of his later assertions concerning the essential contributions of the women's movement.[11]

In spite of such liveliness and development, Anderson points out, what has failed altogether to occur is any "reunification of Marxist theory and popular practice in a mass revolutionary movement" (*THM*, p. 27); this is because of a lack or, as he puts it, "poverty" of strategy rather than of theory. The lack is also Anderson's, and it must be said that his statement of this "failure" comes across as a kind of knee-jerk response to his proclaimed theoretical position. Having a strategy presupposes, after all, having a goal, and Anderson's complaint would be more plausible if he had stated *his* program for such a mass revolutionary movement and suggested who might constitute its participants. It is scarcely sufficient to speak of "the great interventions of Luxemburg or Lenin, Trotsky or Parvus, in the years before the First World War" (*THM*, p. 28), as though—implicitly—world and sociopolitical situations had remained the same. To be sure, Anderson does speak of the development of Western Marxist theory. He does not here consider that its theoreticians' turn away from political and social practice (which he calls "the rout" of the Marxist tradition in "Latin Europe") may well have had to do with (among other things) the difficulty of urging an industrial proletariat toward a revolutionary movement aimed at that very capitalism which, until quite lately, was the apparent source of a fairly dramatic increase in at least the economic prosperity of its major part.

The revolutionary theorist confronting a group that suffers a simultaneous economic and political deprivation faces quite different questions

---

11. I cannot forbear mentioning one person in particular in this context, whose recent book has been reviewed as "exemplary" in combining an extremely detailed sense of people's real life (based on extensive archival research) with a clear presentation of the broad picture and its practical and theoretical dilemmas: Patricia J. Hilden, *Working Women and Socialist Politics in France, 1880–1914: A Regional Study* (Oxford, 1986).

from those to be resolved with regard to a group that experiences relative economic prosperity but virtually entire political dispossession. And since the latter case is almost certainly far more common in the industrial West of the late twentieth century, it is small wonder, that "no working-class or popular bloc in a Western society will ever make [such] a leap in the dark" (*THM*, p. 99). This fundamental change in the nature of the Western industrial proletariat has of course been observed by many for a long time. Anderson is more than justified in dismissing the "rightist' responses of Kristeva, Philippe Sollers, and André Glucksmann (he later adds other "fatuities": *THM*, p. 57), but is wrong, I think, to do so with a kind of nostalgia for some Old Left, be it Trotskyist or other.

However, none of this is his major point. Rather he aims to explore the theoretical trammels into which Marxist critical theory has entered. He intends to dissect its aporias and its opponents, its fears and its hopes. This is the purpose of his second chapter, dealing mainly with France (*THM*, pp. 32–55). Anderson wants to show that French Marxism, formerly the intellectual star in the Western firmament, has yielded the field to complete "intellectual reaction," to the consequences of a "head-on defeat in a rather violent battle with structuralist and poststructuralist ideas (*THM*, pp. 32–33). Actually, he succeeds in showing how, despite their initial "victory," these ideas are fundamentally flawed (some of the flaws have been explored in my earlier chapters) and cannot offer any kind of long-term replacement for the far more powerful intellectual and practical system already available in dialectical materialism—even where the latter has yet to solve a number of vital questions.

The central problem in the battle was "the nature of the relationship between structure and subject in human history and society" (*THM*, p. 33). In France, the exemplary Marxist case was Sartre's, whose *Critique of Dialectical Reason* sought to provide a collectively relational understanding of human society. At the same time, it consciously opposed that search to the singular biographical project of the representative individual, as proposed in Sartre's *Questions of Method* preceding the *Critique* and carried out in his *Baudelaire*, in a short *Mallarmé*, and most massively in the three-volume *Idiot de la famille*. Anderson argues that the 1962 publication of Lévi-Strauss's *Le pensée sauvage* (*The Savage Mind*)—with its ahistorical claim to level human minds and societies to a set of invariant properties and its assumption that human capacities, characteristics, and actual concrete formations and activities are equivalent and equally 'valuable' wherever and whenever they are found—left Sartre without any effective reply. Anderson has no explanation for this silence other than to express surprise that "so agile and fertile an interlocutor, so indefatigable a polemicist" as Sartre should be unable to make an answer (*THM*, p. 37).

But the point is an important one and cannot simply be left in limbo. I think the reason no reply was available was that the anthropologist's reduction of the human to nothing more than a variable in a systematic set of relations was simply too conceptually close to the Sartrean idea of the practico-inert. In itself, this could have been relatively unimportant if Sartre (or someone else) had already been able to develop a strong concept of a collective subject. But he had spent his entire intellectual maturity struggling in vain to develop some notion of the subject beyond that of a willful Cartesian individualism, which had always stood over against the collective (and, here, any authentic role in the practico-inert), just as *Questions of Method* conflicted with the aim of the *Critique* itself. The only reply Sartre could have made, therefore, would have been the reassertion of some kind of Enlightenment individualism—a denial of his own project at the same time.

In fact, Anderson suggests, the second volume of the *Critique* did try to respond to this problem by an "investigation through the medium of the actual historical processes that led from the October Revolution to the apotheosis of Stalin after the Second World War and beyond, in the Soviet Union" (*THM*, p. 71). For diverse reasons, Sartre chose not to publish this second volume during the 1960s.[12] The concrete historical failure of necessity found its echo in theory. In such a case there quite simply *was* no possible response to the structuralist's proclamation of the *dissolution* of "man," which thus became the rallying cry of the next decade (*THM*, p. 37). The seeming inevitability of this theoretical consequence was confirmed in Marxism itself when Althusser emphasized the abolition of the subject in his adoption of structuralist arguments and their application to the principal texts and major issues of dialectical materialism.

Anderson uses his second chapter, however, chiefly to point out the serious weakness of the system upon which the structuralist challenge was based and, furthermore, its inevitable progression toward irrationalism. First, structuralism relies on what he calls "the *exorbitation of language*" (*THM*, p. 40); that is language becomes the foundational universal of everything human, whether it be Lévi-Strauss's exploration of social structures, Lacan's affirmation of the unconscious *as* language, or Derrida's notion of text "as a *universal* suzerain of the modern world" (*THM*, p. 42). This objection contains nothing new, of course, but Anderson does buttress it with some detail. Initially, he puts forward one or two "local" difficulties; one especially reveals a serious problem in his own position.

12. At the time *THM* was published, Sartre's *Critique II* had not appeared, though Anderson had access to the manuscript. For further comments, see Introduction, n. 16, and Chapter 5, n. 31.

Of Lévi-Strauss's work, for example, Anderson observes that the very notion of exchange does not "warrant an elision to the economy." He admits—more than a little oddly—that "speakers and families in most societies may be reckoned to have at least rough equivalence of words and women between them" but asserts that this can never be true of goods, for no economy can be *primarily* defined in terms of exchange: "Production and property are always prior" (*THM*, p. 43). Well, yes, the latter point at least is well taken. But does Anderson really believe that women *can* be defined primarily in terms of exchange? ("Believe," not "think," is clearly the operative word.) And does he really mean to accept, as the quoted phrase suggests, some notion that speakers are male and families chiefly masculine-oriented? (The idea would certainly fit with the dominant 'bourgeois' cultural framework since the European sixteenth century.) There is something more than a little revealing here as to the permanently uneasy relation holding (or not) between feminism and Marxism—a question to which Anderson returns at some length in a postscript (*THM*, pp. 88–96), where he asserts in a decidedly unsatisfactory manner the necessary cooperation yet present incommensurability of the two (I will return to this toward the end of the chapter).

Three other objections must be raised, argues Anderson, to the totalizing use of language: (1) linguistic structures are, among social institutions, exceptionally inert;[13] (2) at the same time, however, the subject (of *parole*) is exceptionally inventive as it moves among those structures in actual use;[14] (3) "the subject of speech is axiomatically *individual*" (*THM*, p. 44). Language thus corresponds in almost no way at all to other social institutions, which tend to be at once far quicker in their development and far more constraining of their subjects. Furthermore, in economic, cultural, political, or military structures, subjects are "first and foremost *collective*: nations, classes, castes, groups, generations" (*THM*, pp. 44–45). (Once again, this enumeration manages to omit women.)

The second "foundation" of the structuralist challenge comes down to the "attenuation of truth." In Saussurean linguistics, truth value was maintained by a dual determination of meaning: relations with other words on the one hand, and reference to something dissimilar—to the idea of something—on the other. Once generalized, the extralinguistic reference

13. This problem was directly addressed during the second quarter of our century by several Soviet linguists. For obvious reasons, language could not be placed at the level of the economic base, yet it did not fit with the kind of transformational properties required of superstructural processes. The debate 'culminated' in Stalin's writings on language published in *Pravda*, June–August 1950. The question is central to the preceding two chapters and indeed fundamental to this whole book.

14. It is precisely this issue that Chomsky's transformational generative grammar sought to resolve, by formulating a limited system capable of unlimited transformability along strict lawful lines.

inevitably disappeared, and the system was taken as entirely closed and self-sufficient. Thus is reached, in Anderson's delicious phrase, a "megalomania of the signifier" (*THM*, p. 45)—from Lévi-Strauss through Lacan to Derrida—and text as a free-floating warm bath.

Anderson is wrong, I think, to include Foucault in this view (a typically Anglo-American conflation, I may add). It is the case that Foucault viewed a *kind* of truth as the consequence of what we may call an epistemic hegemony, a hegemony that is always historically situated and describable in terms of its particular social environment. It is also the case that that leaves him with the problem of where to situate *himself* as subject of understanding—a difficulty the recognition of which hardly required Derridian "acuteness" (*THM*, p. 64). But *that* is a problem of method confronting *any* system of thought that simultaneously questions its own elaboration—including dialectical materialism. We might say, in Anderson's own terms, that Foucault was viewing 'truth' as a superstructural element. But he was far from being unaware of the potential for relativistic irresponsibility that such a view posed, especially in our contemporary atmosphere. And he could of course have responded to Anderson that the latter is simply displacing onto some absolute concept of Truth the very problem Foucault must confront in the Subject: where is that Truth placed (*and* the subject that is taken to 'know' it)?

Derrida is writing of another matter altogether. He does not say that truth is caught up in history. He is making an entirely different and, in fact, a quite contrary claim: that truth has been an *illusion* of Western epistemology since the Greeks (at least). The problem is emphatically *not* one of method but one of axiom. Derrida may be sliding toward "nescience," because history is indeed elided, but Foucault was not. Rather, Foucault wanted to understand the "epistemic" implantation of will, truth, self, reason, and so forth, as hegemonic modes of thought and action. That this poses a number of difficulties is indubitable, but they should not be assimilated into "Derridianism." Foucault, as a matter of fact, was far closer in many ways to the admired Gramsci than Anderson appears to believe.

The third important element in structuralism is "the randomization of history" (*THM*, p. 48): any concept of ascertainable cause is lost; the possibility of describing continuity and development disappears. Again, one cannot make a blanket condemnation. Certainly, some of Althusser's disciples have been known to assert that history is useless for any understanding of the present (see Chapter 9); Lacan, like all psychoanalysts, denied history; Derrida and his followers quite simply ignore it altogether, the auto-undermining of Text being everywhere characteristic. But that Foucault in *Les mots et les choses* (*The Order of Things*) did not manage to develop any idea of epistemic *development* or self-transformation should not be taken to imply the same of his later work (which *Order* is not, though Anderson implies that it is: *THM,* p. 51). He does not yield up the field to chance but relies rather on a concrete portrayal of a kind of transformation (most recently in the second two volumes of *Histoire de la sexualité*). This does not solve the *theoretical* problem, of course, but does make it a rather different one from what Anderson suggests.

Still, making a case for or against Foucault (save as he is one among the "poststructuralists") is not Anderson's chief aim, and I will push the issue no further. The goal is rather the powerful refutation of the more general claims made for and by structuralism and poststructuralism. And the arguments presented appear virtually unanswerable. The idea that language is the universal system organizing all human institutions and actions betrays essential flaws. This fact entirely justifies the assertion that structure, here, is simply a "rhetorical absolutism." That such reductionism has led, through the attenuation of truth (though we should be careful not to equate that with the familiar accusation of relativism) and the randomization of history to a "fragmented fetishism" of the subject (*THM,* p. 57) seems to me irrefutable.

If structuralism and poststructuralism are so internally weak, then how could they "defeat" Marxist theory? Anderson suggests that they could not and did not, that Marxism's failure must be due to some other cause. The search for such a cause becomes the object of his third chapter, "Nature and History" (*THM,* pp. 56–84). This chapter begins with the argument that "structuralist" assumptions need not lead to such aporias as pervade their French versions; indeed, assimilated into a set of concepts drawn at least in part from dialectical materialism, they may lead to such "positive" results as Habermas's concept of the ideal speech situation (*THM,* pp. 58–67). Actually, this notion comes across as rather unsatisfactory, for society so viewed remains disembodied and abstract. Anderson's claim as to the positive value of such an assimilation is therefore quite unconvincing; in fact, it seems to be brought forward only tentatively and with little conviction.

Finally, of course, the reasons for failure must be objective and concrete, rather than in consequence of some discursive confrontation. No doubt that is why Anderson immediately notes a matter discussed in the earlier *Considerations* but until this point left aside in *THM:* the importance of the fate of the international Communist movement. Here, he remarks, we continue to see the series of failures earlier maintained: the aggressive bureaucratization of the U.S.S.R. and the Eastern bloc; the revisionist turn taken by the cultural revolution in China; and a Europe where Eurocommunism (especially in France, Italy, and Spain) has seemed to collapse into a "shamefaced and subaltern" social democracy (*THM,* p. 76). The enumeration essentially repeats that of the earlier book in regard to the series of failures recorded by European Communist movements in the period between the end of World War I and that of World War II. This had enabled Anderson to conclude: "The hidden hallmark of Western Marxism as a whole is thus that it is a product of defeat."[15]

This series of general collapses was due to the aforementioned lack of strategy. We are thus effectively brought back to the need for a satisfactory theoretical treatment of those questions already indicated as concluding *Considerations*. In addition, Marxist critical theory must now confront the challenge of idealism (structuralism), to be sure, but it must further deal with a different opponent: naturalism—in the form of claims concerning biological determinants, most notably embodied in sociobiology (at once "aggressive and conservative, individualist yet inertial": *THM*, p. 81). It must discover some way to theorize the relation between nature and history that avoids the Scylla of relativism and the Charybdis of biological determinism: "the other great crux for Marxism as a critical theory" (*THM*, p. 83).

The three great "issues" of our time that Marxism must deal with and further develop from, argues Anderson, concern "women, ecology, and war" (*THM*, pp. 83–84). Though he returns at greater length to these matters in his postscript (*THM*, pp. 85–105), where he usually refers to the first of them as "the women's movement" or "feminism," his language surely gives him away here, incidentally revealing the reason for the difficulty observed earlier: women remain the infamous "Other." We are not astonished, therefore, to find that the longer discussion of the relation between Marxism and feminism concludes with a commentary on their incommensurability. Class struggle, argues Anderson, can be resolved by political means and theory, but sexual confrontations are so deeply embedded in biological reality and social tradition as to demand solutions yet unperceived (or so it would seem). Among other things, this would suggest that Anderson is coming closer than he claims to Charybdis. In his preface to Anderson's book Frank Lentricchia claims for it a sympathetic treatment of the women's and ecology movements. (Are they really able to be thus equated? After all, the one concerns social, political, and economic *oppression;* the other concerns misuse and is of a rather different order.) But the "treatment" does not appear very "sympathetic" to this reader— and what are the condescending implications of "sympathetic" debate? Whatever the case, this third chapter ends with the rather abstract assertion that in relation to these matters, the subject/structure debate will eventually furnish a strategy, while that of nature/history will provide a morality (*THM*, p. 84).

15. Anderson, *Considerations*, p. 42.

Finally, after discussing the relation between Marxism and socialism in our time, chiefly with regard to the three issues just mentioned, the postscript concludes by setting forth four additional major areas where practical research and proposals are needed: (1) the political structure of socialist democracy; (2) the pattern of an advanced socialist economy; (3) the sociocultural patterns of the "libertarian levelling" that such a society would imply; (4) the kind of international relations that might be maintained between countries of necessarily unequal development (*THM*, pp. 99–100). Anderson rounds off his analysis by suggesting that work by André Gorz and Alec Nove addresses just these issues.[16]

It should be apparent that *In the Tracks of Historical Materialism* is a powerful analysis, whatever my criticism of some of its assertions and arguments. Above all, for the purposes of this chapter, it situates those critical theories that have too easily and unexaminedly come to be the limiting arc of the disciplinary horizon of literary criticism within the argumentative ground that bred them and the historical circumstances that gave them seeming importance and even urgency. It goes further, in that it examines their weaknesses, aporias, contradictions, and failures. Finally, it suggests (whether we can agree with the particulars or not) the kind of fundamental social and historical problem in relation to which our discipline (and any other) must learn to situate its own, more local questions.

Why? Quite simply because without such situation it does not *matter* what anyone may choose to say about some text or other.

This is not a plea, of course, for any superficial 'relevance' of literary reference (for example). Rather is it an assertion, with all its consequences, that what we call "literature" is ineluctably situated in and created by a historical context and social environment, just as are its artifacts and the theories dealing with them.[17] Only there is the matter of our discipline to be found, and only then will our discipline matter. The rest is all sound and fury.

16. Anderson refers to André Gorz, *Adieux au prolétariat* (Paris, 1980), and *Les chemins du paradis* (Paris, 1983); Alec Nove, *The Economics of Feasible Socialism* (London, 1983). Behind the latter's work he situates that of Janos Kornai: *Anti-Equilibrium* (Amsterdam, 1971); *Economics of Shortage* (Amsterdam, 1980); and *Growth, Shortage, and Efficiency* (Oxford, 1982).
17. This is the subject of my *Meaning of Literature*.

For an End to Discursive Crisis

And if such troubles last, it is not long before letters also and philosophy are so torn
to pieces that no trace of them can be found but a few fragments, scattered here
and there like planks from a shipwreck; and then a season of barbarism sets in, the
waters of Helicon being sunk under the ground, until, according to the vicissitudes
of things, they break out and issue forth again.
        —Sir Francis Bacon, *De Sapientia Veterum*

The historical fact cannot be considered as establishing an eternal truth; it can only
indicate a situation that is historical in nature precisely because it is undergoing
change.
        —Simone de Beauvoir, *The Second Sex*

"It is now taken for granted that nothing which concerns art can be
taken for granted any more: neither art itself, nor art in its relationship to the whole, nor even the right of art to exist."[1] Quoting this sentence from Theodor W. Adorno's *Aesthetic Theory*, Jürgen Habermas
criticizes it, gently enough, on the grounds that it asserts a kind of nostalgia for and of a general "aestheticization" of art, its removal from the
everyday concrete. And that is indeed *one* aspect at least of Adorno's
lament, echoing his colleague, Max Horkheimer, who also viewed the
decay of modern culture (as he saw it) with a jaundiced eye and opposed
it to some more 'objective' past form of art. For both of them, this stron-
ger, more confident art certainly included European culture of the Renaissance and Enlightenment: "Once it was the endeavor of art, literature,
and philosophy to express the meaning of things and of life, to be the
voice of all that is dumb, to endow nature with an organ for making
known her sufferings, or, we might say, to call reality by its rightful name.
Today nature's tongue is taken away. Once it was thought that each utterance, word, cry, or gesture had an intrinsic meaning; today it is merely an

1. Jürgen Habermas, "Modernity—An Incomplete Project," [tr. Seyla Ben-Habib], in *The
Anti-Aesthetic*, ed. Hal Foster (Port Townsend, Wash., 1983), pp. 3–15; this reference, p. 10.
This translation is closer to the original than is that in Theodor W. Adorno, *Aesthetic Theory*,
tr. C. Lenhardt, ed. Gretel Adorno and Rolf Tiedemann (1984; rpt. London, 1986). The
phrase opens Adorno's book.

[263]

occurrence."[2] For Horkheimer, the word "once" did not indicate some linear historicity, and Latin poetry in the service of political power was no different from the contemptible mass culture of our modernity, from the "prating" of "German heavy industrialists" in an even more unhappy moment, or literature in the service of any ephemeral social or personal desire. But "a work of art once aspired," he remarked, "to tell the world what it is, to formulate an ultimate verdict." No longer could a work such as Beethoven's *Eroica* do that; its inherent meaningfulness had been lost.[3] It was now but one more fragment among a myriad.

I am of the opinion (provable, I urge elsewhere) that the "ultimate verdict" formulated was *always* so only for the particular sociocultural environment in which it was rendered. That is clearly a fundamental point and one that is central to the argument of this final chapter, to its assessment of reason and understanding; I return to it shortly.

Especially since Schiller, Habermas adds in the short essay to which I referred above—and with Adorno particularly in mind—this "relationship to the whole" (in his quotation from Adorno) has contained some sort of belief in a redemptive power of art whose consequences would have been the pursuit of a "utopia of reconciliation."[4] In my view this sense of an alienated art, of which Habermas speaks with reference to his teachers, is not in fact a matter of art itself (generally speaking, at least, and to the degree in which it is not perceived as in 'revolt' against those foundations of which I will speak in a moment) but *is* the case for certain theories claiming to discuss it (I think especially of certain postscripts to "deconstruction"). Critics such as Marcuse—particularly in his last book, *The Aesthetic Dimension*—and Horkheimer in the quotation just given do show such a result of the Frankfurt School's thinking. As we saw in the last chapter, Western Marxism in general has been accused of an aestheticizing of social life as a whole, though only in the work of Ernst Bloch has it been understood as other than pessimistic. The point is massively important because, as we will see, it implies something very serious about our entire sociocultural environment.

I dare suggest that Habermas is slightly twisting—or at least simplifying—his master's thought and that Adorno was thinking as well of an entirely different aspect of art. In urging this, I recall other aspects of such texts as Horkheimer's *Eclipse of Reason*, and Horkheimer and Adorno's *Dialectic of Enlightenment*. These are works emphasizing how Enlightened reason contains within itself the seeds not so much of its own destruction (we may be reminded here, too, of Georg Lukács's 1961 *Destruction of Reason*, written in that same tradition) as of its deflection—

2. Max Horkheimer, *Eclipse of Reason* (1947; rpt. New York, 1974), p. 101.
3. Ibid., 123, 40.
4. Habermas, "Modernity," pp. 10–11.

a deflection toward goals other than those of the general progress of all humanity: toward an apotheosis of the Self, and therefore not just its own glorification but the glorification as well of its power over others; toward a belief in the superiority of one kind of self over another (be it Aryan, Slavic, or whatever); and of course toward the denial of the very reason that provided the grounding for such belief in the first place. As Arnold Hauser has commented on such origins: "The danger of [Rousseau's] teaching was that, with his one-sided championing of life against history, his escape to the state of nature which was nothing more than a leap into the unknown, he prepared the way for those nebulous 'philosophies of life' which, out of despair at the apparent powerlessness of rational thinking, argue that reason should commit suicide."[5]

Art was from the beginning an integral part of the ideal of Enlightened reason. I have suggested elsewhere, and will shortly demonstrate at some length, that "literature" (*our* modern concept of literature) is the invention, more or less, of the European seventeenth century and that this invention is entirely caught up in a specific political reality, a network of power relations ordered in a particular way. Of this network this literature is part creator, part creature, and always guarantor.[6]

This is not the place to rehearse once again all the complex argument presupposed by this claim, nor the facts providing its proof. Subject to setting forth the complete argument elsewhere, I will merely assert that by the end of the European seventeenth century, literature had been consolidated as an integral part of the cultural response to a general crisis and had as its fundamental task the balancing of four 'goals': epistemological, aesthetic, ethical, and political—of which the last was far and away preponderant at the outset.

This idea of literature as the invention of a particular history, and invested with a specific sociocultural function, immediately suggests a completely different interpretation of Adorno's sentence. For if literature is part of a particular sociocultural environment set in place during the European seventeenth century and the Enlightenment, its "right to existence" must depend entirely on that of its whole environment. And *that*, for Adorno as for many others, has been fundamentally compromised by recent experience. All modern art, therefore, to the degree that it carries on the so-called Great Tradition and corresponds to this compromised civilization of the Enlightenment, must either disappear or be transformed. It would otherwise be the guarantor of a rationalism that has already given too much proof of the unreason it contains (which is not to say that we need throw out the baby with the bath water).

5. Arnold Hauser, *The Social History of Art* (New York, n.d.), III:75.
6. See Reiss, "Environment of Literature"; "Power, Poetry, and the Resemblance of Nature"; and the forthcoming *Meaning of Literature*.

The experience of Weimar and the Third Reich may thus be understood as that of a fundamental *crisis* in Western rationalism and the civilization it supported. It may well be, in fact, that this experience finds a significant precursor (since Rousseau's name has been proffered) in the Great Fear of 1789 and the Terror of 1793, both of them signs of an uncontrolled invasion of 'revolutionary' Reason by a kind of blind and above all *incomprehensible* unreason.[7] The link has perhaps already been indicated by Bertolt Brecht, who in 1938–41 wrote a series of short plays titled *Furcht und Elend des dritten Reichs*; the French translation as *Grandpeur et misère du IIIe Reich* captured the meaning with some precision. Be that as it may, the late years of the Weimar Republic and those of the Third Reich do indeed possess the characteristics of "crisis": in medicine, "the point in the progress of disease when an important development or change takes place which is decisive of recovery or death." Its other essential aspect is that it comes *from within* a system in movement: it is the "catastrophic" mark of a structure that is now undergoing a sudden transformation but that has always been in a gradual process of change.[8]

That said, what can it tell us about the all-too-well-known "crisis" supposedly characteristic of contemporary critical theory for now some twenty years? Of course, if I were a "Derridian," I would play on the words *crisis* and *criticism* to reveal the profundity that it is in the very nature of criticism to be always in crisis. For once, I would have a correct etymology on my side and not simply a play on a surface verbal analogy—a facile joke, but one that will allow me later to make a more serious commentary. Anyway, the case is that this so-called crisis of criticism has indeed been marked (as I observed in Chapter 3) by two main effects: the ever more agitated multiplication of critical discourses assertive of their *difference* and *originality* on the one hand, and the use of ever more esoteric, private, and indeed almost secret languages on the other. Both effects suggest, of course, that we have nothing more to say. In this sense they confirm Adorno's remark and provide a kind of evidence that something was set in place at a specific moment in Western culture which no longer works. (There are those, I am aware, who have urged the agitation and eso-

---

7. For the Great Fear the essential work remains Georges Lefebvre's *La grande peur de 1789* (Paris, 1932). I thank Patricia J. Hilden for bringing this possible parallel to my attention. It may well be that contemporary American Christian fundamentalisms embody the same irrational fear: irrational in the strongest sense, since that sort of belief in some divinity fundamentally denies human reason its efficacy; to note the anti-intellectualism of such beliefs is to scratch only the surface of their fear, compounded, perhaps, from both a terror of the *power* of reason and anguish at its seeming failure—for it can never resolve *everything*; see Chapter 4 above.

8. The reference is to René Thom's topological work and to the concept of inevitable transformation in homeomorphic structures. I do not mean to imply any ethical judgment (though some of my arguments will do so). The preceding definition is from the *Oxford English Dictionary*.

tericism as reason for a return to older familiarities. This has an obvious and highly visible counterpart in some political and social activities of our own time. Both moves represent the very opposite of my own view.)

The dominant analytico-referential discourse slowly consolidated throughout the seventeenth century is characterized among other things by two elements. In *The Discourse of Modernism* I claim to have shown that in order to function well this discourse must play with a basic contradiction between a linear motion assumed to be constant and a stasis conceived as its goal, between process and entropy.[9] That internal and fundamental contradiction is the first element. The second concerns the occulted 'instance' of the irrational.[10] Let me first discuss the implications of the former.

In the science that becomes the very model of this dominant discourse, for example, the discursive subject claims both the right to and the necessity of an endless search. That search proceeds by the discovery (whether inductive or deductive is no matter) of what are in principle endless causal chains. Yet at the same time it proclaims that a moment will come when all possible knowledge will have been acquired (Descartes speaks of "a few centuries," just as Bacon had earlier spoken of a foreseeable though doubtless distant future). This *fact,* this contradiction within scientific discourse which marks its participation in a moment of general discursive formation, shows all the ambiguity—even the falsity—of Louis Althusser's celebrated distinction between "science" and "ideology."

Althusser himself undertook later to criticize this supposed distinction, especially in his *Eléments d'autocritique,* but he did not take it at all as far as he might have done.[11] What he did was point out that he had merely opposed bourgeois ideology to Marxism: that is, a supposed "prescientific" thinking and doing to that *science* of society and history that he understood to have followed upon a sudden rupture. These are now well-known notions: let me just say that Althusser criticized himself for having opposed ideology as such to science as such, as though they existed in some way out of history, as though they were independent of a specific society and its history. He thus charged himself with "theoreticism," with having reduced a real historical rupture to a merely theoretical opposition.

Criticisms of Althusser by John Lewis and especially E. P. Thompson have been directed particularly at this question. Still, I think it worth

9. Reiss, *Discourse of Modernism,* esp. pp. 159, 359–62, and earlier chapters in the present volume.

10. The use of the word "instance" is rather awkward in English, I know, but for sufficiently obvious reasons, I can use neither "presence" nor "absence."

11. Louis Althusser, *Eléments d'autocritique* (Paris, 1974), esp. pp. 41–53.

dwelling on for a brief moment, for the matter is far from being as simple as Althusser himself implies. Then, too, further commentary will permit me to indicate some of the advantages to be obtained from the kinds of argument put forward in this chapter and in the volume as a whole. First of all these arguments make it clear that like literature, science is itself invented by a certain discursive dominance. (Is it necessary to recall, here, that by "discourse" I mean a practice producing meaning through all human action, experience, phenomena, allowing the analysis and understanding of our situation, and all praxis that 'results'?) Therefore, the very opposition between science and ideology would also be the product of the dominance in question. The term "science" would perhaps signal the process I mentioned, "ideology" the stasis.

Thus situated in its historical circumstance, the continuation of Althusser's self-criticism perhaps becomes more interesting. When he makes of ideology a representation "of individuals' imagined relation to their real conditions of existence" and a constant question posed to "the individual as subject," he seems to approach a more fruitful analysis.[12] For then the simplistic opposition between the true and the false is completely modified. We find ourselves simply facing two particular aspects of how *our* discourse works. And that reveals how the human analysis of sociohistorical situation functions *within the specific constraints of a particular historical moment*; "science," then, offers us just one element of such an analysis. Science, for us, would be the dominant way of analyzing the relation to the *other*; ideology would be that which allows us to situate ourselves with respect to what is thus constituted by this science. Science, that is to say, has been our culture's way of justifying its seizure (as a 'truthful' knowledge of what it calls its "objects") of what it perceives as 'different.' Similarly, ideology has become our (totalizing) description of the acceptability of the sociocultural organization inferred from the products of that science—which is precisely why ideology 'lays claim' to a knowledge of *everything*.

Michel Foucault proposed, I think, a similar argument. In a 1977 interview he criticized a too facile use of the term "ideology" on three grounds. I leave aside the second two, those of subject and infrastructure, because they raise questions that would take me far from the present issue. The first dilemma put forward, however, is immediately relevant.

12. Althusser, "Idéologie et appareils idéologiques," pp. 67–125, esp. 97–122. A very useful English-language introduction to many of these questions and others can be found in Ted Benton, *The Rise and Fall of Structural Marxism: Althusser and His Influence* (London, 1984). More recently, Tony Judt has discussed aspects of Althusser's idealism, specifically in connection with the actual activities of the Parti Communiste Français and the postwar conditions of France in his *Marxism and the French Left: Studies on Labour and Politics in France, 1830–1981* (Oxford, 1986), pp. 212–15, 221–33. See also Timpanaro, *On Materialism*, pp. 135–219.

Ideology, Foucault remarked, "always stands in virtual opposition to something else which is supposed to count as truth. Now I believe that the problem does not consist in drawing the line between that in discourse which falls under the category of scientificity or truth, and that which comes under some other category, but in seeing historically how effects of truth are produced within discourses which in themselves are neither true nor false."[13] Our question then must be how our sociocultural environment draws the line between truth and falsehood, and for what ends.

No doubt that all needs to be elaborated, perhaps elsewhere, at greater length. But one can see an immediate benefit in this analysis: it enables us to conceive how reason itself is created within a sociocultural environment *without immediately laying itself open to the charge of relativism*. For reason analyzes itself, here, as *constitutive* of that environment in history. It does not allow us to set aside, for example, moral imperatives, though it does demand that we seek their grounding in the historical establishment of that reason itself. If, for instance, the foundational axiom of that reason is the certitude of the (individual) subject, and if the exteriorization of that subject requires assumptions of equality of action, social and political treatment, access to power, modes of production, and the rest, then it is quite clear that the denial of *any* of these things to *any* subject is the denial of that very reason.

Such an analysis leads to a second point, related to the argument about truth as it is to the discussion of reason and the subject, and that is the question of science and ideology. Once we assert that a particular idea of knowledge corresponds to a culture instituting it, then the end of that culture in its familiar form produces an inevitable consequence. Its knowledge is itself seriously undermined, not as something *known* or as an assured possession (as stasis) but to the extent that it leads elsewhere, toward other areas of knowledge and action (as process)—to the extent, that is to say, that it is (something like) reason in action. We need not worry about the disappearance of the knowledge in question. That remains given as an accomplished fact, the mark of a particular social reality.

We should, however, be concerned about *not* historicizing reason. To the precise degree that we forget that knowledge and reason are historically constitutive and constituted, and believe in their unchanging permanence, just to that degree do we enter upon a kind of infinite pursuit of a language now deprived of contact with the reality that was given as *the* reference place of knowledge. Precisely such a 'scientific' analysis of Stalin by Althusser is what enables Tony Judt to make the amusing retort that

<hr>

13. Michel Foucault, "Truth and Power," in *Power/Knowledge: Selected Interviews and Other Writings, 1972–1977*, ed. Colin Gordon, tr. Colin Gordon, Leo Marshall, John Mepham, and Kate Soper (New York, 1980), p. 118. The ideology/science question was also broached, with reference to literary criticism, in Chapter 6, pp. 191–93.

only the already converted would be likely to believe "this entertaining account of Stalin as the man whose major crime was to pervert the self-understanding of marxism (which is rather like suggesting that Hitler's sin was to give physical anthropology a bad name)."[14] And we may perhaps recall the essay in which Foucault speaks of writing as that activity where humans strive endlessly to postpone the speechless silence that is death.[15] Knowledge as process, that is to say, becomes empty.

We can readily see, therefore, that at a time of crisis, belief in some absolute Reason has consequences that are certainly pernicious and potentially disastrous, for language is then detached from all reference. It discovers itself everywhere and always. It finds nothing else, no way of getting outside itself. It no longer has a grasp on some *other* as such but only as a reproduction of itself. It turns in circles before a mirror reflecting it to infinity: the famous *mise-en-abîme* of so much contemporary literary criticism. When I made fun earlier in this chapter of some of deconstruction's false etymologizing, this was the sort of matter I had in mind. Exactness in this area, however ludic it may be, at least has the advantage of providing something like a fixed link. The aim of the "Derridians" is precisely to deprive us of anything of the kind. In this way Geoffrey Hartman emphasizes the master's play on *ancre/encre* (which picks up exactly perhaps on Benveniste's worry about the loss of an anchor) in *Eperons/Spurs,* and then continues joyfully:

> What gymnastics or abysmatics! "Spurs" is also made to suggest the circumflex on the word *être* (Being), and shows its 'forgotten' *s* through that angular trace. The spur/spoor rides the *e*. If we substitute the *s* and write out *estre,* we can then reconstruct a link between *estre* and *reste,* as if they were anagrams of each other. Being is what remains, not what is. Poetry, as the perfection of writing, is the house of Being, but equally its remains, the disclosure of nonbeing or *Seinsvergessenheit.*[16]

Excelsior, I cry, echoing Edward Thompson's astonishment as he confronts Althusser's idealism.

Here criticism is indeed—as Hartman has himself asserted elsewhere, though with a different view of the matter—in the wilderness, losing both its footing and its head.[17] We need not be surprised that he concludes the

14. Judt, *Marxism and the French Left,* p. 215.
15. Michel Foucault, "Le langage à l'infini," *Tel Quel,* 15 (1963), 44–53.
16. Geoffrey H. Hartman, *Saving the Text: Literature/Derrida/Philosophy* (Baltimore, Md., 1981), pp. xxiii–xxiv.
17. I am referring here to Hartman's *Criticism in the Wilderness: The Study of Literature Today* (New Haven, Conn., 1980). I have discussed this text in conjunction with Fredric Jameson, *The Political Unconscious: Narrative as a Socially Symbolic Act* (Ithaca, 1981), showing how Hartman casts himself up to that nostalgia I have previously mentioned, whereas Jameson seems more akin to Williams in his optimism; see Timothy J. Reiss, "Critical Environments:

passage just quoted: "What survives in this graveyard of meaning is not simply a will, but specifically the *will to write*." Foucault's infinite writing is reduced to absurdity, in a nihilism avoiding all contact with any 'object' potentially able to constitute something called history (whose claim would doubtless be thought of as mere pretension in any case). We must learn to dwell, Hartman implies (after Derrida), in a space of permanent carnival, of an everlasting undoing of what might otherwise construct itself as meaning, in the space of Derrida's archi-literature or of Kristeva's "semiotic," where, as Eugene Goodheart has put it, "the imagination can no longer play its games with confidence, for the deepest knowledge of the critic is of the vacuity on which those games rest." Hartman wants to keep us in a critical wilderness, on the grounds that we have no means of constructing any kind of surety without falling back into old habits. Goodheart, once again, furnishes a reminder: like truth and like subjectivity, like science, literature, and ideology as I wrote of them before, "skepticism is an historically conditioned view of experience, which does not disqualify it as a method or a system of thought, but its historical character should bar it from putting on metaphysical or universalistic airs."[18] Deconstruction wants to dwell in that flux of which Frege was so afraid; Benveniste wanted to find an anchor reminiscent of older habits of thought; Peirce and others wish rather to establish some other form of anchor, equally reliable and actually functional, though doubtless quite different.

One is reminded, too, of Thompson's criticism of Althusser's idealistic Marxism, which has reached an exactly parallel reductionism among some of the French philosopher's disciples—who claim that history itself (or at least its study) is "scientifically" and "politically" valueless![19] Both of these, the Derridian's endless abyss and Althusser's verbose "theoretical practice," can continue forever and at an ever greater distance from that concrete human experience to which they thought, once upon a time, to respond.

In the history of discursive development and transformation, all this is doubtless part of an inevitable and essential moment, a time when all discourse becomes "conscious" of the self-productivity of knowledge and action. But to remain there is to accept pessimism, despair, and the considerable danger of some sort of irrationalism. This is to say that Derrida's work, for example, made sense in 1967–69. It represented a profound questioning of the philosophical presuppositions of a culture now clearly

---

Cultural Wilderness or Cultural History?" *Canadian Review of Comparative Literature,* 10 (June 1983), 192–209.

18. Eugene Goodheart, *The Skeptic Disposition in Contemporary Criticism* (Princeton, N.J., 1984), p. 176.

19. Edward Palmer Thompson, *The Poverty of Theory and Other Essays* (New York, 1978), p. 2.

discontent. But on the one hand, to claim that these presuppositions have their distant source in a (Platonic) rupture between rationality and some kind of ur-Unreason (again, Kristeva's "semiotic" reproduced at a phylogenetic level) is to repeat Althusser's error over a long term and to deprive oneself of all hope of *doing* anything. On the other hand, to pursue deconstruction to the infinite is a mere self-indulgence and, furthermore, one that necessarily leads outside any *real* history.

No doubt Derrida does force us to recognize the limits of any code of meaning: "Derrida's commentary [in *Glas*] . . . is so radical that, despite its reference to our dependence on the words of others, the contained (language) breaks the container (encyclopedic book, concept, meaning) and forces upon the reader a sense of the mortality of every code, of every covenanted meaning."[20] "So what then?" I find myself provoked to ask. For how long, and simply *how*, can we continue to 'awaken' this consciousness? The modern awareness of the issue predates Hartman (and Derrida) by many years. Indeed, at the turn of the century many types of discourse (physics, art, and poetry perhaps especially, but also the development of formal logics) were forcing such a sense upon the reader: it was indeed the project of such as Peirce and Welby. But, further, was it not always an aspect of the dominant discourse of modernism? Did not Bacon, Descartes, and the other 'founders' of our discourse continually repeat it? That is clearly no answer. Nor is it intended to be one. I merely wish to emphasize that the techniques of deconstruction are (avowedly) infinitely iterative. But its aim cannot possibly be.

However sagacious some of its exponents, deconstruction has remained fundamentally a *destruction*, though it is undoubtedly possible to make a nice distinction between the two terms (a distinction that is theoretically a real one, certainly).[21] Worse yet, insofar as its *practical* consequences are concerned, deconstruction has tended implicitly to assert that such (repetitive) destruction is an unavoidable constant of all human action, and that the history of human constructs is that of the successive undermining of previous certainties. Deconstruction provides us with the notion of a conceptual evolution that is in fact forever rendered static by its own skepticism. The so-called "strong" moments of history then become those in which a particular society occults or represses that fundamental incapacity of all human knowledge and action. We are thus provided with the choice between a blind certainty of discursive hegemony or a despair of critical awareness. Such despair cannot but be regressive, just because it disables, because it sees no alternative to the mode of functioning that is now at its critical limit.

20. Hartman, *Saving the Text*, p. xvi.
21. See Paul de Man, *Allegories of Reading: Figural Language in Rousseau, Nietzsche, Rilke, and Proust* (New Haven, Conn., 1979), p. x.

Elsewhere, I have sought to show how the strategies of a Hartman, responding to this impasse, have led directly to some ahistorical concept of the sacred, toward the negation of history and the choice of a vaticinatory 'criticism' clearly publicizing its quasi-religious tone and style (see note 17). This solution echoes the misapprehension of the carnivalesque "Other," already discussed in Chapter 4. It is precisely due (in this case) to the pursuit of textuality (as one might call it) and to an erroneous idea of what constitutes concrete human experience; it leads to a kind of precious plethora whose religiosity is denied in vain. A divinized Text simply replaces the word, a "Monsieur Texte," writes Hartman, that concludes, like *Glas* itself, in the "débris de . . . Derrida."[22] I dare propose a play in similar style, yielding "Derridieu," of whom Hartman's *Saving the Text* is a sacred exegesis, the hermeneutics announced at the outset: Hartman on Derrida on Hegel and Genet, and so on and on (exactly) to infinity.

Such nostalgia is inevitably functionally crippling; it turns its back on human history and any social present. Expressions of despair or approaches to mysticism are the marks of a kind of fragmented anarchy, an assertion that understanding has been disabled, that comprehension has been rendered impossible because the production and communication of meaning have somehow become unattainable. That view implies a consequent inaptitude for action, a sort of escape from praxis of whatever kind, because praxis is inseparable from interpretation, as interpretation is an ongoing access to (and creation of) meaning. But this last idea does not suppose meaning to be divorced from the historical realities of the sociocultural environment. On the contrary, without such embedding, words do indeed come to whirl in some kind of vague ethereality. They do indeed come to find themselves entirely undecidable. And this is so just because deconstruction relies, finally, on that very division of self and other, mind and matter, that it thought it was criticizing so fundamentally: its mind has become entirely dissociated from its environment.

That is doubtless why we arrive at some sort of remaking of a Self. Its games become the only possible standard for such lost-footed play. Hence the importance Hartman ascribes (in *Criticism in the Wilderness*) to the critic's psyche: it is a new anchor for wandering. Just so can Hartman's colleague J. Hillis Miller, as university professor and president of the Modern Language Association of America (in both cases responsible to collectivities), reduce reading to a rigorously individual activity: "Real reading, when it occurs, which may not be all that often, is outside the institution, private, solitary." (The term "real," here, has a deliciously ironic cast about it.) It is this that gives the experience "joy." Nor does Miller pass up the opportunity to remind *his* reader that this joy "of course

22. Hartman, *Saving the Text*, pp. 1–32.

has sensual and erotic overtones" ("of course"?). That individualistic joy of reading has the same purpose as Hartman's wilderness: it marks "a break in time, in that sense anarchic, a dissolution of preexisting orders, the opening of a sense of freedom that is like a new earth and a new heaven, an influx of power."[23]

No doubt. But that power, freedom, dissolution are all entirely and anarchically centered in the individual—even an individual who may be thought of as in the closest possible relation with a community. For more astonishing yet is that teaching also becomes *first and foremost* an active gratification of the self: "A student makes a comment or asks a question that leads the teacher to see something new. . . . Some unexpected insight comes to the teacher in the midst of the class hour." Then teaching becomes "joyful" as a learning process for the teacher, "an active process of invention or discovery." The teacher's primary responsibility is "to the texts being 'read in class' or to the 'material' or the 'things' presented."[24] Since the importance of the text lies in its relation to the individual reading it, this implies that the importance of the whole affair lies in its relation to the individual teacher. Reading and teaching mark the self's wandering off into the wilderness of (erotic, he says) self-gratification. The self, here, is no longer an anchor for collective meaning of any kind but the source of a private language that others may or may not enter. So indeed we do arrive in what Hartman announces as the "graveyard of Western culture."[25] But why on earth dance on the tombstones in some *Walpurgisnacht* of unreason? We confront here an ultimate pessimism that, seeing no future for itself, refuses any further participation in collective reason (like an infant who, finding it cannot win, refuses to play the game).

This erring self, turning away from interhuman communication and action, inevitably finds its only anchor in the sacred. And in this regard I will quote a text that makes the same criticism and elaborates on this argument while contrasting these writers' quest with Ernst Bloch's utopianism (which always remains secular):

> What one discerns today is religion as the result of exhaustion, disconsolation, disappointment: its forms are varieties of unthinkability, undecidability, and paradox together with a remarkable consistency of appeals to magic, divine ordinance, or sacred texts.
>
> When you see influential critics publishing major books with titles like *The Genesis of Secrecy, The Great Code, Kabbalah and Criticism, Violence and the Sacred,*

23. J. Hillis Miller, "President's Column: Responsibility and the Joy of Reading," *MLA Newsletter,* 18, no. 1 (Spring 1986), 2.

24. J. Hillis Miller, "President's Column: Responsibility and the Joy(?) of Teaching," *MLA Newsletter,* 18, no. 2 (Summer 1986), 2.

25. Hartman, *Saving the Text,* p. 9.

Deconstruction and Theology, you know you are in the presence of a significant trend. The number of prevalent critical ideas whose essence is some version of theory liberated from the human and the circumstantial further attests to this trend. Even the revisionist readings of past critics and critical theories— say the current vogue for Walter Benjamin not as a Marxist but as a crypto-mystic, or those versions of such actively radical positions as Marxism, feminism, or psychoanalysis that stress the private and hermetic over the public and social—must also be viewed as being part of the same curious veering toward the religious.[26]

Edward Said is right to ask critics to devote themselves seriously and right away to the search for an answer to such privatization and mysticism, as it comes to overwhelm so much criticism in our time.

Though access to concrete, conceptual, or textual experience may admittedly be difficult (as the very principles put forward here assert), that does not require us to give up on it. On the contrary, the very difficulty demands a constant exchange between the real and whatever awareness we can have of it, and—yes, no doubt—a simultaneous 'creation' of both the real and its awareness (so long as we do not then imagine that 'creation' to result from some free wandering of the mind). Thompson has made the point:

> A historian in the Marxist tradition [and any other] is entitled to remind a Marxist philosopher [here, Althusser] that historians also are concerned, every day, in their practice, with the formation of, and with the tensions within, social consciousness. Our observation is rarely singular: this object of knowledge, this event, this elaborated concept. Our concern, more commonly, is with multiple evidences, whose interrelationship is, indeed, an object of our enquiry. Or, if we isolate the singular evidence for particular scrutiny, that evidence does not stand compliantly like a table for interrogation: it stirs, in the medium of time, before our eyes. These stirrings, these events, if they are within 'social being' seem often to impinge upon, thrust into, break against, existent social consciousness. They propose new problems, and, above all, they continually give rise to *experience*—a category which, however imperfect it may be, is indispensable to the historian, since it comprises the mental and emotional response, whether of an individual or a social group, to many interrelated events or to many repetitions of the same kind of event.[27]

Criticism needs to think this relation between text and society, to think society *as* text, maybe. But that is meaningless if it does not do so in all the concreteness of real experience. Criticism cannot be a permanent ques-

26. Edward W. Said, *The World, the Text, and the Critic* (1983; rpt. London, 1984), pp. 291–92. The growths of forms of religiosity in society at large was commented upon in Chapter 4 and in this chapter above (see n. 7).
27. Thompson, *Poverty of Theory,* p. 7.

tioning of some infinite writing, the remnant of a *process* created to search for what it conceived as the true but now deprived of that fixed point it had called "knowledge." Nor can it simply fix itself in some ultimately entirely private and "anarchic" Self. Either of these would indeed be strictly a form of unreason. For reason (that of the Enlightenment) demanded the play and bond of both analysis and reference, as it did of self and other.

Deconstructive discourse is not alone in depriving itself of an object, in favor of some subject. Others, claiming to be 'scientific' and affecting a certain such style, fall into an exactly parallel trap. When one believes, after filling a page of so-called critical commentary with as complicated and rebarbative a set of equations as possible, that one has clarified a text, one cannot but be deliberately mistaken—a new mystification. I have seen pages of supposedly Peircean semiotics (they aren't) or of Greimasian semiology (they are) that would make you laugh—if only they were not meant to be taken dead seriously (and "dead" may well be the appropriate word). There, too, is a discourse that has lost all contact with the public and the social, straying this time not into undecidability but into a false scientism, a simulacrum. At best, it seeks a static view of what it wants to perceive as 'typically' human (semiotic square or narrative form as elementary structure of meaning—and even of all possible thought); at worst, it throws itself into totally meaningless mathematization—yet another form of private language pursuing its ineffable goals to infinity.

Nor am I altogether convinced that Habermas's "public space," where the "ideal speech situation" may function, is not another example of this effect, inasmuch as it sets aside concrete elements. Indeed, Mary Astell long since made an entirely appropriate response to this sort of claim. Questioning Lord Shaftesbury's assertion in his *Letter concerning Enthusiasm* that rational, ordered debate would always resolve disputed issues, Astell retorted that such might well be the case in an *ideal* situation. Unfortunately, humans are born into power relations whose inherent inequality precludes any such possibility. We cannot simply assume our ability to start again from scratch and create some utopia (a strain as evident in Shaftesbury as it is in Habermas and his teachers): "Were *Matters ballanc'd*, were no other *Force* us'd but that of *Wit and Raillery*, *Reason* wou'd have *fair play*. Mankind wou'd *flourish*. *Wonderful* wou'd be the *Harmony and Temper* from *all these Contrarieties*, they wou'd make up that *right Humor*, which the Letter *contends* for, as going more than half way toward *Thinking rightly* of every thing. And Men *being mildly treated, and let alone*, they wou'd never Rage to that degree, as to occasion *Blood-shed*, *Wars, Persecutions, and Devastations in the World;* which proceed from nothing but their being put out of Humor, by not being permitted to do what they Will."[28]

---

28. Mary Astell [Mr. Wotton, pseud.], *Bart'lemy Fair; or, An Enquiry after Wit, in which due*

Thus was Shaftesbury's rather romantic utopianism turned to mockery. One may well feel that Habermas's ideal speech situation, however attractive, echoes the same contradictory idealism: contradictory, because it assumes philanthrophy in "Enlightened" self-interest. In effect, it is a milder version of Mandeville's discovery of public virtue in private vice, and Habermas's public space would appear to rest on rather similar assumptions. For where, indeed, would such a place for the ideal exchange of various discourses actually function? Still, the hope for this kind of consensus at least represents the pursuit of reason—a social, public, and above all rational will. Indeed, it may offer a pattern something like Peirce's ongoing triadic semiosis, which comes to a temporary halt in the final interpretant, the fixation of habit. It may present a concrete utilization of the multifold language imagined by Cournot and Welby. All that remains still to be seen; at present, Astell's rather savage irony appears quite overwhelmingly convincing.

Yet it seems urgent in our time to strive for debate and consensus, for we are threatened by another element of the irrational. I have spoken first of the contradiction between movement and stasis which is fundamental (as they themselves also are) to the dominant discourse of the Enlightenment, and of some consequences resulting for us today; I have done so because the contradiction in question seemed to preside at the instauration of that discourse: without the successful balance of the two elements, analytico-referential discourse could not have become constituted.[29] At the time of its consolidation toward the end of the seventeenth century, it became necessary to *occult* an element that was not simply contestatory but that once again questioned the very possibility of the discourse of reason.

In the arena of scientific truth this element was manifested in the form of an incomprehensible divine impulse. In the political arena it can be

---

*Respect is had to a Letter Concerning Enthusiasm, To my Lord**** (London, 1709), p. 60. Quoted in Ruth Perry, *The Celebrated Mrs. Astell: An Early English Feminist* (Chicago, 1986), pp. 227–28.

29. The opposition is indeed general and foundational. Earlier in this book we saw it manifest in the opposition between a certainty of knowledge and the flux of its objects (Chapter 2, pp. 57–58, 83–84), an opposition equally often reversed, in the form of reason as process, yet constituting a fixed body of knowledge composed of orderable objects. We saw it, too, in the Saussurean opposition between diachronicity and synchronicity. Psychoanalysis is deeply embedded within it, most notably in the pair *Eros/Thanatos*: pleasure principle or life instinct versus death instinct (on this, see my "Science des rêves," pp. 54–56). Hannah Arendt detected it in Marx's work. Referring to the diverse "inconsistencies" in his writings, she remarked that they were all "minor when compared with the fundamental contradiction between the glorification of labor and action (as against contemplation and thought) and of a stateless, that is, actionless and (almost) laborless society": "Tradition and the Modern Age," in *Between Past and Future: Eight Exercises in Political Thought*, enlarged ed. (1968; rpt. Harmondsworth, 1977), p. 24. She thus indicated the presence of just the same stasis/process opposition within the ultimate liberal politico-social theory itself. See, too, my *Discourse of Modernism*.

seen in the opposition between a monarchy upheld by this same divinity and a network of power relations whose comprehension was in reach of everyone's common sense. In aesthetics it was the inability of the rules to cope with the *je ne sais quoi,* the sublime that is somehow beyond them (eventually to be caught and occulted in the new science of Aesthetics, in the mid-eighteenth century). Everywhere, in fact, it is reason's fear of the wandering, error, and deviation of unreason. The thought of the late seventeenth century and the entire age of Enlightenment succeeded in keeping away this threat of the irrational. The idea of "maturity" used by Kant to define Enlightenment is only a mark of this success.[30]

We need not be surprised, therefore, that Roland Barthes chose to undermine this discourse with what he called a child's (immature) game, a game that can be played only after what seems a series of mystifying simplifications, after a kind of diffusion of attention, an attempt to get rid of (what had been) necessary distinctions. First of all, he took on the concept of power, central to all our discourses. Barthes tried to replace this concept, which is after all historically situated, with a notion of what he called "powers" (*les pouvoirs*). Once again (like Althusser and Derrida) he fell into the universal ("powers" are everywhere and have always existed; thus to look at their actual functioning in specific environments is more than a little hard), and the inevitable irrationality: "The reason for this endurance and ubiquity [of powers] is that power is parasitical on a trans-social organism, bound to the entire history of humanity, and not simply to its historical, political history. This object where power is inscribed, for all human eternity, is: language [*langage*]—or, more exactly, its necessary expression: *langue.*"[31] The only (also permanent) means of escaping this is the "child's game" in question: "I am more and more convinced, whether writing or teaching, that the basic operation of this method of detachment [from powers], is, when you are writing, fragmentation, and, when teaching, digression, or, to use a word whose ambiguity is precious: excursion."[32]

One may well wonder whether such a "disengagement" (withdrawal— or even *failure*—of "commitment," as Sartre might have put it) is not simply the refusal of anything but "desire" (itself become something al-most sacred, a glorification of some Self). The multiplying of places of "power" called for by Barthes (as by Gilles Deleuze and Félix Guattari)[33] is at the same time the refusal of the future implicit in the choosing to

30. This is the central idea of Kant's "Beantwortung der Frage: Was ist Aufklärung?" *Berlinische Monatschrift,* 4 (12 December 1784), 481–94; for English translation, see Kant, *Political Writings,* pp. 54–60.

31. Barthes, *Leçon,* p. 12.

32. Ibid., p. 42.

33. Gilles Deleuze and Félix Guattari, *L'anti-Oedipe* (Paris, 1972); *Rhizome* (Paris, 1975); and *Mille plateaux* (Paris, 1980).

sink into a broken mass of eventually private languages: multiple, too, as they must be to respond to the "powers." Behind that choice, once again, looms the anarchic Self, uttering its very personal language.

This is a refusal of the future because it refuses that public space in which alone some future can be created. Exchange of words demands opposition and conflict (a notion akin, if not identical, to that of "dialogue" as it appears in Lev Yakubinsky, Vygotsky, and Bakhtin).[34] To flee them, as to flee power because it is supposedly everywhere, in fact comes down to accepting them and it. In this case, Barthes actually acknowledges that flight, somewhat obliquely, as he speaks of the Collège de France in terms of a "lieu *hors-pouvoir*"—quite apparently it is anything but such a "place beyond power."[35] It would appear more important to try and change the demands and reach of specific power.

Far from doing any such thing, these thinkers try to slide into the margins, as it were. In Barthes's case the escape route is called "pleasure" (the satisfaction, once again, of personal "desire") "An entire mythology tends to make us believe that pleasure (and especially the pleasure of the text) is a rightist idea. . . . Yet pleasure is not an *element* of the text; it is not some innocent residue; nor does it depend on some logic of the understanding or feeling. It is a wandering [*dérive*], something at once revolutionary and asocial, which cannot be taken in charge by any collectivity, any mentality, any ideolect. Is it then something *neutral*? You can easily see that the pleasure of the text is scandalous, not because it is immoral but because it is *atopical*."[36] Any work, any product, any and all actions, Barthes tells us in his joyfully impish and lugubrious manner, is necessarily recuperated by power (*powers,* rather), by the dominant practices of meaning. The only way to escape is through marginalization in some strong sense ("carnival" in the sense already much used). That he places the following passage in parentheses is intended to mark its flight from *force majeure*: "(On the other hand I understand by *subtle subversion* what is not directly concerned with destruction [in a discourse seeking to escape the clutches of power], what avoids the paradigm and looks for some *other* term: a third term, a term of synthesis, but an eccentric, unheard of, term.)"[37]

The idea is to slide somehow along that edge where silence and power(s) meet. For Barthes, that is what literature, by definition, *does*. "Literature *turns* the forms of knowledge"; it "works in the interstices of science"; it provides us with "this mirage-like movement pushing us elsewhere, to-

<hr>

34. Yakubinsky's book on dialogue is not yet available in translation. My knowledge of its contents is drawn from Wertsch, *Vygotsky* (see Chapter 5, n. 16, above).

35. Barthes, *Leçon,* p. 11.

36. Roland Barthes, *Le plaisir de texte* (Paris, 1973), pp. 38–39.

37. Barthes, *Leçon,* p. 87.

ward some unclassed, atopical place, so to speak, far from the *topoi* of politicized culture."[38] The dominance of analytico-referential discourse was possible because it surrounded and enveloped this internal threat of dissolution, because here too it created a balance. Today there are many who, thinking they have found some solution to a crisis in reason, would like to bring back to life this dosage of the irrational. They would like to place us once again in the presence of unreason.

The general crisis mentioned at the outset of this chapter (and elsewhere) would thus have led to failure of the discourse that supported Enlightenment culture—and was of course supported by it. The balance of this discourse, its *Reason,* implied constant contact between the social and the individual, between the public and the private, between action and thought, and so on. In science we have the notion of *concept* (Locke) explicable through a transparent, "objective," and common language (Condillac, Lavoisier, and others). In political theory we find the argument and assertion of the *contract.* In aesthetics the idea of *taste* provided a bridge between individual appreciation and communal expectations of "beauty."

What we are seeing more and more in our time is thought either retreating before what it views as an inability to grasp what it conceives as reality, or placing itself uncritically at the disposal of powers whose grasp on the world is entirely biased and self-interested. With regard to this last, I am thinking of that current of contemporary thought known as "neoconservative" or even "neoliberal," which has become widespread as much in Europe as in North America and whose counterpart is found in the so-called "pragmatism" of certain socialist or other governments (actually a close regard for the immediate advantages of an individualist "sovereignty").

And do not let us believe that this thinking has no place in criticism. During the 1960s, confronting an aggressive structuralism, it was, for instance, the voice of a Wolfgang Kahler (or even the remnants of the New Criticism). In the 1970s the voices of René Girard and the *nouveaux philosophes* replied to Marxist or sociological critics. In the 1980s, reacting to a sort of confused dispersion that nevertheless does not lack its hesitant and uncertain steps toward resolution, we hear such as John Bayley, Helen Gardner, Murray Krieger, Roger Shattuck. All of them repeat the will to believe in the ubiquitous eternity of the values expressed in and through Western art (or others that may be subsumed under it), which in turn reflects a belief in the perennial value of authoritarian liberal individualism.

38. Ibid., pp. 18, 34.

In a recent public dispute, the precarious balance of Enlightenment reason has once again been disturbed, revealing anew—and in relation to what I have just been saying—what is represented by the irrationalism within it. I am thinking of the confrontation in the pages of the *New York Times Book Review* between Milan Kundera, who appeared as the apostle of Enlightenment, and Joseph Brodsky, who, with an apparently unconscious irony (the implications of which correspond precisely to two of the main types of critical response just indicated), linked the universality of art (especially of literature) to an irrationalism (marked here by the absence of willful interpretation) that according to him would go beyond—and that is my second point—any specific history.[39]

This is no new dispute; it had already become focused, precisely, in the interwar years, in the period of Weimar and the beginnings of the Third Reich. For Joseph Wood Krutch in 1929, the failures of science were cause for profound pessimism. For Edmund Husserl in the 1930s, it led to an attempt to ground all knowledge (and action) afresh. For Julien Benda in 1928, it led to a plea for intellectuals to reaffirm their commitment to Enlightenment.[40] In response to these kinds of reflection, Jaime García Terrés, for example, expressed his astonishment in 1949 at all these volumes asserting that "it is the intellectual, to a greater degree than the rest of humanity, who has responsibility for those situations that the civilized world has recently had to confront."[41] And it is of course the case that while intellectuals may not have seized such responsibility, they have certainly claimed the principal access to *reason.* But we have already seen how the idea of an objective, scientific reason (as opposed to a consciously political and social reason that science claims to exclude) and the claim of universality can indeed lead straight to that irrationalism of which I have been speaking.

In fact, that is just what happens to Terrés, whose polemic against Benda and the rest takes him directly into that irresponsibility which accompanies the irrational. The Mexican writer concludes his argument by asserting that literature is necessarily "free" because of its bond with a kind of knowledge ("literature is a pathway to knowledge [*un camino a la*

39. Milan Kundera, "An Introduction to a Variation," *New York Times Book Review,* January 16, 1985, pp. 1, 26–28; Joseph Brodsky, "Why Milan Kundera Is Wrong about Dostoyevsky," *New York Times Book Review,* February 17, 1985, pp. 31–34 (this exchange and others have now been collected in book form).

40. Joseph Wood Krutch, *The Modern Temper: A Study and a Confession* (New York, 1929); Edmund Husserl, *The Crisis of European Sciences and Transcendental Phenomenology: An Introduction to Phenomenological Philosophy,* tr. David Carr (Evanston, Ill., 1970); Julien Benda, *La trahison des clercs* (Paris, 1928). Husserl's book did not appear until 1954, but parts 1 and 2 were published in the review *Philosophia* (Belgrade) in 1936. In May 1935 he had given a lecture in Vienna entitled "Die Krisis des europäischen Menschentums und die Philosophie," some of whose themes are the same.

41. Jaime García Terrés, *Sobre la responsabilidad del escritor* (Mexico City, 1949), p. 11.

sabiduría]") that reveals, as Goethe's poet has it, "the quickening and calming power of man [*el poder del hombre (que) vivifica y armoniza*]." Here, a 'hidden' relation between literature, knowledge, and power is explicit, yet it remains occulted. For knowledge is above all "free"; it cannot even be specified as to either its structure or its aim. The "power" is that of "man's" mere humanity (as Crusoe might put it). Terrés does admit that this pathway is risky, because along the way all sense of responsibility may disappear (Benda's objection exactly). The mysterious responsibility accompanying this free reason in fact will become simply some extraordinarily vague moral responsibility.[42] In its turn, quite obviously, that morality will belong to universal humanity as construed by the Enlightenment. Any real social role, then—any role applicable to an *actual* environment—is denied to literature as it is to scientific reason in general. Such a position follows naturally from the claim of objectivity and intellectual detachment; indeed, it comes straight back to that treason of which Benda wrote and the eclipse of reason of which Horkheimer, Adorno, Lukács, and others were to speak.

Everything I have been saying till now insists, on the contrary, that art and criticism, science and philosophy, thought and action—the whole praxis of a sociocultural environment—are *always* caught within a specific history. We must be constantly aware of this. For it shows us that any 'crisis,' if there is such a thing, is never that of the 'human mind' or of 'civilization' in general but rather of a particular culture. In the social and cultural arena all forms of human production depend upon historical reason, and we cannot reject it by choosing some mystical irrationalism, by retreating into some false scientism accepted merely out of familiarity and fixed habit, or by selecting some aggressive universalism.

But the consequences of the refusal of reason in favor of one of those choices should not lead us into a no less simplistic recourse to the other side of the familiar equation, with the idea of replying through a reaffirmation of that very reason: "The crime of modern intellectuals against society," wrote Horkheimer, "lies not so much in their aloofness but in their sacrifice of contradiction and complexities of thought to the exigencies of so-called common sense."[43] Such a comment was addressed as much to a Terrés as to a Benda. It is here that we can doubtless situate the simplifications of a simulated scientism, corresponding in their turn to those of an infinite pursuit of the subject's writing: of "desire," or of "pleasure." The end of the European seventeenth century composed a

42. Ibid., p. 119.
43. Horkheimer, *Eclipse of Reason*, p. 86. The two further volumes important for this criticism are Max Horkheimer and Theodor Adorno, *Dialectic of Enlightenment*, tr. John Cuming (New York, 1972); and Georg Lukács, *The Destruction of Reason*, tr. Peter Palmer (London, 1980).

rational balance, set in place a dominant analysis and comprehension of social praxis. But it was a balance that also contained the seeds of its own fall and failure, still in process.

Nonetheless, I would see in that reason the "profound equilibrium, the astonishing success," of which Jacques Ellul spoke in his violent plea on behalf of the values of a culture whose end he thinks is in sight. That end is precisely visible in a certain style characteristic of our intellectual projects, of which three aspects are typical: "negation without any solution"; "directionless" motion involving an "ever more frenetic agitation of the intellect"; and a kind of "satisfaction with [such] acceleration." All this would imply a will *not* to know, and even to assert and rely upon an "absolute incomprehensibility." Thus the irrational would be asserted as the ultimate aim of a 'thought' that is no longer thought at all.[44] The rapid sketch this chapter has just attempted offers some clear examples of the effects of this assertion. The Enlightenment's critical reason would then have taken a definitive cast toward some kind of irrational imbalance rooted in despair, whose echo resonated through the passage I quoted earlier from Edward Said.

The complexity of this old equilibrium certainly demands an equally complex questioning. It will be a questioning that lends itself neither to simplistic answers (in terms of its own familiar "good sense," for instance) nor to the retreat into mystical obscurantist unreason, into undecidable wandering (whether "Derridian" or "Barthesien"), into the pursuit of some disembodied algebraical symbolizing that claims to be "scientific" (what I may call a certain "semiostyle") or even a supposedly objective Althusserian "science." Nor can it be an unthinking repetition of this reason itself (the posture of some "liberal" academic criticism, which thus thinks of itself as sheltered from the winds of theoretical change, conceiving itself as objective practice, as did Terrés and Ellul earlier).

No doubt classical reason's balance did indeed contain all of these. But we now seem to find ourselves in another discursive space—or at least in some moment of passage, of transformation. We go backward at the peril of awakened reason. Or, as Adrienne Rich has put it in altogether neater formulation: "We need to know the writing of the past, and know it differently than we have ever known it; not to pass on a tradition but to break its hold over us."[45]

We must needs rethink that lost equilibrium, therefore, in response to new social, political, artistic, and other demands, but acknowledging the achievement that Enlightenment thought and action were, their particular practico-inert formation—to employ a useful formula of Sartre's, and one

44. Jacques Ellul, *Trahison de l'occident* (Paris, 1975), pp. 219–24.
45. Adrienne Rich, "When We Dead Awaken: Writing as Re-Vision," in her *On Lies, Secrets, and Silence* (New York, 1979), p. 35.

that has the advantage of recalling his own plea for reason.[46] This old formation may even provide us with a good number of elements toward a new one, as Adrienne Rich suggests. In any case, one thing above all seems clear: we can no longer indulge ourselves in a crisis already over, one belonging to an already distant past.[47]

I will draw toward a conclusion by quoting the end of Said's book (cited earlier): "How their discourse can once again collectively become a truly secular enterprise is, it seems to me, the most serious question critics can be asking one another."[48] How, that is to say, can we rebuild a criticism that truly constructs a bridge between what is said or written and what is done and occurs in the public and social world? And here, with regard to this constant idea of generalized 'crisis,' one discovers a quite precise coincidence with Catherine Clément's remark concerning feminism: "Feminine crisis does not truly signify, it does not produce any change: it signals and repeats. Enclosed as an enclave by all of the group and individual constraints, feminine crisis remains enslaved. That women's language must first be a stuttering, when it's about real suffering, is true in fact; can we make a weapon of this shackle? A means must be elaborated to unhinge entire panels of ideology; a rigorous activity is needed which for the sake of rigor must think out and measure its relation to social activities as a whole."[49] The question is essentially the same one that I have been discussing throughout this book. The basic problematics all come together. Our task cannot but be that of responding to them.

I suggest that "ideology" may be understood as the way in which so-called "scientific" modes of social and cultural "understanding" are justified in their forms of *political* dominance. (By "political," here, I mean to

46. Sartre, *Plaidoyer.*
47. To recognize this need is to recognize the full seriousness of the diverse reactions to "critical" circumstances that I have been recording here and before. It cannot allow us to dismiss them simplistically, certainly not with the kind of scurrility used by Roger Scruton in a brief essay in the *Times* of London, itself worth naming as powerful evidence of the kind of retreat and retrenchment already indicated. It is rare, however, to see these occur with quite such vindictive abuse: "As the Seventies wore on, however, the voices of 'liberation' [and *we* must remember they *were*] fell silent. Barthes, living out a fantasy of hedonistic detachment, died in a car crash; Althusser, in a fit of Stalinist paranoia, strangled his wife and retired to an asylum; Lacan confined his public utterances to opaque and muffled seminars, the texts of which were scarcely readable even to his most fervent disciples; Derrida and Kristeva took off to America, there to enjoy the profitable accolades of the world's most gullible culture, while Foucault devoted his spare time to a defence of the sexual practices which were soon—following an injudicious spree in San Francisco—to put an end to his life" ("Paris's Most Evil Fashion," London *Times,* August 12, 1986). Such ugly vituperation speaks poorly for its author and represents an irrationalism from the far right that in its frenetic reactionary trumpeting and demagogic appeal is far more terrifying than the genuine explorations being attempted by the victims of Scruton's shrill bullying.
48. Said, *The World,* p. 292.
49. Catherine Clément, "Enslaved Enclave," in *New French Feminisms: An Anthology,* ed. Elaine Marks and Isabelle de Courtivron (New York, 1981), pp. 135–36.

refer to the ways in which power relations are organized in our environment, whether between state and society; between business, bureaucracy, and individual; or among individuals.)[50] What we call literature has been, since the seventeenth century, one of the primary means of creating and maintaining such dominance. Literary theory and criticism, like philology, political theory, and philosophy, have accompanied it as a process of justification, much more perhaps than as an explanation (though the two may only with difficulty be separated).[51] Increasingly, I think we may find that *some* so-called feminist criticism is the only truly *radical* literary (and other) discourse of our time. This is so because it not only questions the ideology of but seeks to intervene, in a way other criticisms do not (including most Western "Marxist" criticism), in the establishment of the sociocultural environment. It undertakes to question, that is, not so much the science of truth to which our sociocultural environment claims to correspond as the theoretical and practical precision of that correspondence.

Yet such criticism must be a part of a much broader overall critical enterprise, and there it will lose its specifically "feminist" identity. It will become part of an enterprise that will lead—dare one say?—to something like a new instauration, affecting and changing the entire sociocultural environment. The preceding chapters have sought to identify and analyze some of the theoretical aporias, contradictions, and flaws that imply the necessity of renewal. Discussing truth and knowledge, meaning and understanding, science and language, subject and individuality, society and order, these chapters have sought to show (theoretically, at least) how such essential concepts and activities organize and are organized within a particular sociocultural environment. They have also tried to indicate, however fitfully and incompletely, some few of the practical consequences. The harder task is of course the construction whose need they appear to identify.

50. See Chapter 6, n. 32, for the concept of authoritarian liberalism.
51. See, once again, my forthcoming *Meaning of Literature*.

Appendix to Chapter 1

The analysis of cause and effect cited in Chapter 1 (see note 59) is excerpted here from Charles Sanders Peirce, *Collected Papers*, ed. Charles Hartshorne and Paul Weiss (Cambridge, Mass.: Harvard University Press, 1935), 6. 66–87 (pp. 46–66): "Detached Ideas on Vitally Important Topics" (1898); lecture 4, "Causation and Force." Copyright 1935, 1963, by the President and Fellows of Harvard College. Reprinted by permission of the Harvard University Press.

But the grand principle of causation which is generally held to be the most certain of all truths and literally beyond the possibility of doubt (so much so that if a scientific man seeks to limit its truth it is thought pertinent to attack his sincerity and moral character generally) involves three propositions to which I beg your particular attention. The first is, that the state of things at any one instant is completely and exactly determined by the state of things at *one* other instant. The second is that the cause, or determining state of things, precedes the effect or determined state of things in time. The third is that no fact determines a fact *preceding* it in time in the same sense in which it determines a fact *following* it in time. These propositions are generally held to be self-evident truths; but it is further urged that whether they be so or not, they are indubitably proved by modern science. In truth, however, all three of them are in flat contradiction to the principles of mechanics. According to the dominant mechanical philosophy, nothing is real in the physical universe except particles of matter with their *masses*, their relative *positions* in space at different instants of *time*, and the immutable laws of the relations of those three elements of space, time, and matter. Accordingly, at any one *instant* all that is real is the masses and their positions, together with the laws of their motion. But according to Newton's second law of motion the positions of the masses at any one instant are not determined by their positions at any other single instant, even with the aid of the laws. On the contrary, that which is determined is an acceleration. Now an acceleration is the relation of the position at one instant *not* to the position at another instant, but to the positions at a second and a third instant. Let a, b, c be the positions of a particle at three instants very near to one another, and at equal intervals of time, say, for convenience, one second.

Then we may make a table thus:

Dates	Positions	Velocities	Acceleration
0^s	a		
		$(b - a)/(1^s - 0^s)$	$[(c - b)/(2^s - 1^s) -$
1^s	b		$(b - a)/(1^s - 0^s)]/$
		$(c - b)/(2^s - 1^s)$	$(1\frac{1}{2}^s - 0\frac{1}{2}^s) =$
2^s	c		$(c - 2b + a)/(1\frac{1}{2}^s - 0\frac{1}{2}^s)_2$

Or if the intervals are not equal:

Dates	Positions	Velocities	Acceleration
t_0	a		
		$(b - a)/(t_1 - t_0)$	$[(c - b)/(t_2 - t_1) -$
t_1	b		$(b - a)/(t_1 - t_0)]/$
		$(c - b)/(t_2 - t_1)$	$(\frac{1}{2}(t_2 + t_1) - \frac{1}{2}(t_1 + t_0)$
t_2	c		$= [c(t_1 - t_0) - b(t_2 - t_0)$
			$+ a(t_2 - t_1)]/(t_2 - t_1)$
			$(t_1 - t_0) \cdot \frac{1}{2}(t_2 - 2t_1 + t_0)$*

*$(t_2 - 2t_1 + t_0)$ should be $(t_2 - t_0)$ [editors' note].

It will be perceived that there is an essential *thirdness*, which the principle of casualty fails to recognize, so that its first proposition is false. The second proposition, that the cause precedes the effect in time, is equally false. The effect is the acceleration. The cause that produces this effect under the law of force is, according to the doctrine of the conservation of energy, the relative positions of the particles. Now the acceleration which the position requires does not come *later* than the assumption of that position. It is, on the contrary, absolutely simultaneous with it. Thus, the second proposition of the principle of causation is false. The third is equally so. This proposition is that no event determines a previous one in the same sense in which it determines a subsequent one. But, according to the law of the conservation of energy, the position of the particle relative to the center of force, expressed by b, determines what the acceleration shall be at the moment the particle is in that position. That is to say, taking the number b, whose value expresses the position of the particle, we can calculate from this number alone, by the application of a rule supplied by the law of the force, a number which I may denote by Fb, which is the numerical value of the acceleration $\dfrac{c - 2b + a}{(1\tfrac{1}{2}^s - 0\tfrac{1}{2}^s)^2}$. So that we have the equation $\dfrac{c - 2b + a}{(1\tfrac{1}{2}^s - 0\tfrac{1}{2}^s)^2} = Fb$. Now, if we know the positions, a and b, of the particle at the two earlier dates, this equation does enable us to calculate the position, c, of the particle at the last date. But since a and c enter into this equation in the same way, and since the difference of dates in the denominator is squared so that if they are interchanged it makes no difference (because the square of the negative of a number is the [square of the] number itself), it follows that the very same rule, by which we could calculate the value of c, that is, the position at the latest of the three dates, from a and b, those at the two earlier dates, may usually be applied, and in precisely the same form, to calculating the position, a, of the particles at the earliest date, from c and b, its positions at the two later dates. Thus, we see that, according to the law of energy, the positions at the two later instants determine the position at the earliest instant, in precisely the same way, and no other, in which the positions at the two earlier instants determine the position at the latest instant. In short, so far as phenomena governed by the laws of the conservation of energy are concerned, the future determines the past in precisely the same way in which the past determines the future; and for those cases, at least, it is a mere human and subjective fashion of looking at things which makes us prefer one of those modes of statement to the other. Thus, all three of the propositions involved in the principle of causation are in flat contradiction to the science of mechanics. [6.68–69]

Index

In the absence of a general bibliography, the index provides footnote references under an author's name for the first citation of a work (i.e., for its complete bibliographical description). Where several works by a single author occur in different footnotes, each is indicated by a very brief title whose only purpose is to distinguish one from another. Such references conclude entries, following a semicolon. Other footnotes referenced in the index (except those that identify names) contain discussion.

Addison, Joseph, 56, 181, 186, 190

Adorno, Theodor Wiesengrund, 251, 253, 263–67, 282; *Aesthetic Theory,* 263n1; *Dialectic,* 282n43

Agicinski, Sylviane, 21n4

Althusser, Louis, 182, 254–55, 257, 259, 283–84; idealism of, 270–72, 275, 278; science vs. ideology in, 191–92, 267–69; *Eléments,* 267n11; *Positions,* 192n22

Analytico-referentiality, 4–7, 24, 99–100, 102–3, 132; crisis of, 8, 101, 120, 131–35, 143, 223–24, 266; definition of, 7, 19–20, 58–59, 86; dominance of, 7, 58, 149, 188; end of, 263–83; Frege against, 27; literature of, 187–88, 191–94, 268 (*see also* Literature); politics of, 199–200 (*see also* Liberalism, authoritarian); querying of, 36, 58–59, 109–34; reinstatement of, 22; reinstatement of, and political fears, 197n31; in Sartre, 168–69; specific failures of, 10–12, 209–10. *See also* Binarism; Cartesianism; Descartes, René; Linearity; Masculinity; Occultation, discursive; Origin; Other; Reason: instrumental; Science; Truth

Anderson, Perry, 141–42, 251–62; 251n1

Apel, Karl-Otto, 9

Aporia (discursive), 4, 95, 122, 174; of reference, 24–25, 96; in structuralism, 260; of subjectivity vs. objectivity, 63–64, 69–70, 94. *See also* Carnival; Contradiction; Occultation, discursive;

Responsibility of enunciation

Arendt, Hannah, 277n29

Arnold, Matthew, 181, 190–91

Aronson, Ronald, 172n31; 16n14

Artaud, Antonin, 149

Astell, Mary, 34–35, 135, 276–77; *Bart'lemy Fair,* 267n28; *Reflections,* 34n30

Austen, Jane, 193

Austin, John L., 108; 109n20

Ayim, Maryann; 109n21

Bacon, Francis, Lord Verulam, 61n4, 76, 120, 249, 263; on difficulty of communication, 121, 134, 147–48, 234; on limits of knowledge, 81, 107, 130, 272; at origins of modernism, 19, 67, 135, 143–44, 149–51, 224, 238; as precursor of logical atomism, 20, 29; on time to acquire knowledge, 56, 267; on war and state, 198–99; *Works,* 56n1

Bakhtin, Mikhail, 9, 176; on carnival, 136–38, 144, 149; consciousness as social fact, 158–59, 171–72, 175, 246; critique of linguistics, 155, 158, 174; on discourse as process, 119, 122–23, 163, 177, 240, 279; on language and society, 129–30, 163n22, 173, 218–19, 248; *Rabelais,* 137n1. *See also* Carnival; Semiotics; Sense; Superstructure; Vološinov, Valentin Nikolaevich

Barthes, Roland, 9, 61n2, 85n31, 139, 247, 284n47; on constraining language, 140–41, 149, 152, 154n1, 225, 251; and

[289]

Library of Congress Cataloging-in-Publication Data

Reiss, Timothy J., 1942–
   The uncertainty of analysis.

   Includes index.
   1. Truth.   2. Meaning (Philosophy)   3. Culture—Philosophy.   I. Title
BC171.R44   1988   121   88-47741
ISBN 0-8014-2162-4 (alk. paper)